Apple Training Series

Mac OS X v10.4 System Administration Reference, Volume 2

Schoun Regan and David Pugh, eds.

Apple Certified

Apple Training Series: Mac OS X v10.4 System Administration Reference, Volume 2

Published by Peachpit Press. For information on Peachpit Press books, contact:

Peachpit Press
1249 Eighth Street
Berkeley, CA 94710
(510) 524-2178
(800) 283-9444
Fax: (510) 524-2221
http://www.peachpit.com
To report errors, please send a note to errata@peachpit.com
Peachpit Press is a division of Pearson Education

Apple Series Editor: Nancy Peterson
Editors: Schoun Regan, David Pugh
Project Editors: Whitney Walker, Bob Lindstrom
Production Editor: Laurie Stewart, Happenstance Type-O-Rama
Technical Editors: John Signa, Rob Neville
Copy Editors: Elissa Rabellino, Darren Meiss, Joanne Gosnell
Compositor: Kate Kaminski, Happenstance Type-O-Rama
Indexer: Karin Arigoni
Cover Illustration: Alicia Buelow
Cover Production: Chris Gillespie, Happenstance Type-O-Rama

ISBN 0-321-42315-1
9 8 7 6 5 4 3 2 1
Printed and bound in the United States of America

This book is dedicated to Dick and Judy Abrams. In-laws who are not actually crazy. Who knew?

—Schoun Regan

To my beautiful wife, Amanda. You are the reason for the best experiences of my life.

—David Pugh

Acknowledgments

Schoun Regan I would like to first thank Dave Pugh for his assistance. As with Volume 1, this book would not be what it is without his tireless help.

I would also like to thank my wife Susan, my editors Whitney Walker and Bob Lindstrom, Serena Herr and Nancy Peterson from Peachpit, John Signa and John DeTroye from Apple, and the rest of the gang at AFP548.com.

Every day, Apple System Engineers and Consulting Engineers work tirelessly to insure their customers—from all organizations and in all walks of life—are well taken care of. They are a special breed, and they deserve thanks for all their hard work.

Finally, this book might not exist if it were not for the efforts of Mike Bombich, who almost single-handedly kept imaging alive. Mike is proof that one person *can* make a difference. His insights into the issues faced by education gave us several essential tools that are used daily by thousands of administrators literally saving them millions of dollars and untold hours of work.

On behalf of everyone everywhere who has ever used Carbon Copy Cloner, NetRestore, or any of the other tools you freely make available, Mike, I thank you very much.

David Pugh To the entire Mac community, thank you. Without this loyal following, what would we write about?

A big thanks has to go out to Bob, Whitney, Nancy, Serena, and the whole Peachpit gang for the opportunity to work with them.

To my wife, Amanda, thank you for tolerating my late nights, for your support through this and many other projects, and for joining me through all these fun times.

Lastly, I can't express enough gratitude to Schoun Regan for introducing me to a whole new world of speaking and writing.

Contents at a Glance

Getting Started xi

Deployment

Lesson 1 Deployment Strategies 3

Lesson 2 Imaging 21

Lesson 3 Creating and Deploying Packages 51

Lesson 4 Delivering Images and Packages 77

Lesson 5 Testing and Troubleshooting 103

Lesson 6 Maintenance 119

Managing Accounts

Lesson 7 Developing an Account Management Strategy 131

Lesson 8 Creating Accounts 155

Lesson 9 Defining the User Experience 183

Lesson 10 Working with Mobile Accounts 237

Lesson 11 Administering Windows User Accounts 255

Lesson 12 Managing Network Views 277

Lesson 13 Using Apple Remote Desktop 295

Appendix Using Radmind 341

Index. 359

Table of Contents

Getting Started xi

Deployment

Lesson 1 Deployment Strategies 3
Understanding Deployment Scenarios 4
Evaluating Solutions 10
Lesson Review 18

Lesson 2 Imaging 21
Comparing Image Types 22
Creating Your Imaging Environment 23
Creating Hidden Administrator Accounts 27
Including Classic 33
Using Apple Software Restore 36
Using NetBoot Images 40
Lesson Review 48

Lesson 3 Creating and Deploying Packages 51
Why Use Custom Installation Packages? 52
Looking Inside a Package 54
Creating Packages 63
Lesson Review 74

Lesson 4 Delivering Images and Packages 77
Delivering Locally 78
Delivering over the Network 83
Performing Remote Administration 96
Using the Installer Command 98
Using Radmind 100
Lesson Review 100

Lesson 5 Testing and Troubleshooting 103
Testing Images 104
Common Issues and Solutions 111
Lesson Review 117

Lesson 6 Maintenance 119
Automating Client Maintenance 120
Maintaining with Radmind 125
Maintaining with Packages 127
Lesson Review 127

Managing Accounts

Lesson 7 Developing an Account Management Strategy. . . 131
Levels of Management 132
Planning Growth Management 137
Optimizing User Management 142
Documenting Management Policy 147
Creating User Documentation 148
Planning Behind-the-Scenes Account Management 150
Lesson Review 152

Lesson 8 **Creating Accounts** 155
Understanding Account Creation Tools 156
Relocating User Accounts 161
Creating Groups 174
Setting Up a Computer Account 176
Lesson Review 180

Lesson 9 **Defining the User Experience** 183
Managing Preferences with Files 184
Managing Preferences with MCX Settings 188
Defining the User Experience 200
Automating New-User Creation 233
Lesson Review 234

Lesson 10 **Working with Mobile Accounts** 237
Understanding Mobile Accounts 238
Synchronizing an Account 242
Lesson Review 252

Lesson 11 **Administering Windows User Accounts** 255
Unifying User Management Features 256
Setting Up Home Folders and Share Points
for Windows Accounts 263
Isolating and Resolving Windows Management
Account Issues 269
Lesson Review 273

Lesson 12 **Managing Network Views** 277
Examining Flat and Managed Views 278
Planning Your Network View 279
Creating Network Views 281
Viewing the Results 290
Lesson Review 292

Lesson 13 Using Apple Remote Desktop 295
Installing ARD 296
Using ARD 307
Managing Clients with ARD 318
Scripting Remote Desktop 323
Generating Reports 326
Using a Task Server 333
Lesson Review 338

Appendix Using Radmind 341
Understanding Radmind 342
Setting Up Radmind 343

Index 359

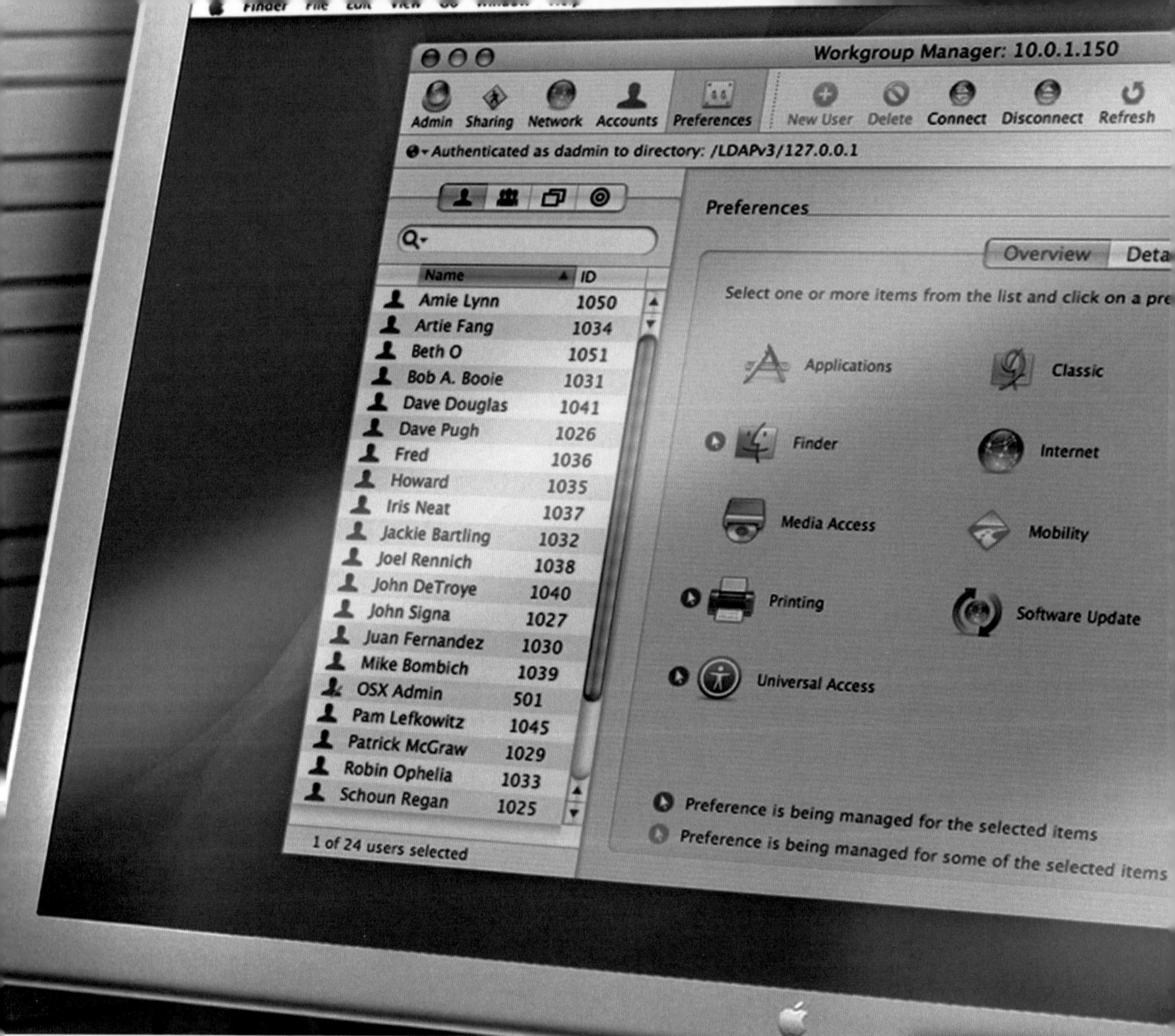
Workgroup Manager: 10.0.1.150
Admin
Sharing
Network
Accounts
Preferences
New User
Delete
Connect
Disconnect
Refresh
Authenticated as dadmin to directory: /LDAPv3/127.0.0.1
Name
ID
Amie Lynn 1050
Artie Fang 1034
Beth O 1051
Bob A. Booie 1031
Dave Douglas 1041
Dave Pugh 1026
Fred 1036
Howard 1035
Iris Neat 1037
Jackie Bartling 1032
Joel Rennich 1038
John DeTroye 1040
John Signa 1027
Juan Fernandez 1030
Mike Bombich 1039
OSX Admin 501
Pam Lefkowitz 1045
Patrick McGraw 1029
Robin Ophelia 1033
Schoun Regan 1025
1 of 24 users selected
Preferences
Overview
Applications
Classic
Finder
Internet
Media Access
Mobility
Printing
Software Update
Universal Access
Preference is being managed for the selected items
Preference is being managed for some of the selected items

Name:
Password:
NetBoot
NFS
Open Directory
Print
QuickTime Streaming
Software Update
VPN
VPN
Web

Getting Started

This book is the second volume of the only Apple-certified reference guide to Mac OS X system administration. Designed as a companion to the Apple Mac OS X Deployment and User Account Management training courses, this comprehensive, self-paced guide will give administrators, support technicians, and ardent Mac users an in-depth look at the technical architecture of Mac OS X and Mac OS X Server. It will teach you various techniques you can use to load and deploy any number of Macs in your organization.

Whether you work with two computers or 2000, in a small or large company, educational system, or government organization, this book will show you how to efficiently manage your system and all the accounts on it. You'll also learn how to handle all types of users, ranging from those with no rights to those with full administrative rights.

The Methodology

Apple Training Series books emphasize hands-on training. The lessons contained within this book are designed to prepare system administrators for the tasks demanded of them by loading and deploying computers and managing the accounts and access rights on each of them. To become truly proficient, you need to learn both the theory and techniques behind each of these topics.

Lesson Structure

This reference guide is broken into two parts, each bringing you into a world of configuration files, mechanisms, best practices, and integration:

- **Part 1, Deployment,** instructs you on techniques you can use to streamline the deployment of multiple computers containing similar configurations. This section begins with strategies used to plan your computer deployment, and it later discusses methods used to install and maintain the software on each computer.
- **Part 2, User Account Management,** shows you how to effectively manage all of your users. You'll start with a number of planning and strategy topics, followed by learning what features the Mac OS X management tools offer you for setting up your users and their environment. You'll also learn about some of the special features available to mobile users and Windows users that can assist in creating a more cohesive computing environment for everyone. Part 2 concludes with information that will assist you in administrating Windows-based user accounts, managing network views, and using Apple Remote Desktop.
- **Appendix, Using Radmind,** gives a short introduction to using Radmind to manage the software installed on your computers.

NOTE ▸ The step-by-step exercises included in the lessons are mostly nondestructive if followed correctly. However, a few exercises are disruptive, in that they may turn certain network services off or on suddenly. Some exercises, if performed incorrectly, could result in data loss to some basic services and even erase a disk or volume of a computer connected to the network on which the Mac OS X and/or Mac OS X Server resides. As such, it is recommended that you run through the exercises on Mac OS X computers that are not critical to your productivity or connected to a production network. Instructions are given for restoring your services back to their initial state, but reasonable caution is recommended. Apple Computer, Inc. and Peachpit Press are not responsible for any data loss or any damage to any equipment that occurs as a direct or indirect result of following procedures in this book.

Prerequisites

Because Mac OS X and Mac OS X Server contain several open-source initiatives, it is impossible to include all the possibilities and permutations here. First-time users of Mac OS X and Mac OS X Server may find the concepts in this book a bit unfamiliar, but that should not dissuade them from learning an integral part of Mac OS X. Seasoned administrators of Mac OS X, Windows, and UNIX will find this book extremely helpful in integrating their various systems to work in tandem.

Before undertaking the lessons in this book, you should have experience in the following areas:

- Apple Certified Technical Coordinator (ACTC) certification or equivalent knowledge
- Network and Internet topical knowledge
- Understanding of the purpose, function, and use of basic IP networking, including IP addresses, subnet masks, ports, and protocols
- Familiarity with the command line and Secure Shell Protocol (SSH)

Hardware Requirements

It is not necessary to have computers set up for this reference guide, although basic configuration requirements are listed in this section for readers who want to locate files, attempt commands, and adjust settings based on the lessons in this book. In order to follow along, you are expected to network your computers and provide basic services without prior instruction.

To complete the lessons in this book, you will need at least two Macintosh computers—one with Mac OS X v10.4 installed and one with Mac OS X Server v10.4—and network cables and a switch to keep them connected via a small private local network. It may be helpful to have a third Mac OS X computer to test images and software created during the first half of this book. Before you set up Mac OS X and Mac OS X Server, you'll want to keep in mind that you should have temporary Internet access to download and install all necessary software updates using the Software Update mechanism in Mac OS X.

You will also need the following items, freely downloadable from Apple or on the Mac OS X/Mac OS X Server CD or DVD:

- Server Admin Tools package
- Developer Tools (Xcode) package
- Latest Mac OS X Server Combo Update package

Set Up Your Client Computer

In this exercise, you will ensure that your Mac OS X computer is properly configured.

1. Do an erase and install of Mac OS X, if this is a computer that can have all of the data on it erased. **DO NOT ERASE a disk with data you wish to keep!**

2. If this is a portable computer, ensure that the power cable is connected.

3. In the Welcome window, select your country of choice and click Continue.

4. In the Do You Already Own a Mac? window, select “Do not transfer my information” and click Continue.

5 In the Select Your Keyboard window, make a selection and click Continue.

6 In the Enter Your Apple ID window, leave the Apple ID and Password fields blank and click Continue.

7 In the Registration Information window, press Command-Q and skip the registration process.

8 In the "You have not finished setting up Mac OS X" dialog, click Skip.

   You do not need to register with Apple for this book.

9 In the Create Your Account window, enter the following information:

   - Name: *Apple Admin*
   - Short Name: *apple*
   - Password: *apple*

   Using the same word for the user name and password does not follow best practices. Because you will be using many different accounts and passwords throughout the book, the exercises use simple, easy-to-recall passwords.

10 Click Continue.

11 In the Select Time Zone window, click your time zone on the map, and then click Continue.

12 In the Set the Date and Time window, reset the time and date if either one is incorrect, and then click Save.

13 Click Continue.

14 In the Don't Forget to Register window, click Done.

   The Setup Assistant will quit, and the Finder will open.

   At this point, your computer should be configured only with an administrator's name and password and basic settings such as date, time, and keyboard settings. Do not configure any network settings.

Configure Preference Settings and Update Software

Because you will be using multiple user accounts, you need to disable automatic login.

1. Open the Accounts pane of System Preferences.
2. Click the Lock button and authenticate as Apple Admin.
3. Click Login Options.
4. Deselect the "Automatically log in as" checkbox.

   Disabling automatic login is a basic security measure. If your computer logs in automatically, any person who starts the computer can access your files.
5. Select "Name and password" for "Display Login Window as."
6. Select the "Enable fast user switching" checkbox.
7. In the Warning sheet, click OK.

   During certain exercises, you will need to quickly switch between different user accounts. With Fast User Switching enabled, you will be able to log in a new user without having to log out the current user.
8. Click the Show All button to return to all System Preferences.
9. Open the Date & Time pane of System Preferences.
10. Deselect the checkbox for "Set date & time automatically" if it's selected.
11. Click the Show All button to return to all System Preferences.
12. Open the Network pane of System Preferences.

13 From the Show pop-up menu, choose Network Port Configurations.

14 Turn off all Port Configurations except Built-in Ethernet.

This will ensure that you are not inadvertently connecting to a network other than the private network you are creating.

15 Click Apply Now.

16 Click the Show All button to return to all System Preferences.

17 Open the Sharing pane of System Preferences.

18 In the Computer Name field, enter *DS Client* and press the Tab key.

19 Quit System Preferences.

20 Temporarily connect to the Internet and run Software Update repeatedly to obtain all current software updates.

21 Download and install Server Admin Tools, if you do not already have them, from Apple's support site (www.apple.com/support).

22 Insert the Mac OS X v10.4 DVD and install the Developer Tools.

23 Install Remote Desktop Admin software if you have purchased it from Apple.

The software is not necessary for this book but may help manage your remote server.

24 Run Software Update repeatedly to update any final tools.

25 Disconnect from the Internet and connect to your local private switch to ensure that you are on a private network.

Configure Workgroup Manager

You can use Workgroup Manager in its default configuration to modify user and group records. However, in this course you will also use it to directly view and modify directory data. In order to do so, you need to enable the Inspector.

1. Open /Applications/Server/Workgroup Manager.

   Typically, Workgroup Manager is used to administer a Mac OS X Server computer. However, you can skip connecting to a server and just manage the accounts in the local NetInfo database.

2. Choose Server > View Directories.

   This command dismisses the Connect dialog and opens a Workgroup Manager window for the local directory.

3. In the "This is not a server directory node" warning sheet, select the "Do not show this warning again" checkbox and click OK.

   The purpose of this warning is to remind you that you are editing directory data on a non–Mac OS X Server computer.

4. Choose Workgroup Manager > Preferences.

5. Select the "Show 'All Records' tab and Inspector" checkbox.

   This option allows you to use Workgroup Manager to directly view and manipulate directory service data.

6. Click OK.

   Notice that an Inspector button (a target) has been added next to the Users, Groups, and Computers buttons on the left. The Inspector is used to modify data directly.

7. In the warning sheet, click OK.

8. Quit Workgroup Manager.

   Workgroup Manager is now configured to allow you to view native directory data.

Perform the Initial Server Configuration

Later on in the directory services section, you will configure Mac OS X Server to provide directory services.

1 Do a custom erase and install of Mac OS X Server, and add the X11 package if this is a computer that can have all of the data on it erased. **DO NOT ERASE a disk with data you wish to keep!**

2 If this is a portable computer, ensure that the power cable is connected.

3 In the Welcome window, select your country of choice and click Continue.

4 In the Select Your Keyboard window, make a selection and click Continue.

5 In the Serial Number window, enter the serial number that came with your server software.

6 In the Administrator Account pane, create an administrator account with these settings:

- Name: *First Administrator*
- Short Name: *fadmin*
- Password: *fadmin*

Using the same word for the user name and password does not follow best practices. Because you will be using many different accounts and passwords throughout the book, the exercises use simple, easy-to-recall passwords.

7 Click Continue.

8 In the Network Names pane, enter the following:

- Computer Name: *C-serverbook*
- Local Hostname: *C-serverbook*

9 Click Continue.

In the Network Interfaces list, make sure TCP/IP is selected for the Built-in Ethernet port and that all other checkboxes are deselected, and then click Continue.

10 In the TCP/IP Connection pane for Built-in Ethernet, configure your connection as follows:

- Configure IPv4: Manually
- IP Address: *10.1.10.1*
- Subnet Mask: *255.255.0.0*
- Router Address: *10.1.10.1*
- DNS: *10.1.10.1*
- Search Domains: *pretendco.com*

11 Click Continue.

12 In the Directory Usage pane, choose Standalone Server from the "Set directory usage to" pop-up menu and click Continue.

13 In the Services pane, leave all services off except Apple Remote Desktop and click Continue.

14 In the Time Zone pane, select your time zone and click Continue.

15 In the Network Time pane, make sure to deselect the "Use a network time server" checkbox if it's selected.

16 Click Continue.

17 Review your settings, make corrections if necessary, and then click Apply.

Server Assistant configures the server according to your instructions and then reboots the server.

18 After the server reboots, log in as First Administrator (password: *fadmin*).

19 Obtain the latest Mac OS X Server Combo update and install that update.

20 Install Developer Tools from the Mac OS X Server CD or DVD.

21 Open the Server Admin application located in /Applications/Server and authenticate as First Administrator.

22 Select your server from the list on the left, click the Settings button, and then choose Date & Time.

23 Double-check your time zone, changing it if necessary, and click Save.

24 Quit Server Admin.

Apple Certification Program

This book is an excellent preparation for the Mac OS X Deployment v10.4 Exam (9L0-609). Successful completion of the deployment exam along with exams totaling five other points earns an Apple Certified System Administrator (ACSA) certification, which requires seven points. Before you take the test, you should review this book and spend time setting up and working with the various deployment tools available through Mac OS X and Mac OS X Server.

You should also download and review the Skills Assessment Guide for the exam, which lists the exam objectives, the total number of items, the number of items per section, the required score to pass, and how to register. To download the Skills Assessment Guide, visit http://train.apple.com/certification.

Earning Apple technical certification shows employers that you have a high level of technical proficiency with Apple products. You'll also join a growing community of skilled professionals—Apple Mac OS X certification programs are among the fastest-growing certifications in the industry, with 300 percent growth in 2004.

Achieving any of the Mac OS X certifications also qualifies you to join the new Mac OS X Certification Alliance, a free benefit program that recognizes and supports the thousands of Mac OS X experts worldwide. For more information, visit http://train.apple.com/certification/alliance.

For those who prefer to learn in an instructor-led setting, Apple also offers training courses at Apple Authorized Training Centers worldwide. These courses, which use the Apple Training Series books as their curriculum, are taught by Apple-certified trainers, who balance concepts and lectures with hands-on labs and exercises. Apple Authorized Training Centers have been carefully selected and have met Apple's highest standards in all areas, including facilities, instructors, course delivery, and infrastructure. The goal of the program is to offer Apple customers, from beginners to the most seasoned professionals, the highest-quality training experience. To find an Apple Authorized Training Center near you, go to http://www.apple.com/training.

Part 1 Deployment

1

Time This lesson takes about 30 minutes to complete.

Goals Describe the challenges in deploying and updating Mac OS X in an organization

Develop and implement a deployment plan for a client management solution

Lesson 1

Deployment Strategies

Welcome to Part 1, "Deployment," designed to address the challenges in deploying and maintaining a large number of computers to provide the optimal end-user experience.

As system administrators, we know you need to do things quickly! Rather than relying on a new employee to configure his or her own system, you must provide a solution that guarantees consistent configuration and a positive user experience. In an education setting, an instructor might need to reset Mac OS X systems back to a "clean" state in preparation for a new set of students coming into a classroom.

Unfortunately, the needs of users and system administrators can sometimes be at odds. People use computers in the workplace or in the classroom to get work done. Meanwhile, system administrators need to provide applications in order for users to be productive, and the simple act of installing and removing applications at will can be disruptive to users trying to do other tasks. This lesson will help you understand the needs of users and system administrators in a variety of situations and provide you with techniques to meet those goals and solve problems that arise along the way.

Understanding Deployment Scenarios

System administrators have to deploy Mac OS X and Mac OS X Server in a variety of scenarios, including the initial setup of the systems, configuration of computer labs, rapid deployment and rollback (which will be defined later in this lesson), configuration of centrally managed home folders, and performing of regular upgrades to hardware and software.

Performing Initial Setups

When people bring home new computers, they usually follow the Mac OS X Setup (or Mac OS X Server) Assistant in order to set up their systems. On Mac OS X, the Installer application is located in /System/Library/CoreServices/Setup Assistant, and on Mac OS X Server it can be found in /Applications/Server/Server Assistant.

Installing Mac OS X on one or two computers with Setup Assistant is easy, but once a lab or department has to have a new system installed or updated, using a single piece of software on each individual system can quickly spiral out of control and be extremely time consuming, as shown in the following figure.

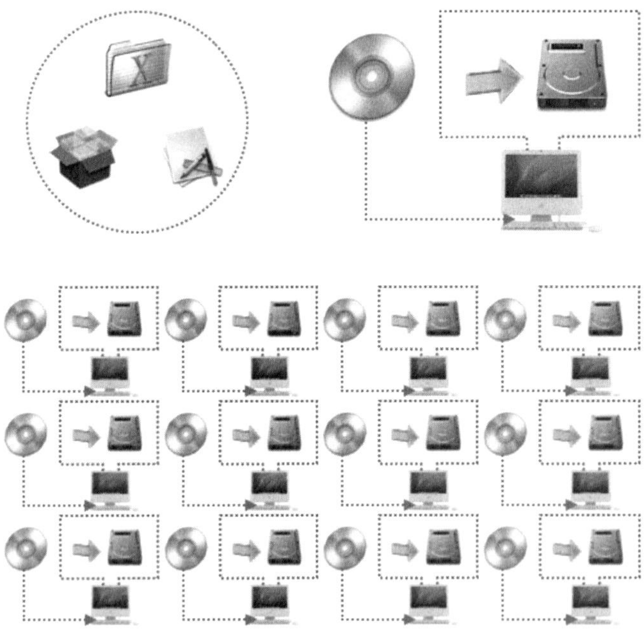

An administrator will use the Mac OS X Installer or Mac OS X Server Assistant, as shown, to install a version of Mac OS X and/or Mac OS X Server on a volume or partition. It is important to do a dry run, rather than blindly clicking buttons to further the process. First you need to read all the options and completely understand the ramifications involved in installing Mac OS X, especially if you are installing on top of an older version of the operating system.

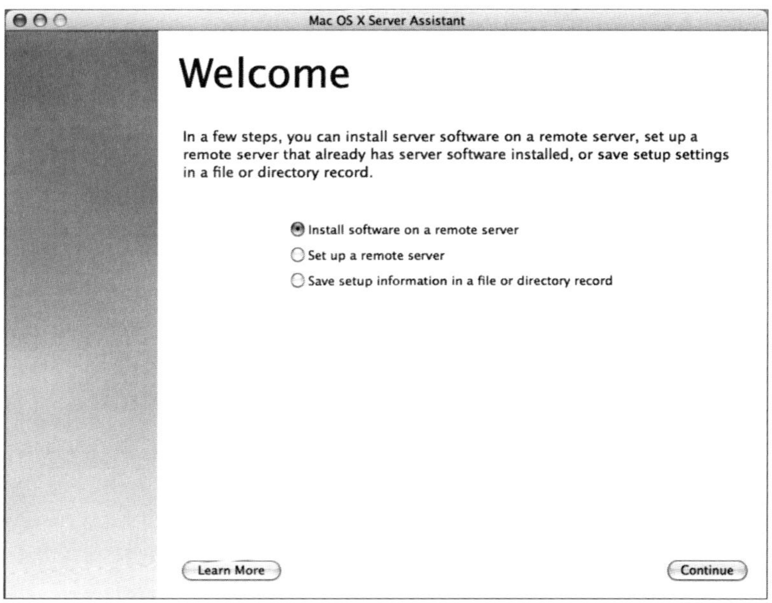

These "auto-start" applications are particularly helpful for new users, as Mac OS X is designed to get home users up and productive in a short amount of time. However, in a corporate or educational environment, the choices offered for basic configuration of a new computer may not match the organization's needs or the user's expectations. Leaving a computer at the initial setup screen also invites the potential for misuse and can be very costly.

To get started, you must determine the initial configuration of a single computer system by looking at what types of computers will be used (PowerPC or Intel-based Macs), what applications need to be made available immediately, how competent you expect the users to be, and how many computers are to be initially configured simultaneously. As you take each of these factors into account, create a plan for deploying Mac OS X initially to individual users or groups of users. Planning what disk images and packages to create, what they contain, how they will be deployed, and how administrators will maintain them is the most important part of running a successful deployment system.

In an education environment, it is common to deploy large numbers of computers in waves. These waves usually coincide with the beginning of a school year or term. The competency of the users and the required applications are as varied as the body of students and faculty at the institution, so you should find a minimal common user experience to use in designing a base system for each user to start with. Further customization to meet individual needs can be scripted or packaged and delivered after the initial setup, reducing the initial number of images necessary for the environment.

You face different challenges in corporate environments where new users are introduced in smaller groups, often one at a time. You might find it easier to craft a basic system based on a set of applications used throughout the company. The competency of users still varies, but it is often addressed on an individual basis. Again, having a base image may reduce the potential number of images.

In the desktop publishing environment, you need to think in terms of a *deployment server* solution, in which the initial installation of Mac OS X and the publishing tools are delivered over the network. Applications that are typically not installed with a standard Mac OS X package can be installed using scripts or a scripted no-load package that automatically executes the commands necessary for a successful install. Base images and packages are the keys to successful deployments regardless of the type of deployment. So, during the planning stage, consider your base image carefully and add everything after that point, as a package. (See "Packaging Certain Files" in this lesson.)

Using Computer Labs

Computer labs can provide a place for instructors to teach concepts in a hands-on environment or a place for users to do research in a library or other resource center. Computers in a lab setting must prevent users from making persistent changes, so that successive users are provided a consistent experience. Using some of the built-in services of Mac OS X Server and some additional third-party solutions, you can deploy and maintain a solution known as *rollback,* in which an image state is maintained each time either the computer is rebooted or a user logs out. As you will see later in this book, rollback can occur at the system level, whether the user is an administrative user or a nonadministrative user, and at the user level with preference manifests, which are new to Mac OS X v10.4. It's best to completely understand how you are going to scale your deployments, and in what order they are going to be built, tested, and pushed out to computers, as shown in the following figure.

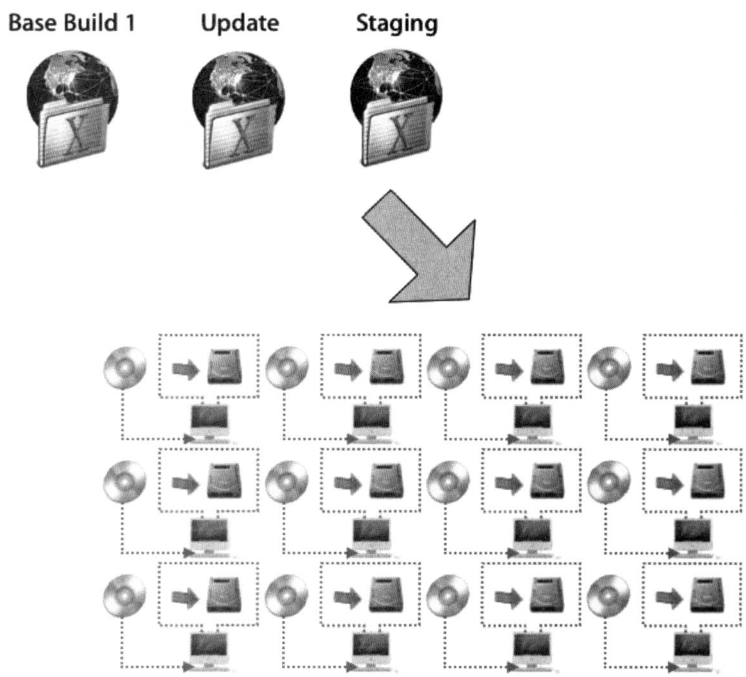

You can also implement computer labs on a smaller scale if you need to maintain a small collection of common workstations to be used by different people in a corporate environment. For instance, specialized printers could be configured to work only with certain computers configured with specific software. This small lab would need to be maintained so that anyone using the workstation could sit down, accomplish his or her task, and walk away without making it difficult for the next user to do the same.

Managing Home Folders

An important challenge facing the system administrator is how home folders are to be deployed. By default, each user account on a local installation of Mac OS X has a home folder that is local to the computer. If you are working with very large files, such as iMovie projects, keeping the files in the home folder on the local drive might be the most efficient approach. However, there are a couple of reasons why this might not be the ideal solution for storing documents. First, unless the user is particularly vigilant about backing up the data on the local computer, the data is vulnerable to being lost. Second, the size and volume of data might require more space than is available on a local computer. Third, a lackadaisical attitude toward security could cause the user to leave his or her computer unlocked and vulnerable to data theft, whereas if the data existed on the server alone, the administrator could automatically disconnect the user every night at a given time, whether or not the user logged out.

Luckily, there are strategies for addressing these challenges. Network home folders can be stored on RAID drives or other high-volume systems. Having home folders on a server on the network that gets backed up regularly improves your chances of recovering lost data and reducing data theft. In the creative and desktop publishing environments, work is often done at home or on the road. With a system of Network home folders, along with local folders that are synchronized with those Network home folders on a server, the user can work locally but update the work to a network volume, which provides both portability and limited data security. This feature is available with mobile user accounts and is a configurable and flexible synchronized directory solution, a feature of Mac OS X Server v10.4.3.

By default, a user's home folder consists of eight directories, as shown in the following figure: Desktop, Documents, Library, Movies, Music, Pictures, Public, and Sites. Users can create additional directories in their home folders, as well.

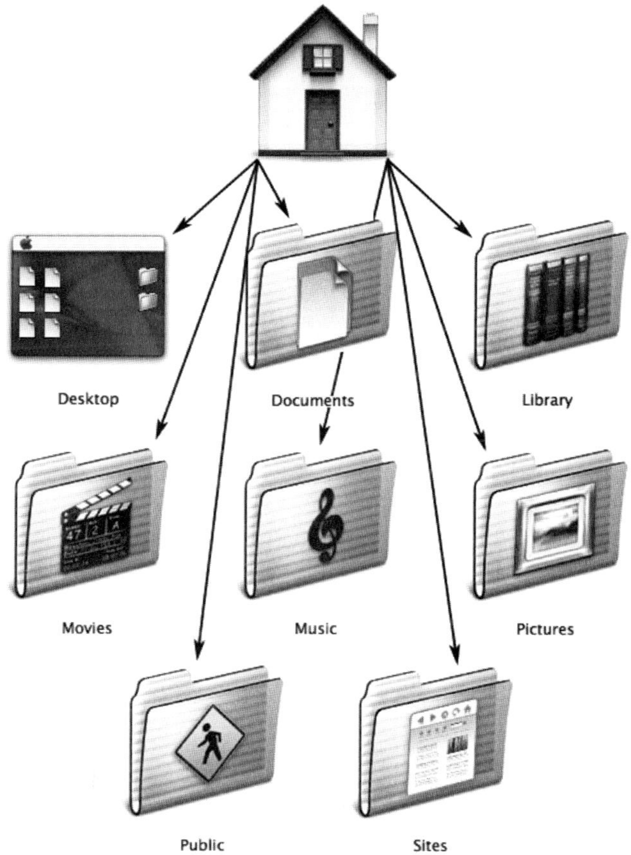

Once you decide how to deploy home folders, develop a plan for configuring the computers to use those home folders. You might have to centralize your user account management or configure each computer to use the synchronization services in Mac OS X. Finally, who will be in charge of the synchronization? You? The user? There are pros and cons for each scenario, as we'll see in later lessons.

Performing Upgrades

Once you have done an initial deployment and have configured your computers to operate according to your needs, it's time to start looking at how you'll perform upgrades to your hardware and software. Each environment has its own unique set of needs, but the common issue is consistency of performance when equipment and applications change.

In an education environment, you might be imaging new computers each school term and need to maintain the existing hardware to keep it compatible with the new hardware, which often involves compatibility issues with existing third-party hardware. However, it also involves keeping the operating system as up-to-date as you see fit on all the computers and having the operating system still remain compatible with the applications you need to use.

Upgrades in the enterprise environment often happen in smaller numbers, usually as new employees are hired. Out of 100 employees, you may have about 20 different computer models, as well as different versions of operating systems. Thus, you want to use tools that report on the state of each computer and deliver the appropriate updates as needed, with proper pretesting being paramount.

In the desktop publishing environment, you face frequent updates of printer drivers and the management of fonts. Again, you want to use tools that can report the state of the printer drivers and fonts on a particular system, and develop a way to ensure that your designers (who often work collaboratively) are using the most up-to-date versions of the software they need to complete their projects.

All this is balanced against the backdrop of expected continuous operation. That is, updates to the operating system and applications should be tested thoroughly before pushing these updates out to the rest of the computers. Listservs are full of administrators who blindly update their production systems without properly testing a proven rollback solution. Testing before deployment is key.

Evaluating Solutions

The solution to these challenges is to develop upgrade plans that are similar to the initial deployment plans. These plans need to incorporate a great deal of testing and staging work that precedes the upgrading of the hardware or updating of the software.

Imaging the Computer

Mac OS X v10.4 and Mac OS X Server v10.4 include software to store and deliver disk images, letting you install the operating system, applications, and documents on those disk images and configure them as startup volumes. You can use this flexible solution to provide remote startup of computers, restore a volume, install software, or run diagnostics. A properly maintained set of disk images lets you quickly bring systems back to a clean state, or efficiently configure new systems with a base set of applications and files. Without third-party software, however, these disk images alone do not provide rollback.

As shown in the following figure, whether the image to be placed on the computer comes from a preexisting disk image pushed from a server, a server-based network install, a server-based network bootable image, or a local disk image, the process of replacing what is on the local volume is paramount.

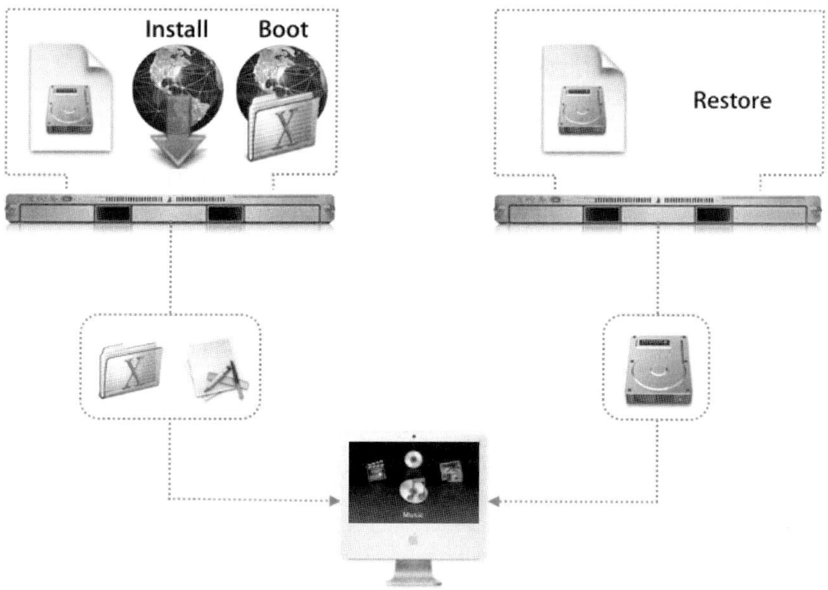

Packaging Certain Files

In Mac OS X, packages are a common means of delivering new software, software updates, scripts, and collections of documents. They are, in effect, documents for the Installer application, which resides in the /Applications/Utilities/ directory. Each package includes the items to be installed, the target locations for each item, and the information to be presented during the installation process.

When installing packages, it is better to have several small packages and group them together into one large package, as shown in the following figure. This enables the administrator to have several combinations of larger packages that are, in effect, nothing more than collections of smaller packages. The benefits far outweigh any additional time involved in creating the smaller packages. When planning your deployment scenario, the best solution is to have one small base image and packages for everything else. Doing so makes it easier to troubleshoot images that contain newer versions of the operating system.

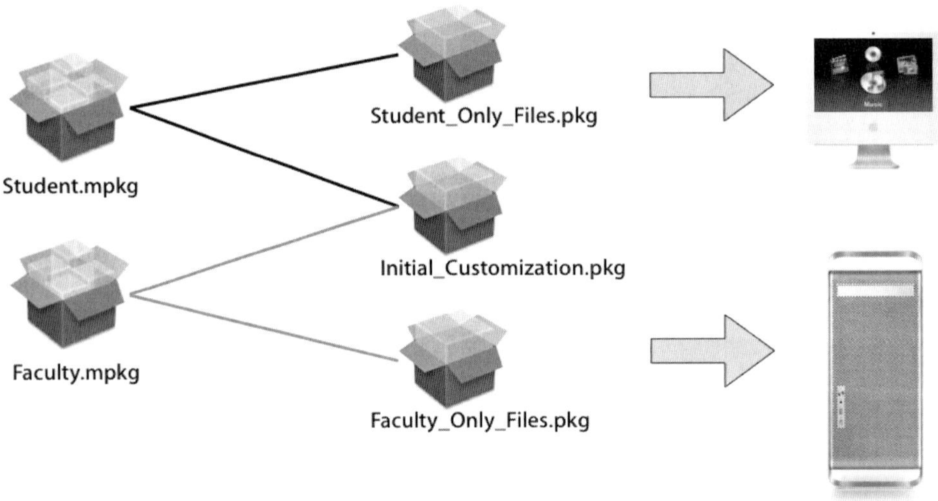

Moreover, packages can be linked together in metapackages. When a metapackage is run by the Installer, the metapackage identifies which packages the Installer needs to reference and install to complete the entire installation. As an option, a list of packages available for installation can be presented and the user can select which ones to install. Packages provide a quick, standard way of distributing applications and documents. One of the applications used to make packages is PackageMaker, which is included when you install the Apple Developer Tools. There is also a third-party tool, called Iceberg (WhiteBox; http://s.sudre.free.fr), that creates packages and metapackages.

Updating Regularly

There are several tools for keeping your systems regularly updated. Mac OS X includes Software Update, located in /System/Library/CoreServices/ and available from the command line as softwareupdate. It is generally launched from the Apple menu or System Preferences. Software Update finds and displays updates for the operating systems and Apple applications, such as iCal, iTunes, and iSync.

The Software Update application, shown in the following figure, will list all updates pertinent to the operating system on the computer, the hardware inside the computer (such as AirPort or Bluetooth), and the computer itself, such as firmware updates based on the type of computer.

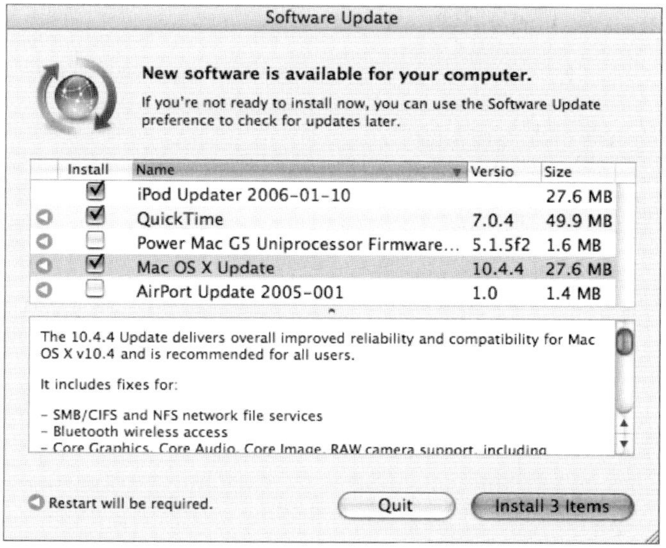

In addition, Mac OS X Server provides a software update service that can mirror the Software Update servers at Apple. With it, you can stage your updates after you have done testing with your particular environment. Rather than downloading updates directly from Apple, your users download the update from a software update server on your local network. A local software update server provides a good solution for closed networks, since you can keep a local software update server inside your firewall. It also lets you deploy only updates that have first been thoroughly tested against your own unique configuration of software and hardware. When you run a Software Update server, almost all available updates are downloaded to the server and listed in the window within Server Admin, as shown in the following figure.

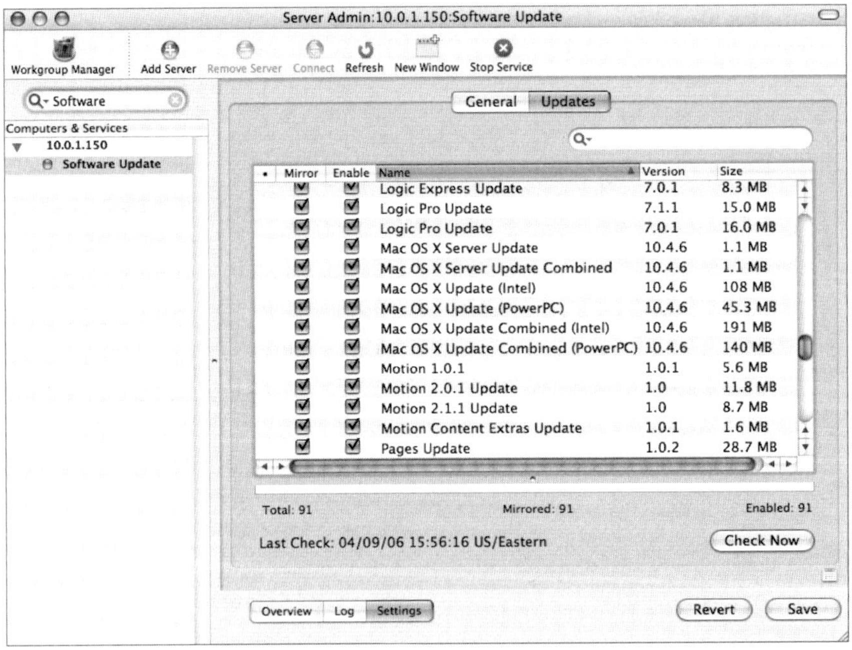

The Research Systems Unix Group at the University of Michigan has developed a tool called Radmind Assistant for Mac OS X. This utility is designed around the Radmind Unix command-line tools to remotely administer the various systems of client files. You can configure it to detect any changes to a managed computer's file system, keep track of those changes, and, if necessary, roll back the changes to a previous *loadset*, which is a Radmind term for each version of changes in a file system. This is, in effect, what free, downloadable software known as *tripwire* does by keeping track of all files on a computer (via checksum values) and notifying the user when any of those files change (open-source tripwire software is freely available from many sources on the Internet).

In an environment where the individual users make many changes to the systems they are currently logged in to, you can use Radmind Assistant or tripwire software to keep track of the state of any computer at any time. As you deploy updates to the operating systems, applications, or other critical files, you have a record of the changes that were made and can roll back the software to a previous state, should an update not work as expected.

It's an excellent solution to mass deployment testing. Say you want to test the latest update, so you send it out to ten different computers with different hardware configurations. Should any of the users have issues, you can simply roll back the machine to a previous loadset.

Radmind provides better scalable update and rollback features than other deployment solutions, and Radmind is free! (For more information, go to http://rsug.itd.umich.edu/software/copyright.html.)

In the following figure, Radmind shows several different loadsets that can be deployed to any number of given computers, depending on the need that particular day. For example, if the computer were used for a programming class, perhaps a loadset with all the developer tools would be wise. Then, when someone needed word-processing software, a smaller loadset with just that software could be deployed to the computer.

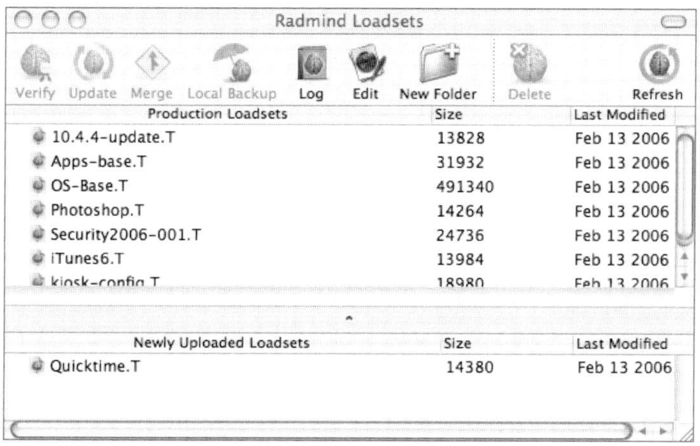

Apple also provides other tools for maintaining your systems. Apple Remote Desktop (ARD) is a remote management tool that can be used to report on the state of computers, deploy changes to those computers, or remotely control those computers. The ARD client software is already built into every installation of Mac OS X and Mac OS X Server. You purchase the administration software separately.

One big advantage of using ARD is that it allows for the gathering of information from each computer system in an overview report like the one shown in the following figure. The information can be a list of all the applications on each system, the hardware configuration of each system, or a comparison of the selected computer systems showing just exactly what is different on each one.

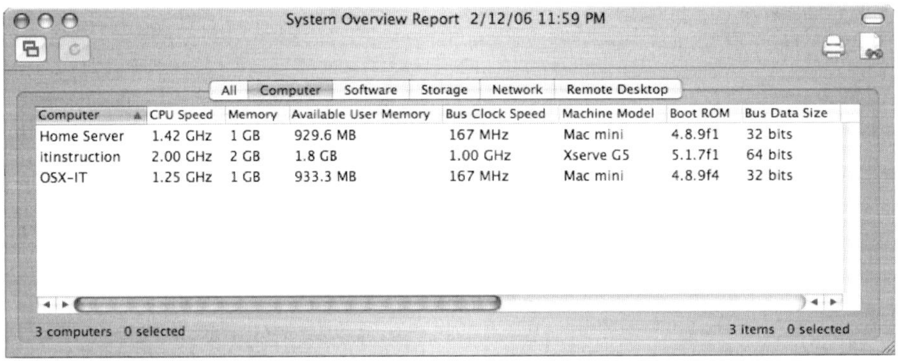

In a corporate or enterprise environment, ARD gives you a tool for quickly reporting on the state of your computers and for deploying changes. If, for instance, you have a new set of templates to use for business communications, you can copy those files to any computer you choose from the list of managed computers.

In education environments, you can use ARD to control how the computer is used. Instructors can monitor the progress of each student by viewing students' screens or lock students out of the computers in front of them during a lecture.

You can also use it to set the boot volume from which the computer starts up to change the learning environment between classes, such as changing it from a local volume to a NetBoot volume.

In desktop publishing, you can use the copy command in Apple Remote Desktop to deploy printer drivers, ppd files, and fonts to the computers in your design and production groups. By specifying the locations of the files on the destination computers, you can stage tests on your local computer to ensure compatibility and functionality. Apple Remote Desktop 2.2 does not support rollback.

Other options for testing and deploying software are: Eggplant (http://www.redstone-software.com), which is to test updates and images, and to test entire workflows and processes on a variety of operating systems; Deep Freeze (http://www.faronics.com/html/deepfreeze.asp), which can automate the management of all deployed computers, among other uses; and FileWave (http://www.filewave.com/top.html), which allows for asset management and patch deployment and rollback.

Overall Deployment Planning Synopsis

Understanding the bigger picture will assist you in your quest for the best deployment solution. If you keep a few key points in mind throughout the entire process, you will emerge with a much clearer picture of the necessary pieces of deployment. Keep in mind that you must start with a plan—based on your organization's needs—that often requires layouts, lists of hardware and software requirements, and current and planned software licensing.

Create the base image with little or no customization, and then create packages to add to the base image. Parallel the creation of the image and packages with continuous testing and use one of the many available tools to automate the process of testing packages and workflows. Once individual packages have been created, assemble metapackages and utilize a method of differentiating the base image and initial packages from different system versions.

Finally, decide how the images will be placed on the computers. All of this requires continuous testing to insure new hardware and software will work when rapidly deployed.

Lesson Review

1. What are the challenges faced by system administrators when deploying initial setups?
2. What are two methodologies available to Mac OS X administrators for resolving deployment challenges?
3. Why would an administrator use a local software update server, rather than rely on users to download their updates directly from Apple?
4. Can you choose what updates are available via a local software update server?
5. What advantage does Apple Remote Desktop offer an administrator when one machine is having technical issues?

Answers

1. Deploying images in computer labs, managing home folders, performing upgrades, and installing updates.
2. Packaging and imaging.
3. Local software update servers reduce traffic from the workplace to the Internet when all users are likely accessing the same files.
4. Yes.
5. You can query several computers and quickly compare results looking for anomalies in the suspect computer system.

References

Administration Guides

"System Imaging and Software Update Administration": http://images.apple.com/server/pdfs/System_Image_and_SW_Update_v10.4B.pdf

"Deploying Mac OS X Computers for K-12 Education": http://images.apple.com/server/pdfs/Deploying_Mac_OS_X_for_K12_Education_v10.4.pdf

Knowledge Base Articles

You can check for new and updated articles in the AppleCare Knowledge Base at www.apple.com/support.

URLs

Visit the following sites for more information:

About Packages: http://developer.apple.com/documentation/DeveloperTools/Conceptual/SoftwareDistribution/Concepts/sd_about_pkgs.html

Distributing Software with Internet-Enabled Disk Images: http://developer.apple.com/documentation/DeveloperTools/Conceptual/SoftwareDistribution/Concepts/sd_disk_images.html

Radmind: http://rsug.itd.umich.edu/software/radmind

Iceberg: http://s.sudre.free.fr/Software/Iceberg.html

2

Time This lesson takes about 1 hour to complete.

Goals

Use various methods of image creation

Create Apple Software Restore images from which Mac OS X can be restored onto a computer

Create NetBoot and Network Install images that can be stored on a NetBoot server and provided by NetBoot services

Configure and test Apple Software Restore and NetBoot-type images

Lesson **2**

Imaging

Disk images are great for distributing software to a large number of computers. You can create disk images of fully configured volumes and then use these images to install the full configuration to a volume on another computer. Alternatively, you can use the images as startup volumes for computers by hosting the images on a server. A properly maintained set of disk images lets you boot systems back to a known state quickly, or configure new systems efficiently with a base set of applications and files.

This lesson will show you how to create, configure, and test Apple Software Restore (ASR), NetBoot, and Network Install images.

Comparing Image Types

Disk image files commonly come in three types; .dmg, .img, and .smi (essentially, .smi is a self-mounting image). When a user double-clicks these files, they mount as virtual disks under the /Volumes/ directory, along with the boot volume and other mounted volumes.

Prior to Mac OS X (specifically, Mac OS 9), disk image files were created using New Disk Image Format (NDIF), a file fork/data fork format. Disk Utility now uses Universal Disk Image Format (UDIF), which permits administrators to created bootable DVD/CDs from disk images.

The following table shows what formats can be obtained via the two file types:

Supported Disk Image Format Options

.dmg Formats	.img Formats
Mac OS X Extended (HFS+)	Mac OS X Extended (HFS+)
Mac OS X Extended and Journaled (HFS+ Journaling)	Pro-DOS
Mac OS X Extended Case Sensitive and Journaled (HFSX)	
Mac OS Standard (HFS)	Mac OS Standard (HFS)
UFS	UDF
MS-DOS	MS-DOS

While Disk Utility can read all three types of images, it can only create .dmg files. The command-line utility hdiutil can also be used to manage disk images. It maintains a wealth of flags and is very useful when scripting disk image manipulation. Using hdiutil, you can script disk creating, verifying, mounting (both in the Finder and not visible in the Finder), burning, converting, segmenting, hybrid creation, resizing, and other functions. Particularly useful to administrators is the ability to use hdiutil to create disk images that do not mount at the root of the file system, but wherever the administrator chooses (along with the flag -nobrowse which hides them from the Finder). This permits images to be mounted at user login—images that appear to be part of the file system but in fact are read-only disk images. This script would appear as

```
sregan$ hdiutil mount /Users/sregan/Desktop/ard_admin_2.2.dmg -mountroot
/Users/Shared/publicmountpoint –nobrowse
```

The command-line tool `drutil` can also be used when dealing with CD/DVD burners and drives.

Creating Your Imaging Environment

As you start to test imaging solutions, consider setting aside three computers for the development process:

1. Production—the workstation where you create and store images, documentation, package installers, and scripts
2. Model—the master on which you build a replica of what your final imaged computers will contain
3. Target—the computer you use to test your deployments by receiving the image and packages you create

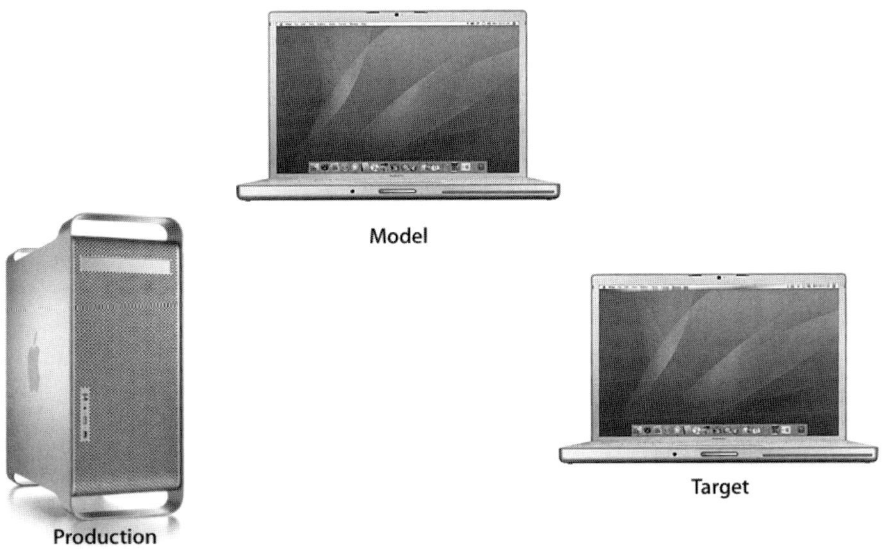

You may choose to have more than one test computer to test simultaneous deployment. Keep in mind that your production computer needs nearly three times as much free disk space as is required to hold each master image. The free space is needed to hold your source files, temporary versions of those files during the build process, and the final product.

If you don't find it practical or don't have the resources to set aside three or more computers, consider setting aside one computer with multiple drives or creating multiple volumes by partitioning a single drive. Maintain three volumes: one production volume, one model image volume, and a third for testing. These volumes can perform the same functions as the three computers described above. Again, keep in mind that your production volume needs nearly three times as much disk space as is required to hold each master image.

The model computer, on which you build your master image, should be the newest and most powerful computer to which you will be deploying. Mac OS X is a remarkably portable operating system, but it is typically more portable from newer hardware to older hardware. If this is not possible, make sure that you have the most recent version of Mac OS X installed on your model computer.

> **TIP** Recently released hardware often comes with a newer build of Mac OS X than is available to older hardware through software updates. For example, you may get Mac OS X v10.4.4 build 8G32 through Software Update, while a new type of iMac might come with Mac OS X v10.4.4 build 8H49 installed. If new hardware has been released since Apple last updated Mac OS X, it's best to use the new computer as your model hardware. Failure to do so could result in that new hardware's being unable to boot from your image.

> **NOTE ►** If you will be deploying both PowerPC and Intel-based Macintosh computers, you will need two separate images for each architecture. The model computer for each image should be the newest for the associated architecture.

You should also choose a computer that has the most hardware options and peripherals. For example, if you have at least one computer with a SuperDrive, use that computer to create your image, even if most other computers don't have that option.

In many cases, when you follow these guidelines, you can use the same master image for all classes of computers of the same CPU architecture. If your image doesn't work properly on a particular class of computers, try creating the image on that class. When a mix of desktop and portable computers is involved, you might need two multiple images.

You can't create an accurate image of the same system you're booted from; therefore, you image your model system by booting it into Target Disk Mode (hold down the T key during reboot) and attaching it to the production computer from which you'll image it. If you're in a pinch and need to create an image of your current system, you can boot from a Mac OS X installation disc and run Disk Utility from the CD/DVD.

Documenting Your Work

The first thing to consider when beginning your image-building process is how you will document your work. Getting the steps down on paper clearly the first time can save you an enormous amount of energy the next time—whether you or someone else is charged with implementing changes, installing updates, supporting new hardware, or creating new images for a different purpose. Without documentation, ideas never become reality.

In order to maintain a traceable process, be sure to answer the following questions in your notes:

1. What was installed and in what order?
2. Which Mac OS X settings, if any, did you change, and if so, in what order?
3. Did you have problems running an application as a particular user or when double-clicking a file? How did you fix the problem?
4. What other problems did you run into? How did you fix them?
5. Did you tweak configuration files by adding or modifying lines?

Problem resolution and troubleshooting are particularly important to document. A problem that took a week to fix the first time could be fixed in minutes the next time, as long as the original solution is documented. You will also want to document any reason for installing a particular package or changing a setting that may not be intuitive to someone repeating the steps. Remember, with your base/master image, customization should be kept to a minimum, as packages are the best way to deliver customized preference and settings files.

In a NetBoot environment, it is common for several images to exist on one or more NetBoot servers. Document ways to distinguish between the images and detail how the images were built.

Use Versioning to Avoid Confusion

Your master image might evolve as you apply updates, packages, and upgrades, so you may find it necessary to distinguish between different versions of your image. This is especially true if you have different classes of computers that you want to bundle with different sets of applications.

It is important to develop a versioning system that makes sense to you. Consider using the version of Mac OS X, followed by one or more letters, to uniquely identify your image: for instance, 10.4.4A.

You also need an easy way to determine the version of an active image. Consider customizing the Desktop image by adding the version string in the upper left corner of the image. In addition, for easier identification, use different image patterns. This will help to immediately identify your image when you're providing support for the user. For instance, use Aqua Blue.jpg for version 10.4.4A of your image and Aqua Graphite.jpg for 10.4.4B of your image.

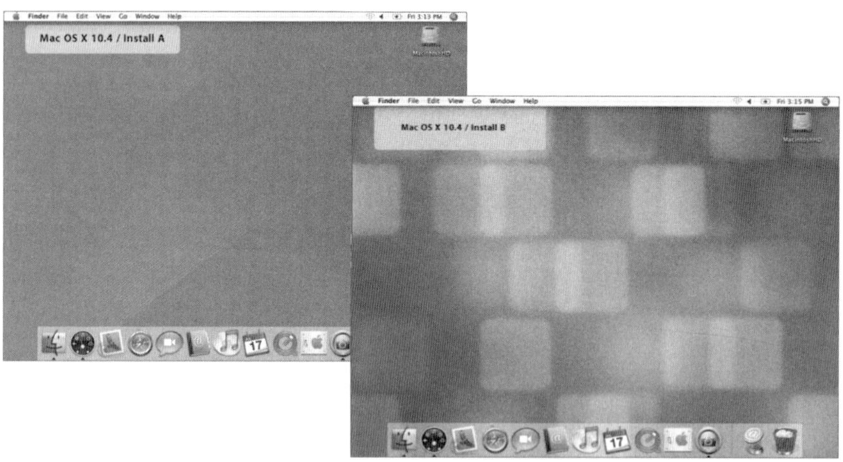

NOTE ▸ The default Desktop picture for the Login window and new accounts is /Library/Desktop Pictures/Aqua blue.jpg. If you want your version-specific image to appear as the default Desktop picture, it must be saved in the /Library/Desktop Pictures/ folder with the name *Aqua blue.jpg.*

TIP ▸ Keep in mind that in most cases, users can change their Desktop background, so it's best not to rely solely on this method to identify your image. You may also want to create a small text file that identifies your image. This file should be placed somewhere in the filesystem that will not conflict with normal operations, such as in /Library/Application Support.

Creating Hidden Administrator Accounts

A hidden administrator account is a functional account that, similar to the root account, is not visible to normal users. It differs from the root account, however, in that privileges can be customized to suit multiple levels of administration. There are two main ways to accomplish this: by modifying an admin account and by manually adding a user to a BSD flat user file.

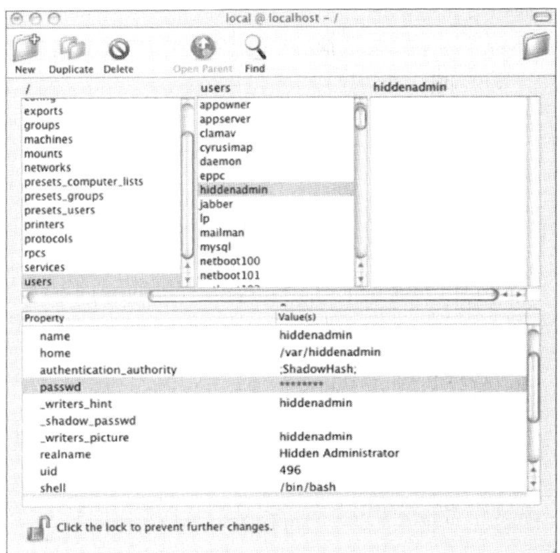

TIP If you don't expect your users to require any administrator access, after you create your hidden administrator account, you can delete the original admin account that was configured when Mac OS X was installed. With this configuration, only Normal user accounts are visible in System Preferences.

Modifying an Admin Account

For the first method, use NetInfo Manager (/Applications/Utilities), an administration tool for configuring and managing NetInfo data to edit the account. NetInfo is the central database for user accounts, groups, passwords, printers, computers, and other configuration information in Mac OS X.

NOTE ▶ NetInfo Manager is an advanced and very powerful application that should be used with care. Do not make changes to the NetInfo data unless you have a specific task to accomplish and understand the changes you are making. Making changes in NetInfo Manager may damage the system and require reinstalling Mac OS X.

Create and configure a new admin user account using System Preferences. Then, in NetInfo Manager, change the User ID (uid) and Group ID (gid) to a free number just below 500. This will keep the account from appearing in System Preferences. Next, change the user's home folder to a location that is not visible to general users—for example, /var/*username*—and then actually move that home folder to the new location:

```
sudo mv /Users/username /var/
```

WARNING ▶ Verify that you are not giving the hidden account an ID that is already used. Because accounts with IDs below 500 are usually system accounts, the result of assigning identical IDs is potentially destructive to Mac OS X. Counting down from 499 is usually safe. You can use the `id` command from a Terminal prompt to check to see if a uid is in use already. Example: `id 499`.

When you change a user's uid number, Mac OS X sees the user as a different user, and the account loses access to its home folder. To fix this, run the `chown` command in Terminal to change the owner and group of the recently moved home folder:

```
sudo chown -R new_uid:new_uid /var/username
```

Once the home folder information, uid, and gid are changed, you will modify com.apple.loginwindow.plist, the preference file for both the Login window and the Fast User Switching list, so that the account will not appear in either list. You will add the short name of the user account you want to hide to the HiddenUsersList key in that .plist file using the defaults command. For example,

```
sudo defaults write /Library/Preferences/com.apple.loginwindow.plist HiddenUsersList -array-add hadmin
```

In order for the hidden administrator account to log in, you must configure the Login window to prompt for a name and password. This is configured in the Login Options of the Accounts pane in System Preferences. Additionally, the user won't appear in the Remote Desktop user list in the Sharing pane of System Preferences. Therefore, if you would like to give this user Remote Desktop access, you must do so *before* changing the user's uid.

When the user is logged in, the account appears in System Preferences, where basic settings can be modified.

Creating a User Account in the BSD Files

The second method, adding a user to a BSD flat user file, requires manually editing the /etc/master.passwd file and enabling the BSD Open Directory plug-in in the Directory Access utility, located in the Utilities folder.

The /etc/master.passwd file contains one user per line, with each line containing ten colon-delimited attributes. For example:

```
hadmin:*:499:499::0:0:Hidden Administrator:/var/hadmin:/bin/bash
```

The first attribute is the short user name (hadmin). The second attribute is the encrypted account password (an asterisk indicates there is no password associated with that user). This value should only be changed on the command line with the passwd utility. The third and fourth attributes are the user and primary group IDs, also known as *uid* and *gid*, respectively (499). The next attribute after the group ID should be the account's general classification. This attribute is often left empty. The next two attributes are for the password change time and account expiration time, followed by the user's long name (Hidden Administrator). The next attribute is the path to the user's home folder (/var/hadmin). Be sure to create a folder here, and change the owner of it using chown. The final attribute is the default shell (/bin/bash).

To change the user's password, use the `passwd` command with the `-i file` parameter to specify that the crypt password should be stored in the BSD flat file:

```
sudo passwd -i file hadmin
```

To direct Mac OS X to allow user accounts in the BSD flat files to log in:

1. Launch Directory Access and select the Services tab.
2. Select BSD Flat Files and NIS, and click the Configure button.
3. In the dialog that appears, select "Use BSD local (/etc) files for authentication" and click OK.
4. In the Directory Access dialog, click the Authentication tab and choose "Custom path" from the Search pop-up menu.
5. Click Add, and then select /BSD/local from the list of available directories.
6. Click Add, and then click Apply.

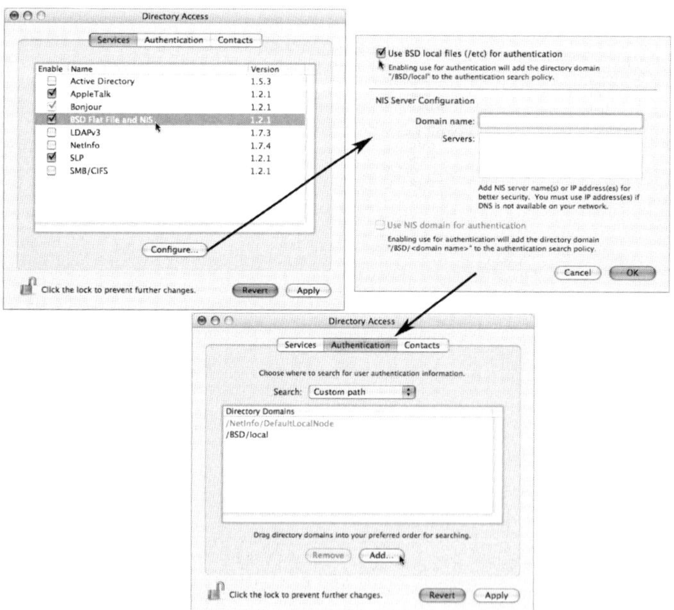

NOTE ▸ User accounts in BSD flat files are not listed in System Preferences because they don't exist in the local NetInfo database; the Accounts pane is not aware of them. If you were to create additional accounts in System Preferences, you could potentially create accounts that had conflicting user IDs or names. If you create user accounts using BSD flat files, use extra caution when managing all user accounts on the computer.

Managing Home Folders

Methods such as NetBoot start up your computer each time with a fresh copy of an image on the network. This fresh image also includes a clean version of the local home folders found under /Users. Any modifications that are made, either to settings or to saved documents, are lost with each restart. This is great news if you wish to present a clean volume for multiple users, but it can present a challenge if you wish to allow users to maintain customized individual experiences or permanently save documents in their home folders.

To allow user customization, you use Open Directory in Mac OS X Server to provide network user accounts and network mounts. This configuration lets users log in to any computer on your network and access their home folders located on a server. When you log in to a computer started up from a NetBoot volume using a network user account, the client computer retrieves the networked user's home folder location from a share point. As shown in the following figure, this share point typically resides on a server other than the one your computer is started up from.

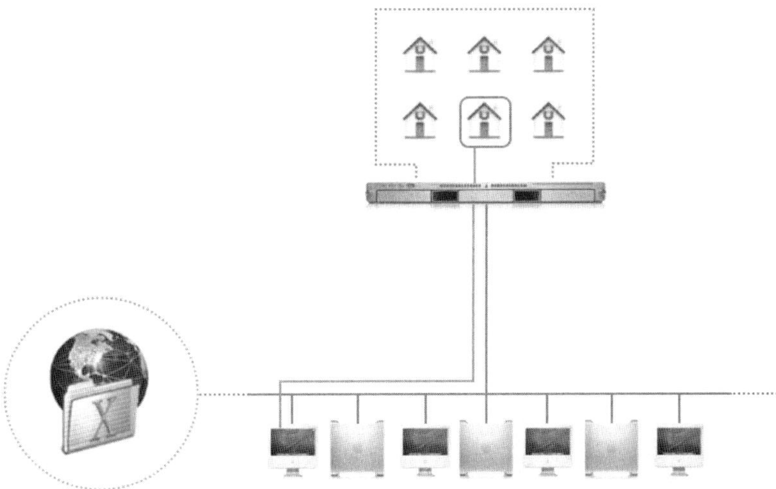

Using Setup Assistant

When deploying images in single-user environments, you may find it useful to force Setup Assistant to run when the user first starts up the computer. This prompts users to create their own unique accounts.

To force Setup Assistant to run, delete the file .AppleSetupDone located in /var/db/ on the startup volume. Use the following command in Terminal for the current startup volume:

```
sudo rm /var/db/.AppleSetupDone
```

If the startup disk you wish to use is not your current startup volume, use the following command:

```
sudo rm /Volumes/startup_disk_name/var/db/.AppleSetupDone
```

You may also want to remove any accounts—along with their home folders—that you added during setup (for example, the admin account).

To delete an account, perform the following commands for the current startup disk:

```
sudo nicl -raw /var/db/netinfo/local.nidb delete /users/account_name

sudo rm -rf /Users/account_name
```

If the startup disk you wish to use is not your current startup disk, use the following command:

```
sudo nicl -raw /Volumes/startup_disk_name/var/db/netinfo/local.nidb delete /users/account_name

sudo rm -rf /Volumes/startup_disk_name/Users/account_name
```

NOTE ▶ The /users/*account_name* at the end of the nicl command is case sensitive: the *u* in *users* is lowercase! This location refers to an entry in the NetInfo database, not a folder in the file system.

WARNING ▶ Deleting an account from the NetInfo database does not remove the user's local home folder, but the above command WILL remove ALL items in the user's home folder and those items will be completely unrecoverable.

Including Classic

When deploying PowerPC-based Macintosh computers, Classic presents lab administrators with a challenge (Classic is not supported on Intel-based Macintosh computers). Mac OS 9 doesn't offer the same security structure that Mac OS X provides. For instance, a user could potentially start up a computer in Mac OS 9 to subvert the Mac OS X security structure and do considerable damage to the Mac OS X system. Even within the Classic environment, a user can inadvertently make modifications that affect the experience of other users.

To reduce the security risk, you might choose not to install Mac OS 9 at all. This situation deters a user from starting up in Mac OS 9, unless the user has a CD or a FireWire drive with Mac OS 9 installed, and the computer supports booting from a Mac OS 9 system (something that most newer Macs do not support). Alternatively, don't install the Mac OS 9 drivers when formatting your drive. This way, users can use the Classic environment, but if they attempt to start up the computer with a CD or FireWire drive with Mac OS 9, they won't be able to see the Mac OS X startup volume.

> **NOTE ▶** To prevent users from starting up the computer with a disk other than the one designated by you, enable the Open Firmware password. This makes it necessary for a password to be entered in order to start up the computer from any other bootable device. Consider implementing this basic security step in addition to any other solutions you use to secure your computers. The pre-Mac OS X v10.4 Open Firmware Password application can be downloaded for free from www.apple.com/support/downloads/openfirmwarepassword.html and the Mac OS X v10.4 version of the Open Firmware Password application must be obtained from the install DVD or CD of Mac OS X v10.4 or Mac OS X Server v10.4.

An additional challenge is that Mac OS 9 requires all users to have read/write access to many common files in order to work as expected. For instance, Mac OS 9 maintains only one set of preferences and one Documents folder for all users. This is one way that one user's actions can affect another user's experience; documents can easily be misplaced and end up in the wrong hands, with security compromised. To further complicate matters, some Mac OS 9 applications require the ability to write back to their own folders.

Managing Preferences in Classic

The best way to manage preferences in Classic is to allow users to store Classic preferences in their own home folders, as shown in the following figure. This can be done easily in the Classic pane of System Preferences by selecting "Use Mac OS 9 preferences from your home," which stores Classic preferences in ~/Library/Classic instead of in the Classic System Folder.

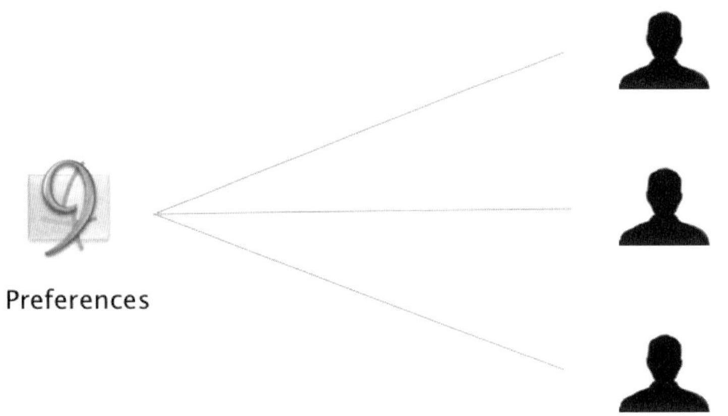

Using Classic on a Disk Image

The Classic environment can start from a disk image, and can even mount a disk image automatically when Classic is started, as shown in this image.

To direct Classic to use a System Folder from a disk image, do the following:

1. Launch Disk Utility (/Applications/Utilities), and choose File > New > Disk Image from Folder to create a disk image.
2. Select a valid Mac OS 9 System Folder as the source of the image, and make the image Read/Write so that temporary files can write back to the image.

3 Save the disk image in /Library/Application Support or some other location where you want it stored.

4 Double-click the disk image to mount it.

5 Open the Classic pane of System Preferences.

6 Select the System Folder in the disk image volume.

7 Close the Classic pane.

 Each time Classic starts, Mac OS X automatically mounts the disk image.

8 Check for each user and set up the image preference if necessary.

WARNING ▶ Once this procedure is accomplished, the Classic pane of System Preferences should be opened only when the disk image is mounted. Opening the Classic pane when the disk image is not mounted may result in Classic's losing track of the System Folder.

NOTE ▶ If a Mac OS 9 application stores its temporary files in the Mac OS 9 System Folder, the disk image may run out of space. You may wish to create a sparse disk image, where you can drag and drop copies of your Mac OS 9 System Folder and Mac OS 9 Applications folder, and then delete them from the local volume. This removes the disk-space-limitation issue.

To address the problem of the system requiring users to have read/write access to common system files, run Classic from a disk image. Script a logout process whereby the Classic disk image file, which contains the Mac OS 9 System Folder, is overwritten with a fresh copy. Additionally, include any applications that need to write to their own folders in the same image.

ShadowClassic (a free open-source tool from Mike Bombich; www.bombich.com) allows you to lock a Classic disk image file to make it read-only, thus preventing users from changing its contents. It mounts the image with a functionally writable shadow file. Instead of applications making changes to the contents of the disk image, the changes are now written to a temporary file. After a logout and login cycle, the temporary file is discarded and the Classic environment is presented to the user in a "clean" state.

There is one caveat to the ShadowClassic procedure: If you launch a Mac OS 9 application that is stored on the Classic disk image prior to launching Classic (for example, by clicking its icon in the Dock or double-clicking an alias of the application), the Finder subverts ShadowClassic and mounts the Classic disk image without a shadow file. To avoid this situation, set Classic to start up on login.

Using Apple Software Restore

ASR is a native Mac OS X application that efficiently copies disk images onto volumes. It is also capable of accurately cloning volumes, although PowerPC- and Intel-based architectures currently each require their own separate images. In Mac OS X, ASR is provided as a command-line tool (asr) with some features accessible through the Disk Utility graphical interface. This feature makes ASR especially efficient and easy to script for mass or repetitive deployment.

As shown in the following figure, ASR requires a properly prepared and created disk image for most efficient operation. This image can be created with the Image from Folder command in Disk Utility or by using Mike Bombich's utility NetRestore Helper (www.bombich.com). These tools can be used to take a volume and create a disk image from that volume and store it on yet a third volume (for later deployment).

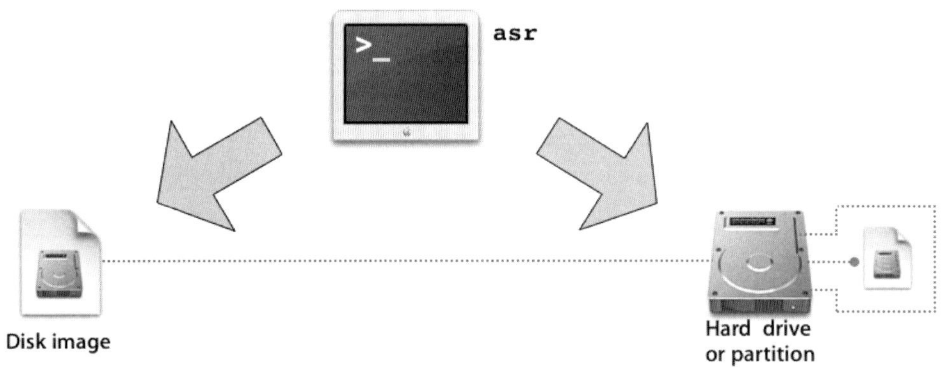

Creating Disk Images with Disk Utility

Once your initial model volume is set up, configured, and clean, you create a disk image of that volume that can be used by ASR. The word *model* is used to support the fact that the image will be used on several computers. Before you create your image, it's a good idea to understand the Disk Utility vernacular: *Volumes*, *drive*, *partitions*, *devices* are all often used interchangeably. When you define a folder, you seldom mean a volume or drive.

Disk Utility has two ways to create images from items: one from devices, one from folders. At first glance, this seems to make sense. However, when creating a disk image for imaging and deployment, the best option is to use the create image from a folder menu option and then select the volume that you wish to image. This will not copy the free space.

Creating an image from a device will actually capture every image, including a device that has been partitioned into several logical volumes, whether it is block-used or not, so it is not incredibly useful when creating model images. Also, if you create an image from a device, you won't be able to perform a block-restore to any volume larger than the one on which you created the image. Creating an image from a folder is slower, but it gives a better (stretchable, defragmented) result.

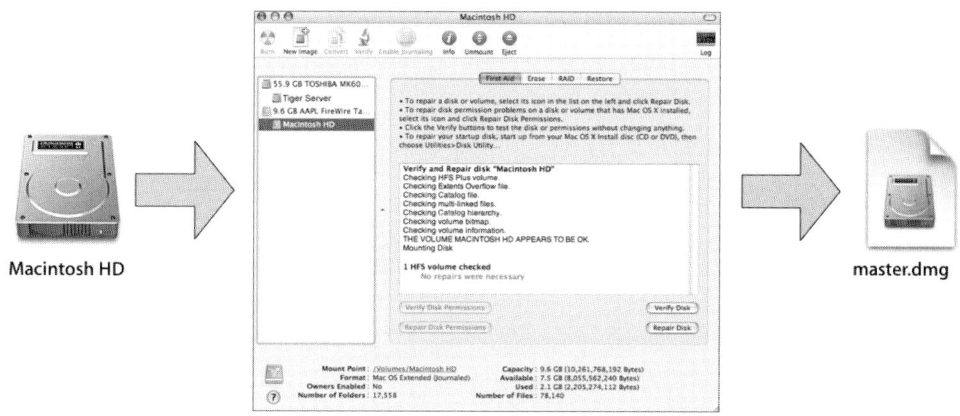

There are four Image Format options: read/write, read-only, compressed, and DVD/CD master. ASR doesn't scan read/write images, so you should save as either read-only or compressed. Compressed images create smaller files that use less disk space and network bandwidth but take longer to decompress, especially on G3-based computers. In general, uncompressed, read-only images are faster for local delivery, but compressed images are faster for network delivery. You'll want to save the image on your production computer (or volume) if you have it set up at this point (you can always transfer it later if necessary).

> **NOTE ▶** This operation requires twice as much free space on the volume to which you are saving the image as you have data on the source.

Disk Utility, as well as the command-line tool hdiutil, removes caches and swap files that would take up extra space on a disk image automatically. This information is unnecessary to restore, since it is dynamic and specific to users or computers. The asr man page explains when and what files are removed. In addition, you might want to remove ssh keys and known hosts if you have used the model computer to make ssh connections.

Once the image is created, run imagescan using the command-line tool asr or by selecting Images > Scan Image for Restore in Disk Utility. imagescan adds checksum information to the image and ASR won't perform a restore operation with a disk image that hasn't had the checksum information added by imagescan. To scan the disk image master.dmg using the command line, type the following command (make sure you are in the same directory as the image or provide the path):

```
sudo asr -imagescan master.dmg
```

Creating Disk Images with NetRestore Helper

NetRestore is an open-source tool (www.bombich.com) that allows you to complete multiple imaging tasks simultaneously. It is based on the Mac OS X–native version of ASR, automating many of the tasks that might otherwise require the command line. NetRestore is not, however, a product that Apple provides support for.

NetRestore is bundled with NetRestore Helper, an application that allows you to create, clean up, and scan an ASR-ready disk image in a single step.

To create an image using NetRestore Helper, follow these steps (as shown in the figure below):

1 Launch NetRestore Helper by double-clicking the icon on the Desktop.

2 Choose the drive from which you want to make an image.

3 If you're using a FireWire hard drive or any G3-based model, choose "Read-only" for faster restores. Or, for faster network restores, choose "Read-only compressed."

4 Choose to enable or disable:

- File-level restore checksumming, necessary if saving to a mounted AFP share point.
- Multicast restore post-processing, which will save time when creating the image if multicast restores will not be used.

5 Authenticate, and then click Create Master Image. You are prompted to save the image.

You need twice the available space on the target volume of the source.

6 If you need to save the image to the same drive that you are imaging, create a Temporary Items folder and save it to that folder on the drive.

The disk capacity cannot exceed 33 percent in this scenario.

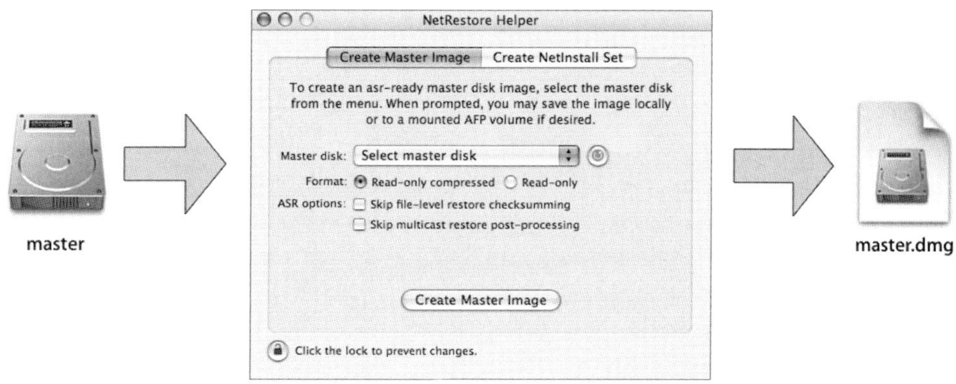

Using NetBoot Images

NetBoot is a service that allows you to start up supported Apple computers from various types of disk images located on a Mac OS X Server, as shown in the following figure. You can create disk images containing Mac OS 9, Mac OS X, and Mac OS X Server system software that can be used by multiple network clients at once Because you can store up to 50 NetBoot/Network Install images on a NetBoot server, NetBoot provides a centralized source for system software you use to configure, test, and deploy.

NOTE ▸ PowerPC- and Intel-based systems each require separate images, thus doubling the amount of space required to host images.

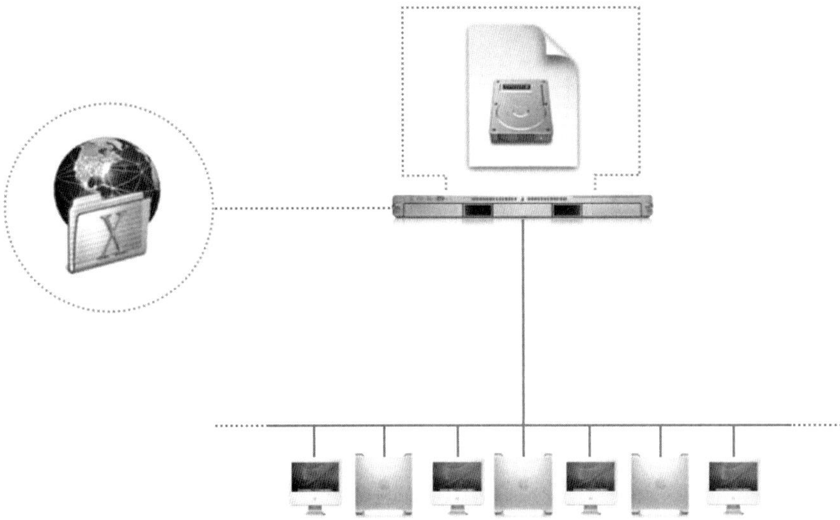

NetBoot is most effective in computing situations where there is a high possibility of user turnover and a large number of computers being deployed with a common set of tasks. NetBoot can also be used effectively in university computer labs, public kiosks, high performance clusters, and computers that are provided for reporters, for example, at sporting events.

As with ASR, NetBoot requires a properly prepared and created disk image for the most efficient operation. This image can be created with the System Image Utility included with Mac OS X Server or by using NetRestore Helper. In this section, you will learn how to prepare and create a disk image to be used efficiently by the NetBoot service.

NetBoot allows you to deploy software in three distinct ways:

- Network Boot (NetBoot)—This method involves starting up the client computer from a disk image maintained on Mac OS X Server. Any changes made to the system by users are stored in a shadow file that by default is deleted when the computer is restarted. NetBoot allows you to quickly deploy an operating system and software to your client computers without installing any software on the actual hard drive. Because you maintain only one copy of the NetBoot disk image, maintenance of the operating system and software is much less time-consuming.
- Network Install—Using Network Install is exactly like starting up from a Mac OS X install disc, except that you are actually starting up the computer from a disk image on a NetBoot server. Network Install image sets are replicas of the installer media that you receive from Apple with the option to add your own packages and customizations.
- Network Restore (Network Install plus block-level restore)—Network Restore is similar to Network Install in terms of the startup method. However, instead of the Installer application using packages to install software, a master disk image is restored to the local volume using a block-level copy. Network Restore is faster and more efficient than Network Install and is, therefore, the fastest method of deploying a disk image to a large number of similar computers.

TIP If using NetBoot or any full disk image restore to boot or load multiple machines running Mac OS X Server, you'll need to obtain a volume license key from your Apple sales representative. This is due to copy protection in place that prohibits multiple servers from using the same serial number. Similarly, if you have machines that came preinstalled with Mac OS X v10.3, you cannot install Mac OS X v10.4 without an upgrade license for each one of the machines set to receive the new image.

NetBoot Image Source

A NetBoot image can be created using the following sources:

- Any volume with Mac OS X installed and configured
- A CD or DVD that is capable of starting a computer, such as a Mac OS X Install DVD or an emergency CD containing some type of disk repair or checking utility.
- A disk image (.dmg) file created from a volume with Mac OS X installed and configured, similar to one created for ASR

When you're creating a NetBoot image using a volume with an installed and configured Mac OS X system, the model computer on which you configure your image should be your newest and most powerful computer. Mac OS X is a highly portable operating system that will work with both newer hardware and older hardware; however, the move from the PowerPC to the Intel chipset will require separate NetBoot images, as neither system will recognize the other's bootable image.

As with ASR images, you should also choose a computer that has the most hardware options and peripherals. For example, if you have at least one computer with a SuperDrive and/or a backlit keyboard, use that computer to create your image, even if most other computers don't have that option.

Diskless NetBoot and the Role of the Local Volume

With NetBoot, many clients can read from the same bootable image, but when a client needs to write anything back to its startup volume (such as print jobs and other temporary files), NetBoot automatically redirects the written data to shadow files on the client computer's file system, as shown in the following figure.

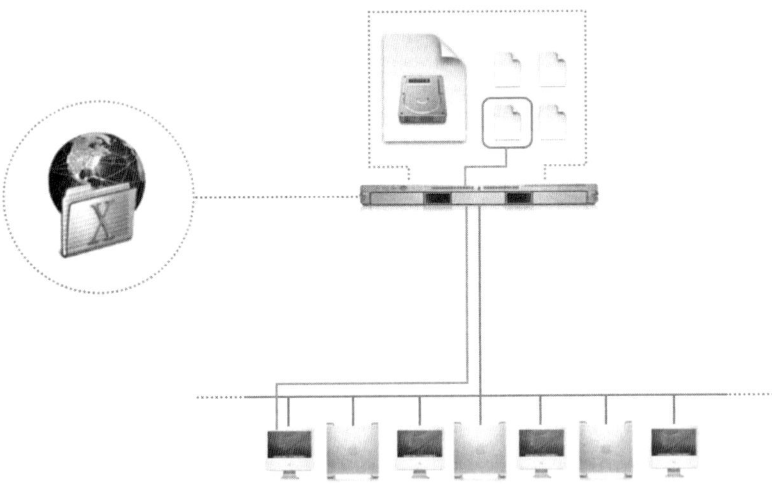

The shadow files preserve the unique identity of each client during the entire time it is started up from a NetBoot image. NetBoot transparently maintains changed user data in the shadow files and reads unchanged data from the shared system image. The shadow files are re-created at startup, so any changes made by the user to his or her startup volume are lost at restart. For example, if a user saves a document to the startup volume, after a restart that document will be gone. This behavior preserves the condition of the environment that the administrator set up. To allow users to save documents, provide accounts on a file server via Open Directory on Mac OS X Server using network accounts and network mounts.

Shadow files are stored on the local startup volume unless the NetBoot image is designated as diskless. In this case, the shadow files are stored on the server. Designating a diskless NetBoot image is necessary if a local hard drive either doesn't exist or must remain untouched by system operations—for instance, if you don't want your users to save any sensitive data to a local hard drive.

Because the shadow files are frequently accessed, system performance can be affected when diskless NetBoot images are used. For this reason, shadow files should be stored on the local hard drive, except where diskless operation is necessary.

Using System Image Utility

The System Image Utility tool allows you to customize your NetBoot or Network Install images. This means that you can open an existing image, make changes, and re-create the image. System Image Utility replaces the older Network Image Utility of previous releases. Located in /Applications/Server in Mac OS X Server or on any computer with Server Administration tools installed, System Image Utility uses any one of the previously described image sources to create NetBoot images.

Each tab of System Image Utility handles a different aspect of the image-creation manipulation process. The following are the tabs for both NetBoot and NetInstall images:

- General: Used to enter the image name, ID, description, location, and deployment protocol (NFS or HTTP). The image name you supply provides the volume name to be listed in the Startup Disk pane of System Preferences. The optional Description text area for administrative notes is a good place to store information that details differences between this and other images stored on your server. The text you type here is visible in the Server Admin application when configuring your NetBoot service.

  NOTE ▶ You can also deliver images over https; however, both the server and the client NetBoot image must contain the certificates being used.

- Contents: Contains image source (disk image, volume, DVD/CD), language to be used, and additional installation or boot packages or scripts.

- Model Filter: Restricts ability to boot or install from the selected image to specific Macintosh computer models.
- Sharing Prefs: Offers the ability to use unique names for the sharing name, derived from a file chosen by you. By default, if the text areas in this tab are left blank, all computers receive the same computer name, -AUTOMATIC-. When imaged computers start up for the first time and find that they have identical names, Mac OS X resolves the issue by creating unique computer names and .local host names automatically. When text is entered in the Computer Name field, a unique name is given to each client based on that name and the client's MAC address. For more explicit names, create a tab-delimited file with the names of the computers and their corresponding MAC Addresses so that the booted computer receives the name that is associated with each computer's MAC address. Any remaining clients are given names based on the contents of Computer Name and their Ethernet (MAC) address. If the field is blank, clients are given the -AUTOMATIC- computer name.
- Directory Services: Applies binding from a local machine running System Image Utility to any computers using selected image.
- Default User (NetBoot only): Lets you choose a default long name, short name, and password for the initial login.
- Installation Options (NetInstall only): Offers Update ByHost preference files (files based on the MAC address of each machine), enables destination verification, and enables automated installation—including selecting, erasing, and restarting specific volumes.

To create a new image with System Image Utility, do the following:

1. Launch System Image Utility located in /Applications/Server.
2. Click New Install for a new Network Install image, or New Boot for a NetBoot image.

   You may want to configure the NetBoot service first. In particular, configure the volumes that will be used to store the images and shadow files. This process creates a NetBootSPn folder in /Library/NetBoot/ and allows you to select that as a destination when creating images.
3. Click each tab (described above) and supply the necessary information.

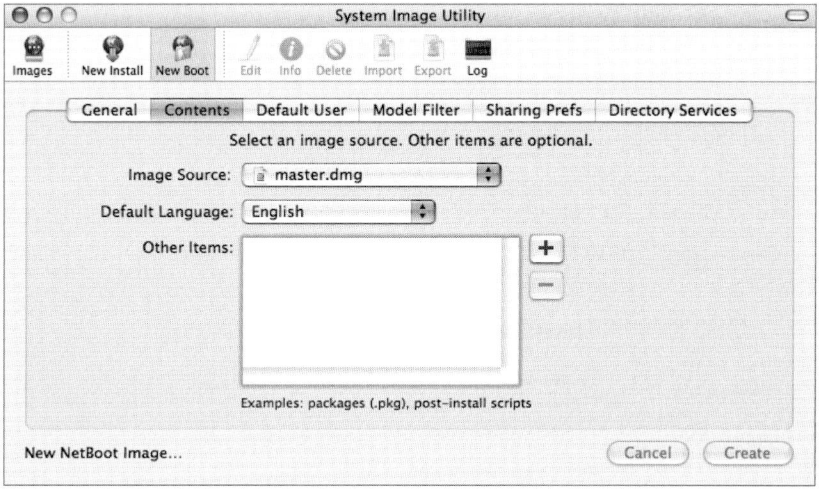

4 Click Create to create the image.

You will be prompted to specify where to store it. For the NetBoot service to recognize the image, it must be stored in /Library/NetBoot/NetBootSP*n*/*imagename*.nbi/, where *n* is the volume number and *imagename* is the name of the image you entered when creating it in System Image Utility.

5 If you have already configured NetBoot service, the Save dialog includes a pop-up menu listing the available volumes.

6 If you choose a volume from that menu, the save location changes to the NetBootSP*n* share point on that volume.

NOTE ► In early versions of Mac OS X v10.4, files and folders that are normally invisible appear when an image is deployed. To remedy this situation, mount the master image as read/write and insert the Mac OS X Install DVD. In the command line, navigate to the following directory

```
cd /Volumes/Mac\ OS\ X\ Install\ DVD/System/Installation/Packages/OSInstall.mpkg/Contents/Resources/
```

Then type

```
sudo ./SetHidden /Volumes/mounted_master_disk_image_name hidden_MacOS9
```

Unmount the image,convert back to read-only, and rescan it for restore.

Using NetRestore Helper

In addition to creating a master ASR disk image with NetRestore Helper, you can create Network Install images that are automatically set up to run NetRestore on startup. Use this to restore your target volume on your computers with your master image.

To begin creating a Network Install image with NetRestore, do the following:

1 Click Create NetInstall Set.

2 Enter a name, image ID, and description on the fields provided.

These fields are similar to those in System Image Utility's General tab.

3 Click Save NetInstall-Restore set.

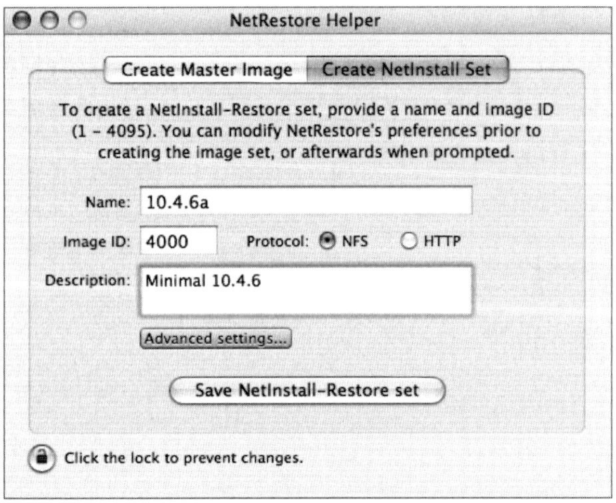

4 When NetRestore Helper finishes creating the image set, you can choose to configure NetRestore.

This launches the copy of NetRestore that has been installed in the Utilities folder of the Network Install-Restore image set, and you are prompted to edit the preferences and configurations.

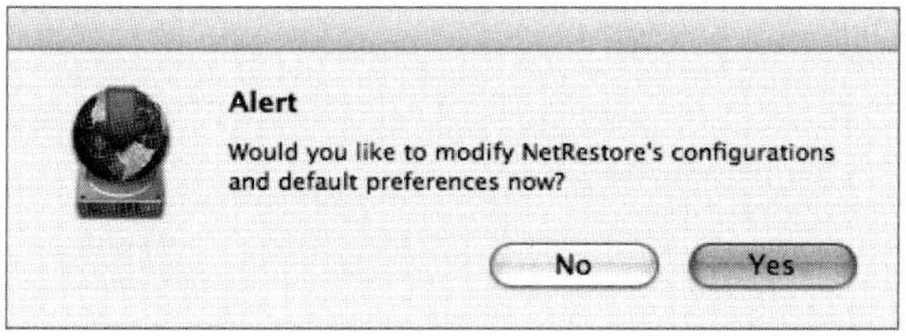

5 In NetRestore, choose Edit Configurations from the NetRestore menu.

Here, you create a configuration that references a master disk image file. The master disk image can be any ASR-ready disk image created with NetRestore or Disk Utility and placed on a file or Web server.

6 Select the configuration in the list of configurations and click Restore.

If the image mounts, then you have set up the configuration correctly.

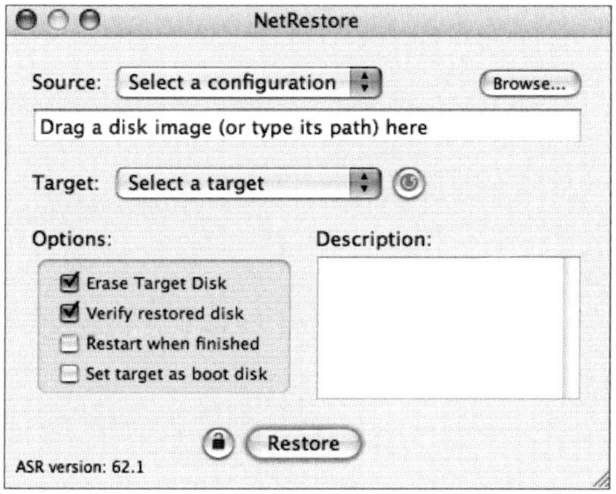

7 Copy the image set to /Library/NetBoot/NetBootSP*n* on your NetBoot server, and enable the image in Server Admin.

8 Reboot your client computer from the server, and restore your master image set.

We've primarily discussed why these methods are a convenient way to administer computers. However, some of them also provide significant security protection for your computers. By using NetBoot or Radmind (see the Appendix, "Using Radmind") in your environment, you ensure that every time your computer is booted, the files in your operating system have not been tampered with and are the original files provided by your image. This significantly reduces the likelihood of malicious software living on your computer, and also protects against unauthorized user changes on public workstations.

Lesson Review

1. What command-line tools are used to work with disk images?
2. What is the process for creating an image that can be restored with ASR?
3. What does `imagescan` do, and why is it important?
4. What kinds of disk images can be served by NetBoot in Mac OS X Server?
5. When would you use an image number higher than 4096 to describe a NetBoot image?

Answers

1. `diskutil` and `hdiutil`.
2. Create an image from a model computer, and then imagescan the image to checksum it.
3. It adds checksum information to the image, and restores cannot be initiated without an imagescan being done.
4. NetBoot images, Network Install images, and Network Install plus block-copy restore images.
5. When you have more than one Mac OS X Server hosting that image, since clients will see only one image and rudimentary load balancing will be achieved.

References

Administration Guides

"System Imaging and Software Update Administration": http://images.apple.com/server/pdfs/System_Image_and_SW_Update_v10.4B.pdf

Knowledge Base Articles

You can check for new and updated articles in the AppleCare Knowledge Base at www.apple.com/support.

"System Imaging Services Overview": http://docs.info.apple.com/article.html?path=ServerAdmin/10.4/en/c0os.html

URLs

Visit the following sites for more information:

Apple Software Restore (ASR): http://developer.apple.com/documentation/Darwin/Reference/ManPages/man8/asr.8.html

Internet-Enabled Disk Images: http://developer.apple.com/documentation/Darwin/Reference/ManPages/man1/hdiutil.1.html
http://developer.apple.com/documentation/DeveloperTools/Conceptual/SoftwareDistribution/Concepts/sd_disk_images.html

Mac OS X Imaging and Deployment Software and Tips: www.bombich.com

3

Time This lesson takes about 2 hours to complete.

Goals Create and deliver custom installation packages for Mac OS X and Mac OS X Server

Describe the differences between packages and metapackages

Lesson **3**

Creating and Deploying Packages

For deployment purposes, custom installation packages can be used with a number of utilities to automate the process of mass software deployment with little user interaction. In single-user environments, where user interaction may be desired, Installer packages allow you to have a professional-looking appearance that is customized to your particular software or configuration.

Custom installation packages can be easily used to upgrade software and related files and can facilitate a customized welcome message, read-me file, and software license to which the user must agree. Your package can also designate whether the computer is to be restarted after software is installed.

This lesson deals with the Apple-specific package-creation utility called PackageMaker, as well as other, third-party utilities. By the end of this lesson, you'll know how to create, customize, and deploy custom packages to computers running Mac OS X and Mac OS X Server.

Why Use Custom Installation Packages?

A common method for installing software is drag-install, in which the application and associated files are copied from the distribution media to the target volume. Although this method is easy and works well when the application files need to be copied to only one or two places in the file system, it is not the most flexible method of installing software. A custom installation package is a better choice because you are able to do the following:

- Verify that a certain version of the operating system is already installed
- Verify that certain components are already in the system
- Start or stop processes
- Put software in multiple locations throughout the system

Custom packages can come in a few varieties, as discussed below.

About Installation Packages

An *installation package* is a collection of compressed files and other information used to install software onto a computer. The contents of an installation package are contained within a single bundle, which has the extension .pkg. The package is created by using the utility PackageMaker, which can be found in /Developer/Applications/Utilities if the Xcode Developer Tools were installed. The Finder displays the package bundle as a single file, but it is actually a special folder that contains all the files needed for a custom install.

> **NOTE ▸** Although the Mac OS X Server Administration Tools disc includes a copy of PackageMaker, you should install the Xcode Developer Tools to get the most recent version of PackageMaker. The Xcode installation package is available from the Apple Developer Connection (http://developer.apple.com).

Installer packages are installed either by the Installer application or by the `installer` command-line tool. Installer will display the custom welcome, read-me, and license information; place the software in its designated locations; and run scripts designated for the installation.

About Metapackages

Metapackages allow you to present multiple packages to the user as a single installation package. A metapackage doesn't install files itself; instead it references other packages to perform the actual installations. You can designate each package within the metapackage as optional or required, allowing your users the flexibility to choose what they want to install.

Just as with installation packages, the user installing a metapackage clicks only one bundle in the Finder and is presented with the same Installer interface, but there is one exception. With metapackages, the user is offered a Customize button, which, if clicked, will display a list of each of the packages being installed, as well as check boxes to enable or disable each package.

Metapackages can be useful if you have files that are common to all users but still allow groups to have their own collections of additional files. For example, you could create a separate package that contains both department files and the files for all users. However, as soon as one of the files used by everyone changes, you need to re-create every department package. The solution, as shown in the following figure, is to create separate metapackages for each department, each also containing a common package for all users. This way, your users will have a single installation experience, but if a common file changes, only the common package has to be updated.

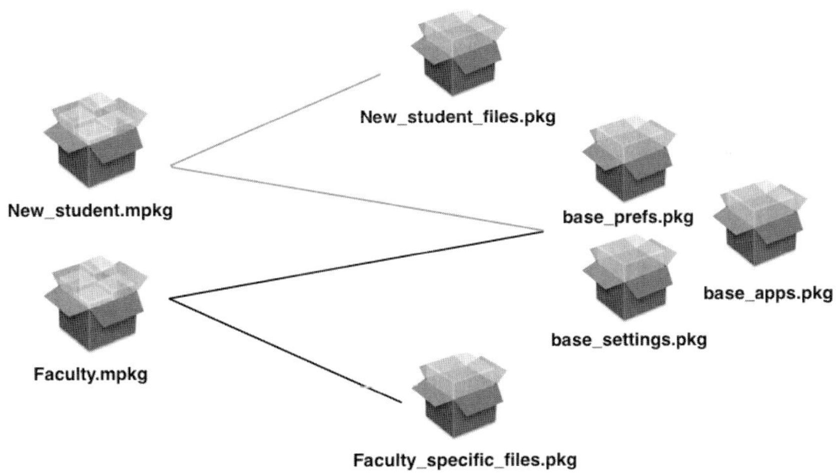

Metapackages are also useful for large software packages, when you have a large set of files you'd like to distribute, but only certain files will be updated. You could create a metapackage that refers to three separate packages:

1. The main application—This package might come directly from the vendor; or, if you were repackaging it, it would be updated with every revision of the application.

2. Configuration presets—This package might include default preferences for all of your users, as well as license code information that you'd rather distribute directly in a file rather than having to type a license code at every workstation. This package would rarely need to be updated.
3. Plug-ins and support files—This package could contain third-party plug-ins and other support files. It would rarely need to be updated. If additional plug-ins were needed later, you would simply add another package to your metapackage.

Looking Inside a Package

A package is made up of a collection of files that tell Installer what to install, how to install it, and how to verify that it was installed. These items reside in the Contents folder inside the package. To view the contents of a package, Control-click the package and choose Show Package Contents from the shortcut menu. This command opens a new Finder window, in which the package contents are displayed. Or, simply `cd` into the package from the Terminal.

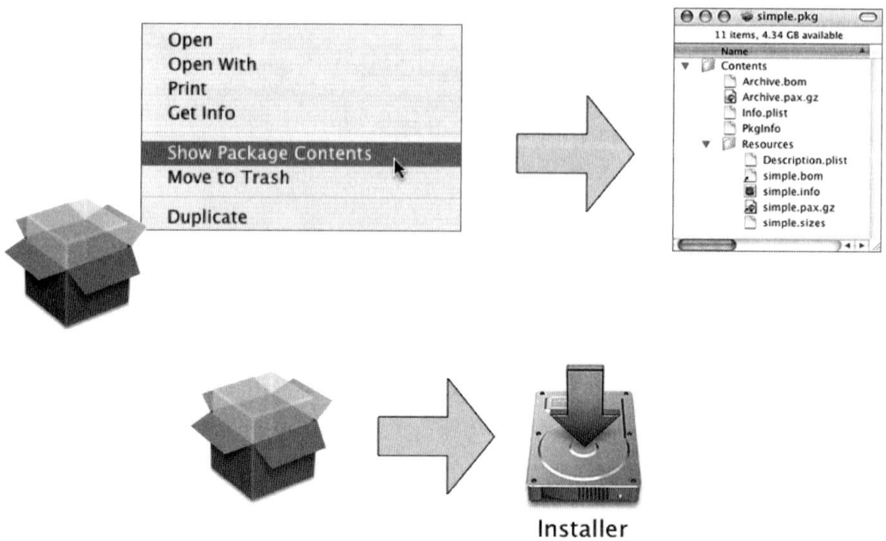

The Contents folder includes a bill of materials (.bom) file that describes the contents of the package. The BOM file contains a list of every file installed by the package, along with the ownership and permissions of each file. You can examine the contents of a BOM file by typing

```
lsbom Archive.bom
```

from inside the Contents folder. This folder also contains an information property list file (.plist) that contains the information entered in the package definition file when it was created. This file contains such details about the package as the authorization required to install and whether the package requires the computer to be rebooted after installation.

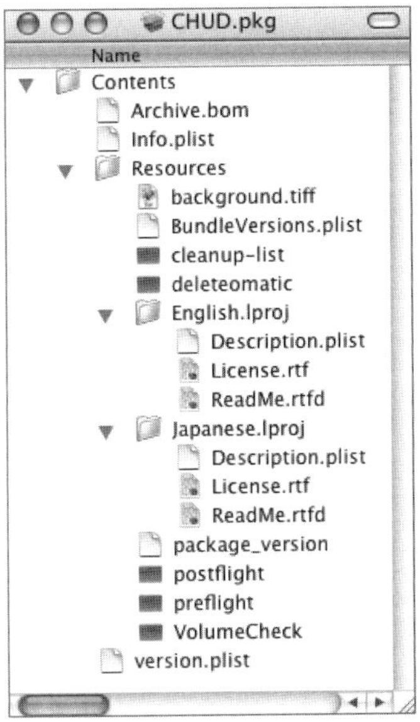

You can view this file in any text editor or with the Property List Editor application included with the Xcode Developer Tools. The archive file contains the set of files to be installed (payload) and is usually compressed (in gzip format) to save space. The size-calculation file is a text file that contains the compressed and uncompressed sizes of the package's payload. Installer uses this to calculate the space required to install the payload.

The Resources folder contains files that customize the behavior and look of Installer during the installation process. Resource files include environment test scripts and installation scripts (described later in this lesson), in addition to text files and a background image. The text files may include an introduction file, a read-me file, and a license file. When your resource folder contains these text files, the program will display the text contained within them in the Installer interface. The files should be in RTF format with the .rtf suffix, so the introduction file will be named Welcome.rtf, the read-me file will be ReadMe.rtf, and the license file will be License.rtf. Installer has the ability to show many types of files, including raw text (.txt), HTML (.html), and RTF directories (.rtfd), which are RTF files with embedded images. The background image, which must be named background.tif, will display in the background of each screen in Installer. The background image can be of any of the following file types: .jpg, .tif, .tiff, .gif, .pict, .eps, and .pdf.

To use localized versions of the resources, create folders with the name *languagename*.lproj, and put the resources for that language in that folder. Note that the scripts cannot be localized, but any of the information presented to the user can be localized.

You enter localized versions of messages in files with the .strings extension. Each .strings file contains messages localized for one language. You then place these files in the appropriate localized-resource directories (which have the .lproj extension). You don't need to create all of the resources. If any resources are missing, either they will be skipped or a default will be presented. For example, if Welcome.rtf is missing, a default pane asks the user to proceed to the installation. If License.rtf is missing, no license pane will appear.

Creating Distribution Scripts

In order to make sure that your software is installed correctly, PackageMaker allows scripts to customize the installation behavior. JavaScript can be used to create a *distribution script* to customize the installation experience. Specific shell scripts can be used in a package to carry out commands before and after the package is installed.

Installer distribution scripts are new in Mac OS X v10.4 and can help verify various hardware requirements prior to installing packaged software. This feature allows you to define the user experience within Installer using a single configuration file. You store this file in either a .pkg file or a .mpkg file, or save it as a .dist file. You can also take a metapackage and convert it to a distribution script. Use distribution scripts to do the following:

- Specify the relationship between packages and the custom selection user interface, allowing creation of complex dependencies

- Exercise full control over the user interface
- Base the behavior of the user interface on the capabilities and configuration of the target computer

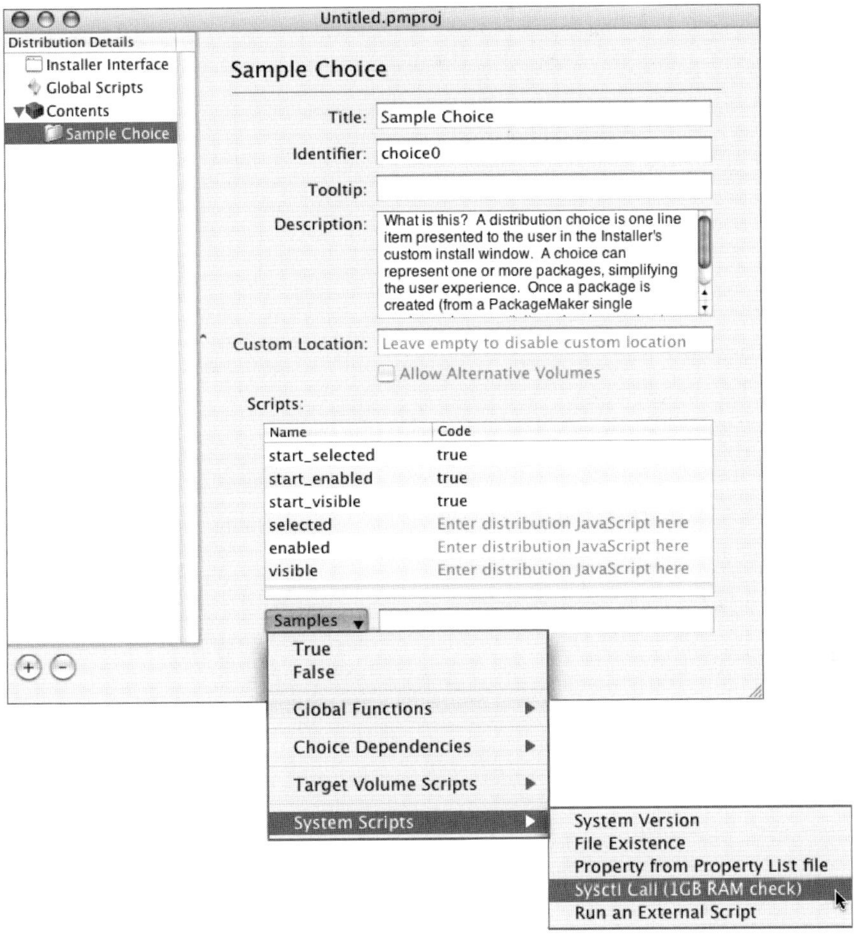

You can now consolidate many of the flags and functions configured by PackageMaker and the included shell scripts (such as InstallationCheck and VolumeCheck) into a single distribution script. The entire range of flags and standard package scripts, plus new features of Installer, are configured using JavaScript within that one file.

For more information on distribution scripts, install the Xcode tools for Mac OS X v10.4 and open /Developer/ADC Reference Library/releasenotes/DeveloperTools/Installer.html.

> **NOTE ▸** Distribution scripts are used only by Mac OS X v10.4 and later. They are ignored by Mac OS X v10.3 and earlier, so you should not depend on their functionality if you need to install on older operating systems.

Running Package Scripts

Scripts are an optional element of an installation package. You add scripts when you need to test certain conditions before installation or when you need to perform special tasks as the installation takes place. (You'll learn to add a script to an installation later in this lesson.)

Scripts can be run before and after the package's contents are installed. You can define two types of scripts: environment-test scripts and installation scripts. Environment-test scripts can determine whether the hardware and software of the target computer meet the package's requirements. Environment-test scripts include the following:

- InstallationCheck—Installer runs this shell script early in the installation process to determine whether the installation should proceed. If the installation cannot proceed, Installer displays a localizable message to the user. Supply this file to check for criteria such as minimum hardware requirements.
- VolumeCheck—Installer runs this script once for each mounted volume to determine whether a particular volume can receive the package's payload. If the installation cannot be done on a volume, Installer communicates this fact to the user, again using a localizable message. Supply this file to check for volume criteria and restrict the volumes on which a user can install. This script is usually used to check for software dependencies on each volume, such as the operating system installed on that volume.

Installation scripts perform tasks you deem necessary to prepare for installation and to clean up after an installation is completed. Use these scripts to create needed files, add configuration options to existing files, start and stop services, and verify that setup is done correctly. These are the default installation scripts:

- preflight—Runs before all other scripts, and before the installation or upgrade takes place
- preinstall—Runs after the preflight script for new installation

- preupgrade—Runs after the preflight script when Installer determines that the installation is an upgrade
- postinstall—Runs after the initial installation
- postupgrade—Runs after an upgrade installation
- postflight—Runs after all other scripts

The following list shows the order in which the scripts are executed and the point at which the actual installation takes place:

1. InstallationCheck—Can cancel the installation.
2. VolumeCheck—Can cancel the installation.
3. preflight.
4. preinstall or preupgrade.
5. Installer extracts and installs the package's contents (payload).
6. postinstall or postupgrade.
7. postflight.

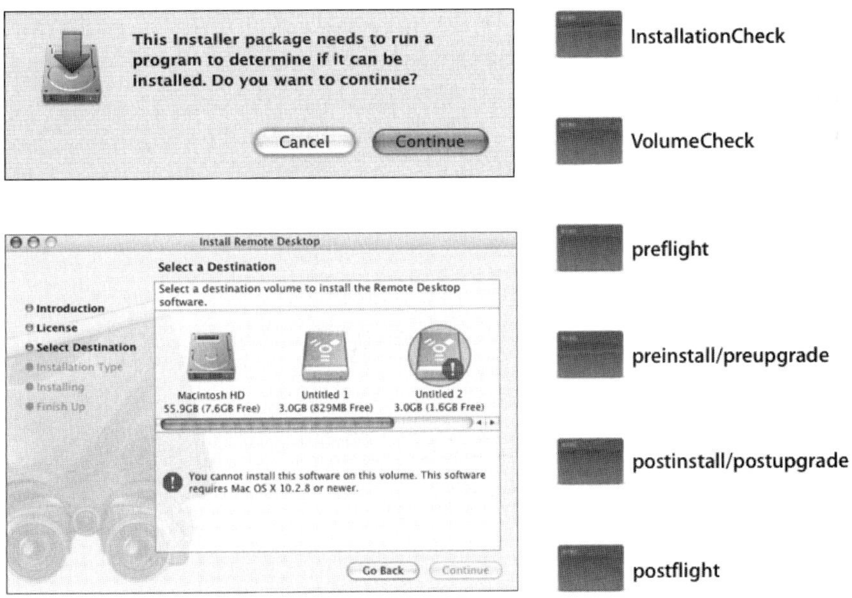

When a package script is run, four arguments are automatically passed to it that contain information useful to the script:

- $1—The full path to the package being installed; for example:

  /Volumes/Projects/Testing/*PackageName*.pkg
- $2—The full path to the installation destination; for example:

  /Applications
- $3—The mountpoint of the destination volume; for example:

  / or /Volumes/External_Drive
- $4—The root directory for the current System directory:

  /

Environment-test scripts and installation scripts can refer to other scripts, but the referred scripts must be included in the package's resources folder. You can see numerous example scripts by examining other packages. The scripts used by packages that have already been installed on your system can be found in /Library/Receipts/*PackageName*.pkg/Contents/Resources.

> **TIP** You should preface most of the paths in your script with the third argument ($3 in a shell script, $ARGV[2] in a Perl script). In most cases, this is all that is necessary to allow your package to be installed on volumes other than your boot volume. Remember that volume names commonly have spaces in them, so you should quote every path.

Using Payload-Free Packages

A *payload-free package* is a package that contains no files to install, so the Installer application uses scripts to automate any process. Payload-free packages are created using the same methods as with regular packages, but with no installed files. Payload-free packages contain only scripts that can automate tasks, as shown in the following figure.

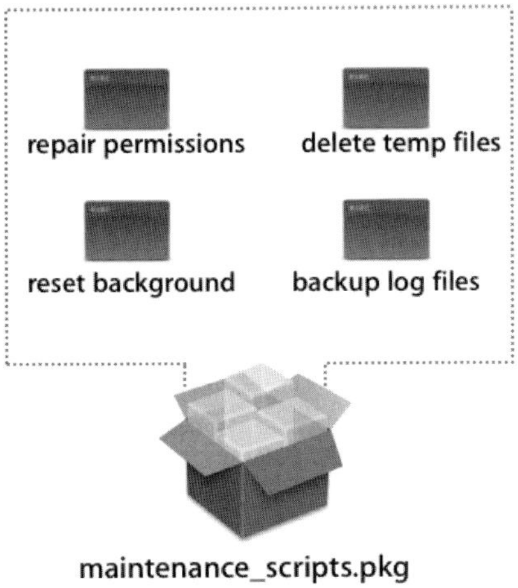

You can populate the resources folder with the same scripts as described in the previous section. This is particularly useful if you need users to run Unix commands on their computers, even if they aren't comfortable working in Terminal. Simply include the command in a postflight script in a payload-free package and ask the user to install the package by double-clicking it.

One way to use this method would be to create a Network Install image from a payload-free package containing a script that runs Apple Software Restore (ASR) over multicast to restore the local volume. See Lesson 2, "Creating and Using Disk Images," and Lesson 4, "Delivering Images and Packages," for information on setting up Network Install images and ASR multicast.

Using Receipts

During installation, Installer creates a package file called a *receipt* that contains the package's resources and a list of the files, permissions on the file with the file size, and a checksum. Note that the receipt doesn't actually contain the files that are installed (the payload), so receipt files are small. For a list of the files that were installed by the package, enter the following command on the command line:

```
lsbom /Library/Receipts/PackageName.pkg/Contents/Archive.bom
```

When Installer is installing a package, it uses the existence of a receipt to determine whether to install or upgrade. If a receipt exists, and version information exists in the software that is being installed, Installer can skip some files that don't need to be upgraded. Installer will also execute the preupgrade and postupgrade scripts instead of the preinstall and postinstall scripts that are run during an install.

As the following figure shows, receipt packages do not contain the actual files that were installed, but they contain the information about those files. Double-clicking a receipt will produce the error message shown below.

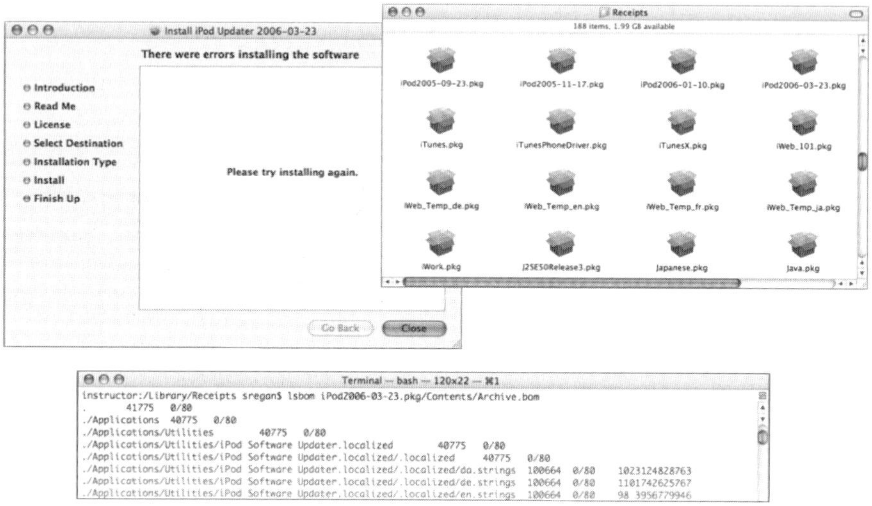

WARNING ▶ If you double-click a receipt for a package installed as part of the Mac OS X or Mac OS X Server installation, Installer will open as if there is a package to install. If you proceed through the screens in Installer, you will uninstall portions of the operating system. The result will be that the operating system will not work correctly.

TIP ▶ If you need to do a full install of a package that was previously installed on your system, delete the old package receipt first. When you do this, Installer no longer knows that you had previously installed the package and will treat the next install like the first. This is particularly useful if you need to replace a file that has become corrupt or is missing.

Creating Packages

With the number of complex files in a package, creating a package can seem intimidating at first. The Apple utility PackageMaker simplifies the process by letting you create packages using a setup assistant, add components to a distribution project, or manually create a package or metapackage project.

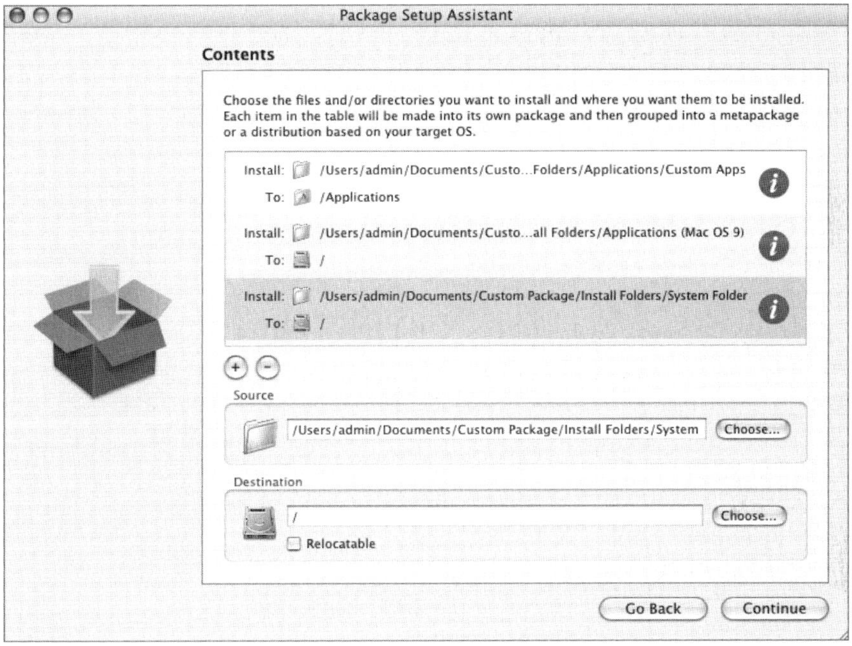

TIP Many of the following features are unique to very recent versions of PackageMaker, so be sure you're using the most recent distribution of the Xcode Developer Tools.

Package Setup Assistant uses a familiar interface for package creation. It is intended to allow for quick and easy package creation with intelligent defaults. If you need different custom settings, simply open the package or metapackage in PackageMaker.

To open Package Setup Assistant, select File > New and click Assist Me. The assistant will walk you through the package-creation process in the following steps:

1. Welcome—Prompts for basic package information.
2. Contents—Prompts for the items to install.
3. Bundle Identifiers—Displays what packages will be created, and prompts for bundle identifiers and versions.
4. Metadata—Prompts for package metadata. Not displayed when creating a distribution.
5. Resources—Prompts for resources (for example, License, ReadMe, and so on).
6. Package Creation—Will create all packages and bundle them in a metapackage or distribution if necessary.

Creating a Distribution Project

Distribution projects can be created for systems that run Mac OS X v10.4 and higher (as well as Mac OS X Server v10.4 and higher). Although a distribution project is similar to a metapackage, it provides more flexibility in customizing the Installer interface. This flexibility is provided by a distribution script, which is XML combined with JavaScript.

To create a minimal, functional distribution project, do the following:

1 Create the packages to be bundled.

2 Using PackageMaker, give the distribution a title in the Installer Interface pane.

3 Create choices for the items you want to install. Multiple packages can be attached to a single choice.

4 Add the packages to the appropriate choices.

5 Make sure the information for each package is correct.

6 Build the distribution by choosing Project > Build.

After the distribution is built, you have the option of verifying the build while still within PackageMaker.

The following figure shows a distribution project window with various authentication and postinstall actions already selected.

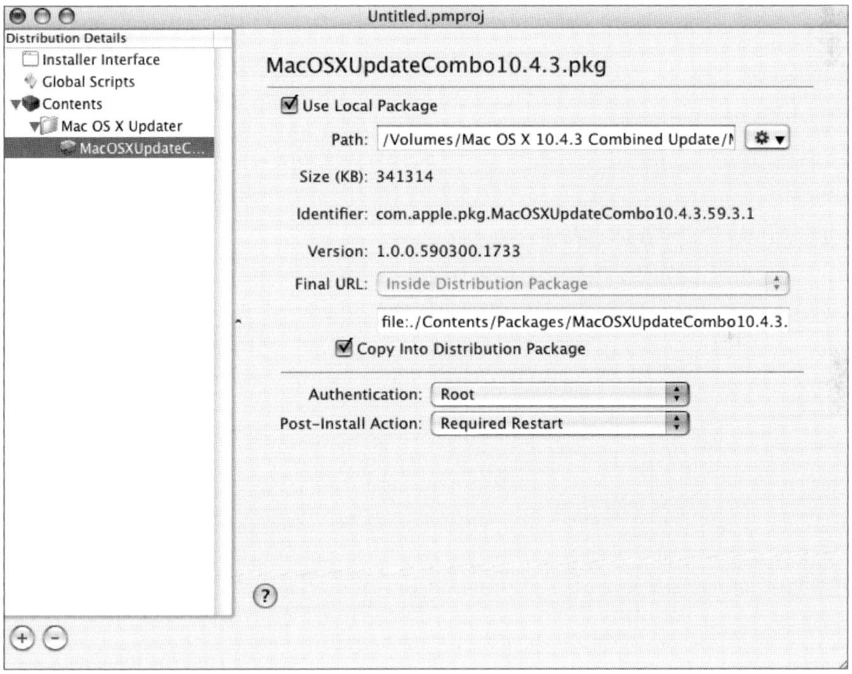

Determining Package File Structure

The first step in manually creating a package project with PackageMaker is to create a folder hierarchy containing the files to be installed. This arrangement should represent the folder hierarchy of the system that will receive the installed files.

Begin by creating a folder that represents the root folder of where your files will be installed, as shown in the following figure. In most cases, your destination root folder will correspond to the root folder (/) of the target file system, but this may not always be the case. If, for example, you were creating a package just to install fonts, the root folder could represent /Library/Fonts. The folder structure for the installer is incredibly important. Folders that do not exist will be created, while folders that do exist can have the existing items replaced by the ones in the package.

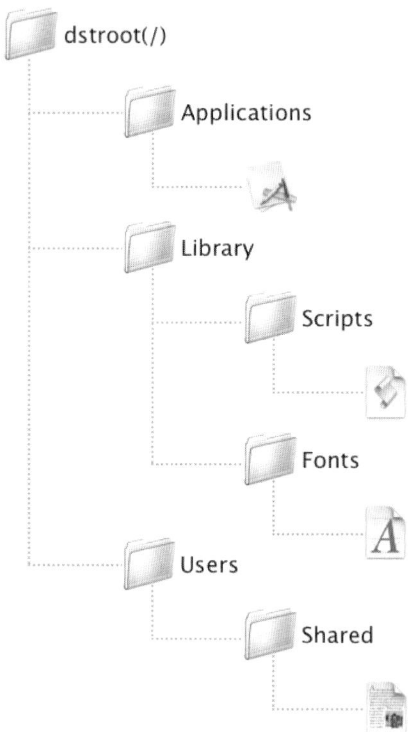

Once you have the destination root folder, you populate it with files that you want installed by your package. The files are placed within a folder structure that matches where they will be placed on the target computer, relative to the destination root. Any folders that are in the destination root layout but are not on the target computer will be created automatically when the package is installed. Only use copies of the files with which you want to populate the folder hierarchy, because PackageMaker will alter the files during the package-creation process.

NOTE ▶ Use caution when naming the folders used in your folder structure. A typo here will create a new folder with the incorrect name, resulting in an installation that may not behave correctly, but also is often very difficult to diagnose later.

NOTE ▶ Take note of folders that are symbolic links or aliases to other folders. Your folder structure should reflect the actual locations of the files, not use paths that include aliases. For example, files that are found in /etc/ actually live in /private/etc/.

Creating a Package Manually in PackageMaker

After you have created the folder hierarchy containing the files to be installed and included the resources, run the PackageMaker utility to convert the folder hierarchy into a package, using the Single Package Project option.

The PackageMaker window has five panes:

- Installer Interface—Allows you to add description information to the package. The Title field allows you to set the title for the Installer window. The title and description will be displayed to the user if the package is delivered as part of a metapackage.

  In Mac OS X v10.4, this pane also includes a button to open the Installer Interface Editor, which lets you drag and drop to change or add new text files and background image resources. Some users may find using the Install Interface Editor more convenient than placing the files in a resources folder.
- Contents—Allows the package builder to point to a folder containing the files to be added to the package. This path is the location of the files that will be stored inside the package. Click File Permissions to examine and change the permissions of the files that will be stored in your package.

NOTE ▶ As you're creating your source folder hierarchy, most files will take your user name as their new owner. Be sure to click File Permissions and change the ownership back to root for most files. Otherwise, a normal user account will become the owner of the new files on the target computer. The File Permissions window contains a button to apply recommended permissions to all of the files. Although these permissions are usually sufficient, you'll want to examine the new permissions assigned to each file before continuing.

The Contents pane also allows you to add file filters and locator definitions (used to locate and identify previously installed software). Generally you will want to compress the archive, so your resulting package will be smaller. In most cases, you'll want to remove the .DS_Store files, but do not discard the resource forks. Including .DS_Store files or discarding resource forks can lead to problems with the appearance and operation of your installed files on the target computer.

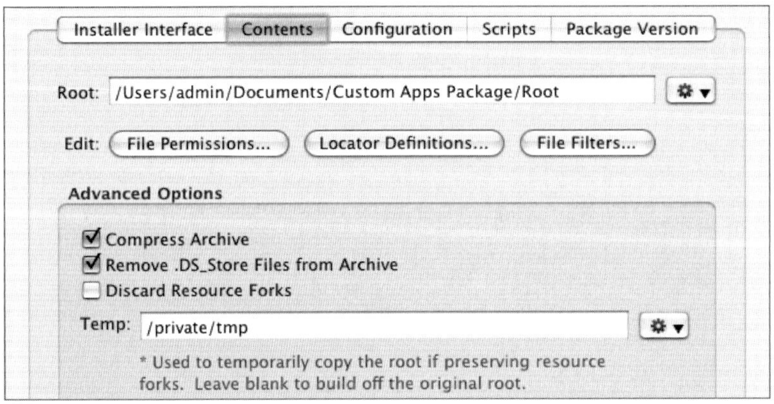

- Configuration—Allows the package builder to configure the installation of the package contents. More details about this pane are included in the next section, "Setting Configuration Options."
- Scripts—Allows the package builder to point to a folder to include any necessary resources to the package, including scripts, tools, and documents such as license or welcome text files.

- Package Version—Allows the package builder to set version and display information. This includes a unique identifier for the package. Since this must be unique, consider using your domain name in reverse dot notation, also known as a Java-style package name. For example, for a package called MyGreatSoftware at Apple, use com.apple .mygreatsoftware as the identifier.

After you fill in the required information in PackageMaker, choose File > Save to save the configuration, and then choose Project > Build to create the package.

NOTE ▸ A symbolic link to the command line version of PackageMaker also exists in /Developer/Tools. It is primarily useful if you want to automate the creation of a package or to create a snapshot, which creates a package based on changes to a specific directory. You can find more information by navigating to the /Developer/Tools directory and typing `man packagemaker`.

MORE INFO ▸ The Help > Online Documentation menu option in PackageMaker provides many details about each of the options in each pane.

Setting Configuration Options

The Configuration pane lists the options on the package. You can specify whether a restart and/or authorization is required. Also, you can set flags that affect the installation.

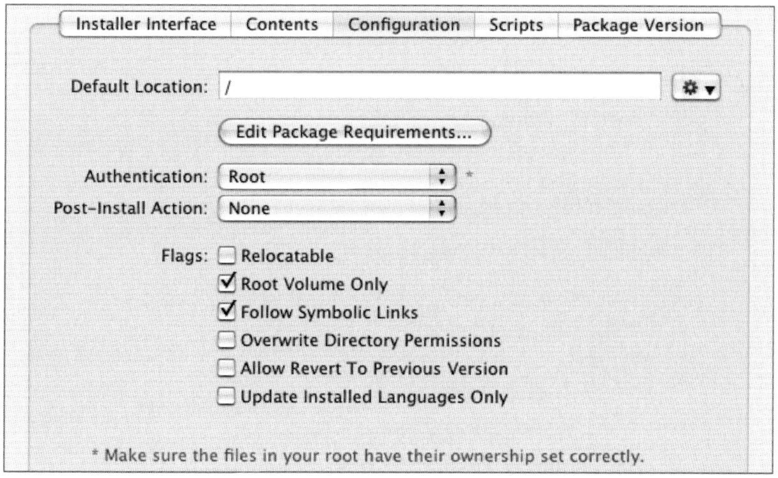

Here are the various options available in the Configuration pane:

- Default Location—The location of the root of the folder structure on the target computer. Note that if you are installing files into multiple folders, this must be the highest enclosing folder. For example, if you are installing files in /private/etc, /Applications, and /Library, you must specify the default location as /.
- Authentication—Specify one of the following options:
  - None—User is not prompted for an admin password, and new files and folders will be owned by the user running Installer.
  - Admin—If the user is signed on as a normal user, the user is prompted for an admin user name and password. Files and folders will have the ownership specified in the package, except when root is specified.
  - Root—All users are prompted for an administrator user name and password. Files and folders will have the ownership specified in the package under all circumstances.
- Post-Install Action—Specify one of the following options:
  - None—Installer can be closed after installation.
  - Recommended Restart—User will be prompted to restart after installation but will have the option to quit without restarting.
  - Required Restart—User will be prompted to restart after installation and won't be able to quit Installer without restarting.
  - Shutdown Required—User will be prompted to shut down after installation and won't be able to quit Installer without restarting.

  TIP Unless it is absolutely necessary, don't force users to restart their machines.

- Flags—Select any of the following options:
  - Relocatable—Allows the user to select where to install the software. Only use this option if the files being installed can be moved from their intended location and if all the files go into one location.

- Root Volume Only—Installer will allow installation onto the volume from which the system is running. Use this option sparingly, as it will prohibit the installation of this package with NetInstall.
- Follow Symbolic Links—If the path to an item to be installed contains a symbolic link and this option is selected, the path will be followed with the link. Otherwise, Installer will replace the symbolic link with a folder. In general, this option should be selected unless you know that you want Installer to replace any symbolic links with folders.
- Overwrite Directory Permissions—Selecting this option will direct Installer to change the permissions on existing folders to match those specified in the package. Use this option with caution, as it can cause unexpected system behavior if permissions are set incorrectly on system folders. Note that this option doesn't address ownership, only permissions.
- Allow Revert To Previous Version—Allows Installer to revert to an earlier version of the package.
- Update Installed Languages Only—Only languages that are currently installed will be updated.

Taking Advantage of Third-Party Utilities

Numerous third-party utilities exist to make package creation easier. There are utilities that cover every aspect of package creation.

logGen

logGen is a command-line utility that you can easily use to display files that were modified on your system. For example, you can compare file checksum values before and after an install so that you'll know what files need to be included in your package. More information is available at the LSA Mac OS X Software site (www.lsa.umich.edu/lsait/admin/mac/software/index.asp.

Iceberg and Composer

These applications provide alternatives to Apple's PackageMaker. Although they simplify many tasks of package creation, you'll want to carefully evaluate which of the three applications is the best fit for your project. Composer, from JAMF Software, can be found at www.jamfsoftware.com/products/composer, and Iceberg is available from White Box at http://s.sudre.free.fr/Software/Iceberg.html. The Iceberg application looks similar to PackageMaker and allows for many of the same options, plus a few more.

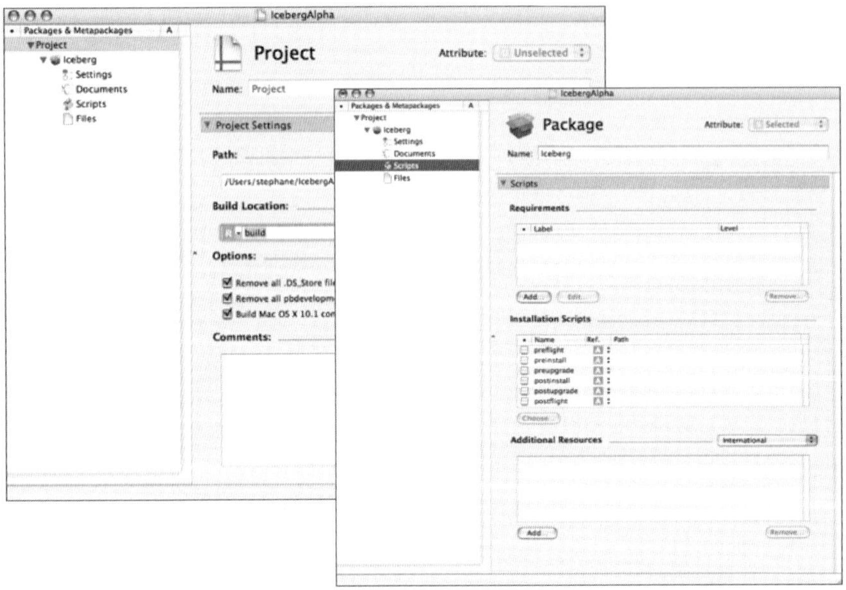

Pacifist

Pacifist, from CharlesSoft (www.charlessoft.com), provides a friendly graphical package inspector. This handy tool provides a quick Finder-like view of the files contained in the payload of a package. That's useful when building packages because it provides a quick way to visually inspect the results of your package building, but it can also be used to extract individual files from a package without installing the entire package. The following figure shows a package and all its contents in a Pacifist window displayed in a Finder-like interface.

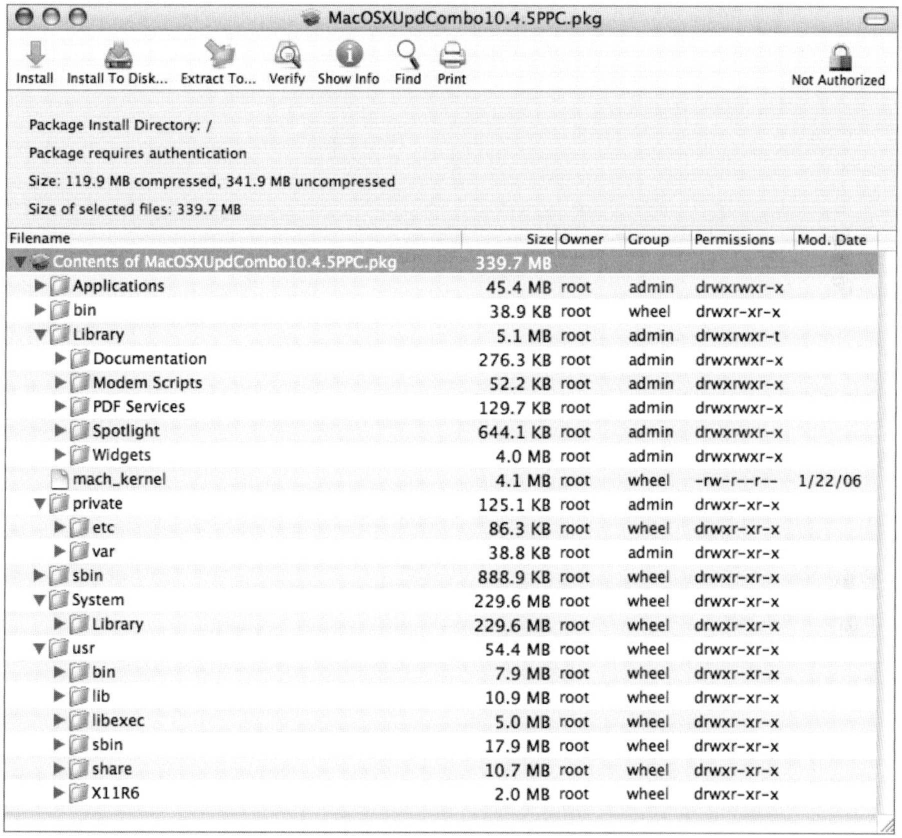

Lesson Review

1. When is it better to use package installation as opposed to drag-and-drop installation?
2. How is a metapackage different from a package?
3. What scripts can be run during installation?
4. Describe the scenarios for how owner and permissions are determined on installed files and folders.
5. How do you localize installation?

Answers

1. It's best to use package installation when processes need to be started or stopped, or the install needs to put software in multiple locations throughout the system. Package installation is also preferred when you need to verify that certain components are already on the system or that a certain version of Mac OS X is being used.

   Another reason to use package installation would be to automate the process of mass software installation. Installer packages allow you to have a professional-looking appearance that is customized to your particular software, is easy to use for users, and can be used to upgrade software.
2. A metapackage contains other packages and metapackages to install.
3. These scripts can be run during installation: preinstall, postinstall, preupgrade, postupgrade, preflight, postflight, InstallationCheck, and VolumeCheck.
4. If authentication is not required, all new files and folders are installed as the user that runs Installer. If authentication is required, ownership is determined by the owner of the files within the package. Permissions always follow the files within the package for new files and folders. Existing folder permissions will not be changed unless Overwrite Permissions is selected in PackageMaker.
5. Put the resources for each language in its own folder called *languagename*.proj.

References

Knowledge Base Articles

You can check for new and updated articles in the AppleCare Knowledge Base, at www.apple.com/support.

URLs

Visit the following sites for more information:

Composer: JAMF Software: www.jamfsoftware.com/products/composer

Iceberg: White Box: http://s.sudre.free.fr/Software/Iceberg.html

Introduction to Software Distribution: http://developer.apple.com/documentation/DeveloperTools/Conceptual/SoftwareDistribution/index.html

logGen: LSA Mac OS X Software: www.lsa.umich.edu/lsait/admin/mac/software/index.asp

Pacifist: CharlesSoft: www.charlessoft.com

PackageMaker Pro Tips: www.macdevcenter.com/pub/a/mac/2003/09/16/packagemaker.html

Technical Q&A QA1281: Correcting a PackageMaker version.plist and BundleVersions.plist Problem: http://developer.apple.com/qa/qa2001/qa1281.html

4

Time This lesson takes about 2 hours to complete.

Goals Install Mac OS X and Mac OS X Server on multiple remote or local workstations using ASR images

Create and deliver custom installation packages for Mac OS X and Mac OS X Server

Configure Mac OS X Server to store and deliver NetBoot and Network Install images through NetBoot services

Configure multiple install packages for use with a Network Install image

Lesson 4

Delivering Images and Packages

Learning how to plan your deployment, create and manage images, make custom packages, and check for software revisions is critical to a successful mass deployment operation. But if the method of image delivery does not work well within your environment (network setup, security, physical location of Macs), time may be wasted, networks may get clogged with traffic, and your entire deployment project may suffer as a result.

In this lesson, you will learn how to install Mac OS X v10.4 on multiple computers by delivering your master image both locally and over a network. You will set up your image for NetBoot startup and perform updates with packages and scripts. The methods you learn in this lesson will allow you to automate the process of image delivery so that you can present a low-maintenance, consistent interface to your users.

Delivering Locally

One of the simplest, most portable, and most flexible methods of local image delivery is through the use of a FireWire drive (Intel-based Macs can also boot over USB with the new formatting structure) as a startup disk. Just configure a portable FireWire (or USB, where applicable) drive with Mac OS X installed, as well as a copy of the disk image you wish to distribute and a utility to distribute the image, such as Apple Software Restore (ASR) or Disk Utility.

You may choose to place a script to initiate the delivery process in a conveniently accessible location on the FireWire drive. To deliver the image, simply start the computer with the FireWire drive and double-click the script. You can even create a script in the /Library/StartupItems folder that will allow users to start up the computer from the FireWire drive, walk away, and return when the delivery is complete. As the following figure shows, using a FireWire drive to deploy an image to a single computer is an easy and network-friendly method of one-to-one deployment.

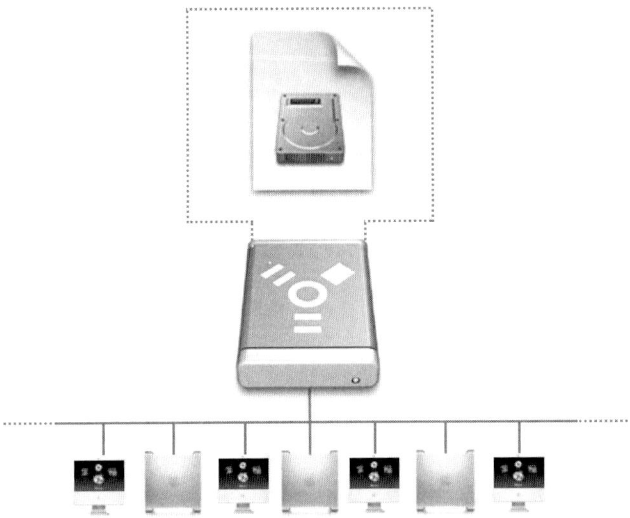

WARNING ► If you create a script that is capable of delivering an image with little or no user interaction, use it with extreme caution. Starting up the wrong computer with the delivery FireWire drive may result in a loss of data.

NOTE ► Intel-based Macs must boot from drives with a GUID Partition Table (GPT), and PowerPC-based Macs must boot from drives with an Apple Partition Map. As a result, you may not currently use the same disk drive to boot both Intel and PowerPC-based Macs.

Using ASR

ASR, which is described in Lesson 2, "Creating and Using Disk Images," is a native Mac OS X application that efficiently copies disk images onto volumes. With an ASR-ready disk image, you can use the command-line tool asr to distribute your image. As shown in the following figure, ASR can be used to push many disk images to many computers or one disk image to several computers.

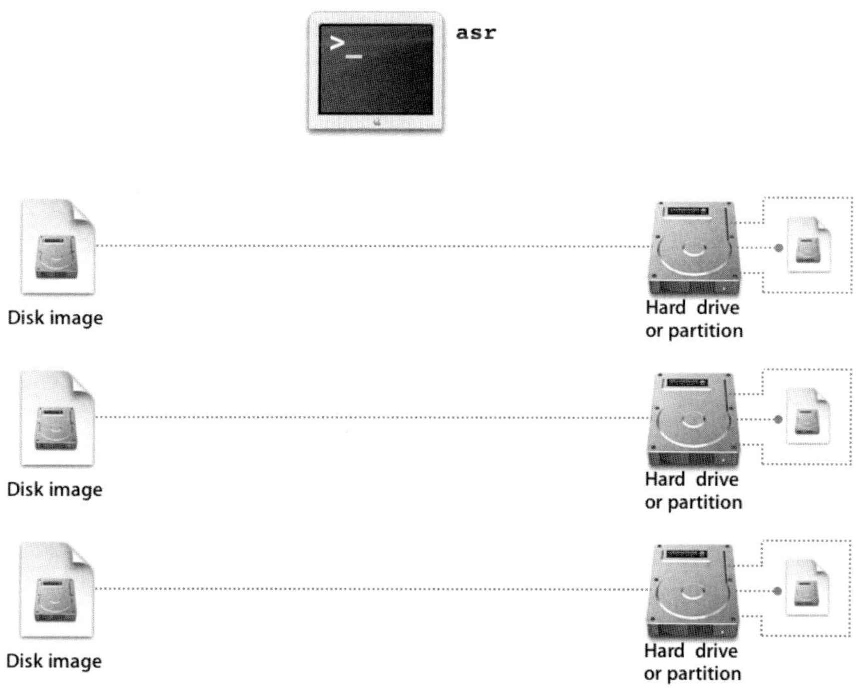

After starting the computer from the FireWire drive, enter the following syntax at the command line or from a UNIX script:

sudo asr -source *sourceimage* -target *targetvolume* [options] where *sourceimage* is the path to your master image and *targetvolume* is the path to the local startup volume for the computer. The optional [options] parameter can be any number of options available to asr as described in the asr manual page. In this example,

```
sudo asr -source /Users/Shared/master.dmg -target /Volumes/Macintosh\ HD/ -erase
```

the -erase option is used, indicating that asr should erase the target volume and perform a fast block copy. By default, without the -erase option, asr will perform a restore in place, which is slower. Type man asr on the command line for details on this option, on block-copy restores versus file-copy restores, and on other features.

Using Disk Utility

Some administrators prefer to use Disk Utility because it has a graphical user interface with drag-and-drop support, and because, unlike ASR, it offers less chance of deleting and imaging a drive unintentionally. As the following figure shows, Disk Utility is a simple, GUI-based version of ASR, so it does not offer a few advanced options that come with ASR.

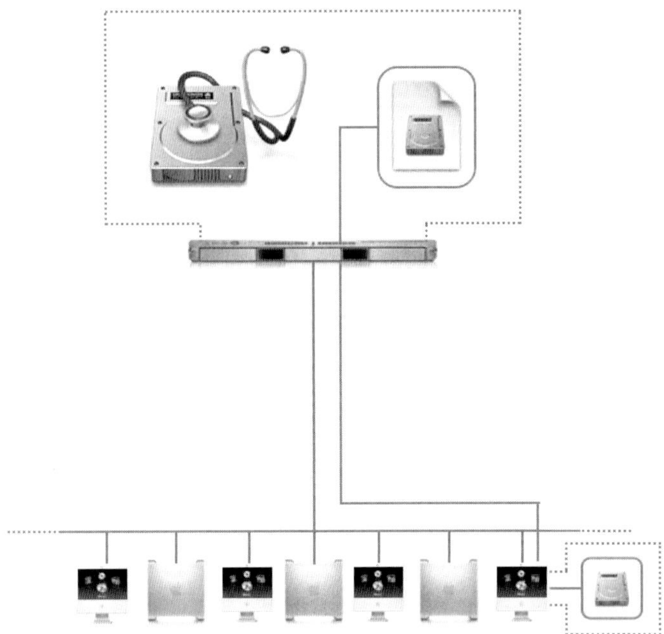

To deliver an image using Disk Utility, follow these steps:

1. Start the computer from the FireWire drive. Alternatively, if you have the images stored on a portable computer, you can boot the target computer in target disk mode and connect it to the portable computer as a FireWire drive.
2. Open Disk Utility.
3. Click the computer's hard-drive icon on the left.
4. Click the Restore tab, as shown in the following figure.
5. Click and drag the master image into the Source field.
6. Click and drag the target-volume icon into the Destination field.
7. Select Erase Destination for a fast block copy, or leave it unselected for a restore in place.
8. Click Restore.

TIP You might find it helpful to set Disk Utility to launch at login.

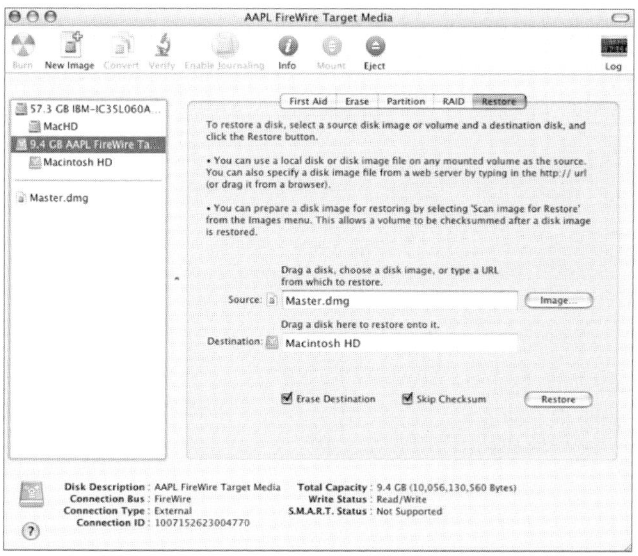

Using a Bootable DVD

Using a CD or DVD to deliver your image has a few advantages over using a FireWire drive. Though not as flexible or easy to set up, optical media discs are inexpensive and can be easily mass produced. Because they are read-only, they also reduce the possibility of corruption or accidental modification.

Due to limited storage size, it is not likely that your master image will fit on a CD, and with a complex modern operating system like Mac OS X v10.4, it is extremely difficult to create a CD capable of starting your computer. DVDs have greater storage capacity, and so they are much more practical. As shown in the following figure, putting the disk image on a bootable DVD allows for a more inexpensive mass deployment solution than that of FireWire drives, but without the ability to update the images without creating new DVDs.

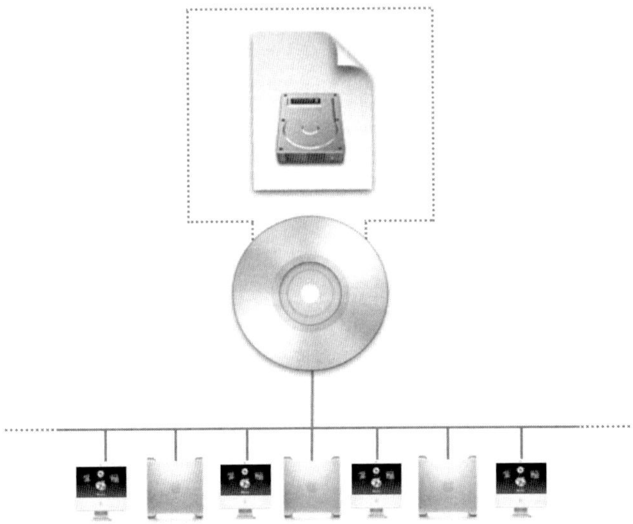

To create a bootable DVD, configure a model and create an install image in System Image Utility (as you would to create NetBoot or Network Install images). Instead of saving the image to your NetBoot storage folder, save the image to a folder in your home folder. Then use the Finder or Disk Utility to burn a DVD of that image. Although Disk Utility can be used to create bootable DVDs, System Image Utility allows you to easily configure a stripped-down version of Mac OS X as the startup volume on the DVD.

Delivering over the Network

Mac OS X v10.4 offers several options for network image delivery, eliminating the need to physically move from computer to computer to deliver images. You can store your master image and update packages on a server on the network. Then you can connect directly, remotely distribute your image to multiple computers simultaneously, or script the process so that your computers will automatically pull images and packages from your server.

Using NetBoot

Client computers that start up from a NetBoot image get fresh system environments every time they start up, eliminating the overhead involved in maintaining local delivery of images, as seen below.

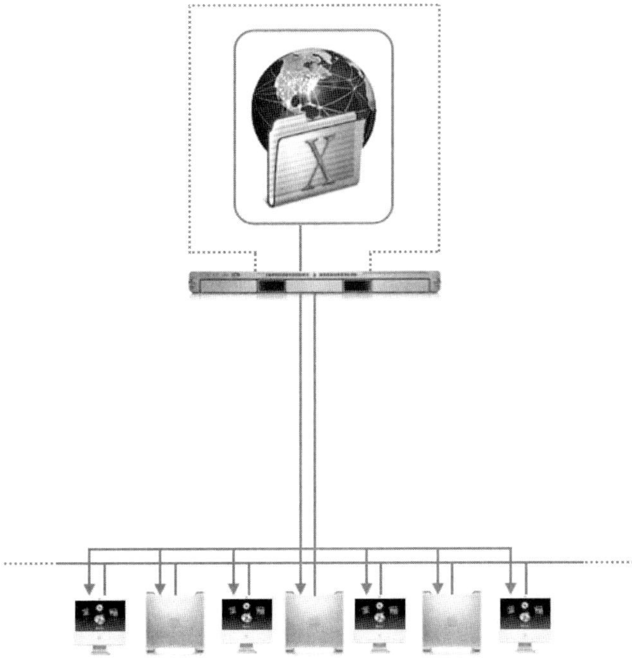

The NetBoot service in Mac OS X Server v10.4 supports Mac OS X computers that have Macintosh firmware version 4.1.7 or later. To start up a computer into Mac OS X v10.3 or earlier using NetBoot or to use Network Install, the Mac OS X computer must have a minimum of 128 MB of RAM and 100Base-T Ethernet or faster network connections. To start up a computer into Mac OS X v10.4 using NetBoot, the client computer must have at least 256 MB of RAM.

For NetBoot deployments of 10 to 50 clients, a 100Base-T switched network is required. Gigabit Ethernet is required for booting more than 50 clients (although Apple has no official test results for configurations beyond 50 clients). Apple does not support the use of AirPort wireless technology with NetBoot clients. NetBooting computers requires a solid network infrastructure.

NOTE ▶ Mac OS X Server v10.4.4 supports Intel-based Mac OS X computers, but the server itself currently must still be a PowerPC-based computer.

MORE INFO ▶ Version v10.4.4, or later, of the System Admin Tools provides Universal applications for administering Mac OS X Server v10.4 from both Intel and PowerPC-based Macintosh computers. It also includes an updated System Image Utility application for creating NetBoot and NetInstall images of Intel-based Macs. For more information, refer to the AppleCare Knowledge Base article "About Server Admin Tools v10.4.4" (docs.info.apple.com/article.html?artnum=302923).

When a client computer starts up from a NetBoot image, the following process takes place:

1. The client places a request for an IP address.

   When a NetBoot client is turned on or restarted, it requests an IP address from a DHCP server. Although the server providing the address can be the same server providing the NetBoot service, the two services don't have to be provided by the same computer.

2. After receiving an IP address, the NetBoot client sends out a request for startup software over the local subnet.

   The NetBoot server then delivers the boot ROM file (booter) to the client using Trivial File Transfer Protocol (TFTP) via its default port, 69.

3. Once the client has the ROM file, it initiates a mount and loads the NetBoot network disk image.

   The images can be served using HTTP (or HTTPS, provided the necessary certificates exist in the appropriate locations) or NFS. Mac OS 9 computers used Apple Filing Protocol (AFP) for mounting during NetBoot.

4. After the NetBoot client starts up from the NetBoot image, the client then requests an IP address from a DHCP server on the local subnet.

   Depending on the type of DHCP server used, the NetBoot client might receive an IP address different from the one received in step 1.

   NOTE ▶ Previous versions of NetBoot server that used AFP to deliver network disk images could potentially run into AFP license restrictions. If you purchased the ten-client version of Mac OS X Server, your AFP license restricted you to supporting no more than ten AFP clients, limiting the number of Mac OS 9 NetBoot clients to less than ten. This would not affect your Mac OS X NetBoot clients, as they use NFS or HTTP and are unrestricted even with the ten-client version of Mac OS X Server.

In order to configure NetBoot on your server, do the following:

1. Place your master boot image created with System Image Utility or NetRestore Helper (as described in Lesson 2) in the /Library/NetBoot/NetBootSP*n* folder.

2. Launch Server Admin and connect to your Mac OS X Server.

3. Click the NetBoot service and then the Settings button to display the Settings pane.

4. Select which Ethernet port(s) provide the NetBoot services.

5 Select which volume(s) provide the image and client data.

6 Click the Images button to display the Images pane, and choose the protocol to serve the image.

7 Select the default image(s). You can select on default one PowerPC-based image and one Intel-based image.

8 Click Save to apply changes.

9 Start NetBoot services.

10 To start any supported computers on the local subnet with this image, select the image in the Startup Disk pane in System Preferences or hold down the N key while the computer is starting up.

Using Network Install

You can distribute and install software, including the Mac OS X operating system, with Network Install images. On Mac OS X Server, use the System Image Utility to create a Network Install image. Create the image by cloning a system that's already installed and set up, or by using a Mac OS X Install Disc.

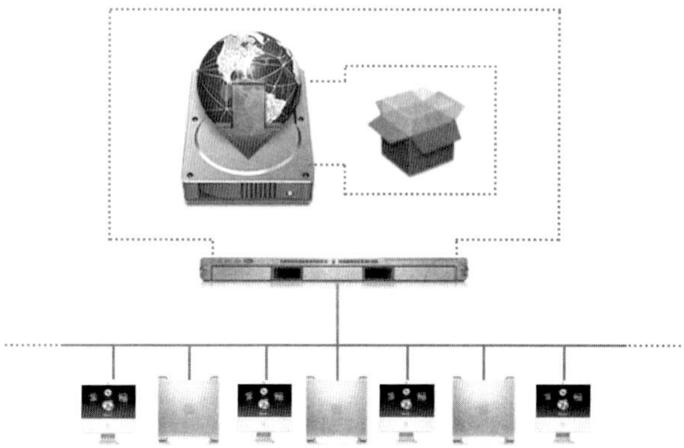

Network Install allows for the installation of packages and metapackages, similar to that of a DVD install, and can be automated to erase the volume set to receive the image or packages. (Note that if you choose to auto-install, you won't have to interact with each computer.) You can also set various ByHost files (specific to an individual computer) to match the receiving computer's MAC address.

For example, when using a Mac OS X Install Disc (you can also use a Mac OS X Server Install Disc when doing a Network Install of Mac OS X Server), you have the option of removing certain packages within the install disc itself. You can also add other packages, such as updates and security updates, and scripts to a Network Install image or image downloaded using Apple Software Update.

NOTE ► You cannot mix and match updates for PowerPC-based Macs and Intel-based Macs and add them to a Network Install image. Doing so may cause the installed operating system not to function. It is best to keep Intel-based Network Install (and for that matter NetBoot) images and PowerPC-based images totally separate.

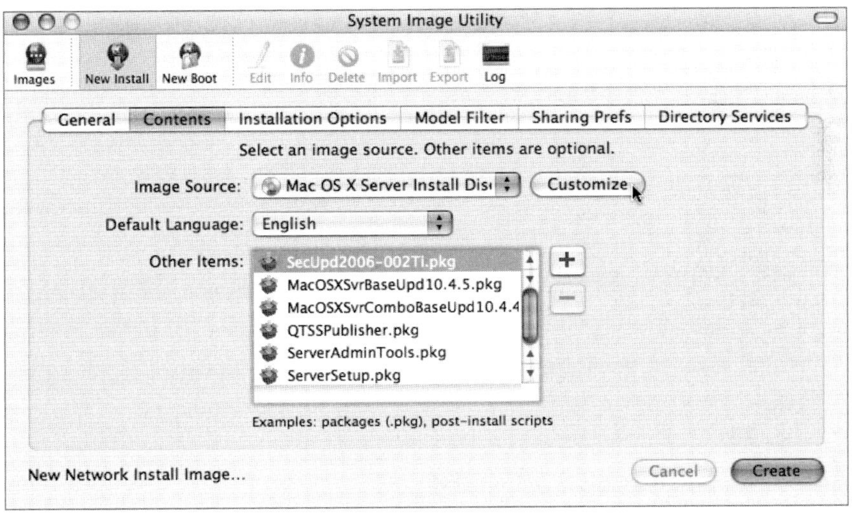

Exploring Other NetBoot/NetInstall Options

NetBoot and NetInstall can be customized in a number of different ways to satisfy the needs of your environment. Network topology, firewall rules, quantities of computers, and other items may require you to make some adjustments to the NetBoot or NetInstall settings.

Serving Your Image over HTTP

NetBoot and NetInstall images are optimally served via NFS because of its speed and low overhead. However, your environment may not allow NFS servers for security reasons. In those cases, you can serve your image via HTTP instead of NFS. To set this option, simply select the radio button when you're setting up your image in the System Image Utility. However, many Web servers are unable to serve files larger than 2 GB.

NetBooting from a Different Subnet

You may need to perform a NetBoot or NetInstall from a network other than the one that your server is on. If this will be a regular occurrence, you may want to have your network administrator forward your broadcast traffic from your network to the NetBoot server. This is commonly changed using DHCP or IP helper addresses.

You also have the option of specifying a particular NetBoot server and image through a number of mechanisms:

- Apple Remote Desktop (ARD) allows you to specify the server IP address and image name from which the client should boot.
- The `bless` command can use options of the following format:

  bless –netboot –server bsdp://*xxx.xxx.xxx.xxx*
- Using the `nvram` command, you can specify both the server and the image file:

  sudo nvram boot-file enet:*xxx.xxx.xxx.xxx*,NetBoot\NetBootSP*n**nameOfNBIfolder*.nbi\mach.macosx

  sudo nvram boot-args rp=nfs: *xxx.xxx.xxx.xxx*:/private/tftpboot/NetBoot/NetBootSP*n*:*nameOfNBIfolder*.nbi/*ImageName*.dmg

  sudo nvram boot-device enet:*xxx.xxx.xxx.xxx*,NetBoot\NetBootSP*n**nameOfNBIfolder*.nbi\booter

Substitute your server's IP address and actual NBI path in the commands above. Once you set the new boot device, reboot the computer to initiate the connection.

You can simplify this using a free application named, appropriately enough, NetBoot Across Subnets, from Mike Bombich (www.bombich.com/software/nbas.html).

Making Advanced Customizations

A number of advanced customizations can be made with NetBoot and NetInstall. The primary locations for making image customizations are the following:

- The bootpd configuration
- NBImageInfo.plist
- Inside the disk image

The bootpd process (started by launchd) handles the reception of the NetBoot BSDP requests and generates the responses to each client. Most of the bootpd configuration is stored in the local NetInfo database. If needed, you can make alterations to this data using nicl. To see your current settings, type

```
nicl . -read /config/dhcp
```

This shows the logging level, any MAC address filtering, and the interfaces for which NetBoot is enabled. You should generally use only the approved NetBoot interfaces to make changes to your NetBoot configuration, including the Server Admin utility and the serveradmin command. More documentation for the serveradmin command is available in the Mac OS X Server Command-Line Administration guide. After you've made any changes to your NetBoot configuration, you'll likely have to restart your NetBoot server for the changes to take effect:

```
sudo serveradmin stop netboot

sudo serveradmin start netboot
```

Further enhancements to the NetBoot server are also made in the local NetInfo database under the /config/NetBootServer entry. The following are some of the configuration options you may wish to use:

- afp_users_max—If you will be using NetBoot with more than 50 machines simultaneously from one server, you may need to raise this number.
- age_time_seconds—Particularly in environments where you're using NetInstall to install machines in assembly-line fashion, you may wish to lower this number. This number indicates how long your server remembers a NetBoot connection.

- machine_name_format—Normally, computers that are NetBooted receive a hostname that is of the format "Net-Boot%03d." You can modify this field to change the format. Note that it should use printf format and contain one number to indicate the machine number.
- shadow_size_meg—This setting controls the size of your diskless client's shadow file. The default, 48 MB, may need to be increased if you have to save more information from a computer while it's NetBooted.

The NBImageInfo.plist file contains all of the details about your NetBoot or NetInstall image. All of the options in this file can be set from the System Image Utility when you create your image, but there may be times when you'd like to make quick changes to some of the options without re-creating your image. Just use a text editor to modify the file and restart your NetBoot service as outlined above. Some of the options you may wish to change include the following:

- Name—The name that appears in the Startup Disk preference pane.
- IsEnabled—A Boolean value indicating whether this image is available.
- IsDefault—A Boolean value indicating whether this image is the default image used when a computer is booted with the N key pressed.

  It's possible to have more than one default image. Although you can't set more than one default image (per architecture) in the Server Admin tool, you may wish to have multiple default images available if you're using different computer model filtering in your images.
- Index—This integer, between 1 and 65535, is used to identify common images coming from multiple NetBoot servers.

  If you have only one server, you can use any number. If you have multiple servers in a load-balancing arrangement, identical numbers under 4096 will be treated by a NetBoot client as different images, and each image will show up in the Startup Disk preference pane. Index numbers of 4096 and above will be treated as identical images, and only one entry will be shown in the Startup Disk preference pane.

Selecting this image on the client will boot the client from whichever server responds first. Subsequent reboots by the client will favor the initial NetBoot server that responded.

- SupportsDiskless—A Boolean value that determines if a NetBoot image can be used on a computer with no disk, or on a computer where you would prefer nothing to be written to the local disk.

  Normally, temporary files and caches are written to /private/var/netboot on a NetBooted system. A diskless NetBoot will instead store this information in a shadow file on the NetBoot server.
- EnabledSystemIdentifiers—An array of each specific computer model that is allowed to use this image.

  You can obtain the identifier for any computer by typing `sysctl hw.model` on the command line of that computer.
- Architectures—An array of processor types that this image supports. Possible values include `ppc` and `i386`.

More details about all of these options can be found in the `bootpd` manual page:

```
man bootpd
```

Creating Utility NetBoot Images

NetBoot doesn't necessarily need to boot into a fully operational Mac OS X system. Through some simple modifications of the /etc/rc files in your disk image, you can make your NetBoot image perform simple utility functions. Some examples of this might include the following:

- Rescue image—An image that contains various rescue utilities such as those pertaining to disk recovery, virus detection, memory testing, or other rescue/diagnostic applications. In fact, Xserve Remote Diagnostics is one such image that has no real user interface but instead might just execute a script to modify the target system and reboot. This is similar to the use of a payload-free package, discussed in the previous lesson.

Using NetRestore

NetRestore, by Mike Bombich (www.bombich.com), extends the features of ASR with a graphical user interface and scripting tools. You can use NetRestore to restore a master disk image to a target volume whether the disk image is hosted locally, on a network via AFP, or on the Internet via HTTP. NetRestore can also be used in conjunction with NetBoot to fully automate the deployment of a lab.

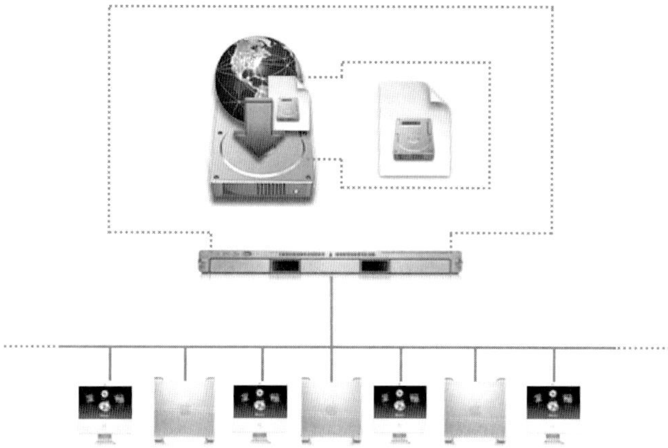

NetRestore does the following:

- ▶ Restores a disk image to a hard drive via block-level or file-level copying
- ▶ Clones local hard drives and restores disk images located locally or across a network
- ▶ Runs pre- and post-restore customizing tools to set computer-specific information
- ▶ Includes a helper application for creating master images and Network Install-Restore image sets
- ▶ Offers extensive user-community support
- ▶ Features easy configurability and support for browsing images and drag and drop for on-the-fly restores
- ▶ Supports post-action customization scripts:
  - Set Open Firmware password

  - Set computer name
  - Set ARD custom field data
  - Fix ByHost preference items
  - Set network configuration (static IP and so on)
- Has full automation
- Works while started up from
  - An external FireWire drive
  - A bootable CD/DVD
  - A network drive (NetBoot)

Using ASR over a Network

ASR provides features that allow restoration of a volume from an image located on a remote server. Through ASR via HTTP or ASR multicast, you can remotely store your master ASR-ready disk image on a file server, rather than copy it to several media devices or spend the time and resources necessary to set up NetBoot services. This solution greatly reduces the amount of disk space necessary for local restoration and allows you to have one centrally located master image that can be maintained with relative ease.

Using ASR over the network is easier than setting up NetBoot, but it still requires a method of starting up your computer from a device other than the startup disk you wish to restore. This device could be a CD, a DVD, a FireWire drive, or a second hard drive or partition. Alternatively, use it in conjunction with NetBoot to provide a complete, network-based image-restoration process. One of the new features of NetRestore is the ability to create a bootable network image that will use ASR multicast to restore the target computer.

With ASR multicast, you can share an ASR image over the network without setting up any other service. This feature allows several clients to connect to the server and simultaneously perform fast block copies of the image to their local volumes.

Use the following command in Mac OS X or Mac OS X Server to set up the multicast:

```
asr -source sourceimage -server configurationfile
```

where *sourceimage* is the path to an image file. The -server option tells asr to multicast the source image over the network. The *configurationfile* parameter is the path to a configuration .plist file that contains the following information:

- Multicast Address—This is the multicast address for the data stream.
- Data Rate—This is the desired data rate in bytes per second. On average, the stream will go slightly slower than this speed but will never exceed it.

To create the .plist configuration file, you can use Property List Editor or run these commands from Terminal:

- defaults write /tmp/myconfig "Data Rate" -int 6000000
- defaults write /tmp/myconfig "Multicast Address" *multicastaddr*

This will create the file /tmp/myconfig.plist. *multicastaddr* will be specific to your network and should be provided by your network administrator.

Finding the correct data rate may take some experimenting. The best data rate depends a great deal on the network hardware you are using. If you're using a network dedicated to loading machines, you'll want to use a fast data rate. If, however, you're using a slow network that is shared by many users, you may want to keep the data rate down to avoid clogging it.

You can also include the following optional keys in the configuration file:

- DNS Service Discovery—Whether the server should be advertised via DNS Service Discovery. It defaults to true.
- Client Data Rate—The rate at which the slowest client can write data to its target.
- Multicast TTL—Time to live on the multicast packets.
- Port—The port used in the initial client-server handshake.

See the asr man pages for more information on server options.

When the server is running, perform a software restore on any client connected to the network with the following command:

asr -source asr://*serveraddress* -target *targetvolume* -erase where *serveraddress* is the address of the server running the asr multicast, and *targetvolume* is the volume you will be restoring. The -erase option is required for multicast restores.

One way to take advantage of this feature is to configure a NetBoot image to be diskless, start up the client computer from that image, and run ASR over multicast. This method offers an exclusively network-based delivery solution that requires no media and can be performed efficiently on multiple computers simultaneously.

To set up ASR over HTTP or HTTPS, simply prepare your ASR-ready disk image and upload it to a folder that is shared by a Web server. As shown in the following figure, ASR Multicast allows a one-to-many setup that is often easier to maintain.

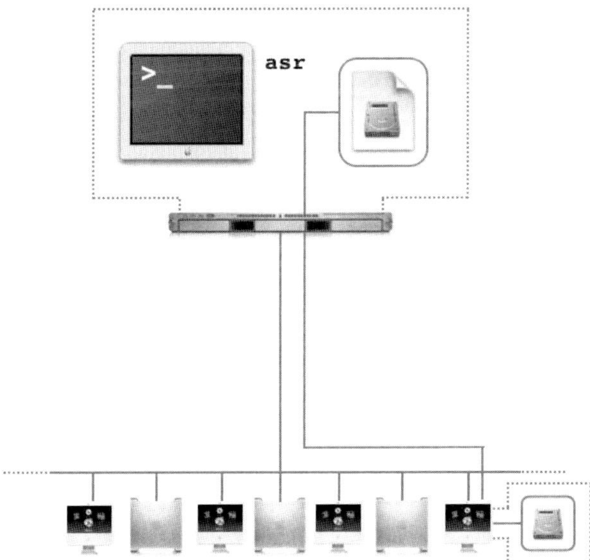

Be sure to do an imagescan before you upload your image:

```
asr -imagescan master.dmg
```

Once your image is uploaded, verify that it is available via HTTP by accessing the URL with a Web browser. For example, if your image is located on a Mac OS X v10.4 Web folder at /Library/WebServer/Documents/image/master.dmg, then type

http://*serveraddress*/image/master.dmg

in your Web browser where *serveraddress* is the address of the Web server where the ASR image is stored. This should result in a download of the image.

Now, restore any volume on any computer connected to the network with the following command:

```
asr -source http://serveraddress/image/master.dmg -target targetvolume [options]
```

where *serveraddress* is the address of the Web server, and *targetvolume* is the volume you will be restoring.

Apple is continuously revising its hardware offerings by releasing new computers and new versions of existing computers, which is great for the end user but presents a challenge to those who maintain disk images used to boot those systems. It is very common for a brand-new computer to be unable to boot from your existing image due to the lack of drivers for a new piece of hardware included in the computer. A good way to check this is to compare the build number of the OS on your image to that of the OS that shipped with the computer. You can use the sw_vers command to see the version information for the booted OS. For example, your image may be built off 8G32, while a new computer might ship with 8H12. A higher letter or number indicates that this is a newer build of the operating system, and you may need to rebuild your image from the newer OS to support the new hardware.

Performing Remote Administration

Apple Remote Desktop is an easy-to-use, powerful, open-standards-based desktop management application for all your networked Macintosh computers. You can remotely control and configure systems, install software, offer live online help to users, and assemble detailed software and hardware reports for an entire Mac network.

The administration utility Remote Desktop lets you distribute software and related files to client computers. You can also distribute and automatically install packages and metapackages. ARD Admin lets you install software and software updates on one or more client computers without user interaction or interruption, whether or not a user is logged in. After installation, Remote Desktop erases the Installer files. If the computers need to be restarted, as they do following an operating-system update, restart them from Remote Desktop.

For example, on your production computer, use Apple Software Update to download an iCal update to the model computer. If the update works as expected and introduces no compatibility issues, copy the install package to a computer running Remote Desktop to distribute to computers that need upgrading. Note that this approach conserves Internet bandwidth because only one copy of the package needs to be downloaded. Use this same method to distribute custom packages you created with PackageMaker.

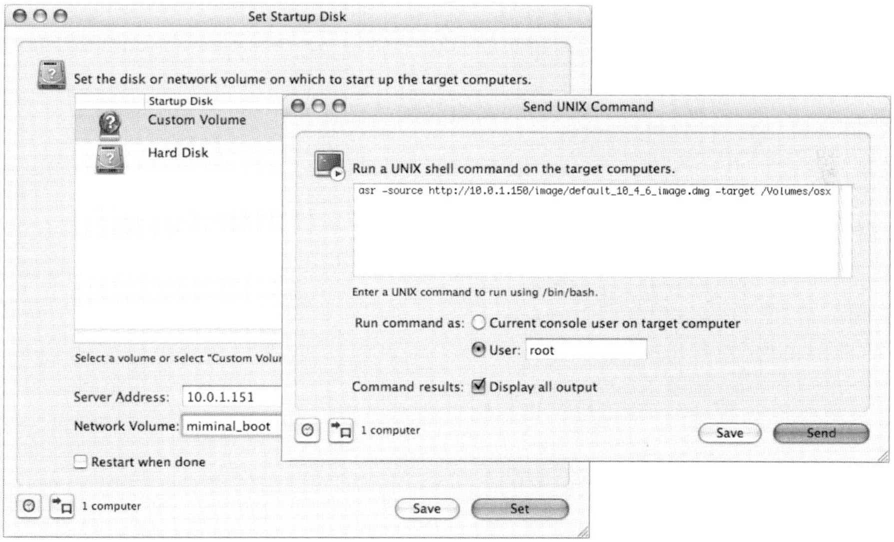

Another example is to use Remote Desktop to set the startup volume of remote client systems to point to a Network Install image, and then remotely restart the clients to initiate installation. Before initiating installations that require computers to be restarted, send a text message to clients using Remote Desktop, notifying them of a pending installation and that you will log them off or lock their screen at a specific time to install an operating-system update.

You can use Remote Desktop to set NetBoot images as the startup volumes of client systems and then restart the systems remotely. With just a few clicks you can reconfigure all the computers in a lab or cluster without having to manually restart and configure each computer individually.

Remote Desktop can distribute and run UNIX shell scripts on client computers. For example, a script can mount an AFP server volume, from which it downloads a disk image to client computers. The script might also download an install package and then perform a command-line install. Remote UNIX commands also provide you with a powerful diagnostic and auditing tool, since you can issue any UNIX command on any number of machines and see the results in one collated list.

Using Remote Desktop, you can distribute and install self-contained (drag-and-drop) applications by copying them to one or more client computers. To check whether an installation has been completed successfully, use Remote Desktop to observe the client computer remotely. Remote Desktop will be the focus of a lesson later in this book.

Using the Installer Command

Similar to the graphical Installer utility, the command-line installer tool can also be used to install Mac OS X. The installer tool installs one package or metapackage per invocation. In the case of the metapackage, all packages in the metapackage will be installed unless disqualified by a package's check tool.

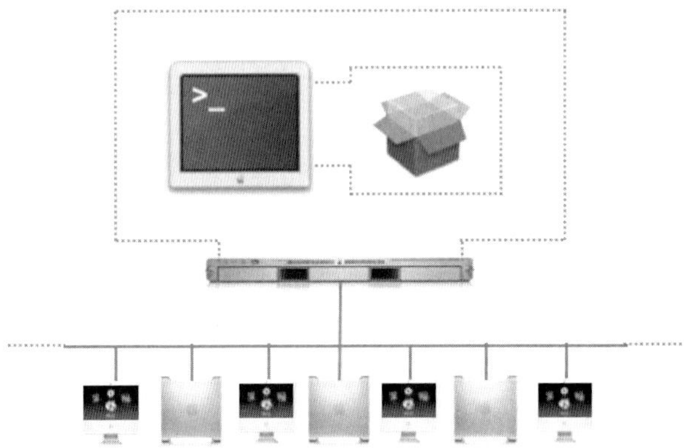

The command-line installer tool provides two main benefits over the traditional method of double-clicking a package to install it in the GUI:

- You can install packages remotely via SSH. Copy the .pkg file to the remote machine, ssh into it, and run the installer tool remotely.
- You can create scripts to automate package distribution and installation. These scripts could make use of other features of scripting languages to create complex tests and methods for package installation. You can use this method with both FireWire and DVD distribution techniques. Simply create a script that runs installer, and make it easily accessible or place it in the startup items.

To run the installer program, use the following command:

```
installer [options] -pkg pathToPackage -target pathToDestinationVolume
```

where *pathToPackage* is the path to the package to install, and *pathToDestinationVolume* is the target volume. For example:

```
installer -verbose -pkg /Users/Shared/master.pkg -target /Volumes/MacHD/
```

In this scenario, installer will install the package located at /Users/Shared/master.pkg to the hard drive mounted at /Volumes/MacHD/. With the -verbose option, installer displays output in a human-readable format rather than the default output, which is formatted for scripting. Type man installer on the command line for details on this option and several others.

One good way to determine whether a package can be installed on a computer is by using the installer command with the -pkginfo parameter. For example,

```
installer -pkginfo -pkg myPackage.pkg -target /
```

In this case, installer will list the package or packages contained within the package myPackage.pkg that can be installed on the current startup volume (/). If for some reason the package can't be installed, it won't be listed. Add this command to a conditional statement in a custom script to verify that a package can be installed before attempting to perform the installation.

Using Radmind

Radmind (detailed more in the appendix, "Using Radmind") can also be used for deploying systems. Generally speaking, radmind isn't well suited for deploying a system with an empty drive, but it is an effective tool for taking a computer that came preloaded with an operating system and bringing it in line with your image configuration. You can use radmind in combination with one of the other methods mentioned above, which is a great solution for maintaining the integrity of the operating system after it has been loaded.

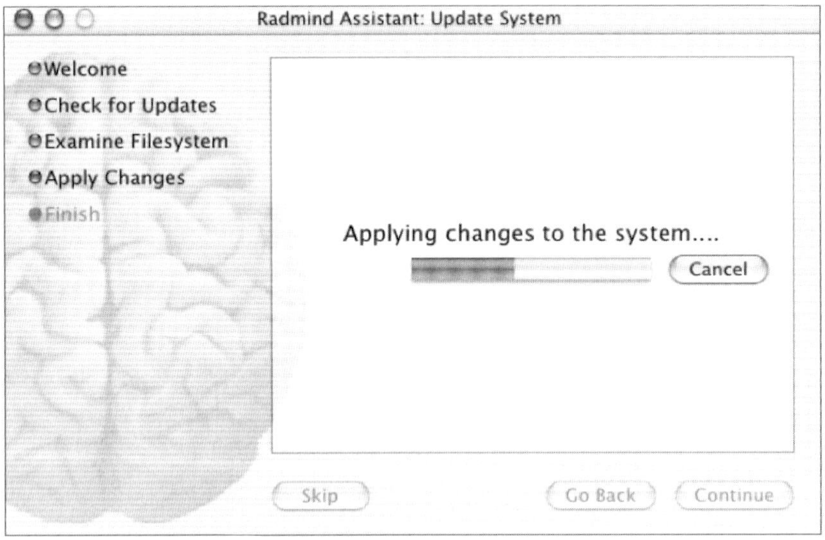

Lesson Review

1. What are some methods that can be used to deliver images locally?
2. What are some methods for delivering images and packages over a network?
3. What method does asr use to deploy a single image to many computers?
4. What protocols of image delivery are available with NetBoot?
5. What must be done to the image before using Disk Utility to image a volume?

Answers

1. FireWire drives, optical media.
2. ASR multicast, NetBoot services, NetRestore.
3. Multicast.
4. AFP and NFS.
5. Scan the image for restore.

References

Administration Guides

"System Imaging and Software Update Administration": http://images.apple.com/server/pdfs/System_Image_and_SW_Update_v10.4B.pdf

"Command-Line Administration": http://images.apple.com/server/pdfs/Command_Line_v10.4.pdf

Knowledge Base Articles

You can check for new and updated articles in the AppleCare Knowledge Base, at www.apple.com/support.

System Imaging Services Overview: http://docs.info.apple.com/article.html?path=ServerAdmin/10.4/en/c0os.html

URLs

Visit the following sites for more information:

Radmind: http://rsug.itd.umich.edu/software/radmind

Mac OS X Management Software and Tips: www.bombich.com

5

Time This lesson takes about 1 hour to complete.

Goals

Isolate and resolve issues with Apple Software Restore, NetBoot, Network Install, and Custom Install images

Isolate and resolve issues with custom installation packages

Use a click matrix to better manage images

Check Installer application log files for errors when installing custom packages

Lesson 5

Testing and Troubleshooting

Consider the following scenario: You build an ASR image containing Mac OS X and some standard applications used in your department. The image also contains a package to install a specialty application from a remote server. You place the image on a file server and use NetRestore to restore the image on the computers in four of your sites. The restoration goes well, and you are able to run a couple of the applications on one computer at each of the four sites. You also test the package installation at one of the sites. The next morning, you get paged to come into each of the sites. The users are able to start up their computers and run their applications, but they are unable to save any work to their network home folders. Furthermore, the application installed from the server using the custom package is unable to access its own template files, making the applications virtually unusable.

Before you distribute images or packages, you must first put them through a series of hardware and software tests for compatibility and usability. This lesson will show you how to develop a plan or checklist that takes into account the variety of systems you support, the network dependencies you work within, and the user accounts that you support.

Testing Images

Images need to be thoroughly tested before deployment. This commonly involves both hardware and software testing. It can be catastrophic to roll out images, only to find that something minor with one machine can quickly escalate into a major issue with all machines. This can be true of application testing, font testing, directory service testing (critically important), and security testing.

> **NOTE ▶** This book primarily focuses on creation of the image and testing related to hardware and software. For information on directory services, security, and file systems, please consult *Mac OS X System Administration Reference, Volume 1.*

Testing Images with Hardware

Because disk images will be deployed on various systems in your organization, you should develop a means of testing representative systems that includes both the basic CPU and any critical peripherals. The goal is to find out how many different images need to be maintained to fully support all the equipment you need to deploy on.

When you test Mac OS X, try the version or versions you plan to use on all of the computer types on which you will be deploying that operating system. Make sure you have tested enough representative systems to be satisfied that these computers meet the requirements of the operating system. If an image doesn't work on a particular system, compare the build version of Mac OS X to the model of computer and boot ROM version of the system, and refer to the Apple Knowledge Base to ensure that the operating-system version is designed to work on that particular system.

TIP Given the hardware differences between desktop and portable computers, you should maintain different disk images for each.

Newer hardware typically requires a new build of Mac OS X. In most cases, this newer build will also work on older hardware. If an operating-system upgrade is needed, create a new disk image with the upgraded software, verify that it works on the affected system, and then test the updated disk image on the other computers. As the following figure shows, several methods should be used to deploy images, each depending on the type of image or package being deployed and the type of hardware that will receive the image.

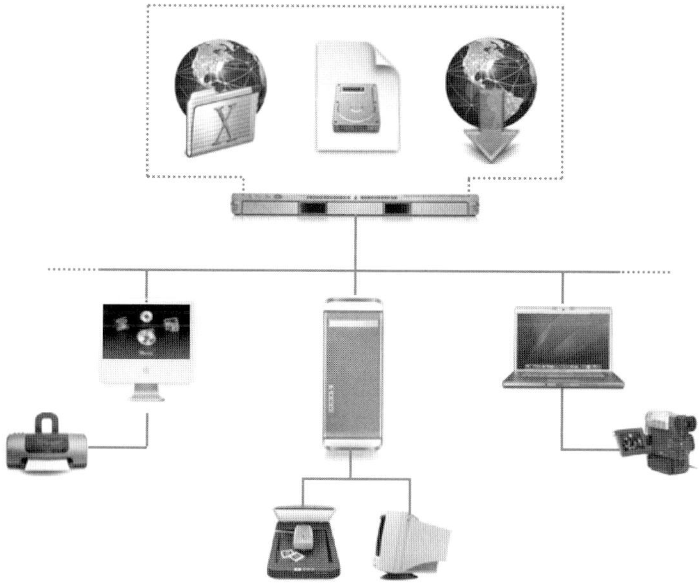

One common and best-practice technique to use when maintaining disk images is to establish a set of base images and then configure customized packages or scripts to run after the images are installed or restored. This technique cuts down on the need to maintain more than a couple of images and on having to constantly update your images. It is less time-consuming to update packages and scripts. For example, you may use the stock Mac OS X installation packages, and then layer your own applications and customizations on top of them. In order to modify parts of the base Mac OS X image, you may wish to take advantage of payload-free packages that just contain postflight scripts to make modifications to the installed system, as discussed in Lesson 3, "Packaging."

If you need to support critical peripheral hardware, such as printers, displays, or scanners, update the driver software on the disk image. In this series of tests, the issues you are looking for are incompatibilities related to the custom driver and the existing drivers on that image. Again, if incompatibilities can't be resolved, maintain multiple disk images and decide how to communicate the compatibility issues to your users, or use custom packages to deliver custom drivers and remove other drivers.

If you need to support laptop computers, be sure to test your image on a laptop. Keep in mind that a laptop computer often has no network connection or may have only a wireless connection. Be sure to verify that your software works in no-network situations. Also be aware that not all laptops support backlit keyboards. If the image is built on a laptop that does not require that specific driver, it may not enable backlit keyboards when deployed to laptops that do support that feature.

Lastly, the type of processor present may also affect the image (depending on software release). It is a good idea to test a PowerPC-based image on an Intel-based image and vice versa. As operating systems and code continues to evolve, this may become a moot issue; however, it should be tested thoroughly to insure maximum compatibility. Generally, one image per chip set is advised. For example, if you maintain four images for your PowerPC-based Macs, you might wish to build and maintain four images for your Intel-based Macs.

Testing Images with Software

Once you have completed the hardware testing, you should test the software that was deployed on the disk image. If you are using NetBoot or Network Install images, verify that the applications run and that documents work as expected while the computer is started up from an image. If you are using ASR images, verify that the applications work as expected after being restored and that the documents are where you intended them to be.

Before testing the application on the images, you might want to create a baseline by determining how the applications work normally. This will help you answer some basic questions:

- Where are the preferences for the application stored?

  After running the application, look in the Preferences folder or an application-specific folder in ~/Library and /Library or in ~/Library/Application Support /Library/Application Support, and sort by date to see what preferences were added when the application was run.

- Are there preferences for each of the application's users?

  Before running the application, take note of the items in ~/Library. After running the application, see if any new items have been created in ~/Library.

- Are the preferences stored in the top-level Preferences folder, or are they ByHost preferences?

- How does the application work when run by a user with administrator privileges versus a normal user?

  This is a simple test to determine what kind of access the application needs when it is running.

- Will the application work differently when run by a network user?

  Some applications are very sensitive to users who have network home directories.

- Where are the components of the application stored?

  Use the package receipt and BOM to identify the location of installed files. Also, open the package to see where items are placed. For applications that don't use Apple packages to install, you can use third-party utilities such as logGen (LSA Mac OS X Software site: www.lsa.umich.edu/lsait/admin/mac/software/index.asp) to find all the areas to which an application is installed.

Your ability to run an application might depend on whether its preferences can be saved to a home folder, a read-only System directory, or a special preferences location. Your ability to deploy an application might depend on whether its components are stored in a single location or across the file system. Once you have a baseline for the application, identify issues when deploying or running it from a disk image.

You should also test any client/server applications to make sure that the network connectivity and performance is what you expect. If you plan to use network home folders, authentication through an Open Directory master (or other directory service), or preference management, test the image in each of the intended scenarios in the following way:

1. Start up the computer from a NetBoot image.
2. Authenticate from a directory running on an Open Directory master.
3. Have your environment predefined by preference management in Workgroup Manager.
4. Verify that your users can accomplish this regardless of which computer they log in from (hardware/software-based testing).
5. Finally, verify that host-specific preferences don't keep users from accomplishing their tasks.

   These include screen-saver, energy, and Software Update preferences. This may require further configuration beyond restoring from disk images or starting up from disk images, such as postinstallation or login scripts.

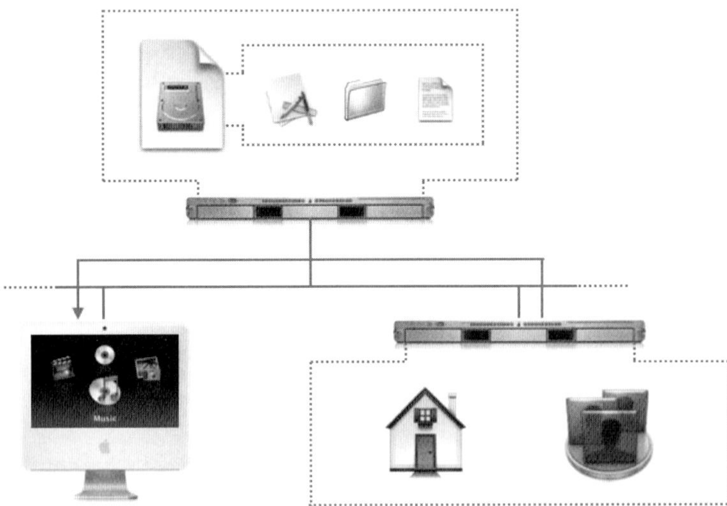

Using a Click Matrix

As you plan what you want to test, start a comprehensive checklist, or *click matrix*, that will include all of the configurations and tasks that need to be completed and validated before the images and packages are ready for use. Each task should simulate the workflow that your users will go through. The tasks should include application, installation, network connection, and hardware tests. If you think it might make a difference in how the computers are used, test it! Each task should be tested carefully and documented, recording which files changed, where temporary files are stored, and if permissions and/or ownership changes. Be sure to document and save your click matrix for the next time you need to rebuild your image or package.

Task: Open Pages and save a file				
Student 10.4.dmg			✓	✓
Faculty 10.4.dmg		✓	✓	
Admin 10.4.dmg	✓	✓		✓

Testing Packages

Installer is an excellent tool for testing packages. Use it to verify that the interface scripting displays properly, that the files and folders install in the correct places, and that the scripting completes the tasks you configured the script to accomplish. In addition, you can test your scripts separately before adding them to the package.

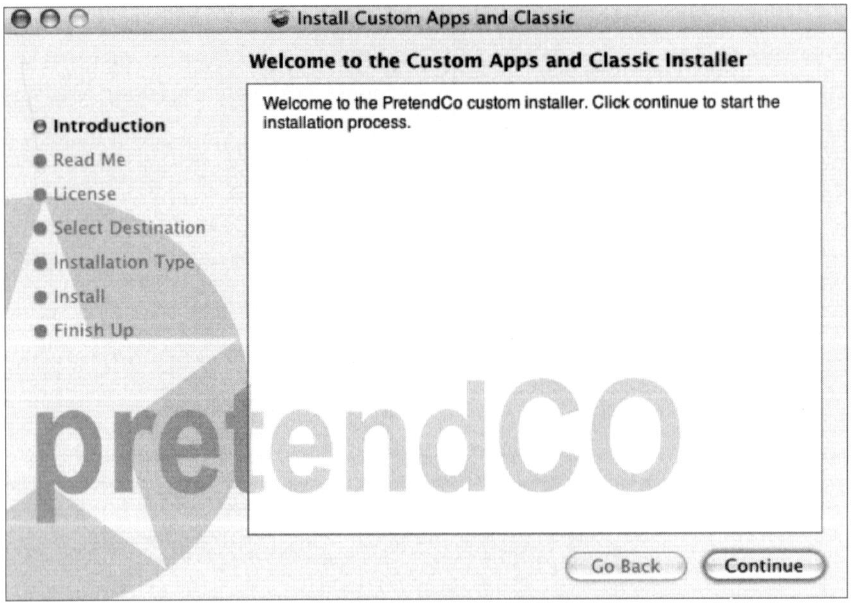

Installer provides a lot of information to work with when you test your packages. The Installer log (Window > Installer Log or /var/log/install.log) will display any error messages or activity that occurred during the installation of the package. Use this information to track down errors in the creation or scripting of the package.

Each time Installer installs a package, it creates a receipt in /Library/Receipts. Receipt files look like packages (.pkg) but include a record of the installation instead of the actual package contents. Included in this receipt is a *bill of materials* (.bom) file. Each .bom file contains a list of the files installed by the package, the proper permissions for each file, the UID and GID for the owner and group, the file sizes, and the checksum. Use lsbom to output the contents of a .bom file. For example,

```
lsbom -p fM\? /Library/Receipts/Java.pkg/Contents/Archive.bom
```

will list specified contents of the bill of materials for Java.pkg. The -p argument specifies which parameters to output—in this example, the filenames (f), the permissions (M), and the name of the owner and group of each file (?). In the example just shown, you must escape the question mark with a backslash since it is a special shell character. Use the .bom files to verify not only that the package installed properly, but also that it registers that it installed properly.

NOTE ▶ Third-party software can automate the testing of packages and workflows, thus reducing the time spent searching for potential errors. Software such as Eggplant from Redstone Software offers this type of testing automation (among other features).

Common Issues and Solutions

There are a number of issues you may encounter as you are testing your method of deploying Mac OS X. Consider these issues and resolutions as you plan.

Requiring Permissions

Some applications require specific permissions on the folders they reside in and the folders they access. As you test your deployment method, part of the testing will include documenting how applications work in a "normal" configuration. Pay particular attention to permissions.

Some applications running in Mac OS X will behave erratically if they are run from a read-only folder. This is common for applications that save preferences to their own folders, rather than to a standard Library folder. If this is the case, copy the application to a folder in the user's home folder or create a folder in /Applications that is read/write for all users.

NOTE ▶ Particularly on multiuser computers, you should exercise extreme caution when giving users read/write access to folders outside of their home folders. Giving them that access can expose the system to the potential for malicious activity and is considered a security risk.

Some Classic applications won't run if the Classic System Folder can't be written to. If you plan on setting the permissions on the System Folder to read-only, test your application before deployment to determine how it will behave with this configuration. If the application doesn't work properly, run Classic from a disk image and mount the disk image with a shadow file using ShadowClassic, from Bombich Software (www.bombich.com), or with the following commands:

```
cd /System/Library/CoreServices/Classic\ Startup.app/Contents/MacOS

sudo mv Classic\ Startup Real\ Classic\ Startup

sudo ditto ~/ShadowClassic.app/Contents/Resources/shadow ./Classic\ Startup
```

Deploying Site-Licensed Software

Many professional applications in Mac OS X use serial numbers to control licensing of the software. In some of those applications, the serial number is user specific, rather than computerwide. If you have configured an application to be deployed using a user-specific serial number, you might find that, although the application was installed/copied to the client computers, users are unable to run the application.

In some cases, you will be working with professional applications that use a serial number tied to the Built-in Ethernet Media Access Control (MAC) address. Again, even though the application may get copied during deployment, it might never run on any computer other than the computer on which it was initially installed. Regardless of where the software is to be used, a work-around may violate software agreements. A better method is to contact the vendor for a site license of the software, and inquire as to the proper method of mass deployment.

Using Firmware Passwords

If a user has set a firmware password for the computer, you won't be able to use the keyboard sequences to start up the computer from a different boot device without supplying the password. This inhibits the ability to use many of the methods described previously, such as changing the NetBoot image from which users are booting.

If you can log in to the computer as an administrator, you can change the startup disk without knowing the firmware password. You can also change or remove the password using the Open Firmware Password utility. If you don't have a copy of the utility handy, you can also use the nvram command to delete the firmware password:

```
sudo nvram -d security-mode

sudo nvram -d security-password
```

If you can't log in as an administrator and don't have the existing firmware password for that computer, you will have to change the amount of RAM in the computer by shutting down the computer, adding or removing memory cards, and then reset the PRAM by holding down the selected keys (Command-Option-P-R at startup) while the computer chimes three times as it boots. For more information, refer to the AppleCare Knowledge Base article "Setting up firmware password protection in Mac OS X 10.1 or later" (http://docs.info.apple.com/article.html?artnum=106482).

Binding to Active Directory

If you are binding your computers to Active Directory for authentication, you'll want to personalize the computer name for each individual Mac OS X computer. (This is taken care of automatically using Windows computers bound to Active Directory.) A workaround for this issue is to unbind your image master computer, still keeping the search paths configured. Once a computer has been imaged from the master image, use dsconfigad as a one-time startup item. Since computers listed in Active Directory must have unique names, have a startup script pull the Built-in Ethernet (MAC) address and use that as the computer name prior to running dsconfigad. For example, the following script pulls the MAC address and uses it for the computer name:

```
#!/bin/sh

MACaddr=`ifconfig en0 | awk '/ether/ { gsub(":", ""); print $2 }'`

dsconfigad -f -a $MACaddr -domain yourdomain -u username -p password
```

Handling Static Network Values

There are a number of computer-specific, sometimes called *static*, values, such as the IP address, computer name, SSH key, and ByHost files. On an ASR image, these values will be the same as those on the computer from which the image was made. When you deploy that image, the values get copied to the target computer. You have a couple of options for resolving this issue. One is to use the System Image Utility to configure computer names to be used on client computers, or to modify host-specific settings such as the directory service that will be accessed and the model of computer the image will be used on. Another option is to use a payload-free package with post-actions or simple shell scripts to change these values on each newly deployed computer. Furthermore, since printers tend to be location specific, consider how to change those settings once an image is deployed. Any files that are based on the MAC address can be changed via the same startup script that binds the computer to the AD domain, simply by locating the ByHost files and changing the names of the files.

Using Non-Package Installers and LogGen

Although Installer in Mac OS X provides a record of what files were installed and where, other installation applications, such as VISE, do not. One solution is to use logGen, a command-line utility that detects file-system changes. It can be run before and after an installation with VISE, and will generate a list of those files that were added, deleted, or modified. Then you can create a custom installation package of the contents using PackageMaker. Or, using the find command, you can create a file just before the installation to act as the baseline for a creation date. After the installation, identify the folders that were created after you created the baseline file.

NOTE ► Another solution is to use the PackageMaker command line utility to take a snapshot of the drive after the installation. Then a package can be created with the differences between before installing the software and after installing it. That package can then be deployed to other computers.

Working with Root-Only Installers

Some applications require that you install to / (root of the volume). If, however, the computer you are installing to is in Target Disk Mode, you cannot install that application because the volume is in /Volumes. There are two possible solutions—one easier but less reliable, and one harder but more reliable. The easy solution is to modify the package requirements to no longer require the target volume to be the currently booted volume. There are a number of places within a package where this check could be made, such as InstallationCheck, VolumeCheck, *packagename*.info, Info.plist, or *packagename*.dist. The drawback to this solution is that pre- and post-action scripts may not be robust enough to work on a non-root volume. This not only may cause application-installation problems, but it also could potentially harm your system. The other solution, although much more labor intensive, is much safer. Using logGen or a similar utility, identify the files that are installed and create a custom package that will put the files in the correct locations.

Using Resource Forks

Although not used nearly as much as they once were, resource forks are still quite common in Mac OS X. If an application or folder is missing a custom icon, typically the resource fork is missing, and there will likely be other problems with your installation. Using extra care to use only resource-fork-preserving command-line tools, such as those supplied with Mac OS X v10.4 and higher, will reduce the possibility of resource-fork problems. Many of the command-line tools included in earlier versions of Mac OS X ignored resource forks.

Another issue to watch for when using .dmg files is that those created in Mac OS X v10.1 and v10.2 often include a resource fork. The result is that when you download them via HTTP, they become unusable. The solution is to provide the affected disk-image file over AFP, which preserves the integrity of a forked file. Alternatively, compress the .dmg file as a .zip file. This will allow it to be downloaded using protocols that don't support forked files.

Hiding Visible Folders and Files

After performing a NetInstall or restoring Mac OS X from a disk image, you may see certain files and folders (such as etc, tmp, and var) at the root level of the Mac OS X volume that are not supposed to be visible. In Mac OS X v10.3 and earlier, these items are made hidden (invisible) by listing them in a file named ".hidden" at the root level of the Mac OS X volume. Mac OS X v10.4 and later do not use this method, but rather hide files by setting certain attributes in the files themselves.

However, in Mac OS X v10.4 and v10.4.1, these attributes are not preserved when you create a disk image. To prevent these files from becoming visible on a NetInstalled or restored system, use the following steps to make them invisible on the source disk image:

1. Create a disk image in read/write format, or convert your existing image to read/write format.
2. Mount the image.
3. Insert your Mac OS X v10.4 Installation DVD into your computer.
4. Open a Terminal window and enter the following two commands:

   ```
   $ cd /Volumes/Mac\ OS\ X\ Install\ DVD/System/Installation/Packages/OSInstall.mpkg/
   Contents/Resources/
   ```

   ```
   $ sudo ./SetHidden /Volumes/mountedImage hidden_MacOS9
   ```
5. Unmount the disk image.
6. Convert it back to compressed format.
7. Scan the image for restore.

You can also create the older, .hidden file at the root level of the volume and place root-level directory, file, and symbolic link names into that file, as well, or use the developer tool, SetFile, located in /Developer/Tools, to hide folders anywhere on the file system. With SetFile, you use the -a flag for attributes and the V flag to make the folder invisible.

For instance, after navigating to the /Developer/Tools directory, you can run this command to make the /Developer folder invisible:

```
$ ./SetFile -a V /Developer
```

Lesson Review

1. How do you verify that images will work properly when deployed?
2. What is a quick means of testing custom installation packages?
3. What are some of the permissions issues you will encounter when deploying images in a network environment?
4. What must be unique when binding a Mac OS X computer to an Active Directory domain and why is that important with imaging?

Answers

1. Test them on representative systems.
2. Use the Installer application.
3. Some applications do not run from a read-only folder; some Classic applications do not run if the System Folder is not writable for the user.
4. The computer name listed in the Active Directory domain must be unique, so a single image cannot possibly have one name to be used for all computers. A method of binding with unique names must be found.

References

Knowledge Base Articles

You can check for new and updated articles in the AppleCare Knowledge Base at www.apple.com/support.

URLs

Visit the following sites for more information:

Application Deployment Problems and Solutions: www.macos.utah.edu/crappyApps.html

ShadowClassic: Bombich Software: www.bombich.com/software/shadowclassic.html

Efficient Practices for a 1 to 1 iBook Deployment: www.afp548.com/filemgmt_data/files/master_1to1_image.pdf

6

Time This lesson takes about 1 hour to complete.

Goals

Deploy and update Mac OS X in an organization

Gather system and software information from Mac OS X systems using Apple Remote Desktop

Update Mac OS X using Apple Remote Desktop

Use Radmind to keep Mac OS X systems updated

Manage the download and distribution of Apple-provided software updates

Lesson 6

Maintenance

For system administrators, it would be ideal to simply deploy Mac OS X to the variety of computers you support and expect that everything will work every time, all the time, forever. Because this is not the case, you need to consider the lifecycle of your deployment.

The lifecycle begins with planning, where you envision what your finished deployment will look like. You go through the trial and error of designing what you hope will be the most functional method of installing, updating, upgrading, and maintaining your operating systems, applications, and files. Next, take some time to test out a few of your ideas in a way that won't impact your current implementation or create any permanent changes. After modifying your plan to reflect any discoveries, move to the implementation or deployment phase. Much of this phase has already been covered in previous lessons. Finally, step back and evaluate whether the plan was successful or not. Look at how you will maintain your implementation over a long period of time. The lessons learned during your implementation need to be captured, incorporated into a revised plan, and used to improve the next iteration.

This lesson focuses on some of the tools you can incorporate into your lifecycle planning to maintain the system of images and packages that you have already deployed.

Automating Client Maintenance

The idea behind successful maintenance of images relies on two key points: updates, and remote access to several machines simultaneously.

Controlling Software Updates

You can use the Software Update utility and the softwareupdate command-line utility (which must be run as root) to automatically download and install the latest updates to Mac OS X. By default, these utilities look to the public Apple update server for the latest software, and users with administrative rights can run them from their machines any time they wish. The softwareupdate command-line utility has a variety of flags with which to manage it. For example, the –l flag lists all available updates, the –d is to download the updates if necessary for later use, and –i is used to install the updates. Updates can be chosen explicitly by name or by using –a for installing all available updates. The line

```
sudo softwareupdate –i –a
```

will install all available updates.

With Mac OS X Server v10.4, you have the option of providing a local Software Update Server to deliver updates that have been collected from the Apple update server. This gives you an opportunity to stage your updates. Rather than having your users download and install the updates as they are released, running the risk of incompatibilities with existing software or third-party hardware, download the update to a testing environment and validate it before allowing your users to install it. Once you are satisfied that the update is safe and compatible with your particular environment, you can enable that update on your local software update server via the Server Admin utility. Environments with tight firewall restrictions can also benefit from using a local software update server. This benefit comes from no longer needing to allow every computer access to the public software update servers. Instead, they only need to talk to one software update server, which may be located inside your firewall. Software Update server handles updates in two different ways. You can choose to mirror an update from Apple and then decide which updates to offer your users. Not all mirrored updates need to be offered. When troubleshooting the Software Update service, all downloaded updates are placed in /usr/share/swupd/html/.

The easiest way to configure a computer to use your local software update server instead of the public Apple servers is to use Workgroup Manager to configure managed preferences in Mac OS X for that computer. If you are not using managed preferences for your computers, you can also issue this command on a computer to configure where it checks for software updates:

```
sudo default write com.apple.SoftwareUpdate CatalogURL http://xxx.xxx.xxx.xxx/index.sucatalog
```

substituting the IP address of your local software update server in the URL.

NOTE ▶ A local software update server can only serve Apple-provided software updates. You cannot add your own packages to the software update server.

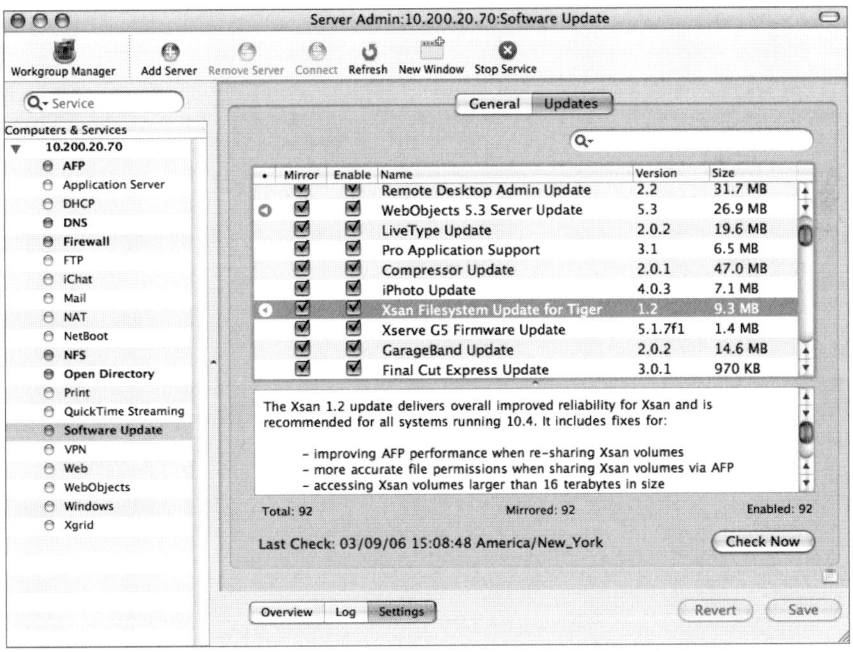

Using Apple Remote Desktop

Apple Remote Desktop (ARD) is another excellent tool for maintaining systems. With it, you can remotely install packages, set the network startup disk, run UNIX commands, and schedule various configuration and reporting tasks.

ARD gives you the flexibility of installing software updates without user intervention (as seen in the image below), installing custom installation packages, or installing packages that simply change user settings. If your user is downloading and installing updates from a software update server, it requires the user to take action. However, as an administrator, you can download the update onto your computer and use the Remote Desktop administration utility to update many other Mac OS X computers with no interaction required by your users.

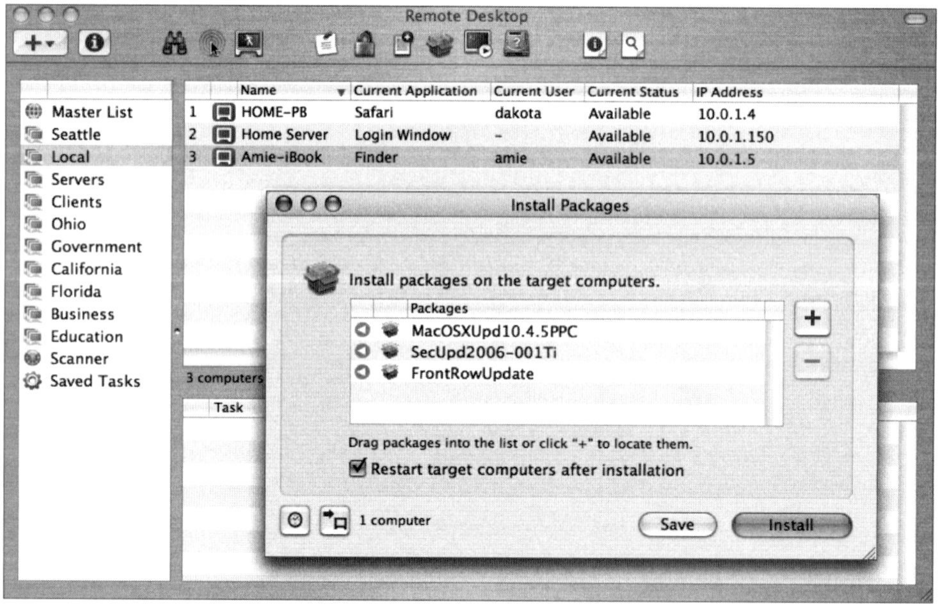

Remote Desktop (the actual application software used to control ARD) also provides a solution for automatically delivering custom installation packages, a feature not supported by the Software Update Server in Mac OS X Server v10.4. This feature allows you to create your own installation packages for the applications and files that are unique to your organization. You can also install packages that modify the settings on other Mac OS X computers. For example, it might be necessary to create a package that configures a Mac OS X computer to bind to a directory service, which is often better than expecting the user to make those configuration changes manually, especially if he or she is not an administrator.

If you configure new NetBoot or Network Install images and want your users to make the transition to those images, use Remote Desktop to change the network startup disk on any of the computers that are managed with the Remote Desktop administration tool. This lets you stage your deployments of updated images and makes the transition transparent to the users.

Remote Desktop allows you to schedule tasks such as delivering updates, running a shell script, or copying files to one or many computers. You can wait until the remote computers are ready to receive updates or information, either at low-usage times or, in the case of portables, when the computers are actually connected to the network. Furthermore, the data reporting in Remote Desktop is automated so that you can collect data on the state of any of your Remote Desktop-managed computers at regular intervals. These reports help you make decisions about which updates are necessary for each system and the best time to deploy changes.

Maintaining with Shell Scripts

Shell scripts are a good option for repetitive tasks to keep systems up-to-date. Many of the tools mentioned previously have a command-line equivalent and can easily be scripted to automate your updates, as shown below. For instance, a machine's crontab can be edited to include the `softwareupdate` command. Use the `softwareupdate` command to search for, download, and install software updates from either a local Software Update server or from the public Apple update server. Putting the command in crontab allows you to specify when the script will be run. You can also put scripts in a number of other locations to have them run automatically. /etc/periodic contains three subdirectories to run scripts daily, weekly, or monthly. Simply drop your script into the appropriate directory, and it will be run on that schedule.

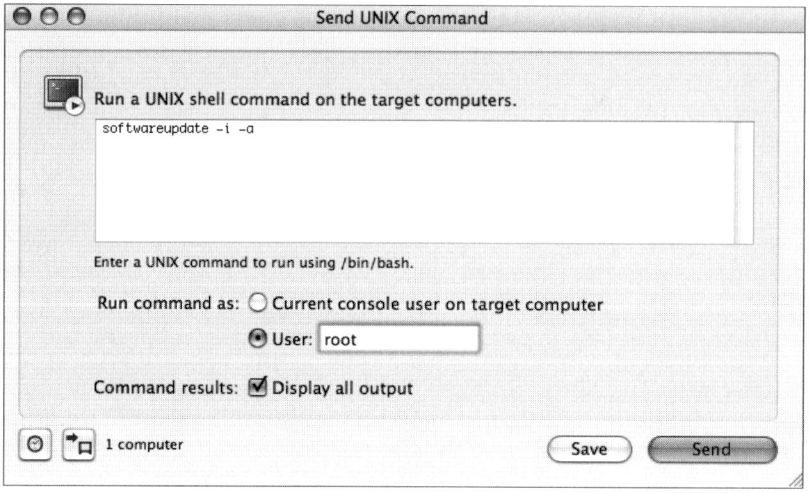

For more control of when scripts are run, third-party utilities such as anacron (www.alastairs-place.net/anacron.html) let you defer scripts to low-usage times. To run scripts remotely, either use ssh or Send UNIX Command in Remote Desktop. The command in Remote Desktop allows you to run a UNIX command, set of commands, or shell script on any number of selected Mac OS X computers. Automate this process by defining these as tasks and scheduling them.

When running UNIX commands, you also have the option to display all the output from the commands. This is the output that normally would be echoed on the screen or sent to the screen via stdout or stderr.

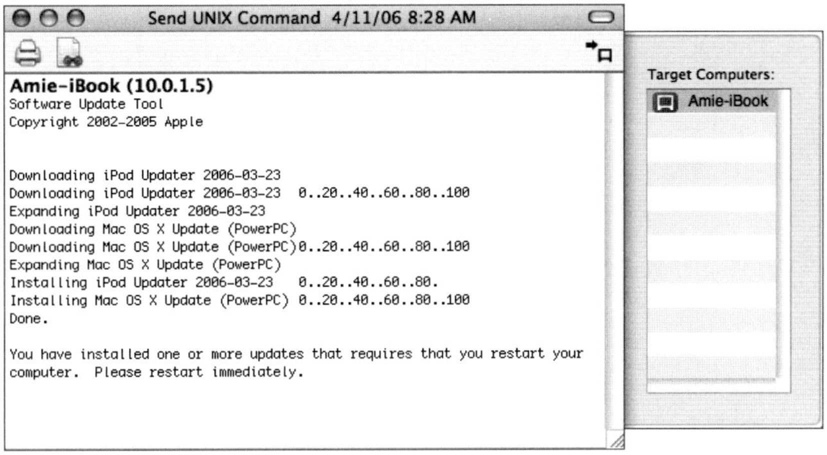

WARNING ▸ Use caution when automating scripts that may affect the user environment because users are not given any warning if a script run from cron will modify their system. The softwareupdate command will not automatically reboot the user's system after an update is installed. After a major update, this could leave the computer in an unstable state until it is rebooted, such as when a kernel is replaced by the update.

Maintaining with Radmind

Radmind can help you maintain a master configuration and then deploy that configuration to multiple computers on a file-by-file basis. When you make changes to that master, the changes can be automatically seen by the clients. You also have the option of reversing the changes, which is particularly useful if you have installed an update prematurely.

Radmind uses loadsets, a collection of files to be maintained along with instructions for Radmind, as the basis for maintaining remote systems. For instance, the base, or initial, loadset contains a working copy of Mac OS X, as well as any applications you want to keep updated on your Mac OS X computers. When you want to deploy new applications or files to your Mac OS X computers, you build a loadset that contains the applications or files and create a transcript for Radmind. You can accomplish all of these tasks using the Radmind Assistant for Mac OS X.

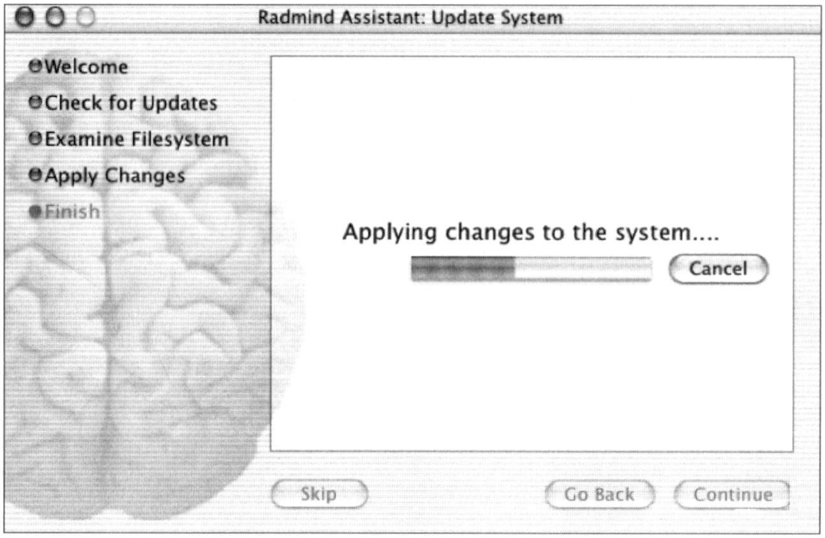

There is also a server component to Radmind. Using the Server Manager, you configure the Radmind server to deploy, serve, and merge loadsets. Please refer to the appendix for more detailed information on Radmind server.

Radmind tracks changes made to a file system after an application has been installed. It can also track changes made by the application itself when it runs. This information is important as you revisit your deployment plan, but is also useful from a security and stability standpoint, since unauthorized changes will be automatically undone the next time Radmind is run.

Maintaining with Packages

Typically, Mac OS X users want to use the latest hardware and software. However, maintaining them can be a challenge. If you are attempting to guarantee functionality for your users, keeping your images up-to-date can be time-consuming, and system administrators often have to limit frequent software or hardware upgrades. Make your users aware of the time it takes to update a set of ASR and NetBoot images every time a new CPU is introduced to the supported equipment. Furthermore, the ASR and NetBoot features themselves change as Mac OS X and Mac OS X Server are upgraded and as new processor types are released.

One solution is to use packages. Packages allow you to create interim updates in response to frequent changes to equipment without having to create new images immediately. Use a package to update a system with a new version of Mac OS X. Deploy packages with updates to hardware drives. Use ARD to make sure that all of your users receive the packaged updates and then keep track of which computers received the updates. This strategy allows you to keep your users up-to-date and still gives you time to test new hardware and software configurations before deploying them. PackageMaker is an application installed with the Apple Developer Tools that can create custom packages.

Lesson Review

1. What are some tools you can use to automate the task of updating computers?
2. What is used to send a single UNIX command to many computers running Mac OS X?
3. What command-line tool can be used to bring Mac OS X computers current with their software?
4. What is one method administrators can use to update existing computers with non-Apple updates?
5. What does Radmind use to image a machine back to a previous state?

Answers

1. Shell Scripts, Apple Remote Desktop, Radmind, cron jobs.
2. Send UNIX Command under the Manage menu of Remote Desktop.
3. softwareupdate
4. Creating custom packages and pushing them out via Apple Remote Desktop.
5. Loadsets.

References

Knowledge Base Articles

You can check for new and updated articles in the AppleCare Knowledge Base at www.apple.com/support.

URLs

Visit the following sites for more information:

Apple Remote Desktop: www.apple.com/remotedesktop/

Radmind: http://rsug.itd.umich.edu/software/radmind/

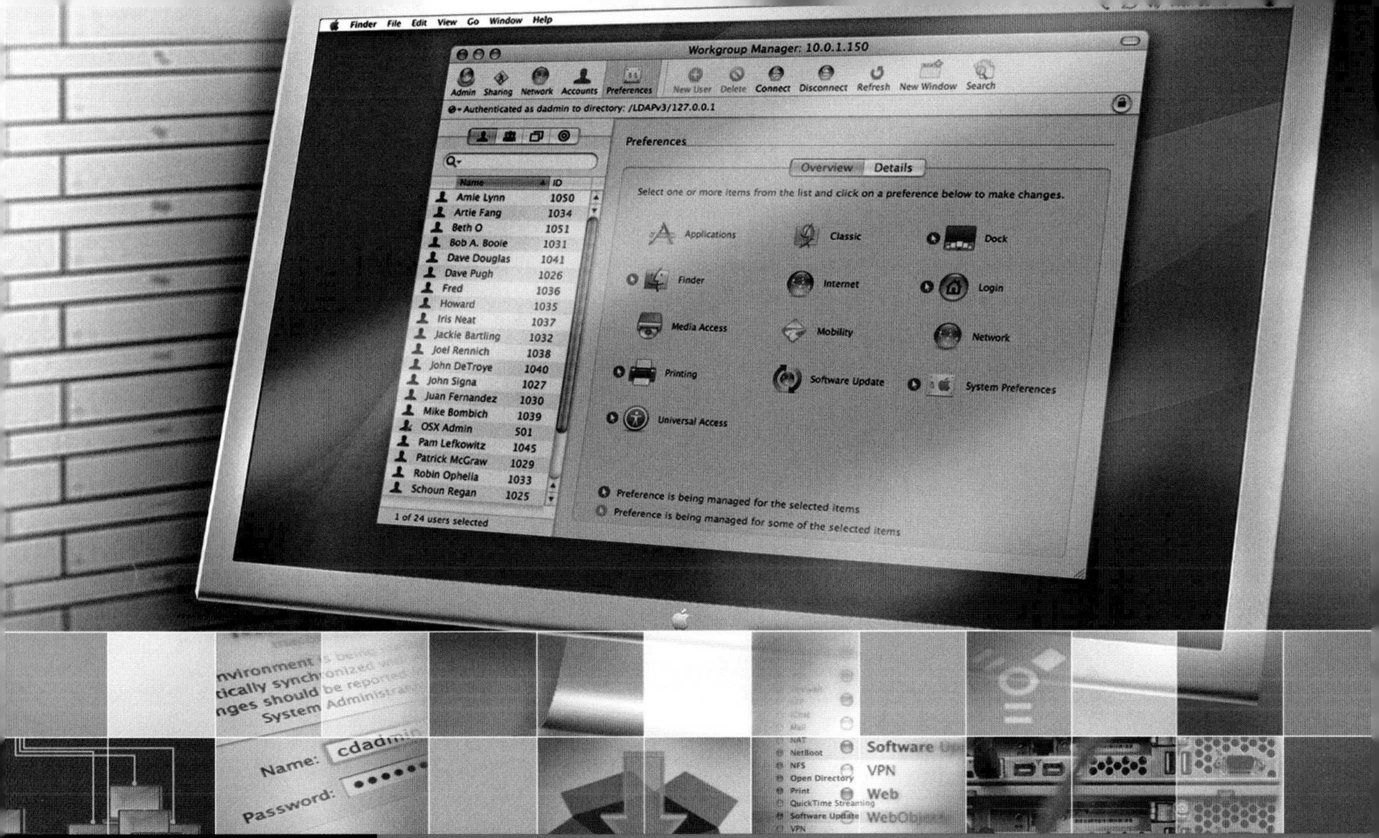

Part 2 Managing Accounts

7

Time This lesson takes about 1 hour to complete.

Goals

Understand the types of managed accounts

Create a plan for managing account types

Evaluate pros and cons of network home folders

Make policies for managed accounts

Create a document for the managed-account process

Import and export user accounts using Workgroup Manager

Lesson 7

Developing an Account Management Strategy

What is account management? Does this mean managing users? Groups? Computers? Access to servers and other systems? Account management is the limitation and control of all types of accounts, whether they are users, groups, or computers. This control can be granular, allowing for limitations to be placed on just one user or group. Mac OS X and Mac OS X Server make account management easy to implement. But without proper planning and testing, account management can easily overwhelm administrators. Before clicking the mouse, develop a management plan.

The best way to think about account management is to examine what your organization wishes to accomplish, and the scope and breadth of the management. Are you planning to manage all users and administrators, or just users? Does your management extend to the company's executives? What is the extent to which you want to manage users? These are a few of the questions that must be asked to ensure a successful implementation of managed accounts.

Levels of Management

Workgroup Manager is used to manage the three account levels:

- User accounts
- Workgroup accounts
- Computer accounts

When you consider managing accounts, think about your organization. You have users, which consist of both standard users and administrators. Among these, the administrators are likely to have various levels of technical acumen and are categorized accordingly by job.

You have workgroups—groups of users, groups of administrators, groups of groups.

You also have computers, perhaps not just Apple computers, but also computers that run other operating systems, such as Windows. These computers might be laptop computers, desktop computers, servers, or small, non-laptop, somewhat portable computers (such as the Mac Mini). These computers may be used by just one person within your organization, or they may be in a computer lab environment.

Each of these levels of management can be used for control and can act independently of each other.

Understanding Account Types

Understanding the levels of accounts that can be managed is a good start. But what types of accounts can be at each level? For example, can you manage a user on a local Mac OS X computer if that computer isn't connected to or bound to a Mac OS X Server? Can groups be managed on Mac OS X as easily as on Mac OS X Server? How many different computer types can you manage? Macs? Windows machines? There are three main account types when dealing with Mac OS X and Mac OS X Server:

- **The local account.** The local account exists only on Mac OS X. There is no connection to any accounts on Mac OS X Server or any other directory service; therefore, user account management is minimal at best. All Mac OS X computers have at least one local account. This is the account that is initially created when Mac OS X is set up without being connected to or bound to a directory service. If the computer on which the local account is located is stolen, is compromised, or has a hard-disk failure, then that user account and all related user information, such as the user's files and data, can be lost (unless it has been backed up to a remote computer or device). One advantage of a local account is that a server need not be present for it to function for the user.

- **The network account.** If a local account does not have any relationship with a directory service, then a network account is the opposite. It exists solely on a server and is used transparently on Mac OS X, allowing for the full complement of account management. Network accounts have no predilection to the computer to which they are bound. If that computer is stolen or a hard-disk failure occurs, only the open files are affected. The user's files and data actually exist on a remote server. However, if the server is not available, the user cannot use the computer.
- **The mobile account.** Mobile accounts combine the advantage of a local account—the freedom to be disconnected from the server (such as with a laptop computer)—with the granularity of account management from a network account. Mobile accounts essentially are new accounts that employ the user account template on the Mac OS X computer to create an account based on the network user account. Any management that is performed on the network account is cached locally on the Mac OS X computer, permitting the user to disconnect from the server to which it was bound when the account was created. This allows for a tremendous amount of physical freedom with regard to the computer's location, as the computer does not constantly have to be bound to the server. However, when the user does reconnect to the network, any changes to that account's management are downloaded to the local computer from the server. A user's data resides locally on the computer on which the mobile account was created. The user's files and data are not synchronized back to the server unless that option is chosen.

Matching Account Types to Individuals

When creating a solution for account management, roles must be clearly defined with respect to users, administrators, and groups. How many groups are required and who should be a member of each group? Mac OS X Server has virtually no limitation on the number of groups you can create. Since you can have as many groups as you like, it is easy to assume that dragging users into their groups is the best solution.

However, removing a user from one group does not remove her from another group. The time spent managing groups can quickly lengthen, and the groups can become difficult to keep organized. Creating nested groups (groups within groups) allows better control of users.

Administrative users are of particular interest because they may be in separate departments within your organization. A one-size-fits-all administrator group may not be the best solution. Within an educational environment, teachers are often placed in control of their students, so they effectively become administrators. However, they may not need or require administrator access to other groups or computers outside of their classroom. Burdening them with additional administrative capabilities when unnecessary is asking for trouble, should their accounts become compromised. It is best to take an organizational chart, evaluate skill levels and specific administrative tasks, and create administrative groups based on these criteria.

Matching User Requirements to Management Solutions

It is important to qualify in advance which management solutions work for each type of user. Defining roles and determining in advance how accounts will be managed removes any doubt or question when setting up accounts. For example, there are probably several skill levels relative to Mac OS X within your organization. Some users may possess more advanced skills than others. A level of account management should respect the fact that some users have earned more freedom to make decisions about their systems. Conversely, new users may merit a more restrictive management solution.

Setting User Management Policies

Regardless of the organization, it is beneficial to create polices early on to use various levels of account management. Doing so defines what is to be accomplished and how deep the management will be.

Setting Account Creation Policy

All organizations have work-related policies, such as vacation policies and lunchtime limitations. To avoid disputes, it is best to plan what types of accounts are to be created, and when. Should a user have a quota on his home folder? If so, how much? And should it depend on the user? These questions and others need answers to avoid confusion.

In no other situation is this more important than when creating administrator accounts. Not everyone should be made an administrator, and doing so can also add liability that did not exist when there were just three or four administrators. Consider the following when deciding on policies for administrator user creation:

- Organizational group
- Job description
- Competency
- Trust

These factors are not set in stone. Each organization will have to decide how to mete out the creation of accounts. The point is that account policies are a critical factor when planning the entire account management structure.

Setting Policy Components

As when you set your account creation policy, you will have to decide on what pieces of the policy deserve a higher priority than others. Examples of policy component issues:

- Can a user create other accounts, and if so, what types?
  - User accounts
  - Group accounts
  - Computer list accounts
- Should the user be able to reset other users' passwords?
- Should the user be able to manage file share points that directly relate to another user's home folder?
- How much restriction should the user be able to place on another user's interface environment?

You can use Workgroup Manager to establish policy priorities to restrict certain administrators to certain groups. This effectively confines an administrator to a given user, workgroup, or computer list. An example of this is a teacher who has total access to her students' accounts, being allowed to manage all their settings and preferences, but is not allowed to manage the computer list settings of the computers that are in her room.

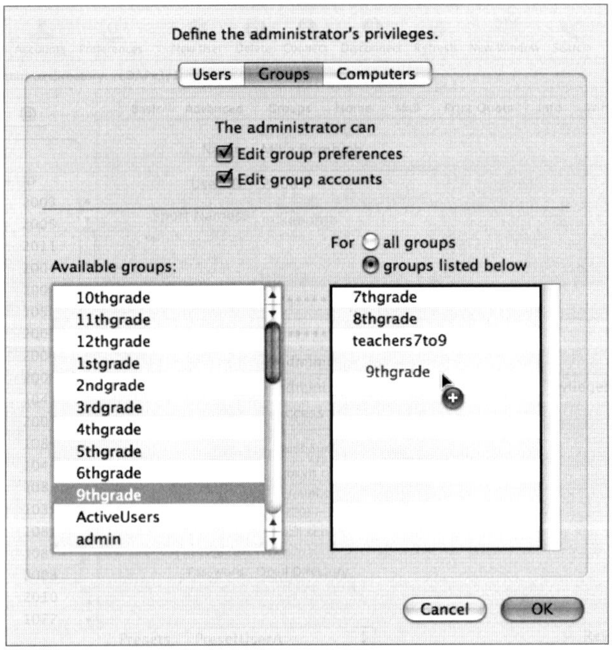

Using Workgroup Manager to restrict an administrator to a given workgroup.

There are usually no easy answers here, and attempting to provide some without an intimate knowledge of an organization's infrastructure would be doing that organization a great disservice.

You must plan not only with computers in mind, but also considering people, personalities, defined roles within the organization, legal ramifications, and long-term goals. This may sound like an overwhelming task, but it is essential to flush out any issues that may arise at the outset, before they become financial and legal burdens later. Proper planning requires that you play the what-if game and provide concrete answers.

Planning Growth Management

Critical to planning your setup architecture is planning for growth. Expansion of hardware, software, network, location of services, and movement of data are all important issues to consider in advance.

Hardware and software should be visited first. For example, 500 users with home folders on one Xserve may be stretching your resources, especially if they all log in within 5 minutes of each other. Available RAM is another consideration. Mac OS X Server should be purchased, if not already owned, and just one copy is not enough. You'll want to make a clone of your directory for reasons you will learn later in this lesson, so plan on purchasing at least one extra copy of Mac OS X Server.

These are some examples of how you should plan for growth with respect to hardware and software. What about accounts? Should you develop an organization-wide account management plan? What benefits will you incur and at what cost? The benefits of this planning include a streamlined path to follow in the future, and fewer questions to answer on the fly.

However, planning comes at a price, which is additional time spent at the onset on the formulation of your plan. If you work in the educational environment, especially within K–12, you are turning over students as they move from one grade to the next, and from one school to the next; as they transfer in, move away, and graduate; and so on. An early decision on how to handle these scenarios will make things easier to manage in the future.

Structuring Organization Management

When setting up your plan, decide how you will structure your server(s) to hold user account information. Students will need a top-level folder for their data. Teachers will need a top-level folder, and will also need read/write access to the student folders. School assistants and office workers will require a separate folder as well, and their access to teachers' and students' folders should be considered.

IT administrators need access to everything—or do they? Some administrators may be allowed to only read all folders and must request that new directories be created, leaving those folders to be created by another administrator. You should scope out all possible scenarios and carefully consider what the folder structure ought to be. Also consider where the folders will exist. How many servers do you have, and where are their locations?

In a business scenario, you take into account some of the newer legal ramifications of giving people unlimited read/write access to all accounts. Directory creation should be documented and limited to a few key individuals to minimize potential duplication of efforts, which can lead to user confusion.

When you are finished with the folder structure, you can move on to creating groups. Who should be a member of which group? Can you leverage the fact that Mac OS X Server can use nested groups?

A very basic school plan might look like this, with a total of 15 folders inside the allgrades folder, 8 folders inside the allstaff folder, and 3 folders in the allitstaff folder:

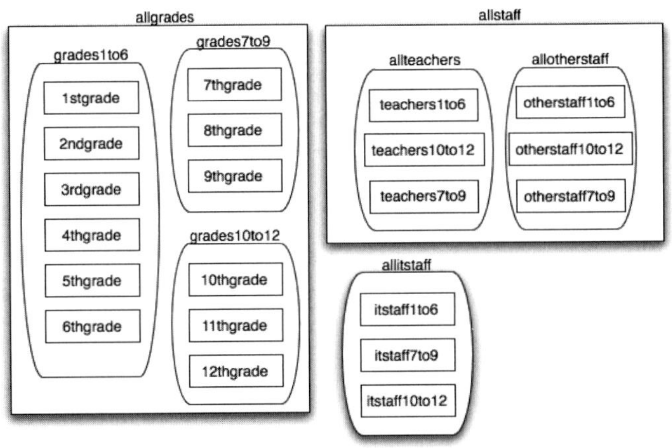

This folder structure, while basic, now requires access to be useful. Creation of groups must now be addressed based on your organizational plan. In this structure, you can create a group for every grade, for every teacher grade set, for other staff, and for IT staff. You can then nest these groups into larger groups and add specific users, such as attaching a first-grade teacher to the 1stgrade group. Again, a concrete plan, while taking longer to formulate, will pay off in the end and can be modified if needed.

Establishing Permissions

Now that you have a basic organization account management plan, what about ownership and permissions? Who will own which folders and what permissions will they have? Mac OS X and Mac OS X Server use both standard UNIX style permissions and Access Control Lists to manage ownership and permissions of folders.

Ownership and permissions are two separate issues, and Access Control Lists introduce yet another layer of planning into your environment (For more information on Access Control Lists, refer to *Apple Training Series: Mac OS X Administration Reference Guide, Volume 1* and *Apple Training Series: Mac OS X Server Essentials*).

At the planning stage, you should layout your read/write permissions for each directory. An excellent guideline to follow is one of restriction: no access is allowed until absolutely necessary, and you document who has access and to which folders. You'll want teachers/project managers to have read/write access to almost all student/user folders, but you may wish to restrict read/write access to student/user folders for teachers/project managers who do not have direct contact with those students/users. Reducing access also allows you to trace back any attacks that may occur in the case of a student or user who obtains the user name and password of a teacher/project manager.

By default, with UNIX-style ownership and permissions, a folder can be associated with only one owner (it cannot be a group) and one group. Access to other folders can be changed, but this is the way UNIX-style permissions are structured in Mac OS X. Each "type" of account has read-only, write-only, read/write, or no access to any folder that the account is associated with, as seen below.

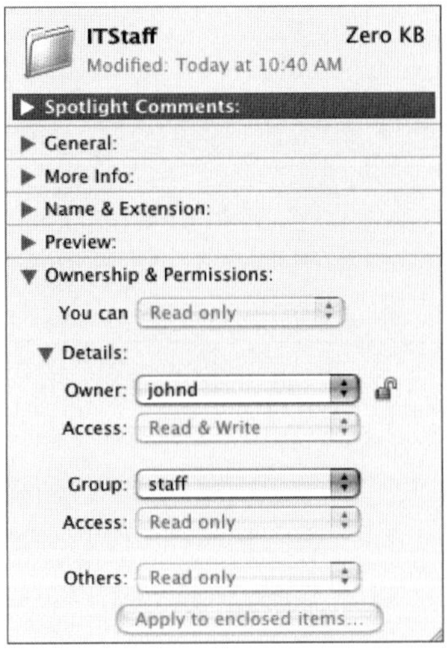

Also take into consideration that items copied to a folder using this permissions model can behave in two different ways:

- They can inherit the permissions of the folder into which they are copied.
- They can maintain their current permissions via the standard UNIX-style permissions behavior.

This decision is based on the Apple Filing Protocol (AFP) server that you have set up as a share point and is not set on each individual folder, unless that folder is also a separate share point. Therefore, creating an account management plan based on these limited ownership and permissions alone is going to be a tedious task. Use Access Control Lists and nested groups to ease the permissions limitations and gain greater control over your folder infrastructure.

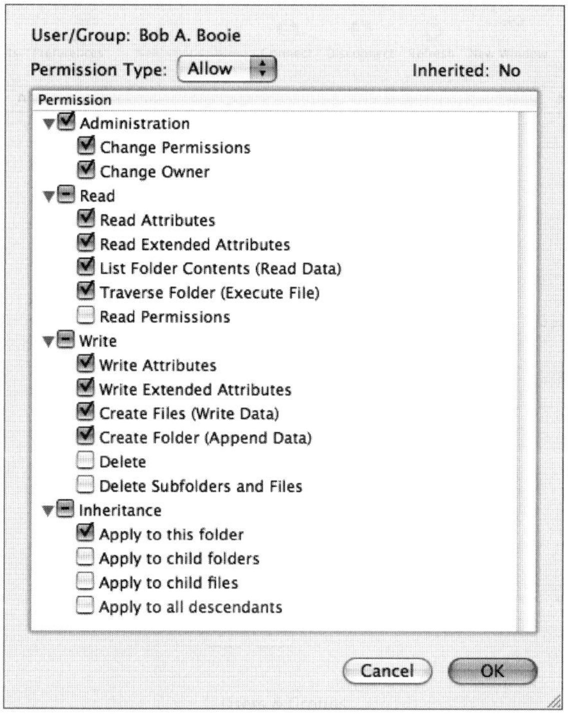

The possible permutations using Access Control Lists for the folder structure.

Implementing Home Folder Management

The location of home folders is another piece of the planning puzzle. Will each user have a local home folder, or should the home folder exist on a server? Or should users have *both* types of home folders and periodically synchronize them? (Apple calls the last two scenarios Mobile Accounts, which will be discussed in Lesson 10, "Working with Mobile Accounts.")

If users are local, they will have local home folders. However, management and control are limited. Users in a remote database, such as an Open Directory master, can have their sessions managed and controlled, and their home folders located on the server. This has several benefits beyond just management of the account. Having the users' work data on the server requires just one server to be backed up every night, as opposed to many single machines. User data growth can be handled easily by moving a user's home folder to a larger drive or RAID array. Also, organizational challenges are easier to handle when users change groups, as their data is more likely to reside on the same physical volume(s).

However, network bandwidth must be available for all users to have an acceptable user experience. A network where each user has a 1 GB connection to her computer is the optimal scenario. If that cannot be achieved across all users, then users with the heaviest data requirements should receive the highest bandwidth.

Network home folders are created using Workgroup Manager, and several folders can be created at once for thousands of users, taking only a few minutes to do so on an Xserve.

Optimizing User Management

Once user accounts have been created, there are a few management options that will assist you in segregating your users into various categories without actually placing them in separate groups. This is useful, as it allows administrators to quickly search an entire database to locate users that meet a certain criterion. You'll also want to use preset values to speed up creation of new user accounts.

Entering Keywords and Comments

Each user and computer account can have keywords associated with it. These can be any words you choose and generally are words that help define users (or computers) that have similar attributes but might not exist in the same group or computer list. An example of a keyword list follows.

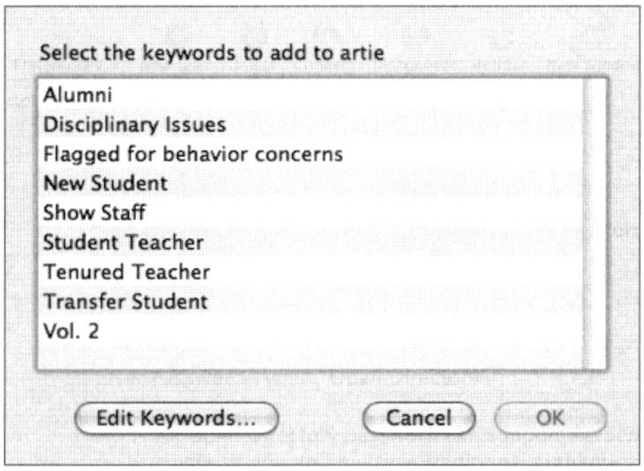

Keywords are defined in the user accounts pane or in the computer accounts dialog, as keywords in one account type can be used in another account type. Once keywords have been defined, searches of user records can show only those accounts with the selected keywords, as seen below.

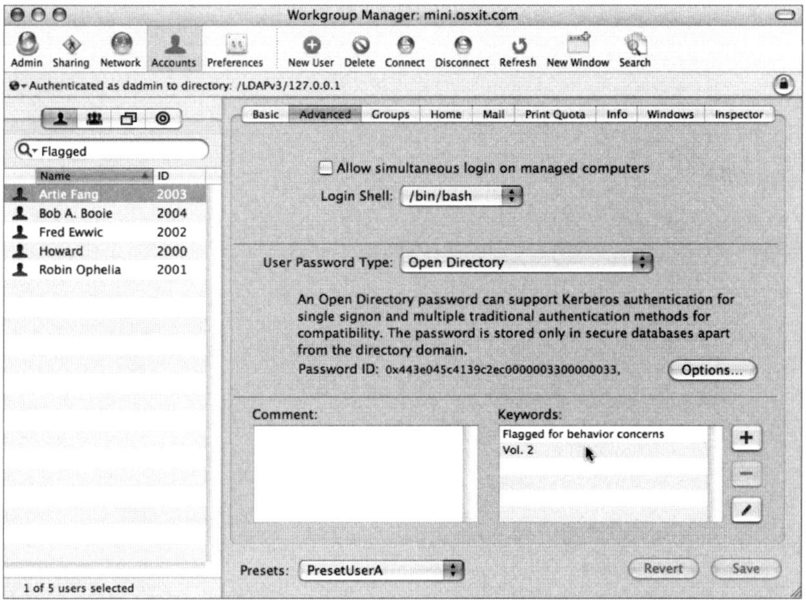

NOTE ▶ Although you can manually add keywords to workgroup accounts using the Inspector pane in Workgroup Manager, there is no mechanism for searching by keyword for workgroup accounts.

Comments are just that—comments. Like keywords, they can be used to identify similar users. Comments, however, can be used for user, workgroup, and computer accounts. Simply select the accounts to which you wish to add a comment, type in the comment, and save the changes.

Use keywords and accounts to keep information about certain account types. It becomes very useful when searching through 10,000 user accounts to locate 50 users with the same keyword or comment.

When searching for user, workgroup, or computer accounts, you have a variety of criteria with which to search, as seen here.

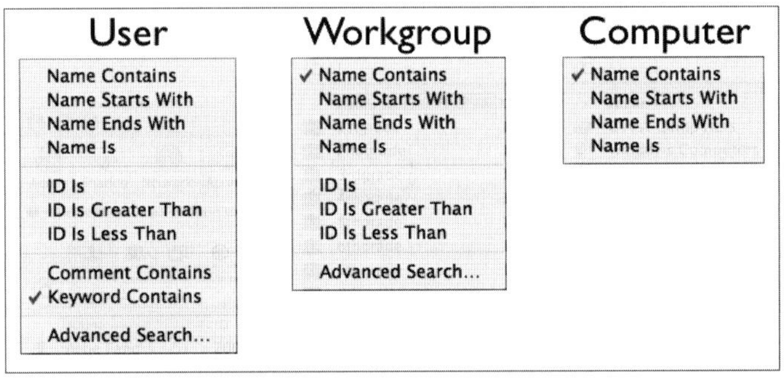

You can also perform an advanced search of users and workgroups by clicking the Search button in the toolbar of Workgroup Manager. Doing so displays the Search dialog.

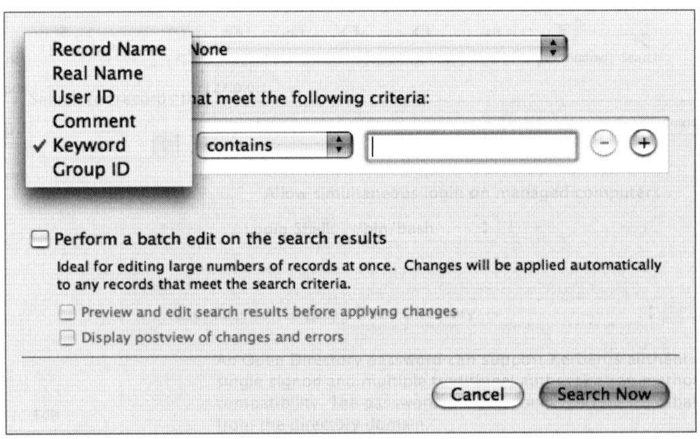

NOTE ▶ You can also perform full batch editing of your search results, such as adding printer quotas or editing account login restrictions. This is a very powerful feature of Workgroup Manager.

Automating Account Creation

When dealing with many account variations, it can become difficult to manage accounts, especially when new accounts need to be created or imported, such as adding new students to a school database every year.

To limit the time spent on configuring new accounts, consider creating an account preset with all the managed preferences. An easy way to do this is to create a separate account, with a name such as PresetUser A, or PresetUser B, that has all the tested preferences entered. Then, when a new account is needed, that preset is chosen before the new account is created, and all the managed preferences are instantly applied to that user account.

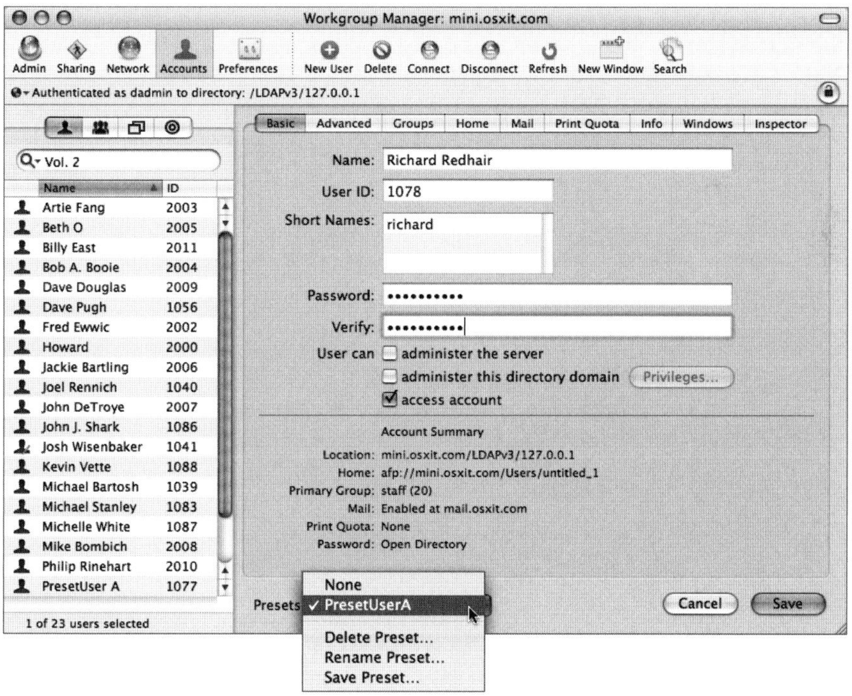

Viewing the Presets menu showing one preset called PresetUserA.

Simplifying User Record Creation

Another way to create (or import) a user is with a third-party application called Passenger (MacinMind Software, www.macinmind.com). Passenger allows you to take any text or delimited file and prepare it for importing into Workgroup Manager. Passenger has many options for assisting in the automatic creation of long names, short names, and passwords. Not only does Passenger define these based on criteria you select, but also you can migrate home folders, batch-change permissions, and preview your data prior to creating a file that Workgroup Manager will import. This allows a student or intern to type all the student information into an Excel file, for example, without giving that student access to the actual Workgroup Manager application.

Documenting Management Policy

All this account management planning can seem overwhelming, and it probably is at first. There are several reasons to carefully document what has taken place during the planning phase of the project:

- Error correction
- Legal concerns
- Privacy assurances
- Staff relocation
- New hires
- IT job reassignment
- Reference guide
- Disaster recovery
- Staff education
- User education

Informing Users

The last two points, staff and user education, are a bit different from the others. It is not necessary to share the entire planning document with all staff members. The entire document should only be accessible to the IT staff, for whom it should be required reading. All others should be given a shorter, condensed version of the document. This helps reduce the risk of the original document getting lost, being misplaced, or falling into the wrong hands. The user document should be shorter still, informing the user of what he has access to, how to report issues, and what he can expect from the user experience.

Identifying Key Documentation Items

There are a few key items that should be specifically documented:

- User account creation presets
- User account restrictions and access via managed preferences
- Person(s) or job descriptions that are permitted to do the following:
    - Create user accounts
    - Reset passwords
    - Manage workgroup accounts
    - Add/remove computer accounts
    - Edit keywords and comments
    - Create new share points

These items are important to the health and well-being of your deployment, so the parties involved in managing this setup should know exactly what their roles are, and what tasks they are permitted and not permitted to perform. Remember, not all administrators should have access to every account.

Creating User Documentation

User documents are created for the same reason that organizations have orientation pamphlets and schools have guideline booklets sent home at the beginning of every school year: They set expectations. Setting the right tone and accurately describing the features is paramount to creating a good user document.

Your users, whether they are students, teachers, librarians, office workers, managers, or interns, all need an accurate description of what to expect. There will be some discussions as roles are redefined, and as some things that may have been previously available are now inaccessible.

In some cases it may be important to state exactly *why* a certain item is not available. For example, "The Restart menu item was removed because shutting the machine down will remove all temporary files, whereas a restart may not." This gives the user an indication as to why the change was made. Depending on the age of the audience, a walkthrough by a teacher in which students comply is acceptable, as is using Apple Remote Desktop to show all students one machine and then having them repeat the process. Either way, there needs to be documentation to support the system.

Selling the Plan to Users

Perhaps the most interesting part of readying a user document is controlling how that document will be perceived. Often, users of pre–Mac OS X operating systems had no management. There simply was no mechanism for putting it into place. With Mac OS X, unless certain specific steps are wisely taken into account, all administrators are created equal. This has been a bit disconcerting to higher-level administrators, as they have often had to redo or fix what other, less well-trained administrators did.

Keeping all that in mind, you must "sell" the account management strategy to your lesser administrators and users as exactly what it is: a robust, scalable, and feature-rich method of securing the privacy and reliability your users expect, while streamlining the process of account creation, management, and backup. It is at this time when you must put your persuasive skills to the test and make them understand that it is in the best interests of all involved that this plan move forward.

Updating and Delivering Documentation

Everything is fluid, nothing stays the same, and your documentation is no different. First, you must have a method for updating and delivering your documentation to all in a timely manner. This allows for more than one person to understand what changes are being made. If the main administrator leaves, another administrator can use the documentation to trace the changes, past and present, and quickly get up to speed. Second, users need to be apprised of changes quickly, so that they can adapt their habits to any changes.

Consider a Concurrent Versioning System (CVS) for your documentation archive. This is better than just updating a document, because it tracks the changes over time. Also, you may have several administrators making changes to the document. CVS tracks all of their changes. To learn more about CVS, refer to

http://ximbiot.com/cvs/wiki/index.php?title=CVS--Concurrent_Versions_System_v1.12.12.1

CVS may be difficult for some administrators, since it is UNIX-based and the syntax carries a learning curve. For those who want an easier, GUI-based approach, any word-processing application that can track and show editorial changes should work.

Planning Behind-the-Scenes Account Management

The personal and political aspects of planning a deployment are important, but without proper hardware planning the whole scenario is in jeopardy. Care should be taken to avoid an overloaded server. It is not realistic to have a single server hold all the account information, handle the authentication duties, and serve home folders for a thousand or so concurrent connections. The tasks must be spread across several servers to insure a quality user experience. This means having at least one Xserve (preferably with an attached Xserve RAID) that is utilized for home folder storage.

Also, there are many dangers in using a single Xserve to run your entire LDAP database with all the associated authentication information. First, a catastrophe could leave the server permanently disabled and the data destroyed. Second, having one access point for both authentication and authorization will soon become a bottleneck for a quality user experience.

Using Server Replication

To solve these issues, replicas should be used to share the load of the directory server and provide redundancy should the Open Directory master have a catastrophic physical failure. Replicas help provide load sharing and redundancy by essentially becoming clones of the Open Directory master's LDAP, Password Server, and Kerberos containers, thereby allowing a computer bound to either the master or any replica to query all servers in sequence and allow the first server to respond to authenticate the user. For more information on setting up replicas, refer to *Apple Training Series: Mac OS X System Administration Reference, Volume 1.*

Archiving Account Data

Using Server Admin, you can create an archive copy of the Open Directory master's directory and authentication data. After you select a location and click the Archive button, Server Admin creates a disk image containing the following:

- An LDAP database and configuration files
- A Password Server database
- A Kerberos database and configuration files
- A Local NetInfo database
- A Local NetInfo users password folder
- Machine networking and service information
- Various launchd items
- Samba configuration information

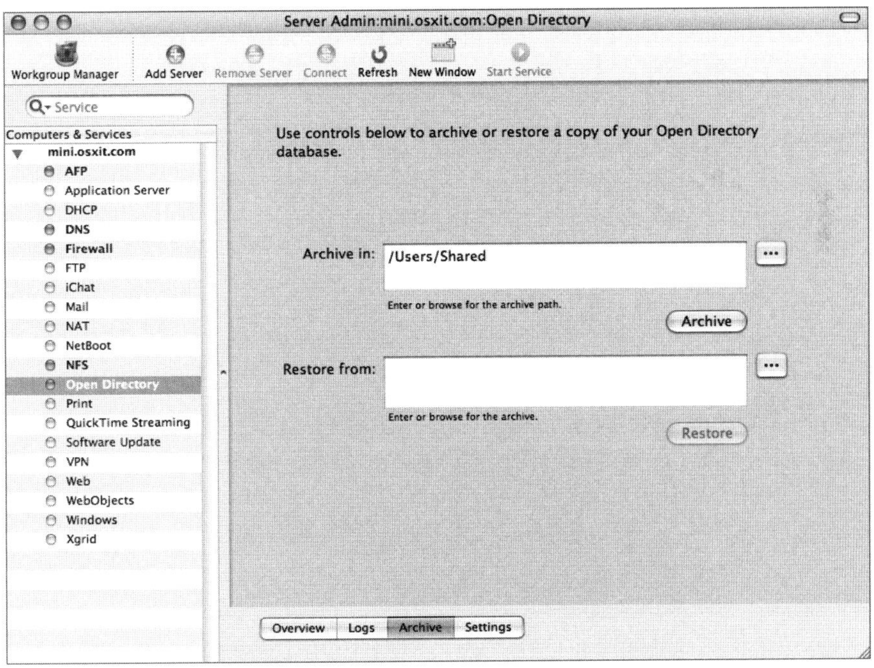

Using Server Admin to create an archive.

Restoring Archived Data

To restore the data, enter the path to the archived image and click Restore. The data from the image will be merged with the existing master's data. If there are conflicts between the master's data and the image, the data in the master takes precedence and the conflict is recorded in the slapconfig log file. To restore from an archive, navigate to the archive using Server Admin and click Restore.

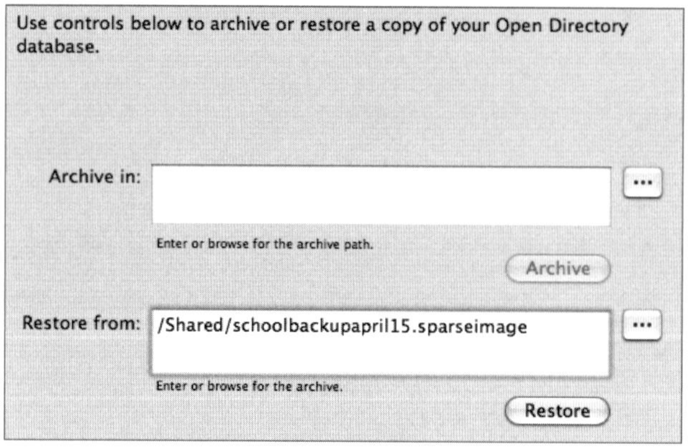

If you have configured Open Directory replica servers to connect to the Open Directory master, you will need to reconnect the replicas after restoring a server from an archive.

NOTE ▸ It is better to promote a replica to a master than to restore a master from an archive.

Lesson Review

1. Name the three levels of management that can be used on Mac OS X when speaking about account management.
2. Can administrators be restricted to modify only certain accounts?
3. What type of accounts can be searched by keywords?
4. What type of file is made when a backup of an LDAP directory is done via the command line and during an archive using Server Admin?
5. What types of accounts can be utilized by users?

Answers

1. User, workgroup, computer.
2. Yes.
3. User and computer.
4. LDIF.
5. Local, network mobile.

References

Administration Guides

"Upgrading and Migrating": http://images.apple.com/server/pdfs/Migration_v10.4.pdf

"User Management": http://images.apple.com/server/pdfs/User_Management_Admin_v10.4B.pdf

Knowledge Base Articles

You can check for new and updated articles in the AppleCare Knowledge Base, at www.apple.com/support.

"Using Mac OS X Server 10.4.4 with Intel-based Mac OS X Systems": http://docs.info.apple.com/article.html?artnum=303127

URLs

CVS information: http://ximbiot.com/cvs/wiki/index.php?title=CVS--Concurrent_Versions_System_v1.12.12.1

MacEnterprise: www.macenterprise.org

AFP548.com: www.afp548.com

Passenger: http://macinmind.com/?pid=2&progid=1&subpid=1

8

Time This lesson takes about 2 hours to complete.

Goals Create user accounts in an LDAP database

Add users to groups

Set printer quotas for users

Manage computer lists

Lesson 8

Creating Accounts

After the plan has been laid out, you should create some users, groups, and computer lists for testing purposes to see how your plan works. The first step is to create some user accounts; however, there are a few options to consider before the accounts are created. Which database should the accounts reside in? Where will the home folders reside? And should there be a user home folder and/or user printer quotas?

Understanding Account Creation Tools

When creating accounts, the logical choice for Mac OS X Server is Workgroup Manager. However, you can also use the Accounts pane of System Preferences and NetInfo Manager to create accounts.

Using the Accounts Preference Pane

The Accounts preference pane can be used on both Mac OS X and Mac OS X Server to create accounts in the local NetInfo database. When accounts are created, you have your choice of the following:

- Long Name
- Short Name
- Password
- Password Hint
- User Picture
- Limited Parental Controls (discussed in Lesson 9, "Defining the User Experience")

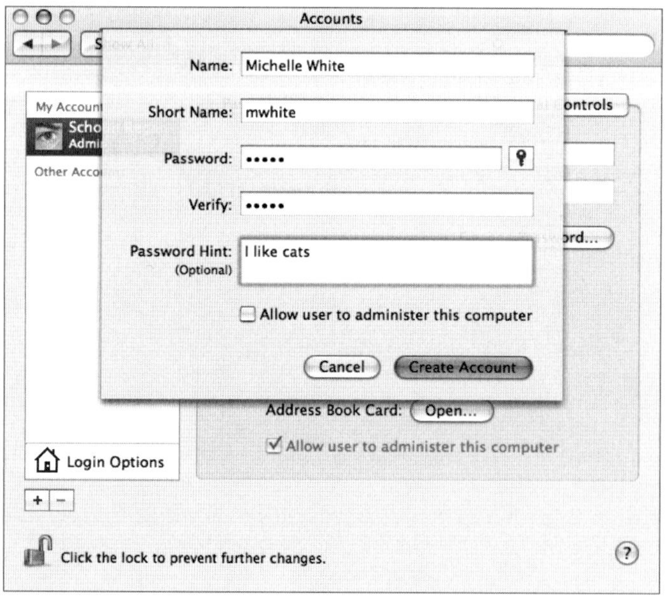

Creating a new account with the Accounts preference pane.

NOTE ▶ Creating accounts information is also discussed in *Apple Training Series: Mac OS X Server Essentials* and *Apple Training Series: Mac OS X System Administration Reference, Volume 1* (both from Peachpit Press, 2006).

What you can't choose are the user ID, primary group ID, and several other attributes. User IDs start at ID 501, which is the first account created when a user first installs Mac OS X. Each subsequent account has an incremental user ID of 502, 503, and so on. The group ID for each user is the same as his user ID. So a user with a user ID of 502 would have a group ID of 502. This is how the Accounts preference pane handles new accounts.

Creating Accounts with NetInfo Manager

Administrators can also create accounts with NetInfo Manager (or its command-line equivalent, nicl). When creating an account using NetInfo Manager, you must ensure that all necessary attributes have the proper values. Normally, the Accounts preference pane does this for you; however, accounts can be created with NetInfo Manager as shown below.

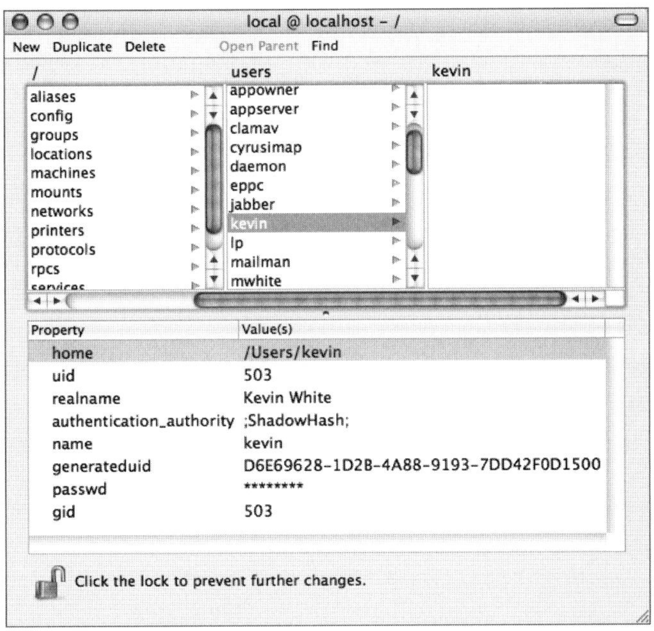

Although you can create users with NetInfo Manager, you should focus your user-creation efforts on another tool, Workgroup Manager. Whereas NetInfo Manager does not create everything a user requires, Workgroup Manager does.

Using Workgroup Manager

Workgroup Manager is preinstalled in Mac OS X Server and can be installed on any Mac OS X computer as part of the Server Admin Tools package available for download in the Support section of Apple's Web site.

Workgroup Manager is the main tool for creating accounts on Mac OS X Server but can be used to create accounts on Mac OS X as well. When you first launch WGM, you are shown a dialog asking you to connect to a server.

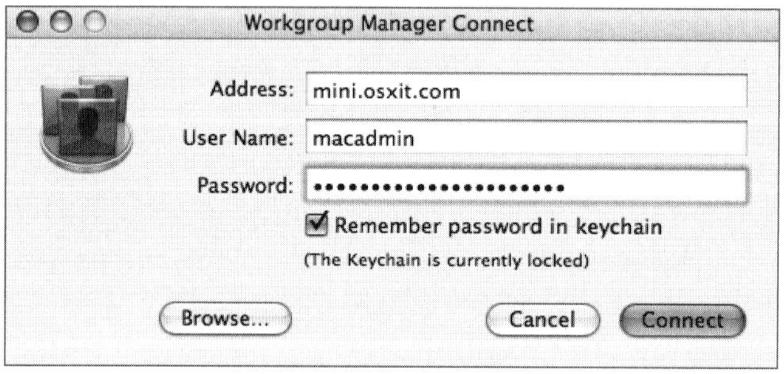

If you are not connecting to a Mac OS X Server, you can ignore this dialog and proceed to the Server menu and choose View Directories. This directs Workgroup Manager to open the NetInfo database. A warning will appear, telling you that this is not a directory server node so some features may not work. Click OK. You are now viewing your local NetInfo database.

In order to manage these accounts, you must click the lock in the top right corner of the window and enter your administrator's user name and password.

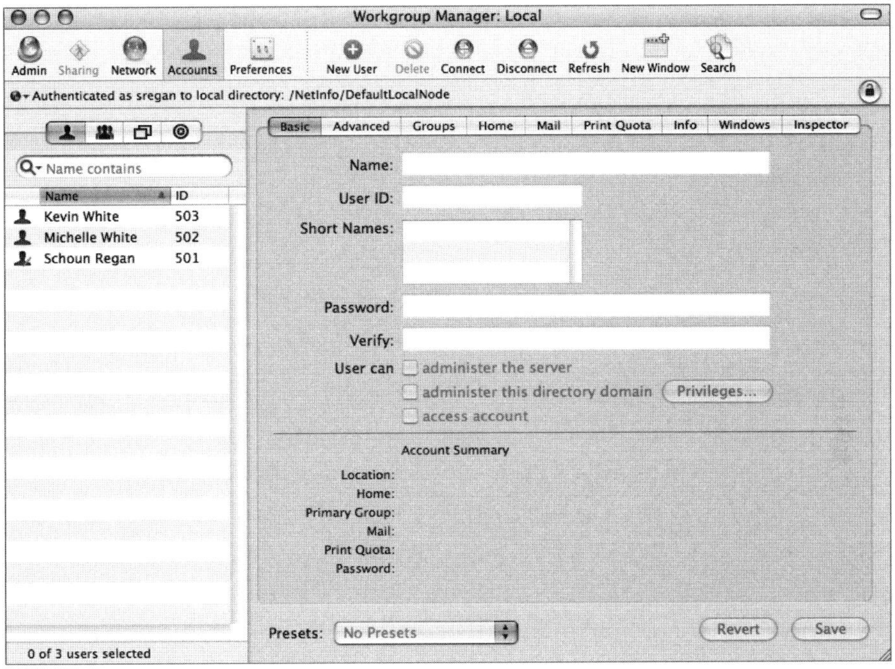

You use Workgroup Manager just like you would use NetInfo Manager, except that Workgroup Manager has a more robust interface and allows a more granular level of management.

One main difference between the Accounts preference pane and Workgroup Manager is that accounts created with the Accounts preference pane identically number user IDs and group IDs starting with 501, whereas Workgroup Manager starts at 1025 for the user ID and the group ID is 20 for every single user created with Workgroup Manager. (The group with an ID of 20 is the "staff" group.)

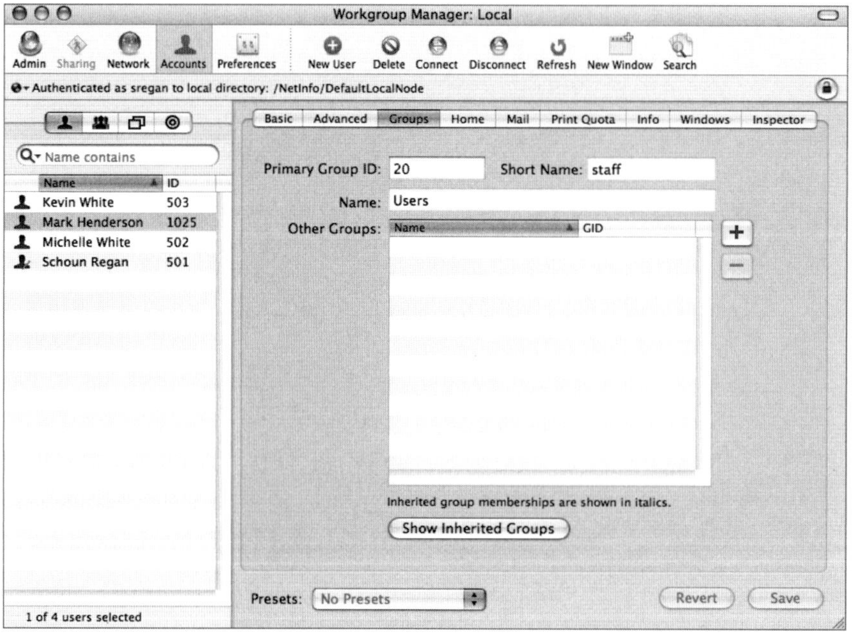

Note the user ID (1025) and the group ID (20) for user Mark Henderson.

Workgroup Manager is also used to create accounts in an LDAP database. These user accounts have the same initial user ID and group ID values as users created in the local NetInfo database. To change to an existing LDAP database, you click the small globe at the left side of the Workgroup Manager window and choose LDAPv3/127.0.0.1 prior to adding any users.

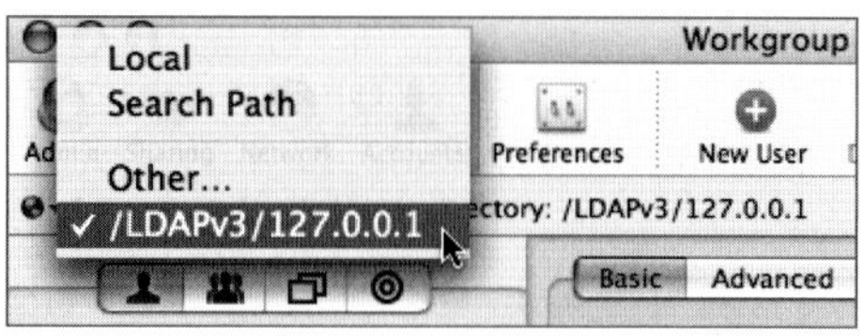

Relocating User Accounts

User accounts are sometimes exported from one server and imported to another, while new server installations may have all users created anew. As mentioned in Lesson 7, user accounts can be imported to a server using a third-party application called Passenger. However, it is also very easy to export LDAP users to another server if those accounts already exist in one location on a Mac OS X Server. There are more advanced methods of exporting and importing user accounts, and you should be aware of the options so you can choose the method that best relates to your organization's situation.

Exporting and Importing Users

Once an upgrade plan is in place, it may be necessary to import users from another directory service. Perhaps an AppleShare IP server was used successfully for several years, and it is time to upgrade both the hardware and software. Or perhaps a Windows NT server is being replaced. No matter what directory service is being replaced or augmented, certain criteria must be met before a user can be imported into Mac OS X Server. These criteria take the form of values, attributes, and records. Values are, well, values, such as *501, mwhite, Michelle White, 123 Main St,* and can include such information as the shell type (`bash` in the case of Mac OS X).

Determining Export Requirements

Servers periodically are replaced. Perhaps hardware is changed or the platform is switched. When dealing with user databases, it is important to understand how to properly export user records.

Exporting NetInfo Accounts

Mac OS X and Mac OS X Server use a NetInfo database (NIDB) to store local (not shared) user records. All user attributes and values are stored there with the exception of the user's password, which is stored as a SHA-1 encrypted password located in /var/db/shadow/hash. The name of the file is the generated unique ID for each user at the time of account creation. That generated unique ID value is also stored in the generateduid attribute. NetInfo uses that value to locate the file of the same name to authenticate the user when necessary.

For example, when a user is created and given a password, her record in the local NIDB may have attributes and associated values such as those seen below.

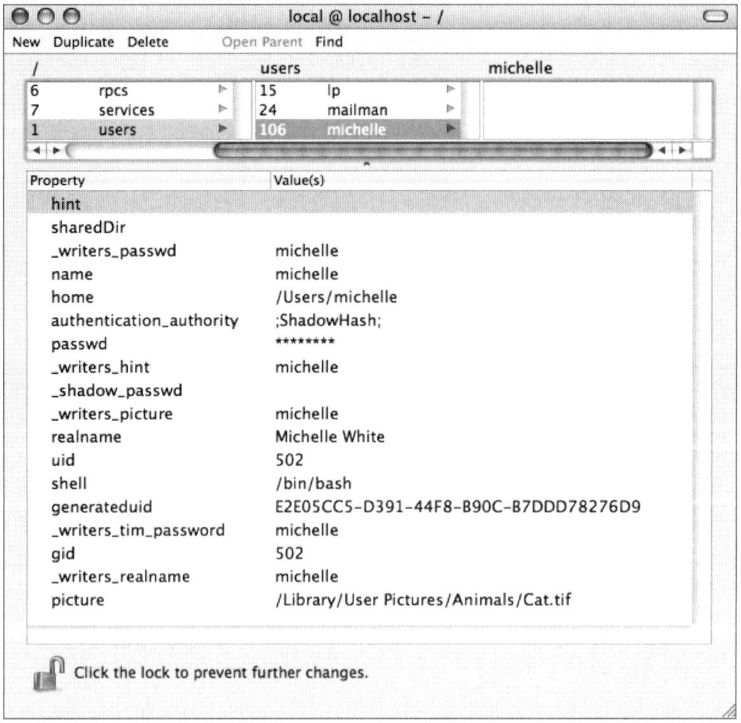

Subsequently, exports of the local NIDB will not grab the user's password, but only the file name of the password (which is the value for generateduid).

When exporting NetInfo data, you can use the `nidump` command-line utility:

```
nidump -r /users / > ~/Desktop/mynidbusers
```

The next step is to archive the contents of the /var/db/shadow/hash/ directory and move it to the new computer. You may also have to change ownership of the newly-moved files, depending on how you transferred them.

Finally, when a user logs in for the first time, his home directory is created, if none exists. If you archived and moved all the users' home directories, then no further action need be taken. You have successfully migrated local NetInfo users from one computer (such as an older server) to a newer server. These users are still in the local NetInfo database with shadow hash passwords.

NOTE ▸ While it is important to understand the process involved in handling NetInfo users, it should only be done in emergencies. Ideally, a Mac OS X Server has all accounts in the LDAP directory, and not the NetInfo directory, as NetInfo accounts cannot take full advantage of the granularity offered by an Open Directory master (which is Apple's terminology for running a Lightweight Directory Access Protocol (LDAP) database, the Password Server, and possibly a Kerberos Key Distribution Center). For more information on Open Directory masters and Open Directory in general, refer to the companion book, *Apple Training Series: Mac OS X System Administration Reference, Volume 1*).

Exporting LDAP Accounts

If you have a Mac OS X Server with LDAP accounts, and you wish to export those accounts, open Workgroup Manager, authenticate, and select your LDAP domain. Select all the users you wish to export from the user's list and choose the Export option from the Server menu, as shown below.

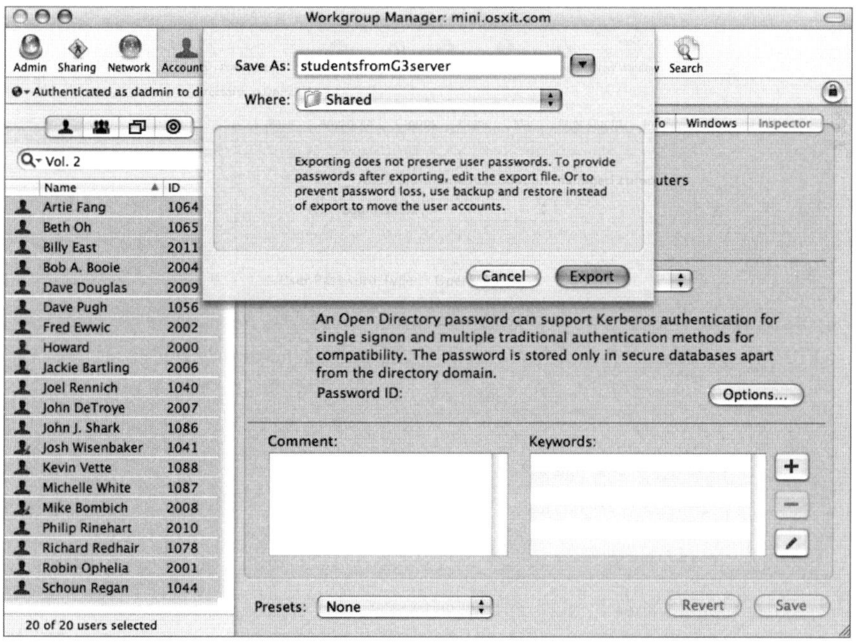

MORE INFO ▸ You can also export group and computer accounts in the same fashion. Since group and computer accounts do not require passwords, there is no real need to custom edit this file.

When exporting users, you are informed that user passwords are not exported, which is for security reasons. This is because passwords are supposed to be secure and nonrecoverable. This is an excellent practice when dealing with security and should not be bypassed. PasswordServer is Apple's process for handling secure storage of passwords for users in a shared (LDAP) database on Mac OS X Server. PasswordServer was designed as a once-in-never-out system. Passwords go in, but they don't come out.

If you wish to set user's passwords prior to importing the users into the new server, you can edit the exported file. You can edit the file after the fact to add user passwords into it. Below is a standard export header from an exported user file:

```
0x0A 0x5C 0x3A 0x2C dsRecTypeStandard:Users 38 dsAttrTypeStandard:RecordName
dsAttrTypeStandard:GeneratedUID dsAttrTypeStandard:Password
dsAttrTypeStandard:PasswordPolicyOptions dsAttrTypeStandard:UniqueID
dsAttrTypeStandard:PrimaryGroupID dsAttrTypeStandard:Comment dsAttrTypeStandard:Expire
dsAttrTypeStandard:Change dsAttrTypeStandard:RealName dsAttrTypeStandard:NFSHomeDirectory
dsAttrTypeStandard:HomeDirectoryQuota dsAttrTypeStandard:UserShell
dsAttrTypeStandard:PrintServiceUserData dsAttrTypeStandard:HomeDirectory
dsAttrTypeStandard:MailAttribute dsAttrTypeStandard:MCXSettings dsAttrTypeStandard:Keywords
dsAttrTypeStandard:Picture dsAttrTypeStandard:MCXFlags dsAttrTypeStandard:SMBHome
dsAttrTypeStandard:SMBHomeDrive dsAttrTypeStandard:SMBProfilePath
dsAttrTypeStandard:SMBScriptPath dsAttrTypeStandard:FirstName dsAttrTypeStandard:LastName
dsAttrTypeStandard:Street dsAttrTypeStandard:City dsAttrTypeStandard:State
dsAttrTypeStandard:PostalCode dsAttrTypeStandard:Country dsAttrTypeStandard:WeblogURI
dsAttrTypeStandard:EMailAddress dsAttrTypeStandard:PhoneNumber dsAttrTypeStandard:MobileNumber
dsAttrTypeStandard:FAXNumber dsAttrTypeStandard:PagerNumber dsAttrTypeStandard:IMHandle
```

Even though it appears that each of these is on one line, in fact there is no carriage return until after the last line, which in this case ends with IMHandle. Examining the top line of the file, you can see—in this example—the number 38, which indicates that there are 38 types of attributes in this user record (which is the record type that is listed at the beginning of the file, shown here as dsRecTypeStandard:Users).

After this section there is a carriage return followed by the first user account and the associated attributes:

```
artie:266E8F7D-E039-4668-8B45-BDFC7CB514A5::isDisabled=0 isAdminUser=0
newPasswordRequired=0 usingHistory=0 canModifyPasswordforSelf=1 usingExpirationDate=0
usingHardExpirationDate=0 requiresAlpha=0 requiresNumeric=0 expirationDateGMT=0
hardExpireDateGMT=0 maxMinutesUntilChangePassword=0 maxMinutesUntilDisabled=0
maxMinutesOfNonUse=0 maxFailedLoginAttempts=0 minChars=0 maxChars=0
passwordCannotBeName=0 requiresMixedCase=0 notGuessablePattern=0
isSessionKeyAgent=0:2003:20::::Artie
Fang:/Network/Servers/mini.osxit.com/Users/artie::/bin/bash::<home_dir><url>
afp\://mini.osxit.com/Users</url><path>artie</path></home_dir>:::Vol. 2,Flagged for behavior
concerns::<?xml version="1.0" encoding="UTF-8"?>\

<!DOCTYPE plist PUBLIC "-//Apple Computer//DTD PLIST 1.0//EN"
"http\://www.apple.com/DTDs/PropertyList-1.0.dtd">\

<plist version="1.0">\

<dict>\

        <key>simultaneous_login_enabled</key>\

        <false/>\

</dict>\

</plist>\

:::::Artie:Fang:::::::::::
```

The first thing to notice is that there is one carriage return right *before* the </dict>\ line. Anything after that line is managed preference information.

Also important to note is the information above that line, which matches one-for-one against the attribute list in the top of the file. If you look closely, you will see instances in which more than one colon appears side by side. A look at the first line of the file shows two colons before the isDisabled=0 value. These empty entries correspond to the actual attributes shown in the beginning of the file.

You can enter attributes in the beginning of the file as long as you enter the appropriate data for each user later in the file. Viewing the following list at the header of a file shows that one attribute was added, dsAttrTypeStandard:AuthMethod.

```
0x0A 0x5C 0x3A 0x2C dsRecTypeStandard:Users 39 dsAttrTypeStandard:RecordName
dsAttrTypeStandard:GeneratedUID dsAttrTypeStandard:AuthMethod dsAttrTypeStandard:Password
dsAttrTypeStandard:PasswordPolicyOptions dsAttrTypeStandard:UniqueID
dsAttrTypeStandard:PrimaryGroupID dsAttrTypeStandard:Comment dsAttrTypeStandard:Expire
dsAttrTypeStandard:Change dsAttrTypeStandard:RealName dsAttrTypeStandard:NFSHomeDirectory
dsAttrTypeStandard:HomeDirectoryQuota dsAttrTypeStandard:UserShell
dsAttrTypeStandard:PrintServiceUserData dsAttrTypeStandard:HomeDirectory
dsAttrTypeStandard:MailAttribute dsAttrTypeStandard:MCXSettings dsAttrTypeStandard:Keywords
dsAttrTypeStandard:Picture dsAttrTypeStandard:MCXFlags dsAttrTypeStandard:SMBHome
dsAttrTypeStandard:SMBHomeDrive dsAttrTypeStandard:SMBProfilePath
dsAttrTypeStandard:SMBScriptPath dsAttrTypeStandard:FirstName dsAttrTypeStandard:LastName
dsAttrTypeStandard:Street dsAttrTypeStandard:City dsAttrTypeStandard:State
dsAttrTypeStandard:PostalCode dsAttrTypeStandard:Country dsAttrTypeStandard:WeblogURI
dsAttrTypeStandard:EMailAddress dsAttrTypeStandard:PhoneNumber dsAttrTypeStandard:MobileNumber
dsAttrTypeStandard:FAXNumber dsAttrTypeStandard:PagerNumber dsAttrTypeStandard:IMHandle
```

When viewing a user account, you can see that an authentication method and password have been added. (In this case, the password is *abc123*.)

```
artie:dsAuthMethodStandard\:dsAuthClearText:apple123:266E8F7D-E039-4668-8B45-
BDFC7CB514A5::isDisabled=0 isAdminUser=0 newPasswordRequired=0 usingHistory=0
```

```
canModifyPasswordforSelf=1 usingExpirationDate=0 usingHardExpirationDate=0 requiresAlpha=0
requiresNumeric=0 expirationDateGMT=0 hardExpireDateGMT=0 maxMinutesUntilChangePassword=0
maxMinutesUntilDisabled=0 maxMinutesOfNonUse=0 maxFailedLoginAttempts=0 minChars=0
maxChars=0 passwordCannotBeName=0 requiresMixedCase=0 notGuessablePattern=0
isSessionKeyAgent=0:2003:20::::Artie
Fang:/Network/Servers/mini.osxit.com/Users/artie::/bin/bash::<home_dir><url>
afp\://mini.osxit.com/Users</url><path>artie</path></home_dir>:::Vol. 2,Flagged for behavior
concerns::<?xml version="1.0" encoding="UTF-8"?>\

<!DOCTYPE plist PUBLIC "-//Apple Computer//DTD PLIST 1.0//EN"
"http\://www.apple.com/DTDs/PropertyList-1.0.dtd">\

<plist version="1.0">\

<dict>\

        <key>simultaneous_login_enabled</key>\

        <false/>\

</dict>\

</plist>\

:::::Artie:Fang:::::::::::
```

Care must be taken if this approach is used, as one small error can affect all the users being imported. A proper template file is useful in this case.

Another method of exporting and importing users is to use the Lightweight Directory Interchange Format (LDIF). Refer to *Apple Training Series: Mac OS X System Administration Reference, Volume 1* for more information on the LDIF format and using the command-line tools. There are plenty of `ldap` options that allow for much finer control of how accounts are exported and subsequently imported, and they are not limited to user, group, or computer accounts, as is Workgroup Manager.

Regardless of how the users, groups, or computer accounts are exported, you should keep a template file handy for comparison purposes, just in case an import of the same file does not go as planned. Comparing a newly imported file with a file that has been successfully imported in the past is the best way to troubleshoot an import issue. To do this, try exporting two test users (who have been created just for this purpose) when your server is working properly. Delete the user accounts from the server and then attempt to import the file to import the users in the file. You'll want to practice this to ensure a smooth export/import, as it's very likely you will be under pressure to perform the task should a catastrophic failure or other serious mishap befall your server.

Establishing Import Specifications

Just as important as exporting accounts is establishing how they are imported. You'll also want to optimize the importation of user data to streamline your process and reduce the potential for errors.

Importing NetInfo Accounts

To import NetInfo users, you can use the command

```
niload -r /users / < ~/Desktop/mynidbusers
```

when the path at the end of the command is the path to your previously exported file.

Care must be taken to not overwrite accounts that may have the same user ID on the new account.

Importing LDAP Accounts

Mac OS X Server's LDAP directory requires certain attributes and associated values when importing users if the user experience is to be satisfactory. When moving from one LDAP database to another LDAP database, the Import and Export menu options under File > Import and File > Export handle most of the duties and is the preferred way of transferring user accounts.

When you are importing users who may not have come from another Mac OS X Server export file, whom you want to make changes to the user IDs and Group IDs, or whom you want to be based on a preset, it is important to choose your options wisely, as seen in the following figure. Also, setting the Logging Detail to Detailed will help provide information when things don't go quite as expected. Choosing a preset is an excellent way to reduce the amount of time spent tweaking each user's settings.

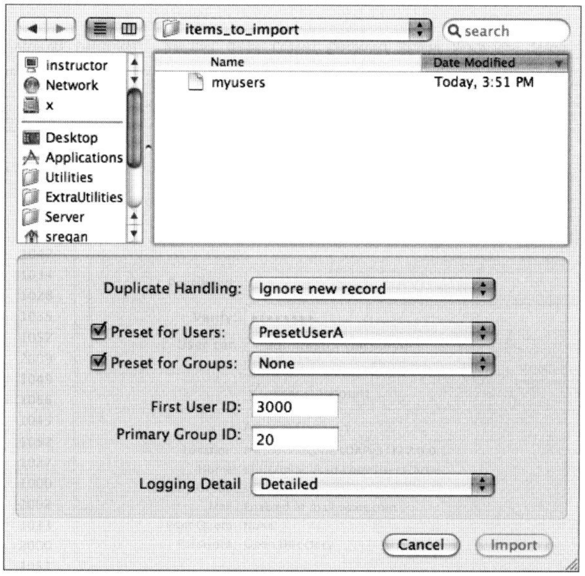

Again, the one component where you will have to make a change is the password. Unless you have specifically set up the file to be imported with passwords, you will have to reset every user's password. This is not as difficult as it seems.

You simply import the file, select all the users, and do a mass change of password to a known single password. Then, you check the box that requires the password to be changed at the next login, as shown below.

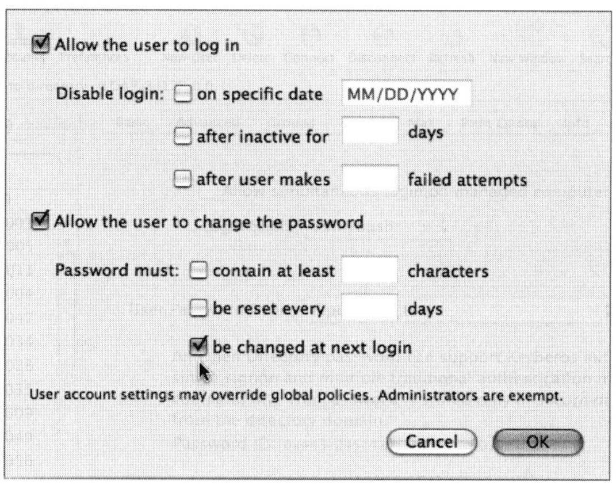

This forces all users, whose passwords currently are all identical, to change their passwords as soon as they log in.

Creating User Accounts

As opposed to importing users, they can always be created from scratch. Before creating user accounts, ensure that you have all the correct information in front of you. It's a good idea not to write down user passwords unless you are certain during the creation process that no one can see the papers and that you can destroy the papers after the user creation is finished.

Adding Basic Information

The Basic pane is used to enter the user's long name, short name, and password. You can add more short names and restrict the user from temporarily logging in, as well as allow various administrative abilities.

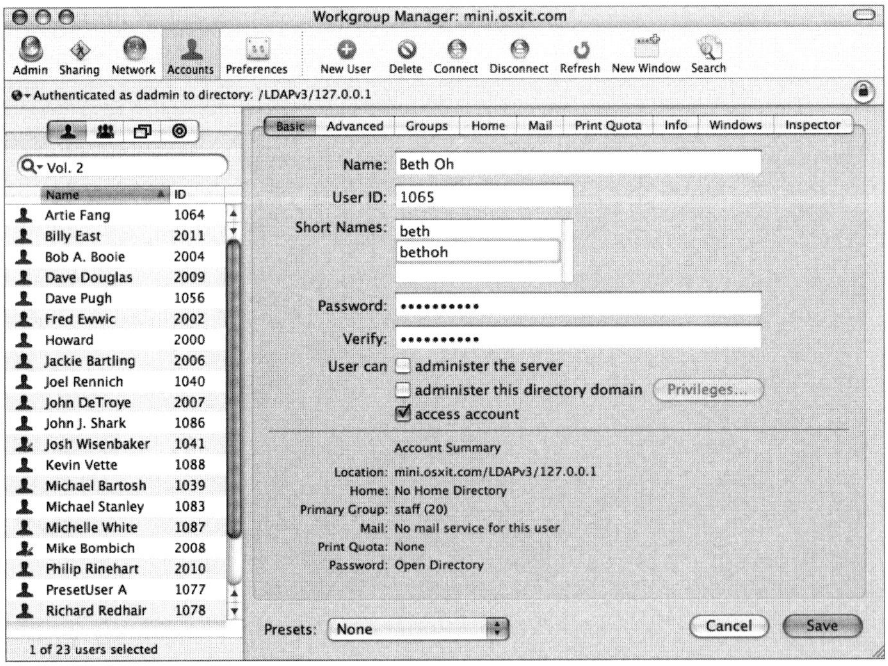

The Basic pane of Workgroup Manager's user account creation pane.

Viewing Advanced Options

In the Advanced pane are the options to change the shell type and password type, and add comments and keywords. You can also adjust the user's password variables by clicking the Options button.

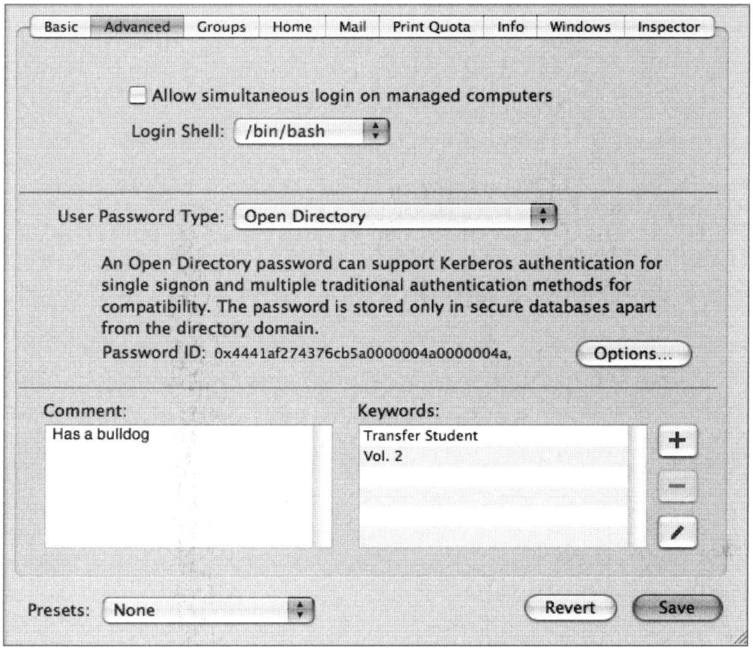

In the Advanced pane are controls for password variables and simultaneous logins, among other options.

Viewing Group Association

The Groups pane shows the groups of which the user is a member, and includes the option to show any nested groups, as shown in the following figure. You can also change the user's primary group ID.

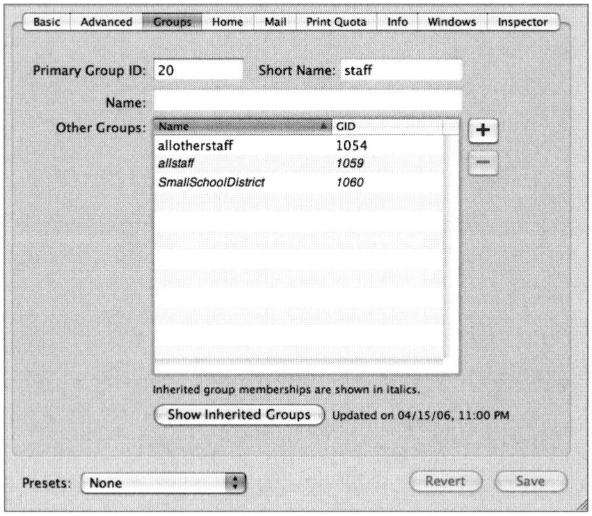

Locating the Home Folder

The Home pane is used to direct the user account to locate its home folder by providing a path to that folder. (This setting is managed by the server administrator.) Every possible location for a home folder that is initially listed must be a share point on the server; however, the home folder can be located on any folder on any server, over the AFP, SMB, or NFS protocol.

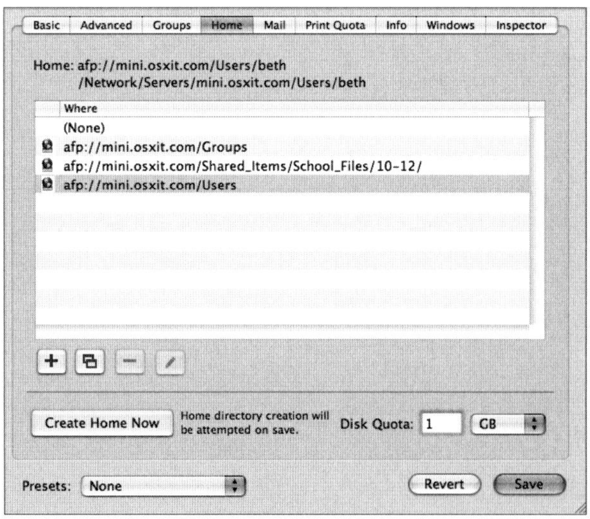

Once you choose a folder location, clicking the Create Home Now button automatically will create the home folder template when you click the Save button. A quota can also be placed on every location where that user has write access on the volume containing her home folder.

Setting Mail and User Information

The Mail and Info panes are used to add an email address (or forward email to another address) and to enter user information such as address, city, state, zip code, and phone number.

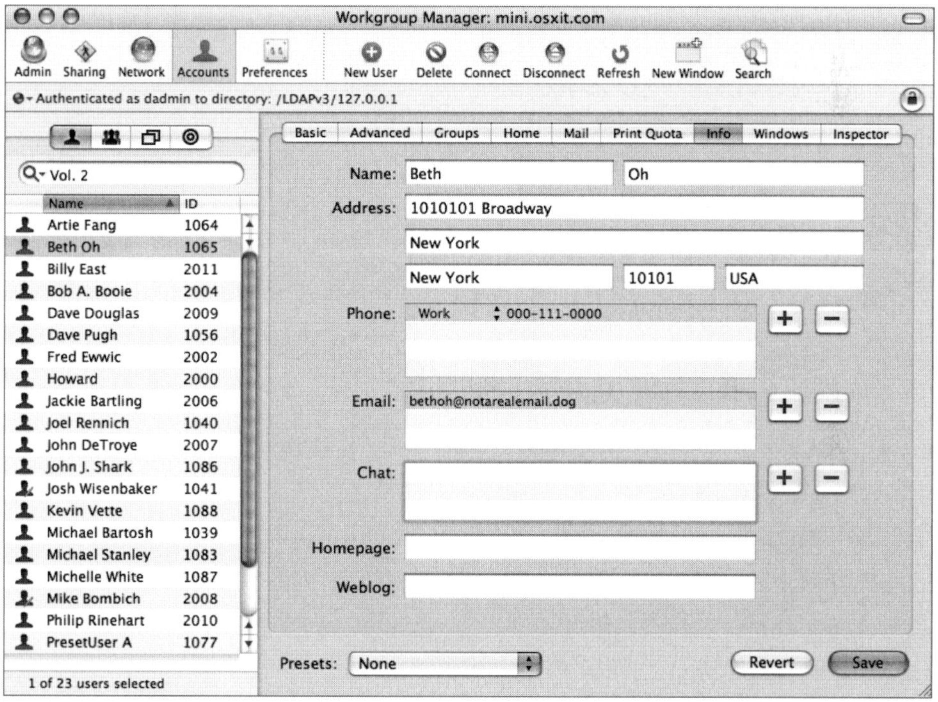

Setting Printer Quotas

Each user can have printer quotas; that is, users can be restricted as to the printer queues to which they can print and the number of pages per printer. Quotas that have been exceeded can be reset by clicking the Restart Print Quota button.

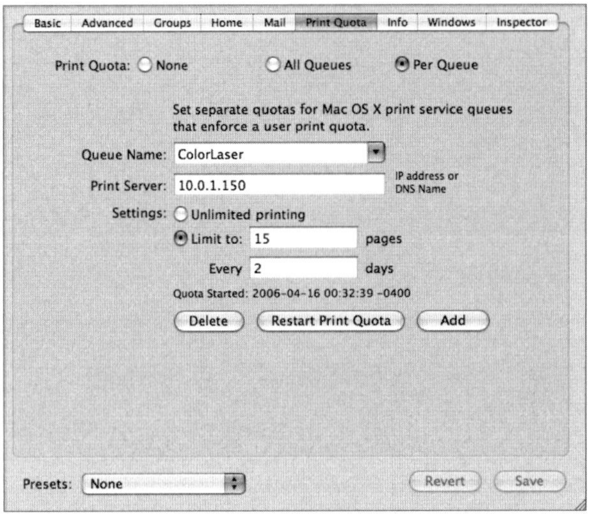

Creating Groups

Groups are collections of users, and users have no realistic limitation on the number of groups to which they can belong. When creating a group, you have to provide default group information, such as the group's long name, short name, and group ID, image, and image path.

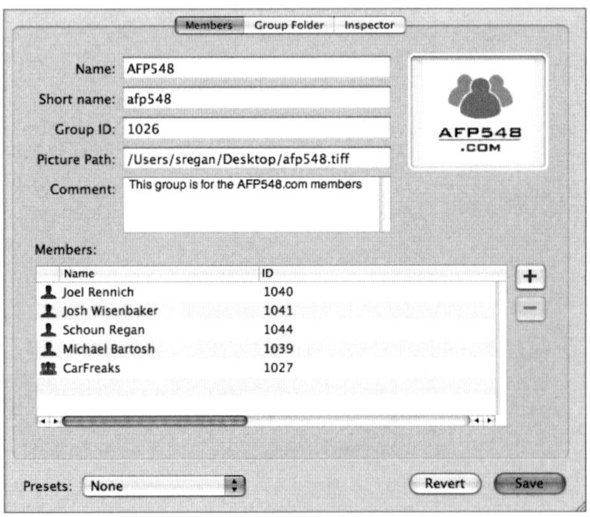

Members of groups can include users and other groups. In the Group Folder pane, you can assign a folder to the group. The folder to be used to house the new group folder must be a share point on the local volume to initially show up in the list, as seen below. You must define an owner for the new group folder. Once it's set up, either you can wait for the new folder to be created automatically by a task that runs periodically on Mac OS X Server, or in Terminal you can type

```
sudo CreateGroupFolder
```

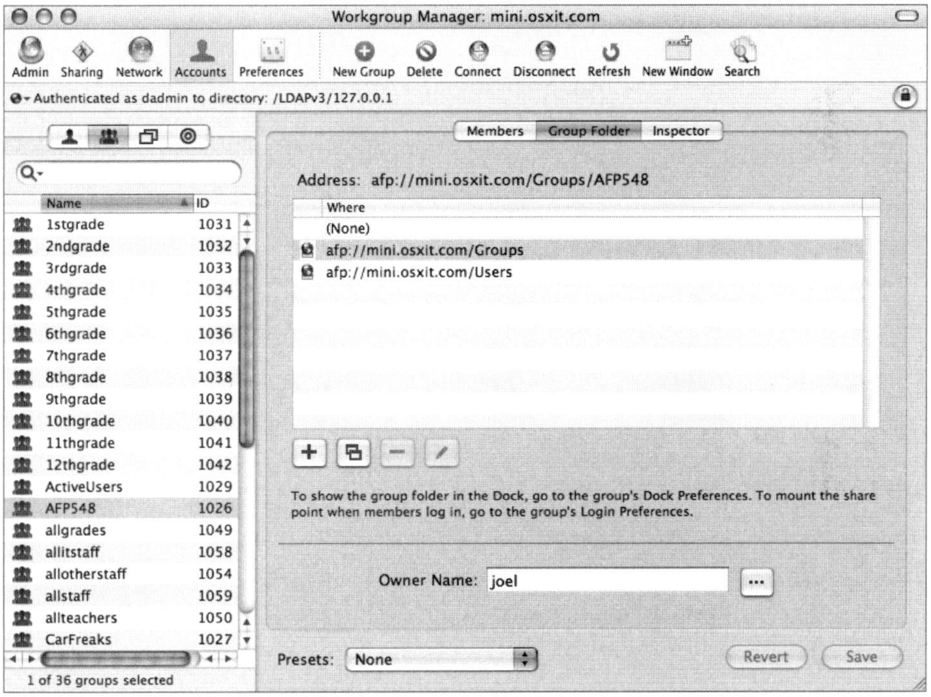

To set up a group folder in Workgroup Manager:

1 Select the workgroup and click the Group Folder tab.

  A common mistake is to not assign an owner to the folder. This will result in errors.

2 Select a listed share point to set up a group folder in it.

If the predefined Groups share point or any other existing share point is not listed in the Group Folder pane, create a mount record for it in the Network Mount pane of the Sharing window in Workgroup Manager.

3 Next to the Owner Name field, click the Browse (…) button to choose an owner from a list of users in the current directory domain.

The group folder owner is given read/write access to the group folder.

4 Click Save.

The group folder is named using the short name of the group with which it is associated.

5 Create the group folder using `sudo CreateGroupFolder` in Terminal on the server.

6 It is important to check the permissions for the newly created folder, because they may not be exactly what you want for your setup.

TIP There are at least two ways in which you can facilitate a group member's access to the group folder when the user logs in: You can set up Dock preferences to make the group folder visible in the Dock, or you can set up login preferences so that the share point in which the group folder resides appears on the Desktop.

Setting Up a Computer Account

A *computer list account* is a list of computers that have the same preference settings and are available to the same set of users and groups. You create and modify these computer lists in Workgroup Manager. Computer lists that you set up appear in the searchable list on the left of the Workgroup Manager window. Computer list settings appear in the List, Access, and Cache panes on the right of the window.

When you set up a computer list, make sure you have already determined how computers are identified. Use descriptions that are logical and easy to remember. (For instance, the description might be the computer name.) You must use the "onboard," or built-in, Ethernet address for a computer's address information. This information, often called the MAC address (which is short for Media Access Control), is unique to each computer. The client computer uses this data to find preference information when a user logs in.

An easy way to add computers to a list is to use the Browse (…) button. When you select a computer from the browse list, Workgroup Manager automatically enters the computer's Ethernet address and name. It is best to use a computer list for resources in a specific area, as well as for computers of a specific type, such as portables. For example, all kiosk computers might have the same login preferences or all computers in a lab might have the same default printer preferences.

When a computer starts up, it checks directory services for a computer list record that contains its Ethernet address. If it finds one, it uses settings for that computer list. If no record is found, the computer uses settings for the default Guest Computers computer list. You can add up to 2000 computers to a computer list, but a computer cannot be a member of more than one computer list.

Creating a Computer List

To set up a computer list account in Workgroup Manager:

1. Click Accounts.
2. Below the toolbar, click the globe icon on the left and open the LDAP domain.
3. Click the lock and enter your user name and password.
4. Click the Computers tab.
5. Choose Server > New Computer List, or, in the toolbar, click the New Computer List button.

6 Type a list name in the List Name field.

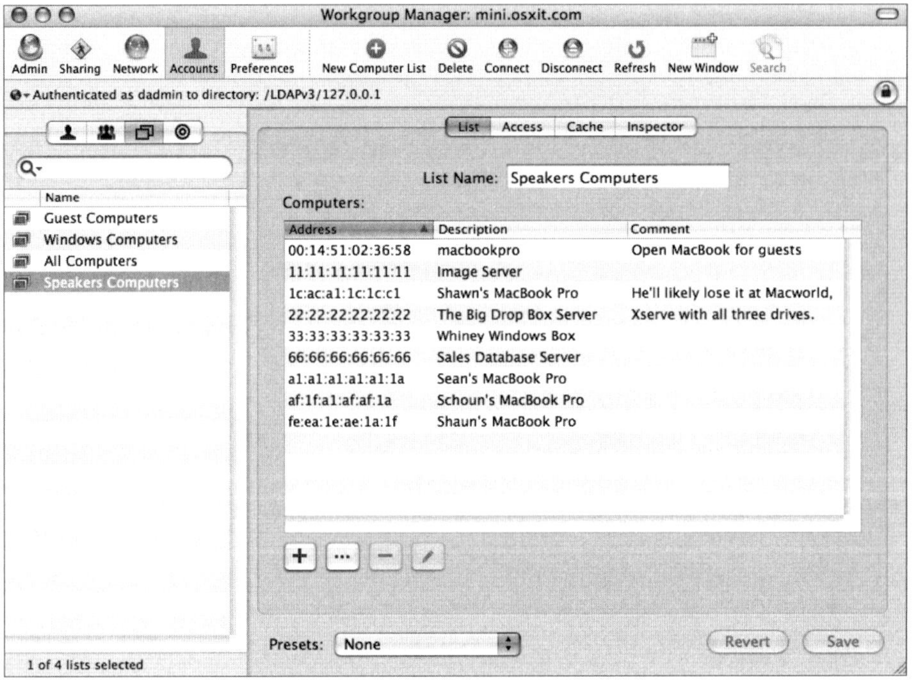

7 Click the Add (+) button to add a computer to the list, and type the computer's Ethernet address in the Address field of the dialog that appears when the button is clicked. Alternatively, you can click the Browse (…) button, and Workgroup Manager will enter the computer's Ethernet address and name for you.

8 Type a description, such as the computer name, and type a comment.

Comments are useful for providing additional information about a computer's location, configuration (for example, a computer set up for individuals with special needs), or attached peripherals. You could also use the comment field for additional identification information, such as the computer's model or serial number.

9 Continue adding computers until your computer list is complete.

10 Click the Access tab. To restrict computer access to certain workgroups, select "Restrict to groups below" and add workgroups to the list.

11 Save the account.

NOTE ▶ Computers added to the computer lists at this stage are available in the Managed Network View section of Workgroup Manager. Resources may reside at specific computers (for example, Web or file servers).

TIP ▶ When there are only a few computers to manage, it is useful to enter them into a computer list or lists. In this way they are accessible to the multiple mechanism of management. This list is also less likely to change frequently.

Controlling Guest Computers

If an unknown computer (one that isn't already in a computer list) connects to your network and attempts to access services, that computer is treated as a guest. Settings chosen for the Guest Computers account apply to these unknown or guest computers. Using the Guest Computers list (or just a single computer list) is not recommended for large numbers of computers. Most of your computers should belong to regular computer lists. This makes managing them easier.

During server software installation, a guest computer record is automatically created in the original directory domain only. Afterward, you can create additional Guest Computers accounts in other directory domains. After the account is created, "Guest Computers" appears in the list of computer lists. Each directory domain can have only one Guest Computers list. Depending on network organization and setup, you may not be able to create a Guest Computers list in certain directory domains.

Select the "Define Guest Computer preferences here" option in the List pane if you want to set up managed preferences. Click Access and select the settings you want to use. Then, click Cache and set an interval for clearing the preferences. Select the "Inherit preferences for Guest Computers" option in the List pane if you want guest computers to have the same managed preference settings as the parent server. Finally, to restrict access to the Guest Computers account to certain groups, use the Access pane.

Lesson Review

1. Identify the differences between user accounts created with the Accounts preference pane and accounts created with Workgroup Manager.
2. What must be done before users can use a just-created group folder?
3. How many computers can be in a computer list?
4. Can a user be a member of more than 16 groups?
5. What are inherited groups?

Answers

1. The Accounts preference pane uses the same number for both user ID and group ID, whereas Workgroup Manager uses a different number for the user ID and 20 for the group ID.
2. The CreateGroupFolder command must be run either as root or with sudo preceding the command.
3. 2000.
4. In Mac OS X v10.4, yes; prior to Mac OS X v10.4, no.
5. Inherited groups are groups that you are a member of simply because your group is nested inside their group.

References

Administration Guides

"User Management": http://images.apple.com/server/pdfs/User_Management_Admin_v10.4B.pdf

"Deploying Mac OS X Computers for K-12 Education": http://images.apple.com/server/pdfs/Deploying_Mac_OS_X_for_K12_Education_v10.4.pdf

Knowledge Base Articles

You can check for new and updated articles in the AppleCare Knowledge Base, at www.apple.com/support.

"About the Mac OS X 10.4.6 Server Update" (specifically Workgroup Manager related): http://docs.info.apple.com/article.html?artnum=303160

URLs

Visit the following sites for more information:

Passenger: http://macinmind.com/?pid=2&progid=1&subpid=1

9

Time This lesson takes about 3 hours to complete.

Goals

Understand the differences between parental controls, property lists (plist) files, and MCX settings

Preconfigure a user's environment

Restrict the capabilities of a user

Understand the three types of manageable accounts

Use presets to save time when adding several users

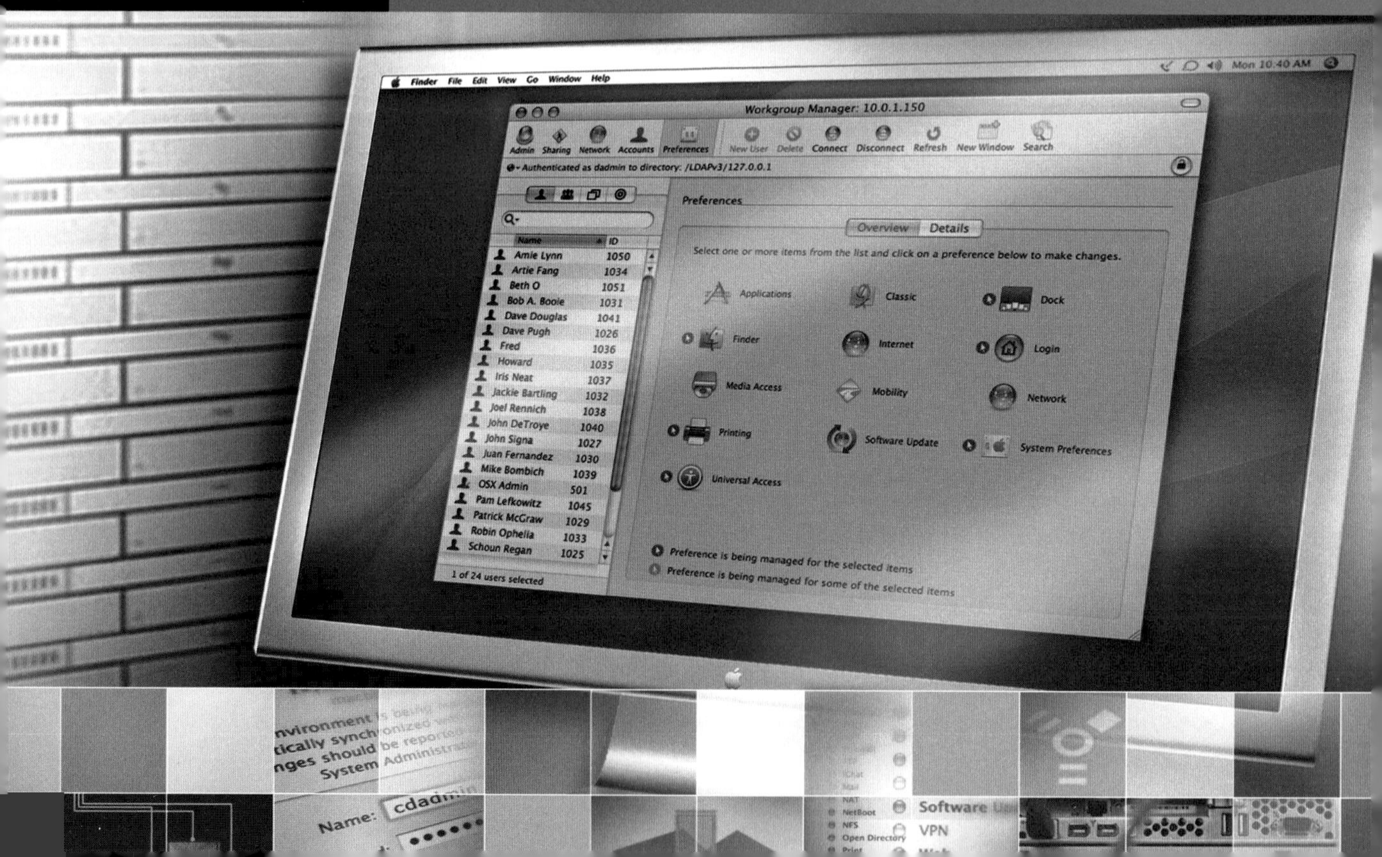

Lesson 9

Defining the User Experience

There are three main reasons to define the control, the look, and the feel of your computers for the users. The most obvious reason is to prevent users from doing things you don't want them to do, such as people using a kiosk station, students working in a computer lab, or children sitting at a home computer.

The second reason is to provide a preconfigured environment that is convenient for your users and lowers support costs in all its forms. You might choose to configure the basic look and feel of a new employee's workstation, but still allow the individual to make changes. Mac OS X and Mac OS X Server offer many different methods for controlling aspects of the user experience.

The third reason is to direct users to focus their activities and access where you want them. Parental controls are one good example of this. However, in this lesson you'll see that you have a wealth of other tools and options available to you for defining the user experience.

Managing Preferences with Files

Before you tackle the managing of preferences, it's important to understand where preferences can be stored. The normal location for preferences are in a *property list*, or *.plist*, file. Although preference files can be stored in many locations, they are most commonly found in

- ~/Library/Preferences/
- /Library/Preferences/
- /Network/Library/Preferences/

Property list files are generally named using the reversed form of the domain name of the software creator, followed by the application's name, and they have a *.plist* extension. For example, Safari's preferences are stored in com.apple.Safari.plist. Preferences that apply only to the specific computer on which they were created live in a subdirectory called ByHost and include that computer's Ethernet MAC address in the filename. This is done to allow the presence of multiple host-specific preference files in a network home directory environment.

Property list files are XML-formatted and typically store settings in key-value pairs. If you've installed the Xcode Developer Tools, you can look at any .plist file simply by double-clicking it, which will open it in Property List Editor:

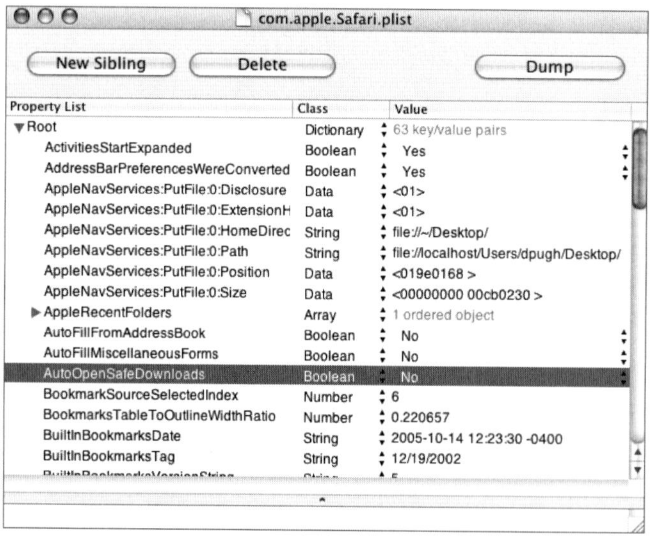

You can also view .plist files from the command line in Terminal. Property list files can be in a human-readable XML plain-text format or in a binary format that Mac OS X can process more quickly. Although Mac OS X can read either format, plists are created in binary format by default. To look at a plist from the command line, you must first convert the file from binary back to a simple XML text file in the Terminal window using commands like this:

```
plutil -convert xml1 ~/Library/Preferences/com.apple.Safari.plist

cat ~/Library/Preferences/com.apple.Safari.plist
```

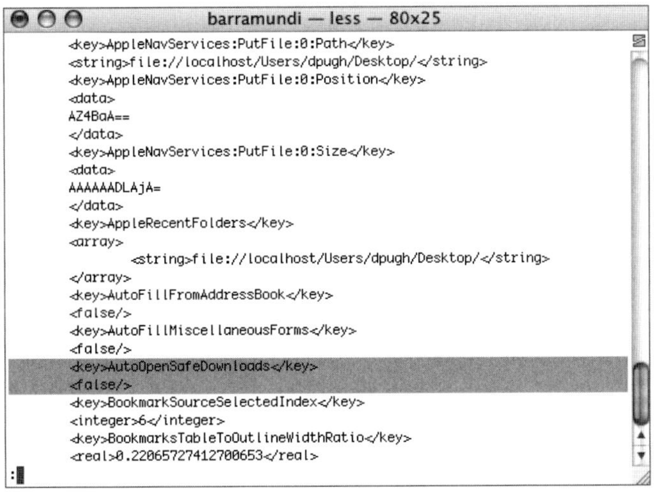

When an application needs to know the value of a specific preference key, it will consult each of the preferences files until the value is obtained. This allows you to layer preference files. For example, you could create a Safari preference file at /Library/Preferences/com.apple .Safari.plist that contains only the AutoOpenSafeDownloads key with a "false" value. All new users on the system would see that new preference setting without having it affect their other Safari settings.

However, since the preference domain system uses the layered approach, users can override the preferences stored in the top-level /Library/Preferences directory with those stored in the Preferences directory inside their home folders, at ~/Library/Preferences/. Each of the user-specific preferences is stored here, including those that override the preferences set at the system level. This makes the use of preference files suitable for preconfiguring a user's environment, but not for restricting access. One example of this is the login window plist.

Opening Preference Manifests

Most of the preference keys have self-explanatory titles. However, you may not always know exactly what something does, or what the possible values for it are. New in Mac OS X v10.4 Tiger are *Preference Manifest* XML files that describe the possible keys and values for an application's preference file and make them available for management by Workgroup Manager

A Preference Manifest file is located within the application's bundle in the ./Contents/Resources/ subdirectory. Using Safari as an example, you can look at the Preference Manifest file from the command line:

```
cat /Applications/Safari.app/Contents/Resources/com.apple.Safari.manifest/Contents/Resources/
com.apple.Safari.manifest
```

Inside this file you'll see a list of each of the keys you may wish to preset for your users, along with descriptions and possible values. Here is a sample of one of those keys:

```
<dict>
 <key>pfm_description</key>
 <string>TRUE to automatically open downloaded files that are of certain well-known safe types\, such
as images\, PDF and text documents\, etc.</string>
 <key>pfm_domain</key>
 <string>com.apple.Safari</string>
 <key>pfm_name</key>
 <string>AutoOpenSafeDownloads</string>
 <key>pfm_title</key>
```

```
<string>Open Safe Downloads Automatically</string>
<key>pfm_targets</key>
<array>
<string>user</string>
<string>user-managed</string>
</array>
<key>pfm_default</key>
<true/>
<key>pfm_type</key>
<string>boolean</string>
```

In this example, the AutoOpenSafeDownloads key defaults to being true, and is of type "boolean."

Preference Manifests don't control any settings themselves, but only describe the settings that can be managed. You'll learn later in this lesson how to use these settings through Workgroup Manager if you don't wish to modify preference files directly.

NOTE ▸ Safari and the VoiceOver Utility are currently the only applications included with Mac OS X that have Preference Manifests.

MORE INFO ▸ For more information, consult the man pages for plist, plutil, and defaults or the following developer document: "Introduction to Runtime Configuration Guidelines" (http://developer.apple.com/documentation/MacOSX/Conceptual/BPRuntimeConfig) and "Preference Manifest Files for Managed Clients Overview" (http://developer.apple.com/documentation/MacOSXServer/Conceptual/Preference_Manifest_Files).

Managing Preferences with MCX Settings

In the previous section, you learned about using preference files for preconfiguring a user's environment. You also learned that they can't be used for restricting access, since user preferences take precedence over System Preferences. The Managed Client for Mac OS X (MCX) settings are used here. These settings are stored in a key called *MCXsettings*, but are sometimes referred to as *MCX rules* due to their restrictive nature. MCX settings are used to apply preferences to workgroups, computers, or individual users. Most commonly, preferences are applied easily across your organization through the use of a network Open Directory server, but can also be set locally on a single machine.

Using Parental Controls

MCX settings are commonly used in two main ways. The first use is for parental controls. Many applications in Mac OS X have built-in parental controls, and still other parental controls can be handled in the specified standard nonadministrator user account in the Accounts preference pane of System Preferences, as in the following ways:

- Looking up what some would consider profane words with the Dictionary application
- Determining which email addresses the user can access
- Limiting whom the user can converse with on iChat
- Setting Finder and system controls
- Burning CDs and DVDs
- Changing a password
- Modifying printers and Dock items
- Restricting use of System Preferences panes and applications
- Controlling site access with Safari

When parental controls are put in place for a given user, his or her user record is modified to contain MCX settings. An example of this would be the parental controls for Safari. The Safari parental controls prevent a user from connecting to any Web site that isn't already bookmarked. You can enable this feature on any nonadministrator account by opening Safari's preferences window. Click the Security button, and check the box for "Enable parental controls":

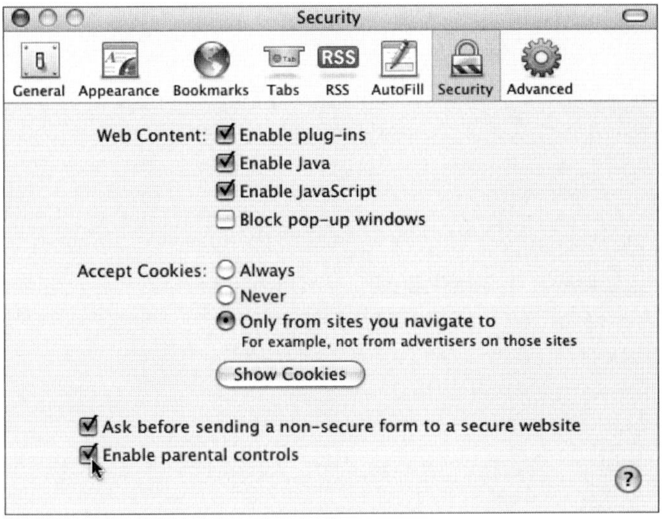

After this box is checked, that user's record in NetInfo will have a mcx_settings attribute added to it:

```
mcx_settings: <?xml version="1.0" encoding="UTF-8"?>

<!DOCTYPE plist PUBLIC "-//Apple Computer//DTD PLIST 1.0//EN" "http://www.apple.com/DTDs/
PropertyList-1.0.dtd">

<plist version="1.0">

<dict>

 <key>mcx_application_data</key>

 <dict>
```

```
<key>com.apple.safari</key>
<dict>
<key>Forced</key>
<array>
<dict>
<key>mcx_data_timestamp</key>
<date>2006-09-21T09:21:02Z</date>
<key>mcx_preference_settings</key>
<dict>
<key>ParentalControlEnabled</key>
<true/>
</dict>
</dict>
</array>
</dict>
</dict>
</dict>
</plist>
```


The mcx_settings attribute has data that looks very similar to the XML data found in a preference file, but rather than having every application's preferences stored in separate files, they are all placed in this single user attribute. You'll notice that Safari's settings are still identified by com.apple.safari, that the settings are Forced, and that ParentalControlEnabled is set to true. Later, you'll see that MCX settings can also be applied in less restrictive ways that will allow users to make changes when they desire.

Setting preferences in files or through NetInfo isn't particularly scalable in a large organization. You'll see in the coming pages how you can use Workgroup Manager with a network Open Directory server to easily deploy similar settings throughout your organization.

Using Workgroup Manager

Workgroup Manager—part of the Server Admin tools—allows you to access many more MCX settings, and all from one place. Workgroup Manager can manage the preferences of users both on your local system (even a nonserver version of Mac OS X) and in an Open Directory database.

To manage settings on a local, nonserver version of Mac OS X:

1. Launch Workgroup Manager.
2. When the Connect dialog appears, click the Cancel button.
3. Select Server > View Directories.
4. A warning will appear, telling you that some features may not work because this is not a directory server node. Click OK.

   If you're managing settings on your Open Directory server, connect in the same manner you would normally use to access your user records.
5. In the top right corner of the Workgroup Manager window, be sure the lock icon is unlocked to indicate that you are authenticated. If not, click it and authenticate.
6. Select the user to whom you wish to apply the settings.
7. At the top of the window, click the Preferences button.
8. Select the Details tab.
9. Click the Add button.

10 In the file-selection pane that appears, find Safari in the Applications folder, select it, and click Add.

11 You should now see the com.apple.Safari preference listed. Select it, and click the Edit button.

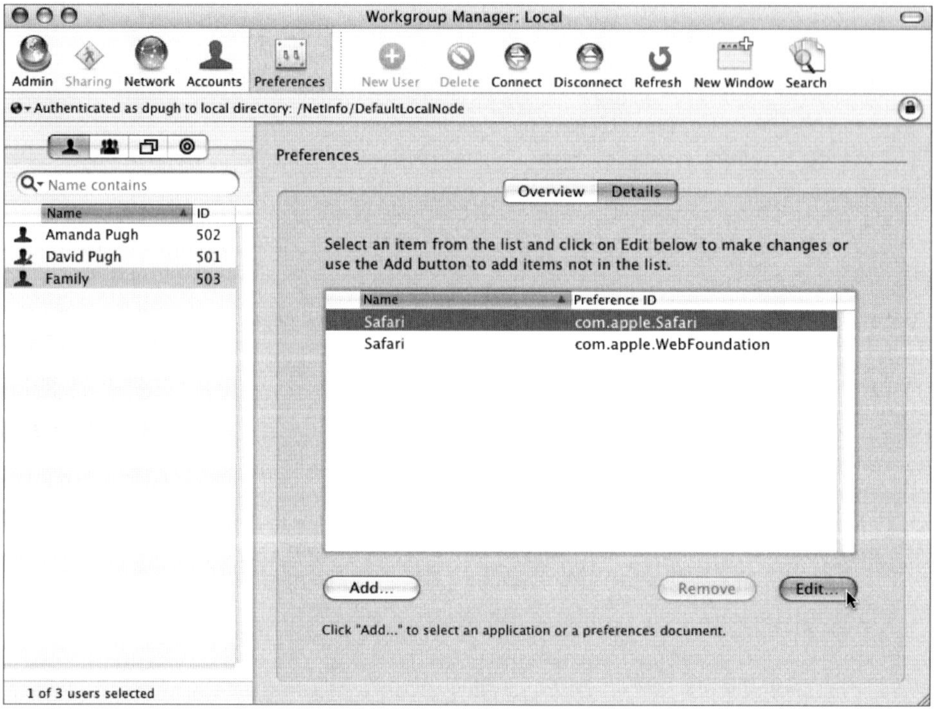

12 A new window should appear containing Once, Often, and Always. Select Always, and click its disclosure triangle.

13 Click the New Key button.

14 Click the New Item text.

15 Choose Open Safe Downloads Automatically.

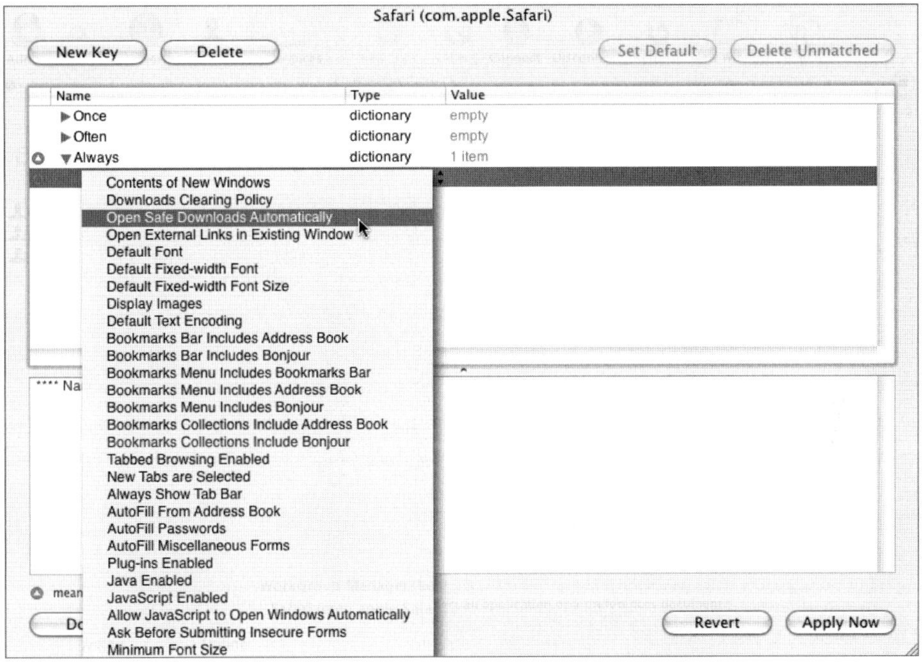

Notice the descriptive text that appears in the bottom pane of the window. The list of fields and their accompanying text come from Safari's Preference Manifest.

16 Change "true" to "false."

17 Click the Apply Now button.

18 Click the Done button.

You've now used Workgroup Manager to disable the AutoOpenSafeDownloads feature of Safari that you saw earlier in the preference file. This illustrates not only the alternate ways you can apply settings, but also the numerous other options you have available to you through Workgroup Manager. Plus, you've observed the descriptive text that accompanies each setting thanks to the Preference Manifest found inside Safari's application bundle. If you try some of the other options, you'll see that the Preference Manifest controls the values you can set for a given key, reducing the chance for error.

You'll also notice that there is no mention of parental controls in the Preference Manifest for Safari. The Preference Manifest is not required to contain an entry for every possible setting you may place in the preference file or MCX setting for a user. It is up to the developer of an application to include a Preference Manifest and to choose what settings are made available for customization. This can be a bit onerous, as you cannot manage a setting if you do not know what that setting is called. In addition to Apple provided Preference Manifests, you can also manage certain third-party applications that abide by the Preference Manifests. As developers continue to modify their applications, Preference Manifests will start appearing, allowing you to manage those applications with the same level of granularity that you find now in Safari. In the meantime, you can use the same interface to add rules for items found in an application's plists, even without a Preference Manifest. You'll just need to do some extra research to determine the options and behavior given the absence of a descriptive Manifest.

If you'd like to view the MCX settings field for the account you just modified, you can follow these steps:

1. Open Workgroup Manager > Preferences.
2. Check the box to Show "All Records" tab and inspector.
3. Click OK, and then quit and relaunch Workgroup Manager.
4. Click the Accounts button at the top of the Workgroup Manager window.
5. Click the All Records tab (bulls-eye icon) above the list of users.

6. Choose Users from the pop-up menu if it isn't already selected.
7. Select the user to whom you just applied the Safari settings.
8. In the inspector window, select the MCXSettings field.

9 Click the Edit button.

A new window will appear, displaying the contents of the MCXSettings attribute for that user, as shown in the following figure.

10 When you are finished looking at the record, click the Cancel button.

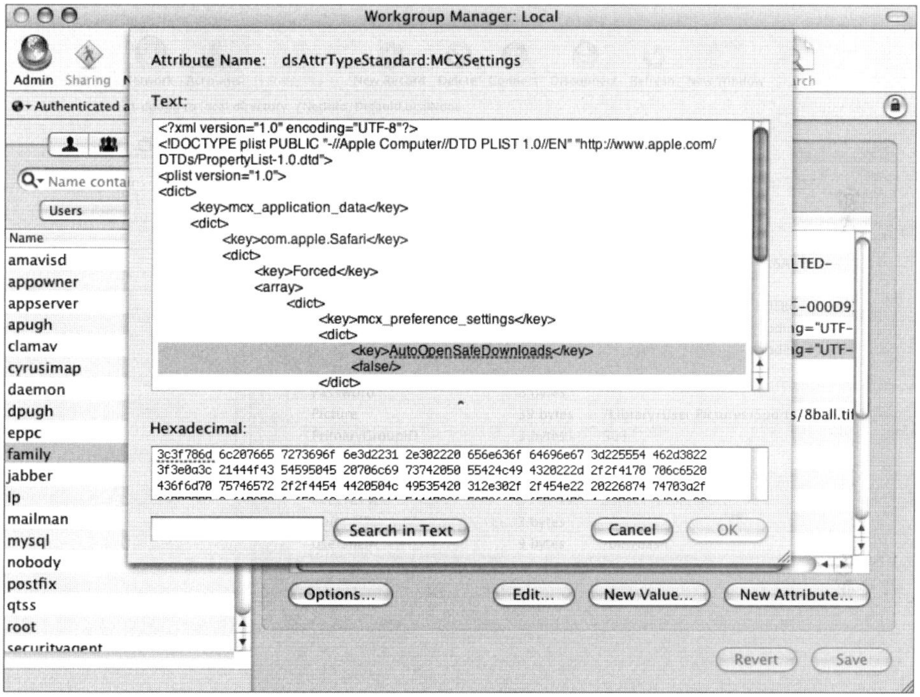

MCX Information Locations

It is important to note that not only are MCX records stored in the user's NetInfo record, but also Managed MCX preferences show up in the following locations:

- NetInfo database/config/mcx_cache
- NetInfo database/mcx_cache/(all records)
- NetInfo database/users/managed_user_short_name/mcx_flags
- /Library/Managed Preferences/(all files)
- ~/Library/Preferences/com.apple.MCX.plist

You can delete and remove the last three in this list, but if you do not get the MCX config and cache records removed (the first two), then the managed preferences will return, whether or not the computer is connected to the server that initially set the managed preferences. This is by design, as you would expect preferences to be managed when users with laptops disconnect their computers for travel or home use.

Therefore, if you have the firmware protected from booting into single-user mode, you have denied access to both Terminal and NetInfo Manager, and the user is not an administrator, it is next to impossible to remove the cache and disable the managed preferences, even if the computer is disconnected.

Managing Users, Workgroups, and Computers

So far, we've only been talking about managing the preferences of individual users. But what if you have thousands of users? If you're making nonrestrictive changes to the user environment, you could use the preference file method and drop the desired preferences in the /Library/Preferences folder on a machine. That would apply the presets to every user on that machine. If you wanted to apply the setting to many machines that have a shared /Network/Library folder, you could put the preference files there. However, neither of those options will place any forced restrictions on the users, since users can override those settings with preferences in their home directories.

Using Workgroup Manager, you can apply managed settings via the Preferences button to users, as well as workgroup records and computer lists. By applying MCX settings to a group of users, you can, for example, give office staff one set of preferences and students another. If a user belongs to multiple workgroups, he or she will be prompted at login to decide which workgroup's settings should apply to that session.

You can also apply managed settings to lists of computers to provide a given look and feel, or restrictions, to different classes of machines. For example, a kiosk computer in a hallway might have access to Safari and no other applications, while computers in a classroom might have access to a restricted set of applications or might prepopulate the Dock with those applications. If your DHCP server sends out your Open Directory configuration, it's possible that outside computers brought onto your network would bind to it. These computers would inherit any of the MCX settings applied to the Guest Computers list. You'll explore the settings you might want to apply to different users, workgroups, or computers in the remainder of this lesson.

Managed Preference Precedence

It is plausible—but not recommended—that you must manage Dock settings for both a specific user and three or four workgroups. However, the user may also be a member of one of those workgroups. Perhaps there are managed Dock settings for a computer list and a person with a managed user account happens to sit down and log in to a managed computer with a managed workgroup account. Depending on the Dock settings, what happens? There are three scenarios that can result from this.

The first precedence is to *inherit*, in which the user inherits managed settings, as in the following chart. Each type of management shows up only once, and even though they exist in different types of managed accounts, the end result is that the user's experience is managed as expected.

	Login	Dock	Finder
Workgroup	Address Book	"Not Managed"	"Not Managed"
Computer	"Not Managed"	Right	"Not Managed"
User	"Not Managed"	"Not Managed"	Snap to grid
Result:	Address Book	Right	Snap to grid

The next type of managed precedence is *combine*, in which managed settings appear cumulative even though they exist in different categories of management, as shown in this illustration. Again, this is generally expected and can be planned for under certain circumstances.

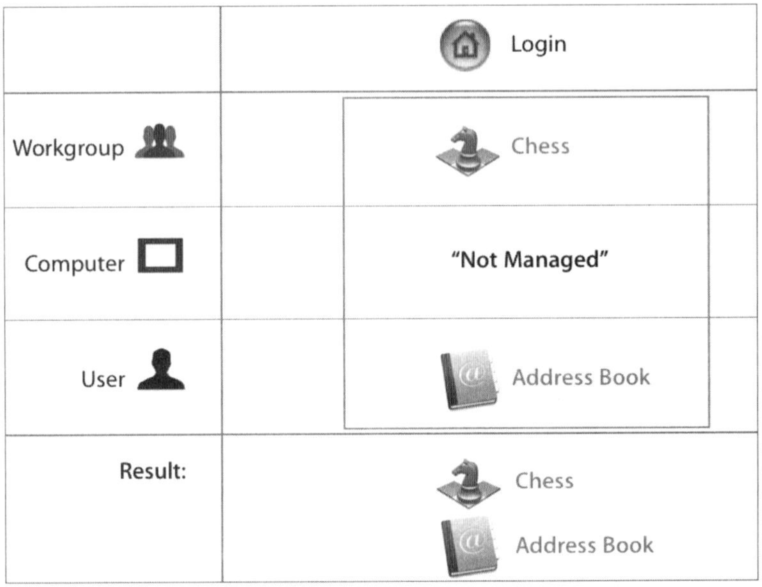

The last precedence scenario is when two competing managed settings are set differently, such as when a user's workgroup's home page is one site, and computer list managed settings have the home page listed as a different site, as seen in the following chart. This is an *override* situation, where the computer list managed preferences override the user's workgroup's managed preferences. The behavior is expected in situations where you manage settings for computers or workgroups, and use individual user settings to override them when needed, such as for a teacher in a classroom.

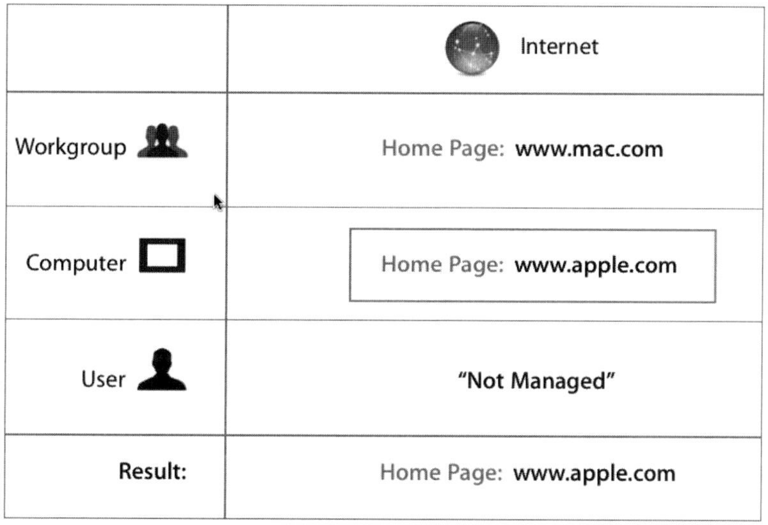

Determining How Often Settings Should Apply

Each of the managed preferences allows you to specify how often you want your MCX choices pushed onto the user, group, or computer. Not all of these are available to every managed preference, however. The settings are as follows:

- Never—Does not apply any MCX rules to the selected user, computer, or workgroup. However, by applying the previously mentioned precedence rules, the user may have MCX rules applied by a different level (user, computer, or workgroup) than what you have selected.
- Once—Configures the user's settings based on the MCX rules you set but allows the user to change things in the future. This is useful when you want to preconfigure a user's environment for his or her convenience but don't want to restrict the user.
- Always—Sets the MCX settings to have complete control over this aspect of the user's environment. The user will be unable to make any changes to this aspect of his or her session. This is the most restrictive setting.

- Often—When creating MCX settings based on Preference Manifests or other preference settings set manually through the Details tab in Workgroup Manager, you will be presented with an Often setting. These settings are similar to the Once settings but are applied every time the user logs in. This allows the user to make changes to the application during his or her login tenure, but the next time the user logs in, the preferences will be set back to their initial state.

  NOTE ▶ If you're using the Once setting in your organization and you make changes to a group or computer record, users who have customized their settings prior to the change may have their configurations overwritten by your new Once settings. Always test Once settings before enabling them for all users.

Defining the User Experience

As you've learned, there are multiple methods for managing the user experience through multiple levels of MCX settings. These methods target different users on different machines and at different frequencies. Now that you have an idea of the methods you can use to manage the user experience, you'll explore a sampling of the preferences you can set for your users, groups, and machines. Some preferences can't be applied to all three categories, but that's generally only the case when you wouldn't want to apply them anyway. An example of this is your inability to apply power-management settings to a user record—they can be assigned only to computers.

For each of the areas outlined below, follow these steps to define the settings:

1. Open Workgroup Manager.
2. View the directory that contains your user records, and authenticate, if necessary.
3. Click the Preferences button at the top of the Workgroup Manager window.

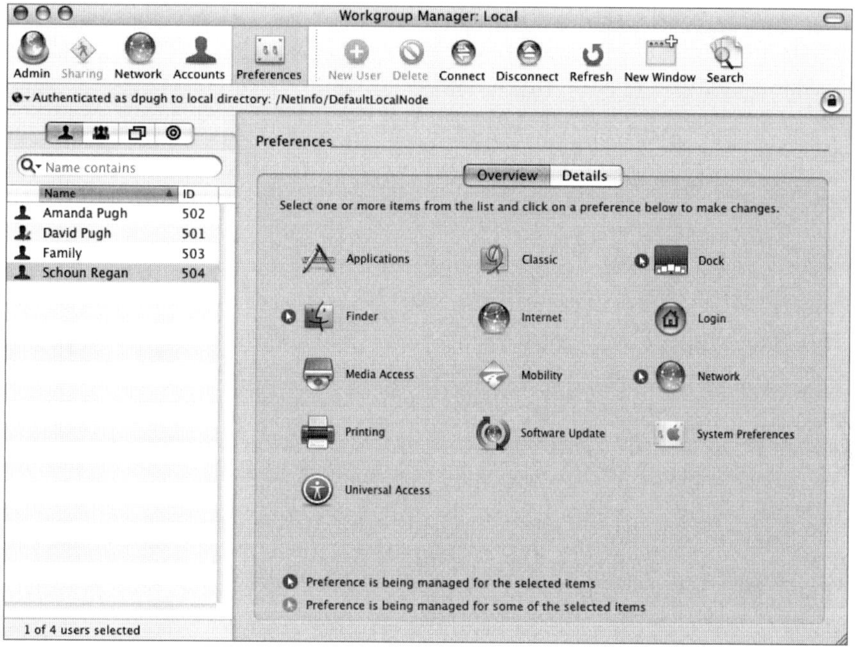

4. Select the users, workgroups, or computers tab (on the left), depending on whom you want to apply the settings.
5. Select one or more entries in the users, groups, or computers list.
6. Click the icon of the preference you want to set.
7. Click the radio button to indicate whether you want to manage these settings just once or always for that user, group, or computer list.

Once an item is managed with a Once, Often, or Always designation, an arrow will appear in the main preferences overview pane, as seen in the above figure.

Setting Finder Preferences

The Finder preferences offer you a number of choices for configuring the appearance of the Finder. At the most basic level, you have the choice of using the normal Finder that you're accustomed to seeing, or setting up the computer to use a Simple Finder, in which the user isn't able to navigate to anything but is presented with just a Dock and very limited pull-down menus (as in the following figure). The user is restricted from navigating on the computer and, for the most part, can only run the applications on his or her Dock. You may wish to customize this setting using the Dock preferences.

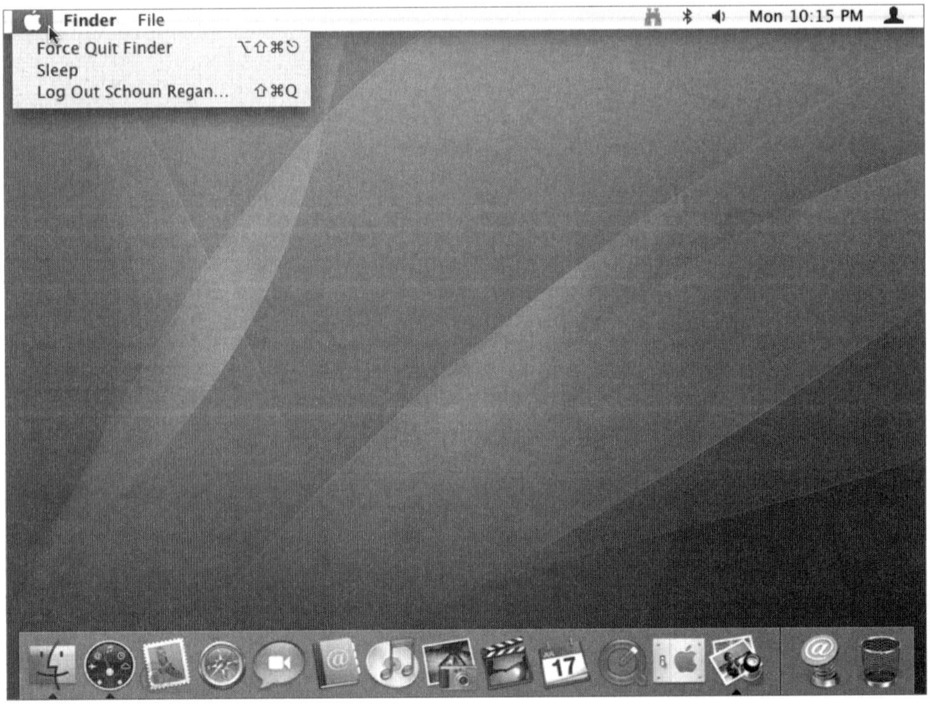

If you wish to continue to use the normal Finder, you have many options for configuring the look and access of the Finder. You can select check boxes to determine whether the hard disks, removable media, or servers show up on the user's Desktop. You can also configure such Finder behavior as what happens when the user opens a new Finder window or empties the Trash.

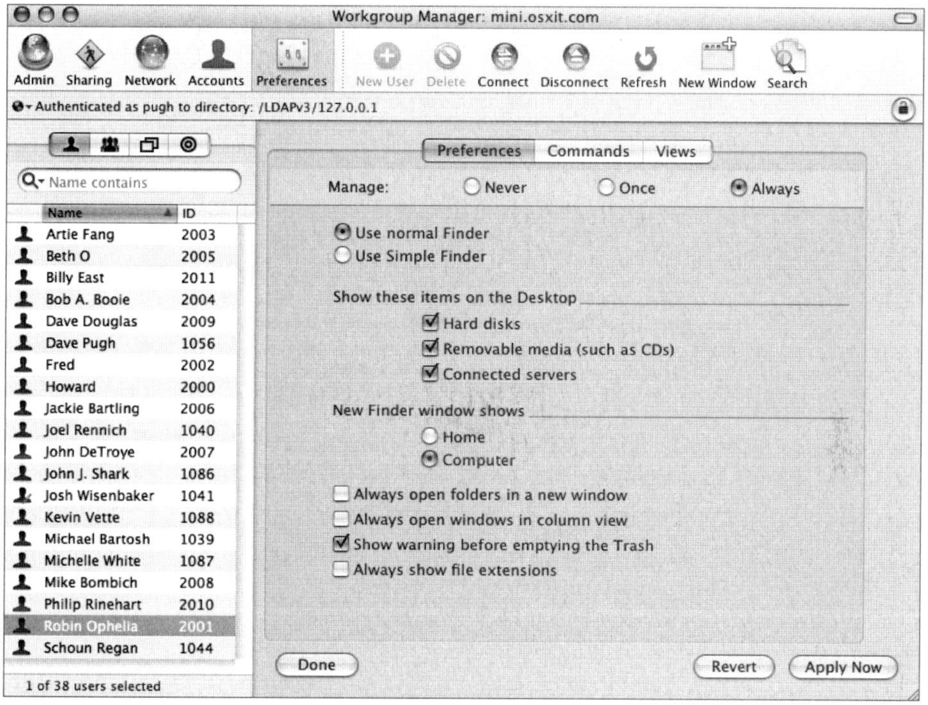

In the Commands pane of Finder preferences, you'll find the following capabilities that you can make available or unavailable to users:

- Connect to Server
- Go to iDisk
- Eject (media and volumes)
- Burn Disc
- Go to Folder
- Restart
- Shut Down

These settings are very important when you want to restrict access to areas of the local computer or of the network. If the user has the Go to Folder ability, he or she can navigate to almost any location on the computer, even if the hard-disk icon isn't shown on his or her Desktop. By removing the ability to burn discs or connect to remote servers, you prevent the user from easily stealing licensed software that may be installed on a computer lab machine. Without access to external servers, it's also a bit more difficult to install additional software or files on the machine. By limiting Connect to Server, iDisk, and Safari access (as shown with Preference Manifests), you can create a a more restrictive computer environment in which users don't have unauthorized network access and can't transfer files to or from the machine.

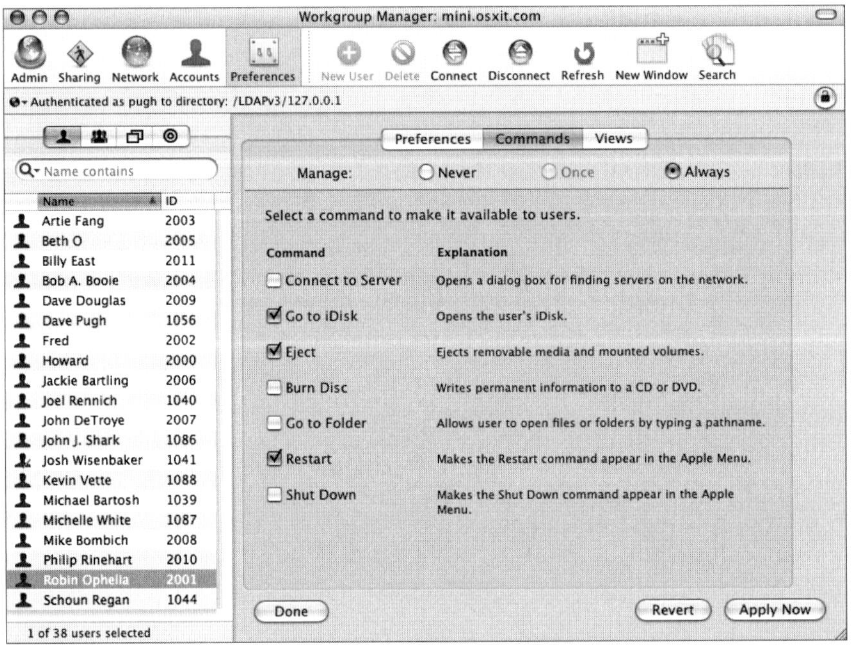

Restricting commands a user can access using the managed Finder settings.

Finally, the Views pane can be used to configure the icon properties in the Finder. For the Desktop, default Finder windows, and Computer view, you can set the icon size, arrangement, and snap-to-grid behavior. These presets can be useful for enlarging icon views for young children or those with poor eyesight.

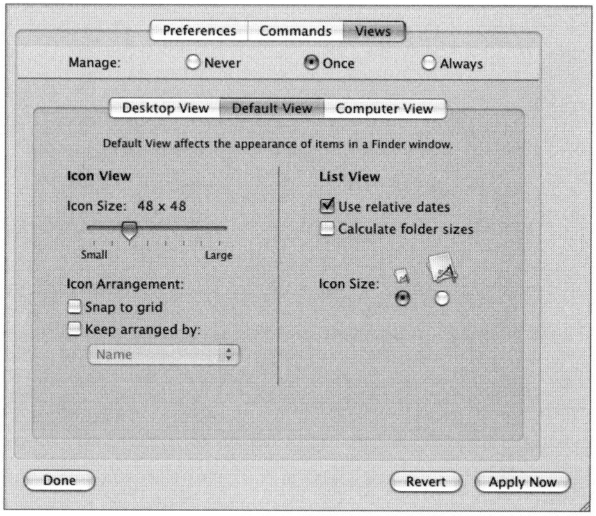

Setting Media Access Preferences

The Finder preferences concentrate primarily on controlling how the user sees objects already on the computer or on restricting the ability to connect to network shares. You can use the media preferences to restrict how a computer behaves when external media are plugged in.

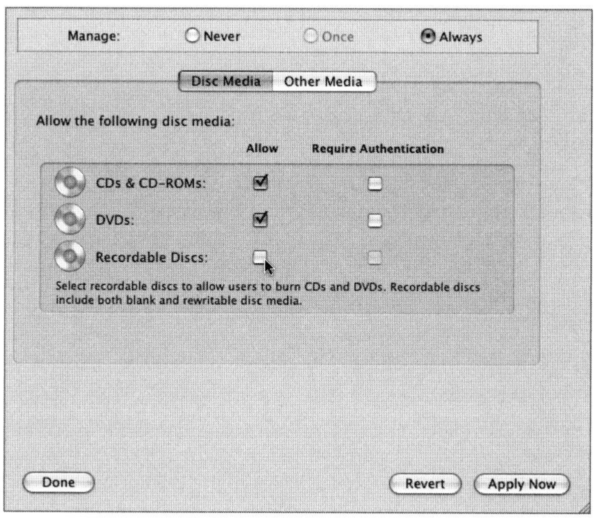

The following media are listed:

- CDs and CD-ROMs
- DVDs
- Recordable Discs
- Internal Disks
- External Disks, including FireWire drives and keychain flash drives

In the Other Media pane, an option is also available that will eject all removable media at logout. This is a particularly good feature to enable in a computer lab situation to help keep users from leaving CDs in the drives.

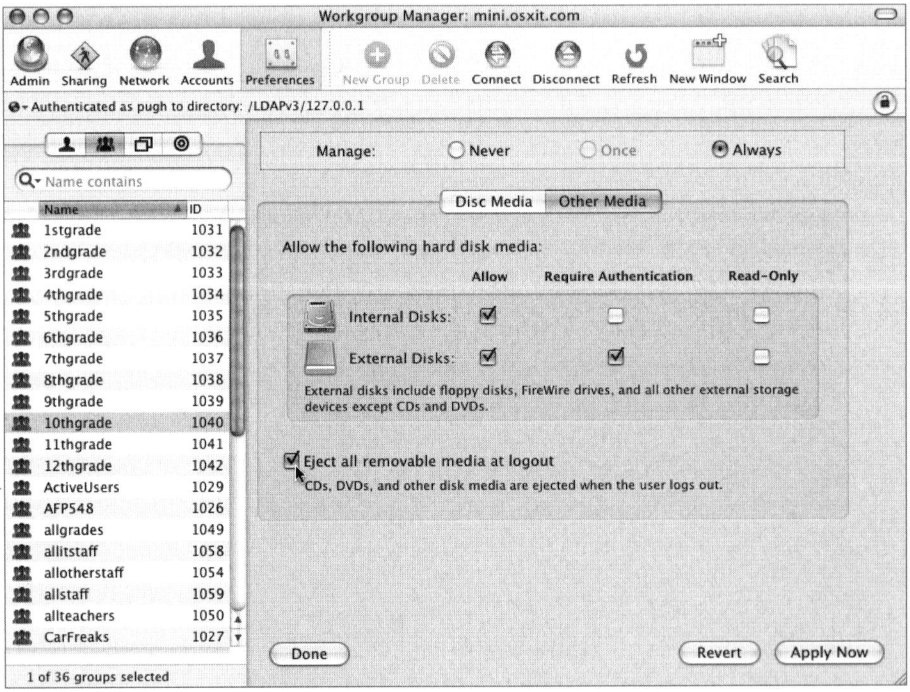

Setting Dock Preferences

Setting the look and feel of the Dock goes hand in hand with configuring the user's Finder preferences. This is especially important for Simple Finder users who can only run the applications found in their Docks. In a classroom, you may also wish to remove some applications from the Dock such as Safari, Mail, and iChat.

The Dock preferences offer two tabs. The first tab opens a pane where you control the items that appear in the Dock. Just as a normal Dock is separated into two parts, one containing applications, and the other containing documents and folders, the preferences for the Dock also manage these preferences separately. You can add items to and remove items from the list as you see fit. Checking the box for "Merge with user's Dock" will combine what you define in the lists with whatever the user may already have in his or her Dock preferences. This is important if you're applying the Once setting and don't want to overwrite the items that users may already have in their Docks. Options are also present to dynamically add a user's Applications, Documents, and Network Home folders. If you're managing a group's preferences, and that group already has defined a network group share, you can check the box to automatically add that to the Dock.

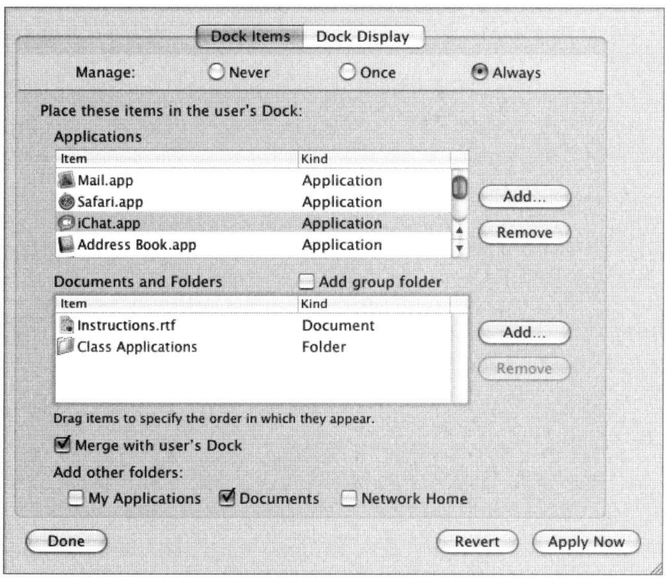

Managing the contents of the selected group's Dock.

The second tab for the Dock preferences opens a pane where you control the Dock's behavior. This includes the size, position, magnification, and minimizing style.

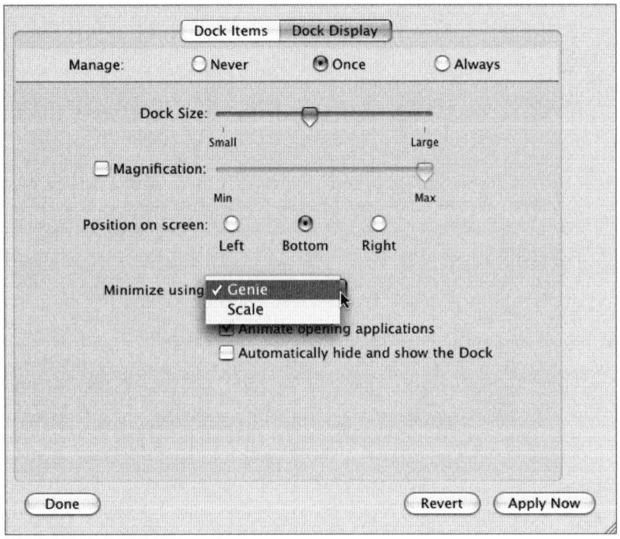

Creating Group Shares

If you'd like to configure your Dock settings to automatically contain a group share, you must first create the group network share point, which is also done in Workgroup Manager. The network group share can be used for collaborative purposes, to share documents or other common files used by members of the group.

1. Open Workgroup Manager.
2. Connect to the LDAP directory containing your groups, and authenticate, if necessary.
3. Click the Sharing icon, and select the Groups folder from the Share Point list.
4. Click the Network Mount tab, and click the lock icon.
5. Enter your LDAP directory administrator's short name and password.
6. Select "Enable network mounting of this share point," and click Save.

7 At the top of the Workgroup Manager window, click the Accounts button.

8 Select the groups tab on the left side.

9 Select the group(s) for which you'd like to define group folders.

10 Select the Group Folder tab, and click the Refresh button in the toolbar to refresh the view.

11 Select the share point that already contains or will soon contain your group folders.

If the share point isn't in the list, you can add it using the Add (+) button. If you're adding a new share point, just list the root level of the share point as the URL, and identify the remaining portion of the path (without the leading slash) in the second field.

For example, to reference the group shared folder at afp://server17.pretendco.com/GroupShares/finance/budget, you'd put *afp://server17.pretendco.com/GroupShares* in the URL field and *finance/budget* in the Path field.

12 Specify the owner of the group folder using the Owner Name field. This user will have full access to the group folder.

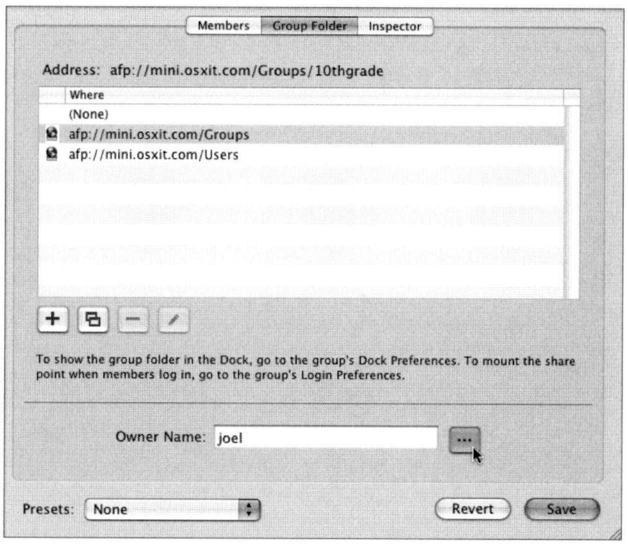

Using the Apple default Groups folder to host the group share point.

After you've defined all of your group share points, you can have the server create and populate each of the group folders with this command-line utility:

```
sudo CreateGroupFolder -v
```

This will create the folders, set their permissions, and set up Documents, Library, and Public folders (complete with Drop Box) for each group. The -v option sets the command in verbose mode, allowing you to see the output.

If you'd like the members of this group to automatically see their group folders, you can either select the checkbox in the Dock preferences for "Add group folder", or you can create a login item that automatically mounts their network folder.

Setting System Preferences Access

MCX settings can also be used to control which System Preferences can be accessed. Simply click the Preferences button and select each of the System Preferences that the user is allowed to access.

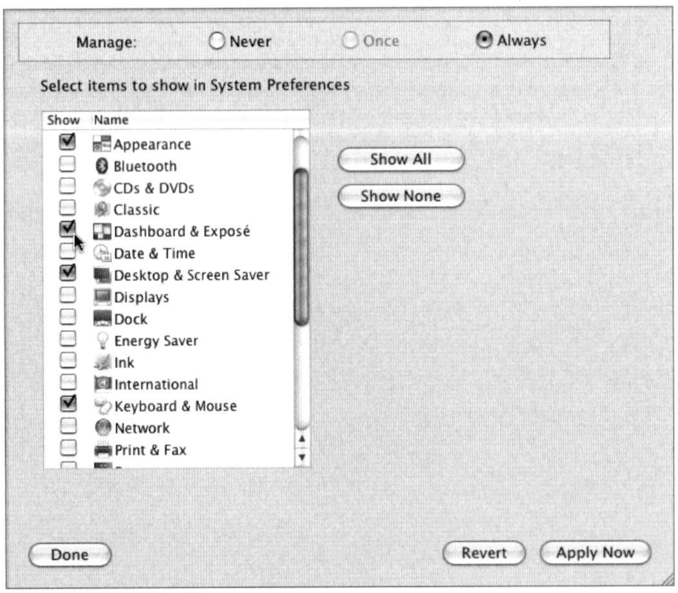

The primary benefit of this setting is security. Any items that users can't access according to their MCX settings are disabled and dimmed when they open System Preferences.

Setting Login Preferences

The login preferences offer many options in four panes. In the Login Items pane are options that control the traditional login items for the user. You can drag applications into this list with the option of hiding them, as you can with the login items available to users through the Accounts preference pane. At the bottom of the Login Items pane, you have a few options controlling the user's ability to modify this list or bypass it altogether. The option "Mount item with user's name and password" is used after selecting "Add network home share point" (if managing a user record) or "Add group share point" (if managing a group record).

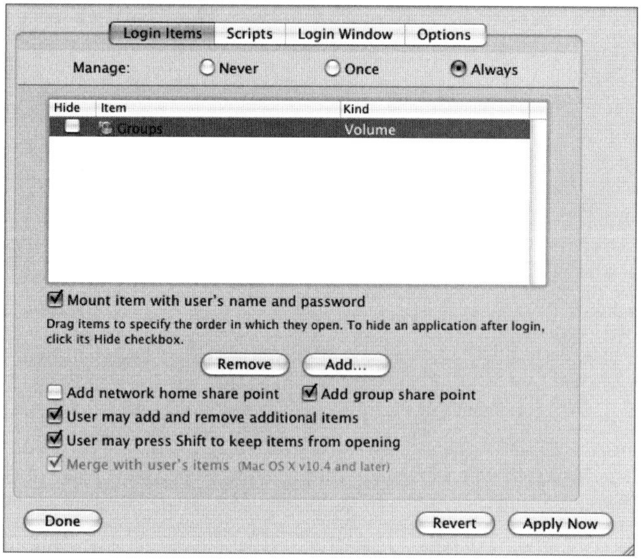

The Scripts tab can be used only when editing the MCX settings for a computer list. This pane offers options to execute login and logout scripts.

Before enabling these scripts, you must first enable MCX script execution on the client. This is disabled by default as a security precaution.

```
sudo defaults write /var/root/Library/Preferences/com.apple.loginwindow EnableMCXLoginScripts -bool TRUE
```

You must also set the trust level:

```
sudo defaults write /var/root/Library/Preferences/com.apple.loginwindow MCXScriptTrust PartialTrust
```

The MCXScriptTrust setting can be any of the following:

- Anonymous—will run scripts from any directory server configured in Directory Access (least secure)

- DHCP—will only run scripts from the directory server given to the client during the DHCP negotiation
- Encryption—will only run scripts from directory servers configured in Directory Access to Encrypt all packets
- Authenticated—will only run scripts from directory servers with a trusted binding between the client and server
- PartialTrust—will only run scripts from directory servers configured in Directory Access to Digitally sign all packets
- FullTrust—will only run scripts from directory servers configured in Directory Access to Digitally sign all packets and Block man-in-the-middle attacks (most secure)

NOTE ▶ If you're using Active Directory for your directory services, you can only use PartialTrust, as most AD servers cannot support the requirements of FullTrust.

Once you've enabled scripts on the client, you need to use Workgroup Manager to define the scripts. Compose a shell script on your local machine, and then use Workgroup Manager to select that script. Scripts must be smaller than 30 KB, since the script itself is stored inside the directory entry.

Additionally you can use these settings to enable or disable the traditional `loginhook` and `logouthook` scripts. These scripts are defined using the following two commands:

```
sudo defaults write /var/root/Library/Preferences/com.apple.loginwindow LoginHook /path/to/script
```

```
sudo defaults write /var/root/Library/Preferences/com.apple.loginwindow LogoutHook /path/to/script
```

Any of these scripts could be used to modify the user's environment. The scripts are run as root and have the user name of the user that is logging in passed as the first argument. These scripts could be used for such things as preconfiguring Mail, adding items to the user's Desktop, recording login auditing information, or preconfiguring any other aspect of the user's session.

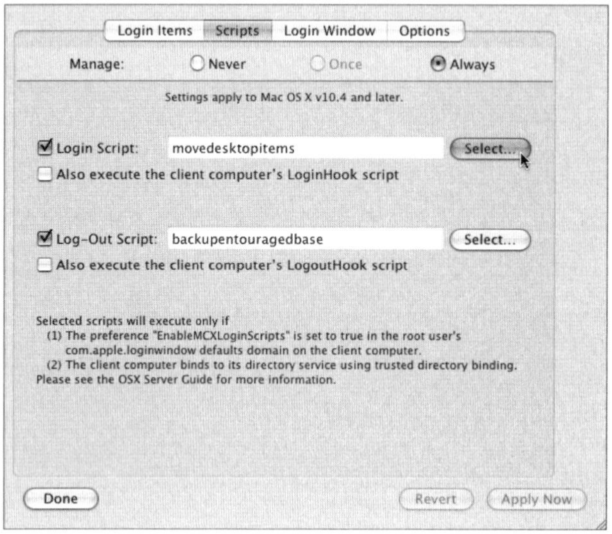

Adding scripts to a computer list that force the scripts to be run at login and logout.

The Login Window pane can be used only when editing the MCX settings for a computer list. The options in this pane control the look and behavior of the Login window on the client computer.

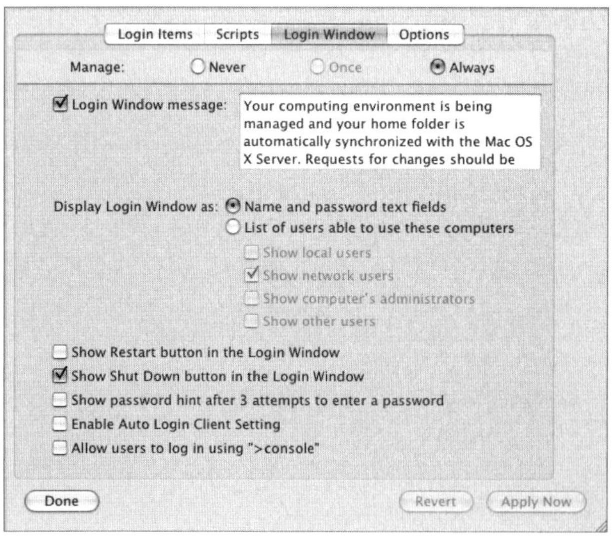

Options here include items available through the standard Accounts preference pane as well as some additional items normally only available through preference files. You can define whether to use name and password entry fields or a list of users, and you can also define which types of users should appear in that list.

Settings are also available to determine whether the Restart and Shut Down buttons are present, whether auto-login is enabled, and whether password hints should be shown. If desired, you can provide a small amount of text to be included in the Login window, as shown in the following figure. This text can be used for anything ranging from implied usage agreements to contact information for users that are having trouble using the machine.

Finally, you have the option to disable the >console option. Users can normally type >console in the user-name field of the Login window, which will drop them out of the GUI environment and into a text-based login prompt. Other similar shortcuts are available in the Login window:

- >power—Shuts down the computer.
- >restart—Restarts the computer.

- >console—Exits the GUI session and drops to a text-based login prompt.
- >exit—Restarts the Login window. This is useful when making changes to /etc/authorization or other settings that affect the Login window.

The Options pane in the login preferences has only two options:

- Enable Fast User Switching
- Log out users after: *N* minutes of inactivity

As with the previous two panes, these options are available only when editing MCX settings for a computer list, as shown in the following figure:

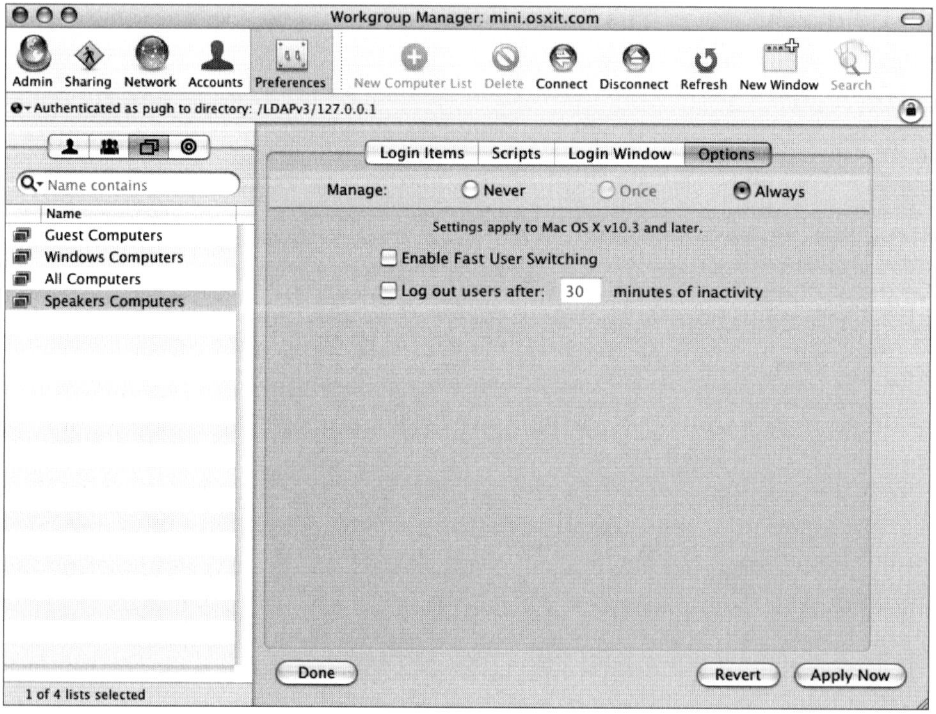

Limiting Application Access

After the user logs in, you may wish to control what applications he or she can run. You can do just that with Workgroup Manager's Application preferences. These settings can apply to users, groups, or computer lists, and can specify a list of applications the user is allowed to use or a list of applications the user is prohibited from using.

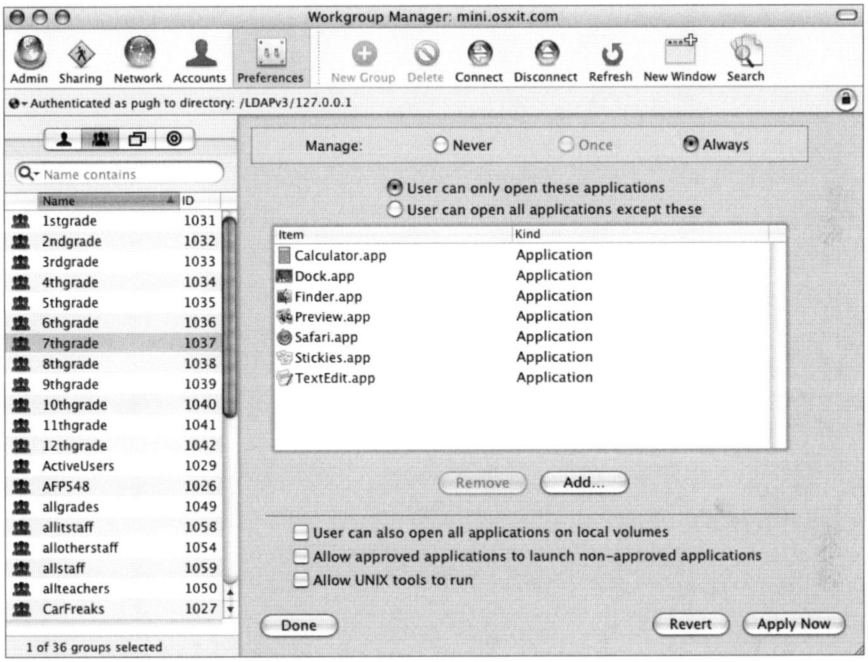

If you don't see an application in the list, you can add it. If you're trying to maintain tight control of which applications the user can run, you should be aware that a number of applications have the ability to launch other applications. Deselect "Allow approved applications to launch non-approved applications" if you'd prefer this. Note that some helper applications are required by other applications, so in this case you must add the specific helper applications to the main list of allowed applications.

Similarly, you can remove the user's ability to execute UNIX utilities. Although this is a good idea for high-security environments, many applications also use UNIX tools as helpers. Those applications may not be fully functional if this setting is unchecked. Depending on what your users should be doing, this may be good or bad.

NOTE ▶ A creative user can find ways to circumvent the application access settings, so consider this setting more of a guideline that just keeps honest people honest.

Setting Classic Preferences

Macintosh Classic applications run inside the Classic environment. This, too, can be managed with Workgroup Manager. If your users are frequently using the Classic environment, you may wish to automatically start Classic when they login. For those users who don't need Classic regularly, you can enable a setting to warn users when the action of opening a document causes Classic to start.

Your environment may use multiple Classic configurations. By using Workgroup Manager's Classic preferences, you have the option of selecting which System Folder is used by this particular user, group, or computer. Leaving the "Use this System Folder when Classic starts" field blank will cause the regular location to be used.

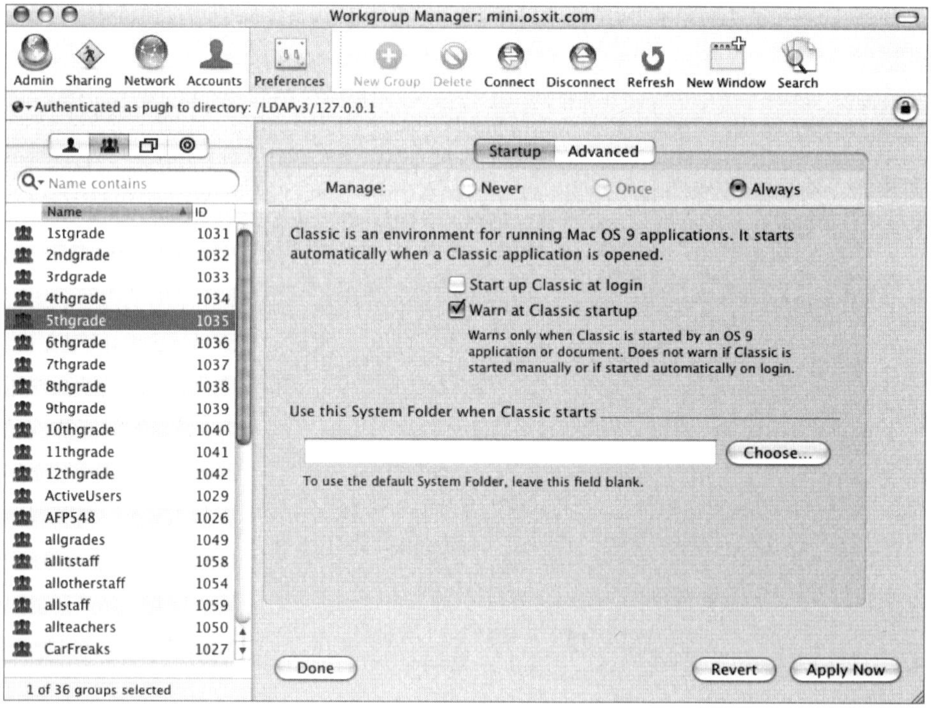

The Advanced pane of Classic preferences includes some options related to security and other behaviors of Classic. If you'd like to ensure a consistent and secure Classic environment, you'll probably want to disable the special startup modes that disable extensions, as well as hide the Chooser, Network Browser, Control Panels, and other Apple Menu items. Other options in this pane help to bridge the gap between Classic and Mac OS X by storing the Classic preferences found in the user's Mac OS X home directories and control when the Classic environment will sleep if not in use.

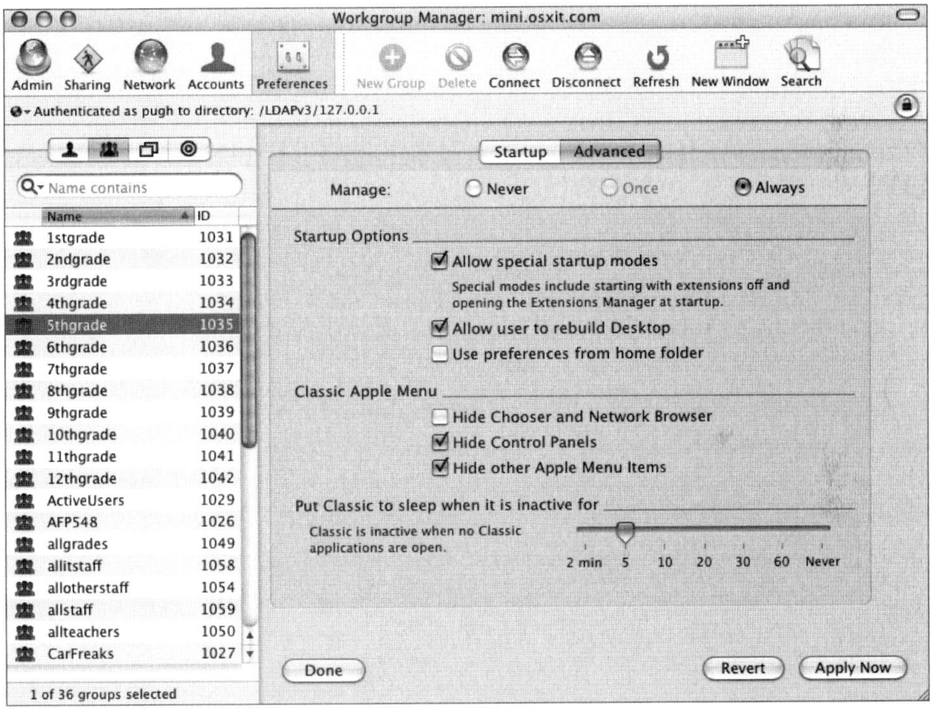

Keep in mind that printing from Classic generally requires access to the Chooser. It should also be noted that your Application access preferences can also apply to applications running in Classic mode.

NOTE ▸ Classic applications will not function on Macs using Intel processors.

Configuring Universal Access

Among the preferences available for management in Workgroup Manager are the Universal Access preferences. In most cases, they are used only to preconfigure systems for users with special needs. Through MCX settings, those users will be able to use different machines with the same Universal Access settings on each one. Since Universal Access is provided as a convenience for the user rather than as a restrictive security measure, you'll probably want to use the Once setting, rather than Always, which will allow the user to modify the extent to which he or she customizes the environment. For example, users may wish to alter the amount of screen zoom, repeating key delays, or mouse speeds.

Visually impaired users may need the Zoom features turned on, allowing them to zoom in on portions of the screen using Command-Option-+ (plus) or Command-Option-– (minus). Users who have difficulty distinguishing between colors have the option of removing colors from the GUI to create a higher contrast environment. Users who are visually impaired can also modify the icon-size settings, available through the Finder preferences.

Hearing-impaired users have an option in the Hearing pane for the screen to flash when the alert sound is played. This can help to notify them to error conditions or new mail delivery.

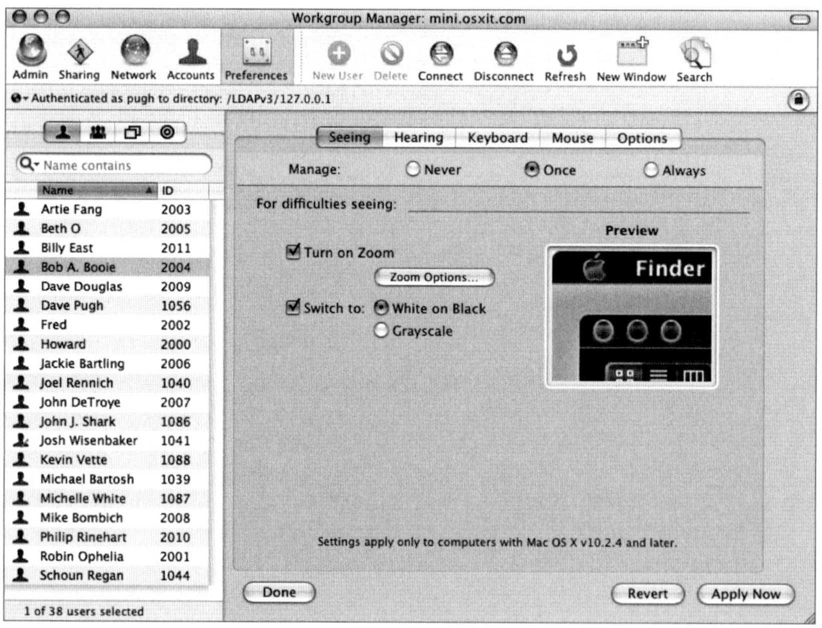

TIP The zoom feature is also great for presentations when displaying tiny text on a projection screen.

Keyboard-based options are available in the Keyboard pane of Universal Access preferences. Users who are unable to press two keys simultaneously, such as the Command-S key combo that saves a file, can turn on Sticky Keys. With this option, a user can press a modifier key (Command, Option, Control, Shift) and then release it. The next key pressed will be treated as if the user had pressed the modifier and key simultaneously. Pressing a modifier key twice in a row will create a caps-lock-like state, in which the user can press the final key multiple times to repeat an action. One use of this feature is for multiple successive undo actions. If it is enabled, an image of the enabled modifier key will be shown in the corner of the screen.

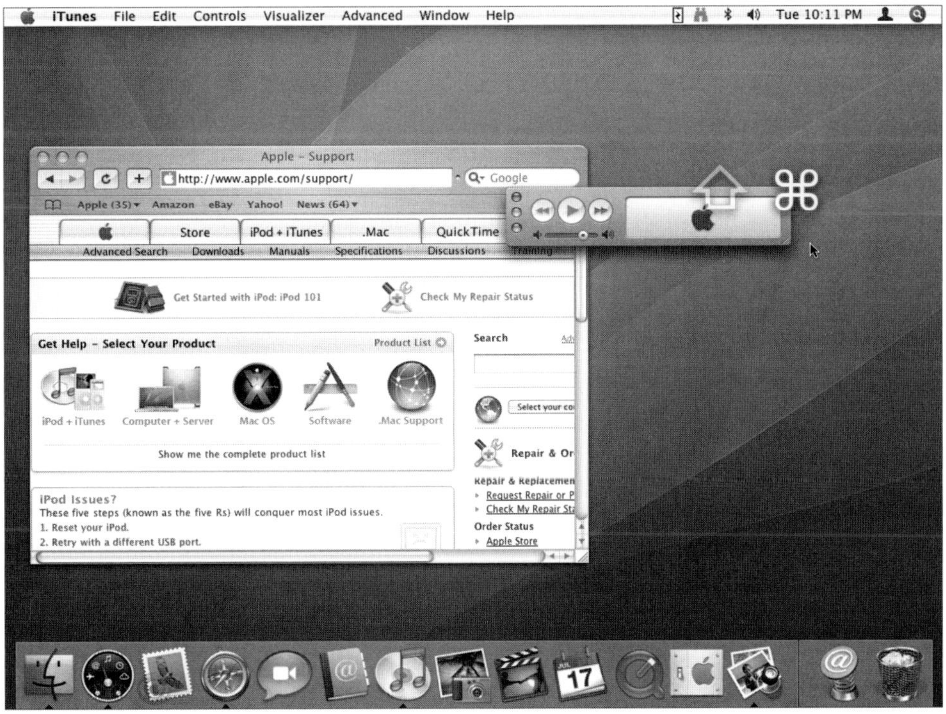

Other users may be unable to tap keys and may hold keys too long. The Keyboard pane of Universal Access also addresses these users with Slow Keys. This setting will help avoid repeated keystrokes due to held keys.

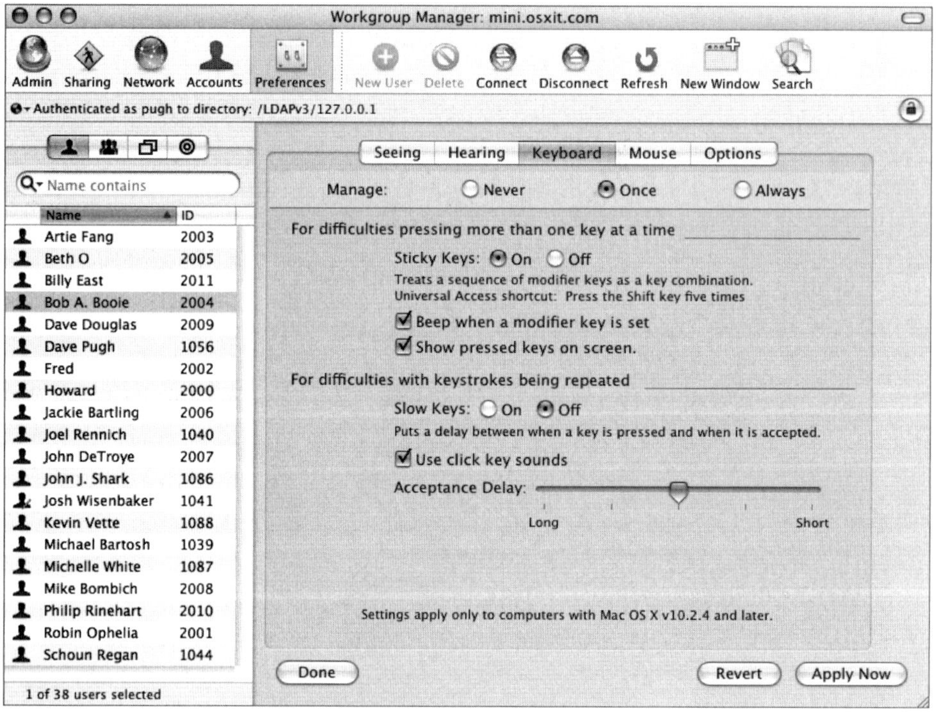

Users who have difficulty using a mouse can use the numeric keypad to move the pointer around the screen. Settings are also present to control the speed at which the mouse moves.

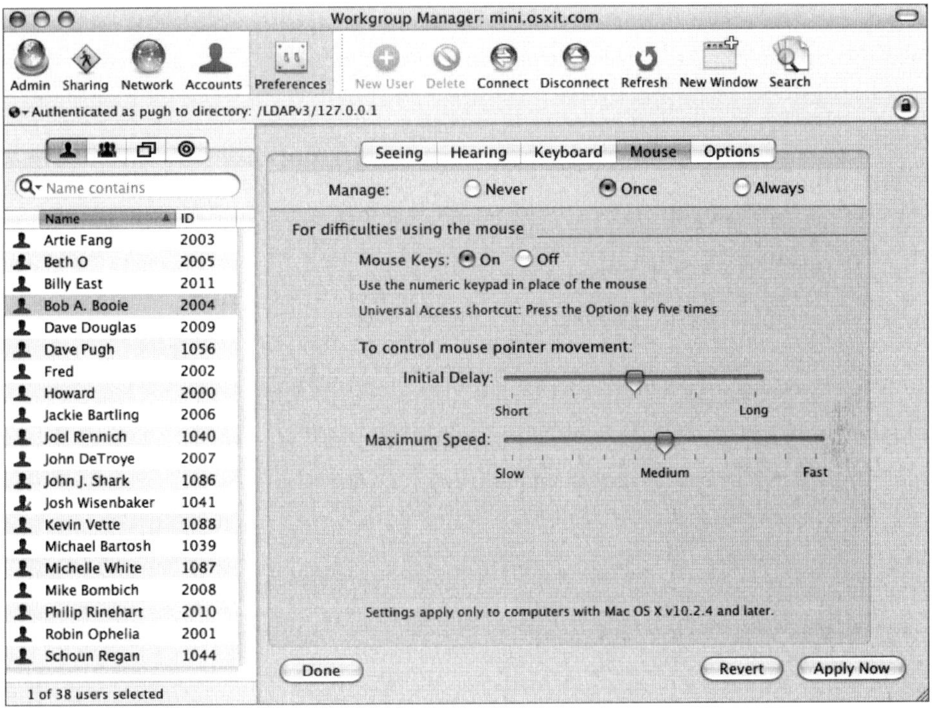

The Options pane contains a box than can be checked or unchecked to enable or disable the keyboard shortcuts that turn each of these accessibility options on or off. Some users may prefer to have these shortcuts, while others will prefer to use the Preferences pane for management.

If you're applying Universal Access settings for a computer list, the Options pane also contains a box you can check to enable access for assistive devices on that computer. A text reader would be one such device. Note that to enable this feature, you must select Always for the frequency that you wish to manage this option.

Setting Network Preferences

The Network preferences can be used to configure the proxy settings for users, groups, or computers. These settings are the same settings found in the normal System Preferences Proxies pane and allow you to configure which intermediate servers provide the path to various Internet traffic.

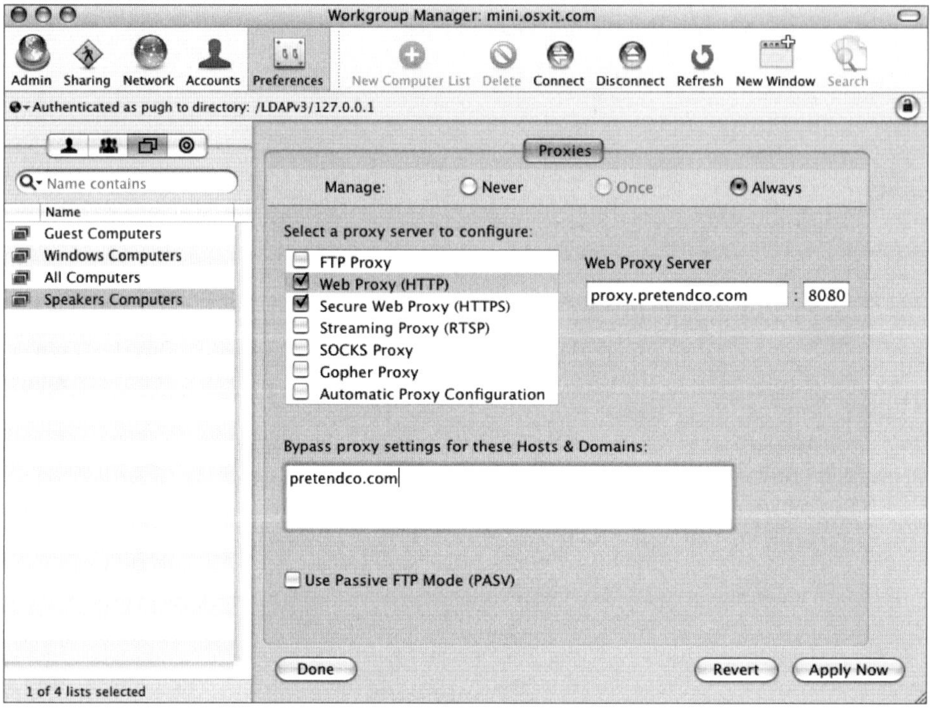

Setting Internet Preferences

The Internet preferences can be set to preconfigure email and Web settings. These settings include the user's default email-reading and Web-browsing applications. Email-configuration parameters such as the user's email address and mail servers can also be configured here.

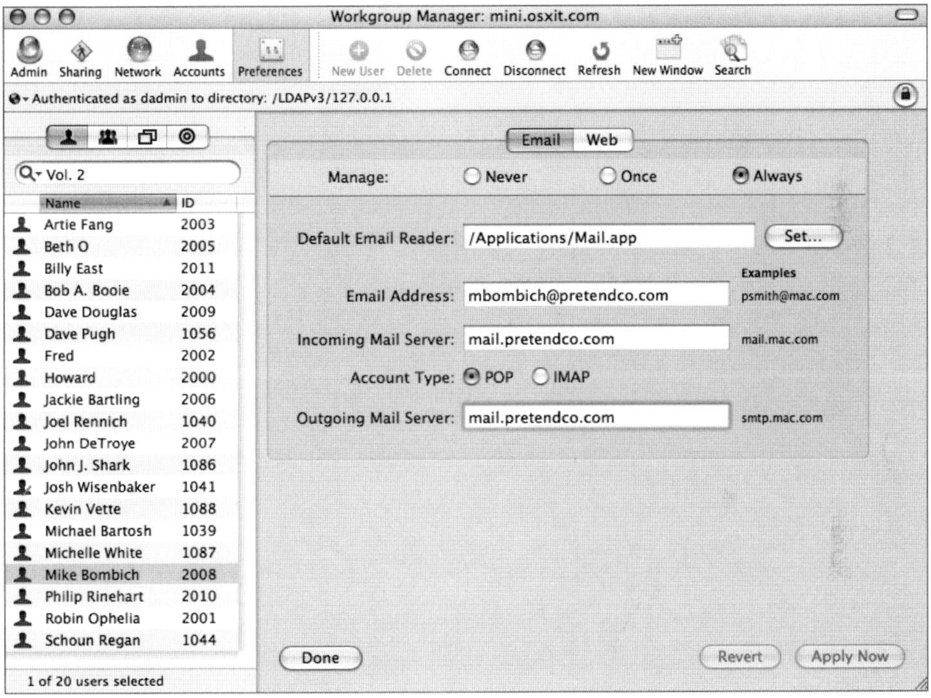

The Web pane allows you to set the user's home and search pages and also define where his or her downloaded files are stored. These settings can help maintain a consistent environment throughout your company, or can be used to maintain correct settings on a kiosk machine.

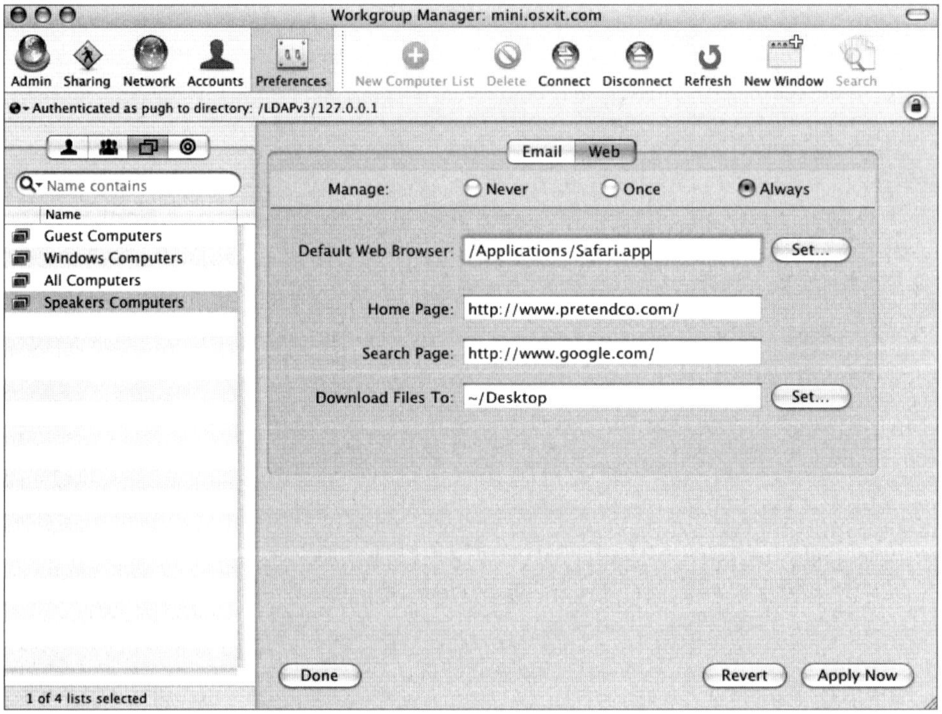

Setting Printing Preferences

Depending on the printing habits of your users, you may be using the printing preferences for a variety of reasons. You may set up the lists of printers for the convenience of your users by defaulting their printers to the ones located closest to them, or you may use these MCX settings to restrict which printers the user can access.

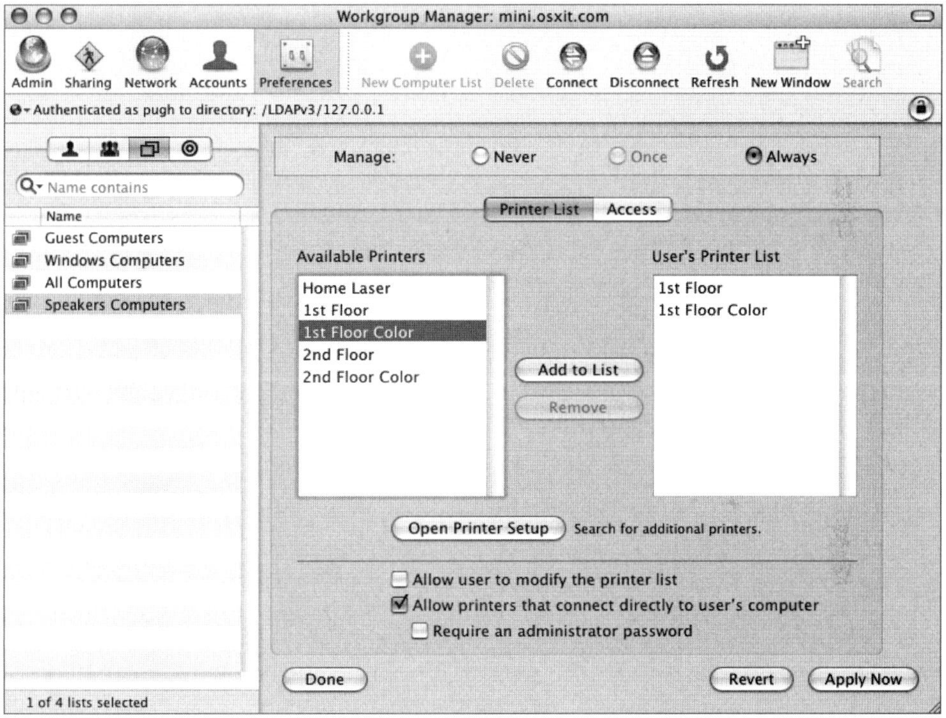

Options are available on these preference panes that can restrict the ability for the user to change these settings.

Setting Software Update Preferences

Some organizations may have a local Software Update server hosted on a Mac OS X Server. This might be done for a number of reasons:

- Internet bandwidth savings—Your client machines all obtain their updates from a local server rather than each going to the Internet for its updates.
- Work around firewall settings—A tight firewall at an organization may not allow software update traffic outside of the organization. By mirroring updates, client machines don't need to talk to the public Apple Software Update servers.
- Approve updates—Some software updates may break functionality critical to an organization. The Software Update server allows the server administrator to test and approve updates before the client machines see them.

Before you can restrict accounts to a specific Software Update server, you must first set up that server as a Software Update server.

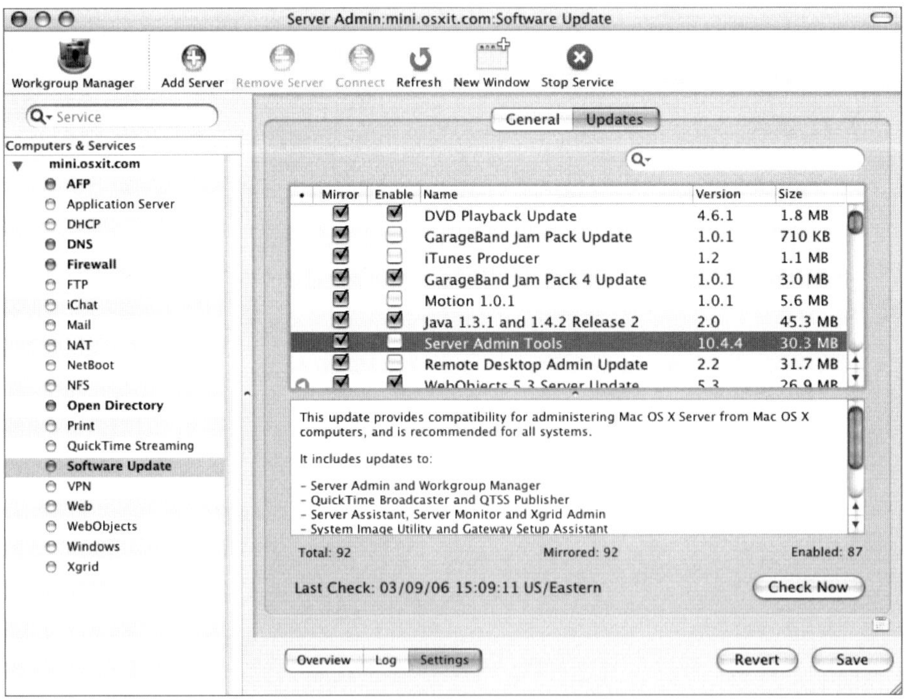

See Lesson 1, "Developing a Deployment Strategy," and Lesson 6, "Maintenance," for information on setting up a Software Update server.

To configure clients to see your local Software Update server, enter the URL of your server.

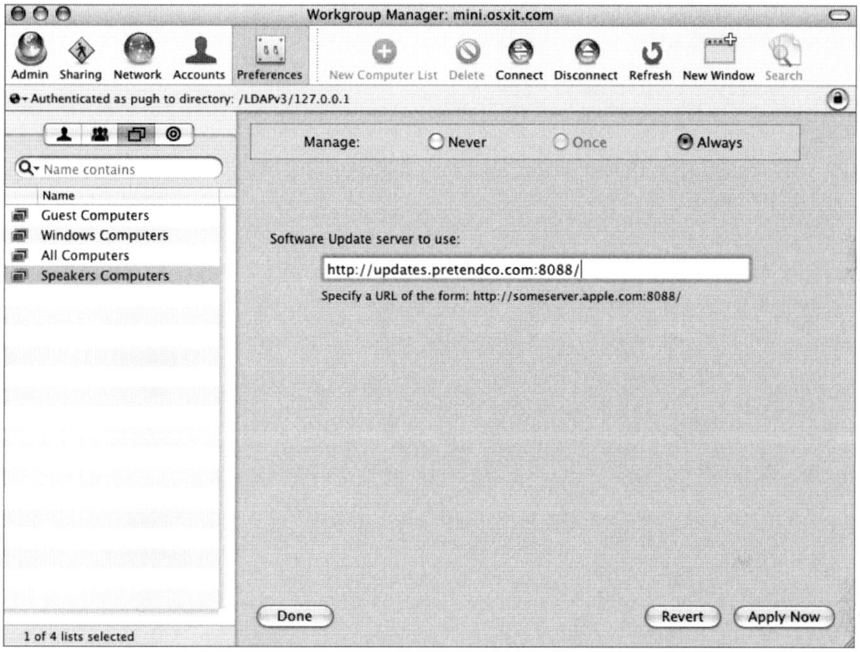

You can also specify this on unmanaged computers from the command line:

```
sudo defaults write com.apple.SoftwareUpdate CatalogURL http://your.server.name:8088/index.sucatalog
```

NOTE ► The Software Update server is not intended to host non-Apple software updates. Each software update is signed by Apple. Without this digital signature, the client on your network will not recognize an update. There are some work-arounds published on the Internet, but they involve replacing the public certificate on each of your clients and re-signing every Apple update. Not only is this tedious, but it could also be insecure. A much better approach is to use Apple Remote Desktop (ARD) to push out your non-Apple software updates.

Setting Energy Saver Preferences

The Energy Saver preferences are available only if you're assigning MCX settings to a computer list. The button will not be visible if you're looking at users or groups. This pane allows you to assign power-management settings to the computer. Note that there are separate tabs for Desktop and Portable. These panes are functionally identical, except the Desktop pane has a menu where you select whether you're using Mac OS X or Mac OS X Server, while the Portable pane allows you to set different options depending on whether your laptop is plugged in with the power adapter or is on battery power.

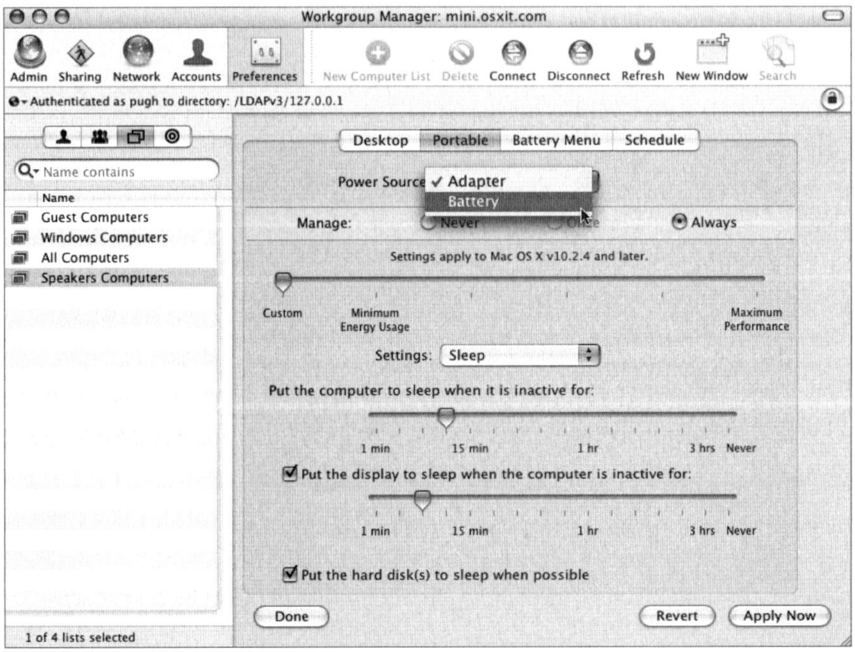

For each configuration, you can either set a preset configuration based on minimum energy usage or maximum performance, or move the slider to the left and use custom settings defining the computer sleep time, display sleep time, and whether the hard disks should spin down when not in use. By choosing Options in the Settings menu, you also have the following options available:

- ▶ Wake when the modem detects a ring
- ▶ Wake for Ethernet network administrator access (Wake-on-LAN)
- ▶ Restart automatically after a power failure
- ▶ Processor performance: Highest/Reduced/Automatic

The Battery Menu pane only contains an option to show the battery status in the menu bar. The Schedule pane allows you to configure Mac OS X or Mac OS X Server to start, sleep, or shut down the computer at specified times, as shown in the following figure:

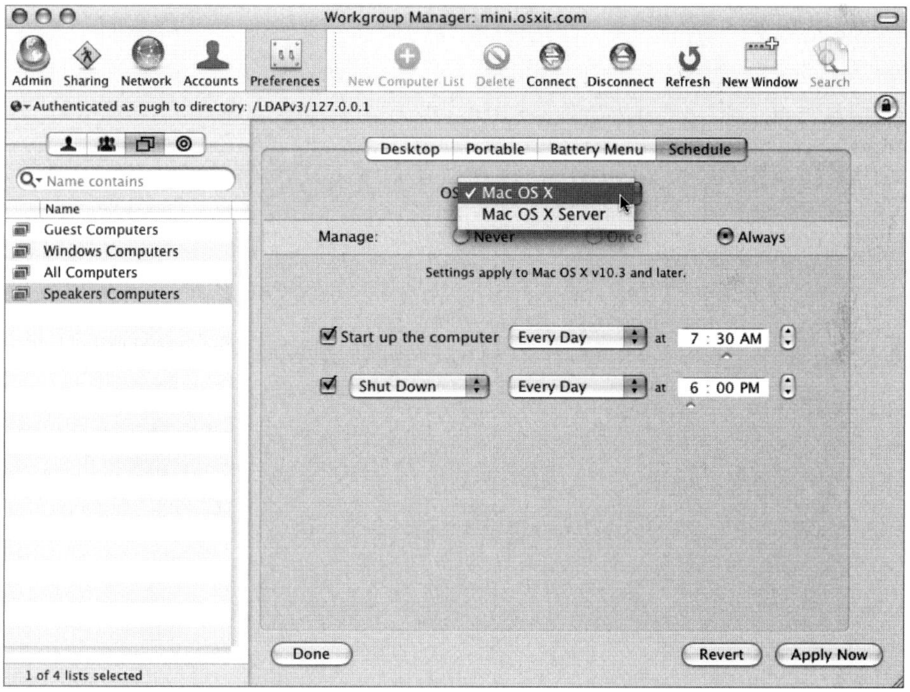

Configuring the Shell

Workgroup Manager can also be used to configure aspects of the user's environment through the Accounts panes. These settings are not MCX rules, and can only be applied to individual users. After selecting a user in Workgroup Manager, you can click the Accounts button in the toolbar and then the Accounts tab on the left side of the window. Select a user or users there prior to changing that user's (or those users') account information. In the Advanced pane, you can change the user's login shell, as shown in the following figure. This has an effect on the behavior of the user's Terminal and SSH sessions.

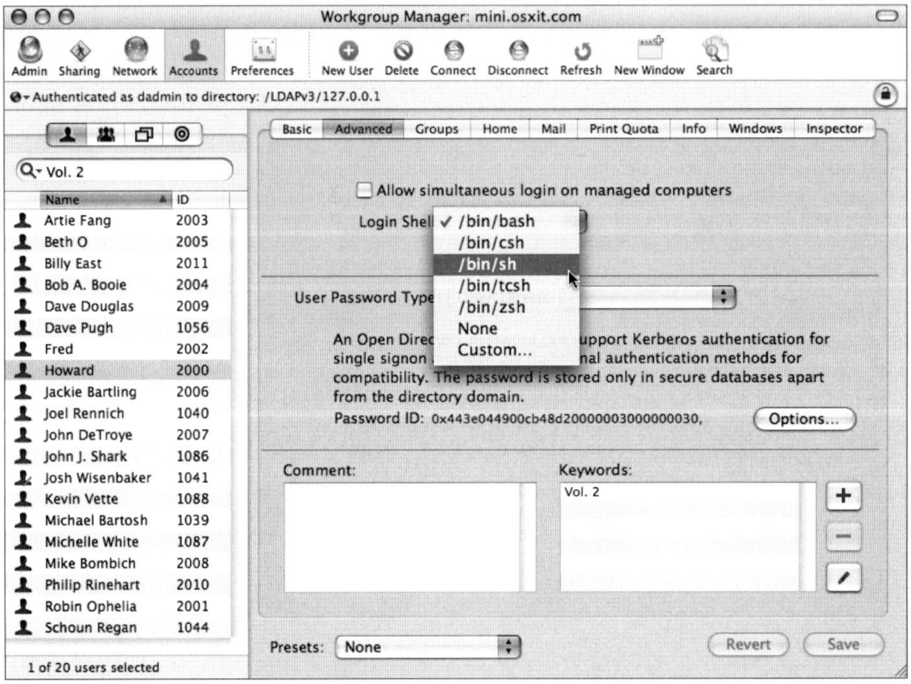

There are two main variants of shells—those based on the Bourne shell, including /bin/sh, /bin/bash, and /bin/zsh, and those based on the C Shell, /bin/csh and /bin/tcsh. Setting the user's shell to None sets the shell to /dev/null. This disables any Terminal shell access but does not disable the user's ability to run commands. He or she just can't do it from a shell prompt.

The default shell in Mac OS X is /bin/bash. Users may have a preferred shell, or your organization may wish to standardize on an alternate shell.

Automating New-User Creation

When dealing with many different account variations, it sometimes becomes difficult to manage accounts, especially when new accounts need to be created or imported, such as when new students are added to a school database every year. To help limit the time spent configuring new accounts, consider creating an account preset with all the managed preferences already set. An easy way to do this is to create a separate account, which may be called PresetUser A or PresetUser B (see Lesson 8 on creating new users), that has all the tested presets already done. Then, when a new account is needed, that particular preset is chosen before the new account is created, and all the managed preferences are instantly applied to that user account.

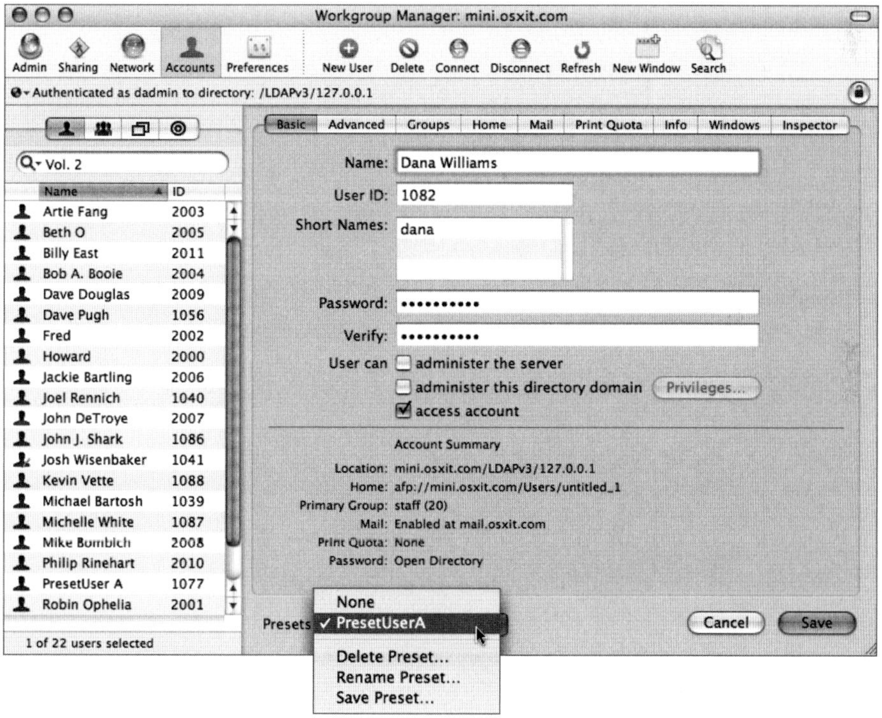

Viewing the Presets menu showing one preset called PresetUserA.

Lesson Review

1. List the directories where the system looks for preference lists.
2. What is a Preference Manifest?
3. List the four frequencies at which a preference setting can be applied to a user's session.
4. What is the difference between a Simple Finder and normal Finder?
5. What are some ways to limit a user's access to a UNIX command line?
6. Name the three situations that might arise when similar preferences are managed by more than one account type.
7. How do you set Software Update to recognize a different Software Update server if the account is *not* managed?

Answers

1. ~/Library/Preferences/, /Library/Preferences/, /Network/Library/Preferences/.
2. A Preference Manifest is a plist that describes the options and possible values for an application's preference list.
3. Never, Once, Often, Always.
4. The Simple Finder can only run items in the user's Dock, has no Desktop or file-navigation abilities, and has a much smaller set of pull-down menus.
5. Use the Simple Finder, disallow use of the Terminal application, disallow UNIX tools to run, or set the user's shell to None.
6. Inherit, Combine, Override.
7. `sudo defaults write com.apple.SoftwareUpdate CatalogURL http://your.server.name:8088/index.sucatalog`

References

Administration Guides

Mac OS X Server User Management: http://images.apple.com/server/pdfs/User_Management_Admin_v10.4B.pdf

Deploying Mac OS X Computers for K–12 Education: http://images.apple.com/server/pdfs/Deploying_Mac_OS_X_for_K12_Education_v10.4.pdf

Apple Knowledge Base Documents

Numerous Knowledge Base documents pertain to this chapter. Visit www.apple.com/support and search on *managed client* for a complete list.

URLs

Preference Manifest Files for Managed Clients Overview: http://developer.apple.com/documentation/MacOSXServer/Conceptual/Preference_Manifest_Files/Preference_Manifest_Files.pdf

10

Time This lesson takes about 1 hour to complete.

Goals

Define a mobile account

Create mobile accounts

Synchronize mobile account user data

Define synchronization parameters

Lesson **10**

Working with Mobile Accounts

System administrators often have to make many choices and trade-offs when dealing with laptop users, such as how to back up data, what to back up, and how to deploy a directory infrastructure that works on computers that may or may not be continuously connected to the organization's network.

In this lesson, you'll learn how to set up and manage accounts that may not always be within your reach. Apple calls these *mobile accounts*, although they can be used as easily on desktop computers as they can be on laptop computers.

Understanding Mobile Accounts

Mobile accounts essentially are copies of network accounts that simultaneously exist in your directory domain (such as Open Directory, OpenLDAP, or Active Directory) and in the local domain (NetInfo) of a Mac OS X computer. Certain attributes are used to define a user account, and some of these attributes are copied to the local domain when a mobile account is created. This may seem confusing at first, raising such questions as "Where is the *real* password stored, on the server or the local computer?" or "How can a remote user be managed?"

Before implementing a mobile account, it is important to see the variety of ways in which such an account can be used, so that all the ramifications of a mobile account can be addressed, reducing the possibility that costly mistakes will be made.

Using Mobile Accounts

There are a couple of ways a mobile account can be used. First, a laptop, which contains only a local administrator account, can be imaged and given to a new user. When the laptop is connected to the local network before it is started up for the first time, a directory binding can be made to a directory service. The user types in a user name and password supplied by the directory administrator, and the following takes place:

- Certain user attributes are copied and/or created from the shared directory domain to the local NetInfo directory.
- A home directory is created and appears. This home directory is not a network home directory (it does not exist on a network server) but is a locally created home directory, based on the user template located in /System/Library/User Template/*language*.lproj, where *language* is the name of the localized language set for that particular laptop.

  The second way a mobile account can be used is similar to a laptop account except that, instead of being used on a laptop computer, it is used on a desktop computer. It may seem strange to create a mobile account on a computer that is constantly connected to the network containing the shared directory domain, but it has several advantages. For example, you could create a disk image that is deployed to hundreds or thousands of computers with nothing more than a single administrator account. When the image is deployed to a computer and initially booted, a user with a network account can log in and get a home folder created for her based on the local computer's user template. This keeps all user-created data local while the mobile account is a cached version of the network account.

NetInfo caches the mobile user account and its various attributes.

Should a problem with the local account occur, the local administrator can simply delete the locally cached NetInfo account for the mobile user and log out as the administrator. The user whose account has been deleted then logs in again. Once more, the account is cached locally. Since the administrator did not delete the user's home folder and the user's UNIX ID did not change, the user still has access to all her data. This is an extremely efficient way to manage thousands of users while allowing them to store their data locally on their computers.

In either case, when the mobile user logs in and the computer is connected to the network on which the original account is stored, the account name, MCX settings, and password are updated on the mobile account.

NOTE ▶ Mobile accounts are not good for users who may log in to three or four different computers during the day. Each time the user logs in, he or she will get a new local home folder, and the files created by the user will be on each computer, not housed in one location, such as a network home folder.

Implementing Mobile Accounts

Mobile accounts are created based on user, workgroup, or computer list accounts, depending on the types of accounts you wish to manage. For example, you may have a workgroup that contains all users in your company. You assign mobile accounts to the group, so any user who logs in as a member of the group will get a mobile account. Mobile accounts are handled equally regardless of whether you have 1 user or 10,000, 1 workgroup or 50, a computer list that contains all the Macs in your company, or just 5 laptops.

To implement a mobile account for a user:

1. Launch Workgroup Manager.
2. Connect to your directory server and authenticate.
3. In the top right corner of the Workgroup Manager window, be sure the lock icon is unlocked to indicate that you are authenticated. If not, click it and authenticate.
4. Select the user(s), workgroup, or computer list to which you wish to apply the settings.
5. At the top of the window, click the Preferences button.
6. Click the Mobility icon.

7 Click the Always button in the Synchronization pane and select "Synchronize account for offline use."

8 Click Apply Now.

Doing so will permit a local account to be created the next time that user logs in to a computer bound to that directory server.

NOTE ▶ An option also exists to permit a dialog to appear requiring confirmation when creating a mobile account.

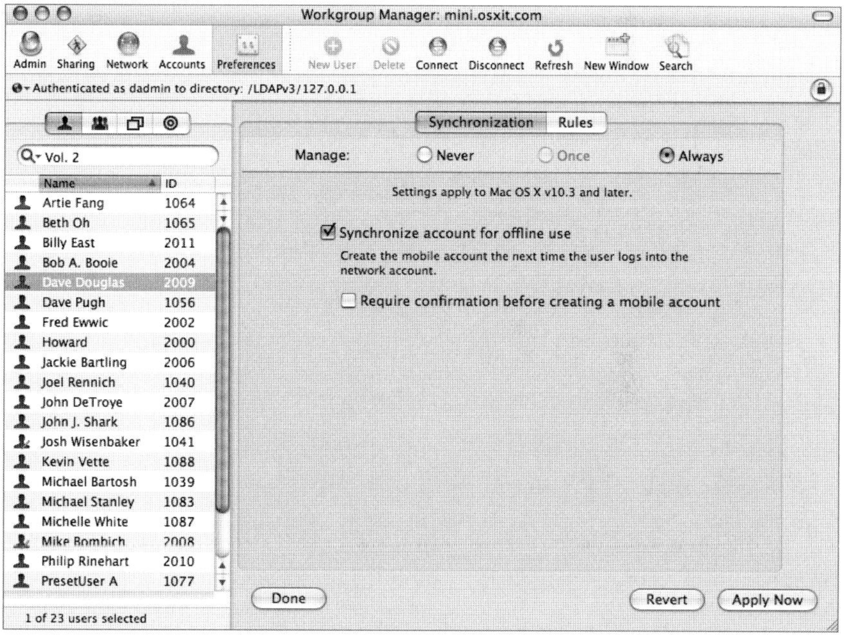

This can be done for many users, a group of users, or computer lists. Doing so will affect several accounts, not just one, as shown above.

But what happens when a computer with a mobile account is removed from the network? What if the password policy required the user to change his or her password every 30 days? How will the local account behave if the user attempts to log in on the 31st day?

When computers containing mobile accounts are disconnected from the network on which they were born, they act independently of the network because all their MCX settings have been cached locally. In the case of a password change, the user will still use his old password beyond 30 days until he can reconnect the laptop to the network. At the next login, he will be asked to change his password.

Mobile accounts can be combined with directory services to produce some versatile scenarios.

One option using mobile accounts is called the *OD/AD* (Open Directory/Active Directory) *triangle*. This consists of a Mac OS X Open Directory server as one corner of the triangle, an Active Directory server as another corner, and a Mac OS X computer as the third corner. The goal of an OD/AD triangle is to have the Mac OS X computer bind first to the Active Directory server and bind second to the Mac OS X Open Directory server. First the Mac OS X server binds to the Active Directory server, and then it binds to itself. In this fashion, users log in to a Mac OS X computer with a user name and password that exist on the Active Directory server and subsequently obtain a mobile account managed by a Mac OS X Open Directory server. Refer to *Apple Training Series: Mac OS X System Administration Reference, Volume 1* for more information about connecting to an Active Directory server and the OD/AD triangle.

Synchronizing an Account

Once a mobile account is created, a user has a local copy of her attributes and values, but the data that user works with every day—word-processing documents, Keynote presentations, and other document types—is stored on the computer on which the local account was created. Also, any preferences for the applications that create those files and settings, such as the Dock or Finder preferences, are stored locally as well, and not stored on the server where the original account is located.

While MCX setting changes are propagated down every time a user logs in when connected to the network on which the original server is located, user-created data and preferences are not. Therefore, a plan must be put into place to handle the user-created documents and preferences. Synchronization backs up user-created data, preferences, and other items related to the user's work environment into the network home folder of that user.

Before synchronization can occur, a home folder for the user must be created on the network for that user and listed in the user's attributes. This is done using Workgroup Manager. Please refer to Lesson 8, "Creating Accounts," for more information on creating home folders for network user accounts.

Setting Up Synchronized Accounts

After setting the managed preference for mobile accounts, choose how the initial synchronization will take place. (If no synchronization is set, the user-created data is never written back to the server.)

When setting up synchronization, you must define which parts of the user's home folder will be synchronized. When testing a new account with no user-created data, it's best to synchronize the entire home folder and leave all the defaults in place. Remember that the shortcut for a user's home folder is represented by a tilde (~).

To set up synchronization on login and logout:

1. Launch Workgroup Manager.
2. Connect to your directory server and authenticate.
3. In the top right corner of the Workgroup Manager window, be sure the lock icon is unlocked to indicate that you are authenticated. If not, click it and authenticate.
4. Select the user(s), workgroup, or computer list to which you wish to apply the settings.
5. Click the Preferences button at the top of the window.
6. Click the Mobility icon (not shown).
7. Click the Rules tab, and in the Rules pane, click Always.
8. Next to the "Synchronize at login and logout" portion of the window, click the Add (+) button and add a tilde (~) in the new line.

9 Leave all other defaults as they are for now.

10 Click Apply Now.

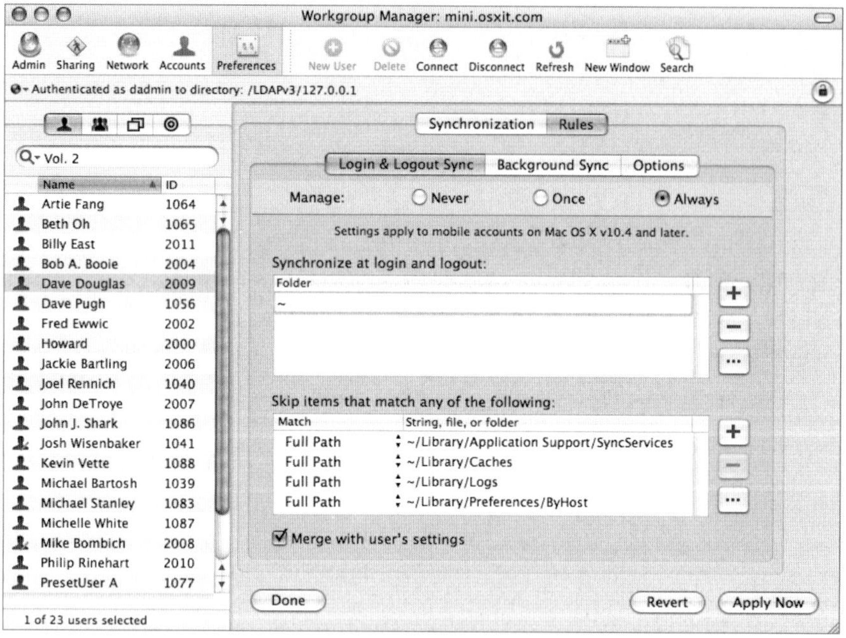

When the user with the mobile account initially logs in to a computer bound to the directory server, a new home folder is created and a dialog appears, informing the user that the mobile account is being synchronized.

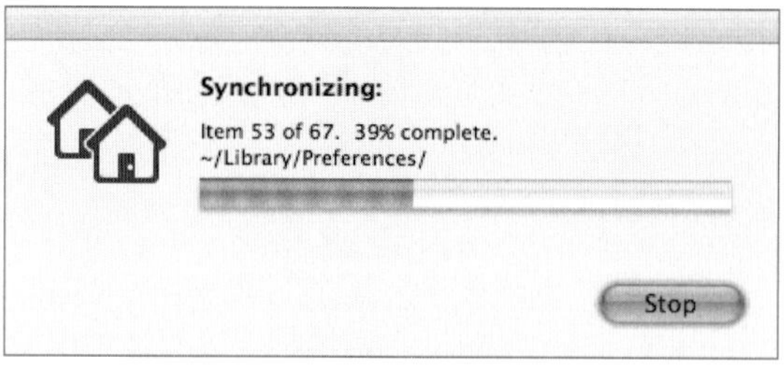

After the login, another icon appears in the menu bar, indicating that the user can immediately synchronize his home folder whenever he wishes and perhaps also control which folders are synchronized.

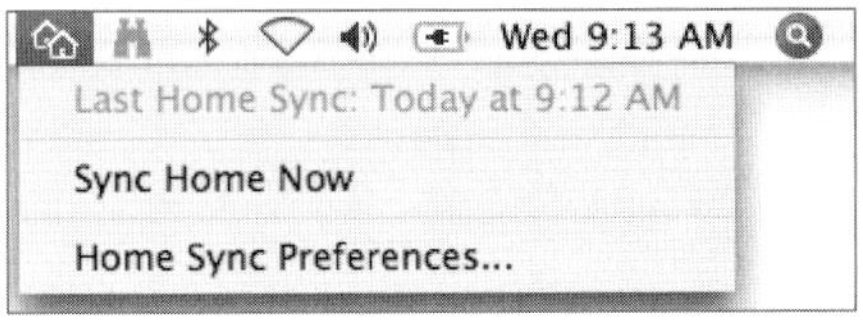

Managing Synchronized Folders

Another aspect to consider when setting up synchronized accounts is whether users should have their data synchronized in the background, and how often that synchronization should occur. Second, should users decide this or should administrators? If users decide, are they also permitted to decide which folders are synchronized?

The options related to overall synchronization are as follows:

- Login, logout, and background syncing
- Merging with user settings
- Time interval for background synchronization

Regardless of whether the synchronization takes place at login and logout and whether background synchronization is involved, you have the option of merging new settings with the user settings. This permits preferences that the user has set, such as Dock preferences, to not be overwritten unless management is strictly enforced on those settings.

To enable merging with user settings, click either the Login and Logout Sync or Background Sync tab (depending on which you are doing), and check the box (if it's not already checked) at the bottom of the window.

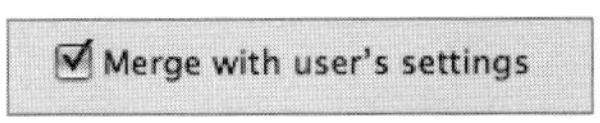

Then click the Apple Now button. (It is checked by default when setting up new mobile accounts with synchronization.)

The login and logout synchronization is exactly what it sounds like. Synchronization takes place only when the user logs in or logs out. Choosing to always manage this setting does not permit the user to allow what is synced. If you choose to manage the item once as opposed to always, when the user logs in, she can manage which folders are synchronized by using her Accounts preferences pane (within System Preferences) and clicking the Configure button that opens the Synchronize dialog.

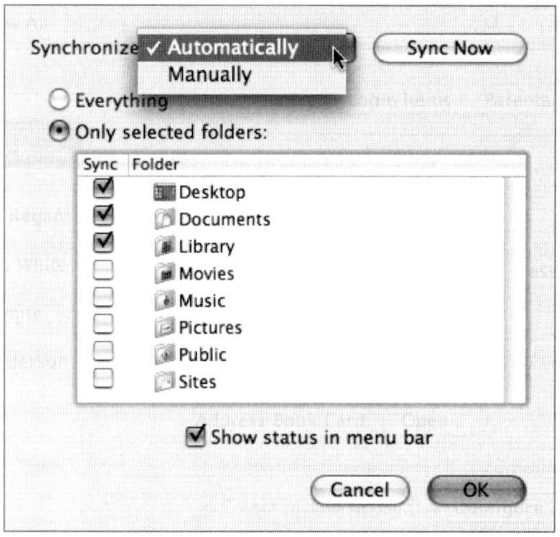

Users can control when they synchronize during their logged-in session and exactly which folders they want to synchronize.

Background syncing is simply the permitting of synchronization to take place at predefined intervals. Background syncing can be managed never, once, or always, and if it's managed only once, the user then has control over when the account is synchronized while he or she is working.

Also, as you learned earlier in this lesson, merging these settings with the user's settings will permit the user to keep the settings that were configured prior to the initial syncing.

Once background syncing is enabled, you must use the Options pane to decide how often to synchronize the information.

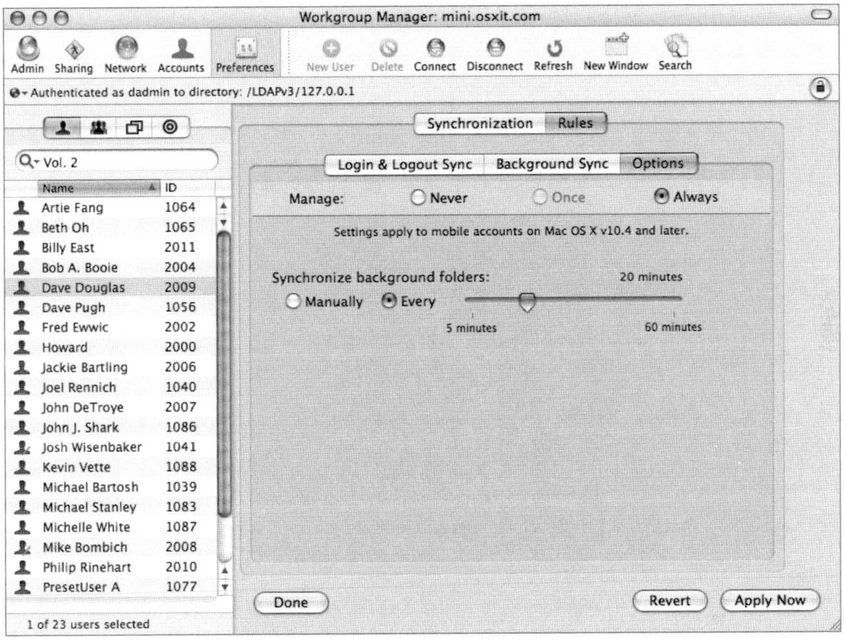

Optimizing Synchronized Content

Once you decide how synchronization takes place, you must decide what to synchronize. Earlier in this lesson, you synchronized the user's entire home folder, as represented by the tilde (~). However, you can specify with a high level of granularity exactly what is synchronized. For example, at login and logout you can choose to synchronize the user's entire home folder; however, you also can set background syncing to synchronize the user's Documents folder every hour. Both the Login & Logout Sync pane and the Background Sync pane have the same interface when dealing with exactly what to synchronize.

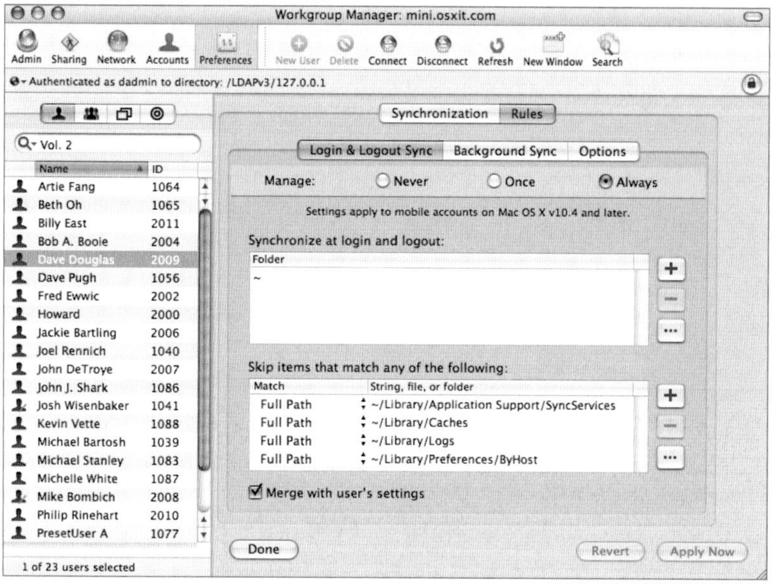

The Login & Logout Sync pane.

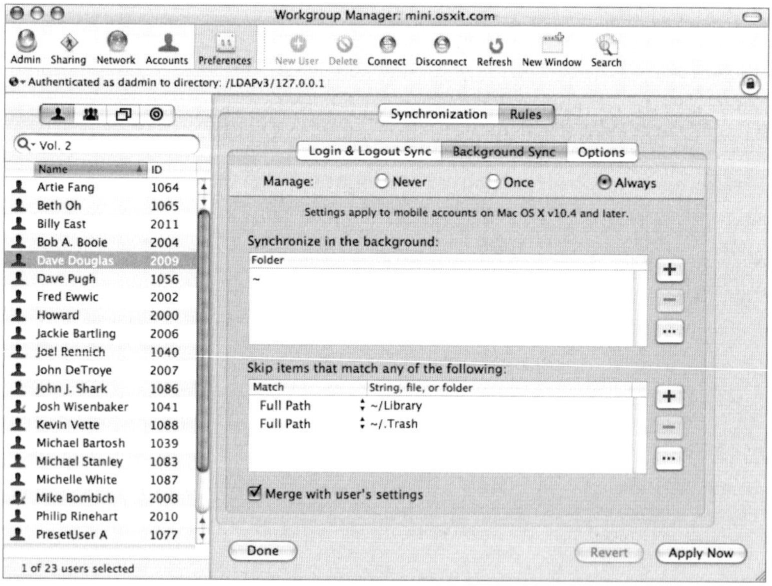

The Background Sync pane.

While it is readily apparent what is skipped during background syncing (which is the user's Library and Trash in the preceding example), the window showing items that are skipped with login and logout syncing does not scroll, so you see only a few skipped items.

Here is the list of Apple's default skipped items when doing login and logout syncing. The full paths of items are skipped.

- ~/Library/Logs
- ~/Library/Caches
- ~/Library/Printers
- ~/Library/Safari/Icons
- ~/Library/Preferences/ByHost
- ~/Library/Application Support/SyncServices
- ~/Library/Preferences/loginwindow.plist
- ~/Library/Preferences/com.apple.dock.plist
- ~/Library/Preferences/com.apple.iChatAgent.plist
- ~/Library/Preferences/com.apple.sidebarlists.plist
- ~/Library/Preferences/com.apple.systemuiserver.plist

Items starting with the following text are skipped:

- IMAP-
- Mac-

You can change exactly what is synchronized by adding to the synchronize list. Before you do, you should remove syncing of the entire home folder and then add back only the folders you want to sync. You do this by clicking the Add (+) button and manually adding a path, or by clicking the Browse (...) button and navigating to the location you want to synchronize.

Not only can you choose what to sync, but you can also choose what *not* to sync. As discussed earlier, there are a set number of items that are skipped by default when syncing.

The defaults are just suggestions and can be modified or deleted, depending on usage. You have available several methods of locating items that you want to skip:

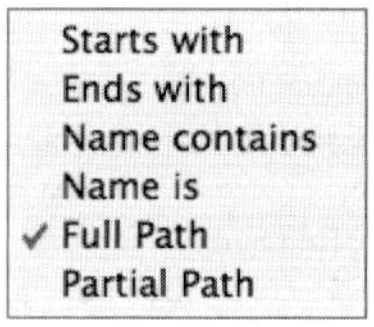

By using qualifiers such as "Name contains" or "Ends with," you can skip items such as all files inside the home folder with names ending with the .mp3 or .m4a filename extension. You also could skip any item whose name contains *movie*. The level of detail is left up to you, but, using this method, you can skip large files and focus on syncing only those files germane to the organization.

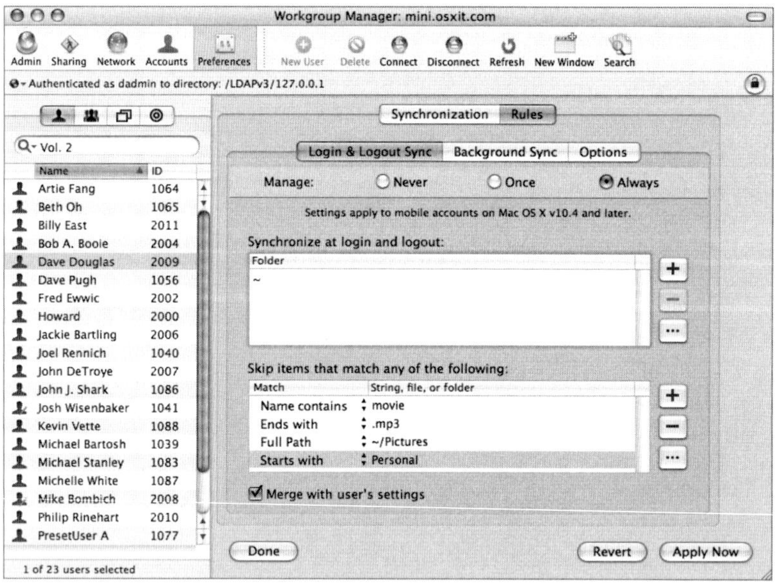

Dealing with Synchronization Issues

What happens when users complain of slow login times, or your network administrator comes knocking on your door? Is the number of items being synchronized too high? What about items that appear synchronized but are not synchronized, or fail to synchronize at all? Examining some known issues and correcting for them will result in a richer user experience when using mobile accounts with synchronization.

Bandwidth Considerations

Depending on what is synchronized and the number of users doing synchronization, it is possible to saturate your network with all that synchronization traffic. Music, movie, and large image files that may take up several hundred megabytes will cause the user experience to appear sluggish, and they should be avoided unless the network can handle the bandwidth. One example of this is a Microsoft Entourage database that may be several hundred megabytes in size. Even if the user receives only one email during login, the entire database is synchronized. As you have seen, you can dictate with considerable precision the items that get synchronized. Testing, monitoring, and efficient management of items to be synchronized are the keys to keeping your network from being overwhelmed.

Synchronization Irregularities

It is possible for folders to get out of sync. An error message will appear stating that items cannot be synchronized. If the network home folder is not available, or if there has been an authentication issue, these errors will prevent synchronization from taking place. Attempting to log in via Connect to Server will test whether the home directory can be mounted with the proper authentication. Related to this type of error, disruption in the AFP service will also cause synchronization to fail.

One of the primary causes of conflicts is multiple logins of the same user account. For example, a user has several accounts on separate computers, and all those accounts are used at the same time. This can happen when a generic account is used for several users. To prevent this, in Workgroup Manager uncheck the box for "Allow simultaneous login on managed computers" in the Advanced pane of the generic user.

If a user logs in to her computer, and syncing occurs but the home folder on the server becomes unavailable during the session, she must log out and log back in when the server becomes available to synchronize her files on the server.

One way to prevent students from creating multiple mobile accounts (logging in to several different computers each day and having a mobile account on each computer) is to use computer lists and force a specific computer to a specific user. This prevents other users from logging in to any computer other than the one to which they were assigned. Should multiple accounts occur and the user's data is expendable, the user and his associated mobile home folder can be removed from all the computers. This can be done using the Accounts pane of System Preferences or by using NetInfo Manager. The shell script below can be sent out via Apple Remote Desktop to automatically remove mobile accounts, while keeping the local administrator account on each computer.

```
#!/bin/sh

#This script deletes mobile account user and their home directories

PATH=/bin:/sbin:/usr/bin:/usr/sbin export PATH

Users=$( nireport . /users name original_home | grep -v NoValue | sed -e's/[ ,].*$//' | sed –e'/^$/d')

for users in $users; do

echo Removing home folder of $user

eval hd="~$user"

if [[ "$hd" !="/"]]; then

        rm –r "$hd"

fi

echo Removing $user from NetInfo

niutil –destroy . /users/$user
```

Finally, if a serious error occurs and it appears that the mobile accounts home folder has been erased, look to the server hosting the network home folder, delete the local mobile account in NetInfo and the mobile account home folder, and allow the user to log in again and synchronize again from the beginning.

Lesson Review

1. What options are available for skipping items when synchronizing folders?
2. What does "Merge with user's settings" do?
3. How do you allow a user to control which folders within his or her home folder are synchronized?

4. Will mobile accounts work for users running Mac OS X v10.3?
5. What three items are updated when a mobile account user logs in to a computer connected to the network on which the server that stores the original account is located?

Answers

1. "Starts with," "Ends with," "Name contains," "Name is," "Full Path," and "Partial Path."
2. Allows previously created preferences not to be overwritten when synchronizing.
3. Set the synchronization managed level (either login and logout or background or both) to Once instead of Always.
4. Yes. Mobile accounts will work; however, synchronization is not supported.
5. User name(s), password, and MCX settings.

References

Administration Guides

"User Management": http://images.apple.com/server/pdfs/User_Management_Admin_v10.4B.pdf

"Deploying Mac OS X Computers for K–12 Education": http://images.apple.com/server/pdfs/Deploying_Mac_OS_X_for_K12_Education_v10.4.pdf

Knowledge Base Articles

You can check for new and updated articles in the AppleCare Knowledge Base, at www.apple.com/support.

About the Mac OS X Server 10.4.3 Update ("Managed Users" section): http://docs.info.apple.com/article.html?artnum=302089

URLs

Visit the following sites for more information:

MacEnterprise: www.macenterprise.org

Portable Home Directories without Open Directory: http://managingosx.wordpress.com/2006/03/15/portable-home-directories-without-open-directory

AFP548.com: www.afp548.com

11

Time This lesson takes about 1 hour to complete.

Goals

Learn how to set up Windows accounts

Set up security policies for Windows accounts

Configure Windows file services on Mac OS X Server

Set up a Windows share point

Create a Windows computer list

Lesson **11**

Administering Windows User Accounts

Account management is not confined to Mac OS X accounts. Mac OS X Server can also host Windows accounts and home folders. While full manageability does not compare equally between the two types of accounts, a reasonable user experience for Windows users can remove the need for a Windows server in some situations. To provide home folders for Windows users, Mac OS X Server must be able to share folders (and/or volumes) over the default Windows sharing protocol, *Server Message Block* (SMB). Both Mac OS X and Mac OS X Server include Samba, the open-source alternative to Windows Server Message Block. This enables Mac OS X and Mac OS X Server to offer share points to Windows users. Before a share point can be accessed, authentication must take place. Mac OS X Server can authenticate users with various methods, including popular Windows methods such as NTLMv1, NTLMv2, Kerberos, and even LAN Manager for older Windows 95 clients. In this lesson, you will learn how to set up and manage Windows accounts, Windows share points, and Windows computer lists.

Unifying User Management Features

It is important to note the differences between Mac OS X accounts and Windows accounts, especially if Windows accounts are moved to a Mac OS X Server. For example, you must understand what Mac OS X Server offers in the way of security policies, how Windows users can be managed, how to configure a basic Windows account, and how to set up a Windows computer list. While you may routinely do all these things for Mac OS X users and Macintosh computers, Windows accounts and computers often represent a new challenge for Mac OS X administrators.

Comparing Security Policies

Mac OS X Server has various security policies when dealing with user accounts. Password policies can be user specific or global. User-specific policies will override global policies.

Here are the Mac OS X Server user authentication policies:

User Authentication Policies

GUI Password Policy Option	Usage	pwpolicy Command-line Equivalent
On Date	Disables an account on a set date, such as when a contractor is set to leave a job site	usingExpirationDate usingHardExpirationDate expirationDateGMT hardExpireDateGMT
After a set number of days	Disables an account after a set number of days, such as when a student has access for the number of days in a grading period	maxMinutesUntilDisabled
After a period of inactivity	Disables an account after the user doesn't log in for a set number of days, such as when a user stops using a particular file server	maxminutesOfNonUse

GUI Password Policy Option	Usage	pwpolicy Command-line Equivalent
After a set number of failed login attempts	Disables an account after a user or hacker attempts to enter incorrect information a set number of times	maxFailedLoginAttempts
Length Policy	Dictates that a password must be at least a set number of characters long	minChars
Letter Policy	Requires a password to contain at least one letter	requiresAlpha
Numeric character policy	Requires a password to contain at least one numeric character	requiresNumeric
Account name policy	Requires the password to be different from the account name	passwordCannotBeName
Reused passwords policy	Requires a password to be different from previous passwords	usingHistory
Password change policy	Requires a password to be changed after a set number of days, weeks, or months	maxMinutesUntilChangePassword
Be reset on first user login	Require a new password at next logon	newPasswordRequired
Allow the user to change the password (in WGM)	Allows the user to change their password	canModifyPasswordSelf
(No GUI equivalent)	Requires a password to have both upper- and lowercase letters	requiresMixedCase

Almost all these policies can be accessed via the Server Admin tool, under the Open Directory service.

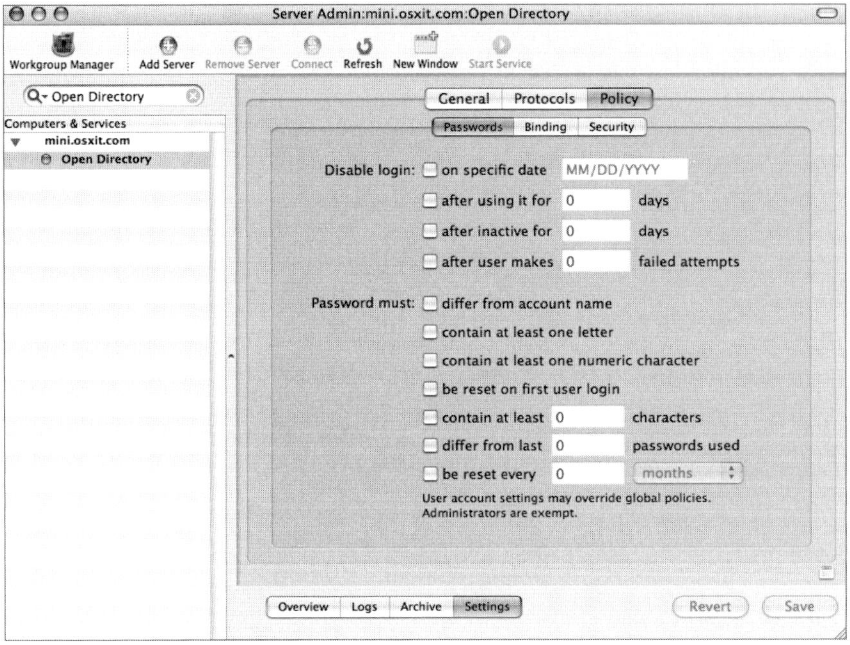

You can also manage password policies on Mac OS X without a connection to Mac OS X Server. You do this by using the pwpolicy command from Terminal. Before you can see all the policies, you must actually set a policy.

To set the policy of requiring a minimum of eight characters for a user's password:

1. Enter the following command in Terminal on Mac OS X:

   ```
   pwpolicy -n /NetInfo/DefaultLocalNode -a davedoug -setglobalpolicy minChars=8
   ```

2. Enter your password when asked. You now can enter the command

   ```
   pwpolicy -n /NetInfo/DefaultLocalNode -getglobalpolicy
   ```

which returns this result:

```
usingHistory=0 canModifyPasswordforSelf=1 usingExpirationDate=0 usingHardExpirationDate=0
requiresAlpha=0 requiresNumeric=0 expirationDateGMT=12/31/69 hardExpireDateGMT=12/31/69
maxMinutesUntilChangePassword=0 maxMinutesUntilDisabled=0 maxMinutesOfNonUse=0
maxFailedLoginAttempts=0 minChars=8 maxChars=0 passwordCannotBeName=0
requiresMixedCase=0 newPasswordRequired=0
```

Since there is no GUI for changing these parameters, you would use the command line to change them for local-only accounts.

Therefore, it is important to understand that both Mac OS X and Mac OS X Server have very similar security policies.

In contrast, Windows 2003 and Windows XP have the following password policies:

Policy	Security Setting
Enforce password history	0 passwords remem...
Maximum password age	42 days
Minimum password age	0 days
Minimum password length	0 characters
Password must meet complexity requirements	Disabled
Store password using reversible encryption for all users in the domain	Disabled

The one policy that is not clearly defined in the preceding image is "Password must meet complexity requirements." When this option is enabled, the password must meet the following criteria:

- It must not contain all or part of the user's account name.
- It must be at least six characters in length.
- It must contain characters from three of the following four categories:
  - English uppercase characters (A through Z)
  - English lowercase characters (a through z)
  - Base 10 digits (0 through 9)
  - Non-alphanumeric characters (!, $, #, %)

When considering whether to create accounts that will be accessed from computers running Windows, the focus is not on local account password policies but on those policies residing on Mac OS X Server. As you can see, password policies vary slightly from system to system, but the basic objective of forcing a user to create a better password remains the same on both systems.

Configuring Windows Accounts

A Windows account is configured much like a Mac OS X account. One main difference is the Windows tab for each user.

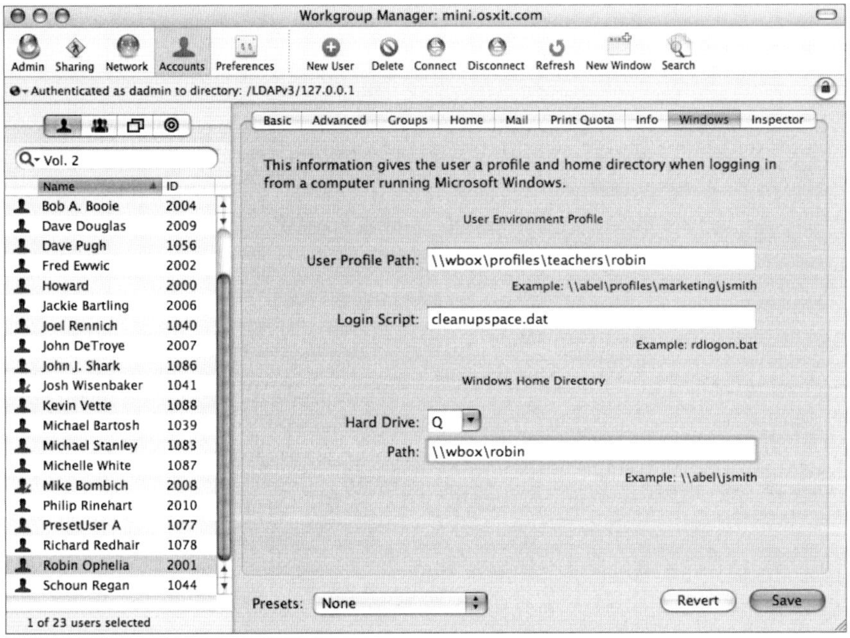

The following entries (all of which are generally entered under a user's profile tab of Active Directory) can be used by users logging in from a Windows computer:

- User Profile Path—the location of the user's profile setting
- Login script, if used
- Hard drive letter—the letter that appears when the user has a home directory
- Path—the path to the user's home directory

When created, the OpenLDAP attribute names are

- homeDrive for the drive letter
- profilePath for the path to the user's profile
- scriptPath for the location and name of the login script
- smbHome for the location of the user's SMB home mount

The Open Directory attribute names are

- SMBHomeDrive for the drive letter
- SMBProfilePath for the path to the user's profile
- SMBScriptPath for the location and name of the login script
- SMBHome is the location of the user's SMB home mount

Assigning Login Scripts to Windows Accounts

A login script can be used to execute certain commands when the user logs in. This is done for Windows-related viruses and worms, or to remove cache or temporary files. Writing a Windows batch file is similar to writing a standard UNIX shell script, although the syntax is slightly different. Writing batch scripts is beyond the scope of this book, but be aware that you do have the ability to define the script that runs for a user, and you can change or rotate the scripts that run without informing that user.

Creating a Windows Computer List

The Windows computer list is used to let a Mac OS X Server that is acting as a Primary Domain Controller (PDC) know which computers are to be part of the domain, based on their NetBIOS names. Once a computer is added, it is given a unique ID and a shared Group ID. To add computers running Windows to the Windows computer list in Workgroup Manager, do the following:

1. Open and authenticate to Workgroup Manager.

2. From the domain pop-up menu, choose your LDAP domain.

3. Click the Accounts button in the Toolbar and then click the Computer tab.

4 Select the Windows computer list and click the Add (+) button to add a computer, filling out the fields as shown in the figure below.

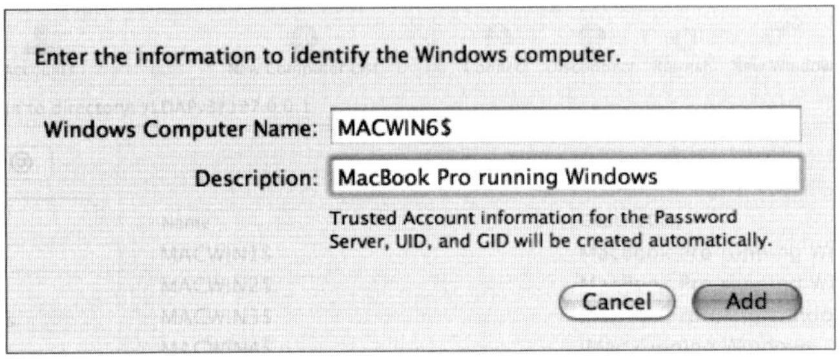

5 Enter the appropriate information, including adding a dollar sign ($) at the end of the computer name, and then click Add.

6 When you are finished entering all the computers, click Save.

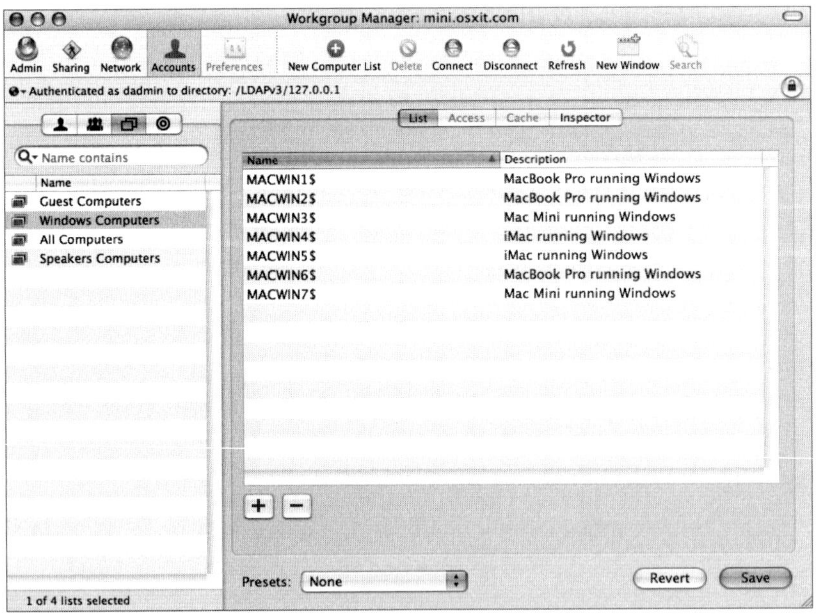

You must also enable Windows sharing and promote your Mac OS X Server to a PDC using the Server Admin utility to allow these computers to be part of the trusted domain.

Setting Up Home Folders and Share Points for Windows Accounts

Once the user accounts are set up and the Windows pane is filled out accordingly, you'll want to set up share points for Windows users to access. Before doing so, you should examine exactly what is involved in setting up a share point for Windows access.

Identifying Windows vs. Macintosh User Account Requirements

When dealing with Windows users, the requirements for a user experience similar to that of Mac OS X are varied. This is because each operating system handles restrictions and permissions in slightly different fashions. It is important to understand that Mac OS X does not contain all of the same attributes as Active Directory. You cannot expect Windows users to have the same user experience with an account that resides on Mac OS X Server compared to an account that resides on Microsoft Active Directory.

For example, Mac OS X Server uses a generated unique ID to identify every user, and Microsoft uses what is known as a Secure ID (SID). Mac OS X uses MCX information to control the user experience, while Microsoft controls the user experience differently. The basic requirements for both users are as follows:

- Long name
- Short name
- Password location and type
- Home directory location
- Home directory local mount point
- Unique value (UUID and SID)

Enabling SMB Services on Mac OS X Server

In order to plan and create share points that Windows users can access, you must use Server Admin to start the Windows SMB service and then use Workgroup Manager to enable the share points.

Before starting the Windows service, you should be aware of the ways in which Mac OS X Server can provide Windows services. Mac OS X Server can be a

- Standalone server, which just allows for file and print services.
- Domain member, which allows for file and print services and also permits the hosting of profiles and home directories. It does not provide authentication but defers that to another server. The Mac OS X Server must know about a PDC prior to becoming a domain member.
- PDC, which allows for file and print services, hosts profiles and home directories, and provides authentication services. The Mac OS X Server must be an Open Directory Master prior to becoming a PDC.
- Backup Domain Controller (BDC), which allows file and print services, hosts profiles and home directories, and is a backup for authentication services on the PDC. The Mac OS X Server must be an Open Directory Replica prior to becoming a BDC.

Each of those options is available in the Windows service Settings pane.

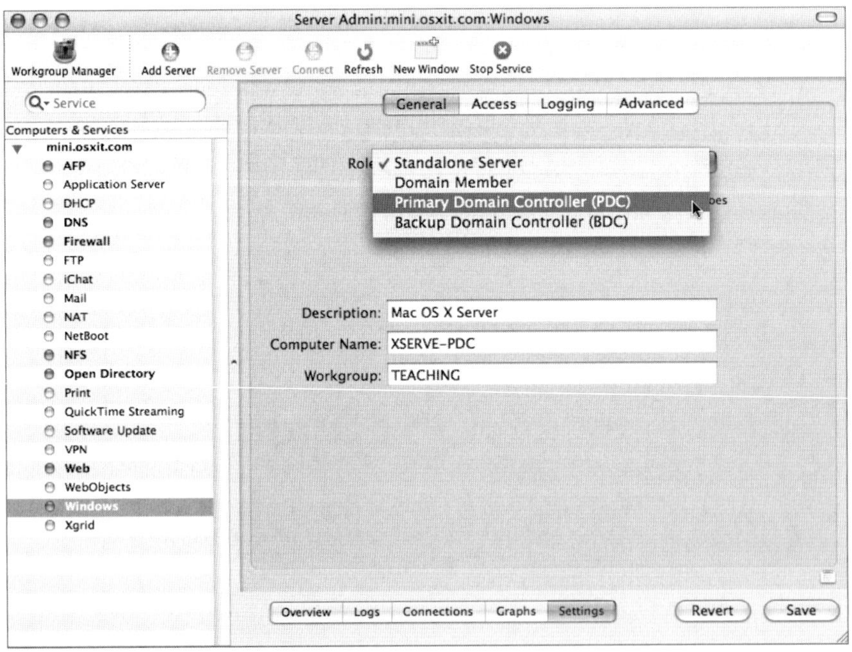

Addressing Security Policies with Windows Accounts

Once you choose a role for your server, you then can choose the authentication methods for your Windows computers. Older versions of Windows will require less secure authentication methods, while newer versions of Windows can take advantage of Kerberos. LAN-Manager is the authentication method used for Windows 95. Any version of Windows later than Windows 95 but prior to Windows 2000 uses NTLMv1. Starting with Windows 2000, NTLMv2 and Kerberos are used for authentication.

> **NOTE ►** It is important that you discuss the options surrounding the Windows service settings with your network administrator and Windows administrator. Mac OS X Server can overtake or conflict with settings on Windows servers, so careful planning and discussion should take place prior to enabling the Windows service on Mac OS X Server.

The choices to allow different authentication methods and to allow guest access are made in the Access pane.

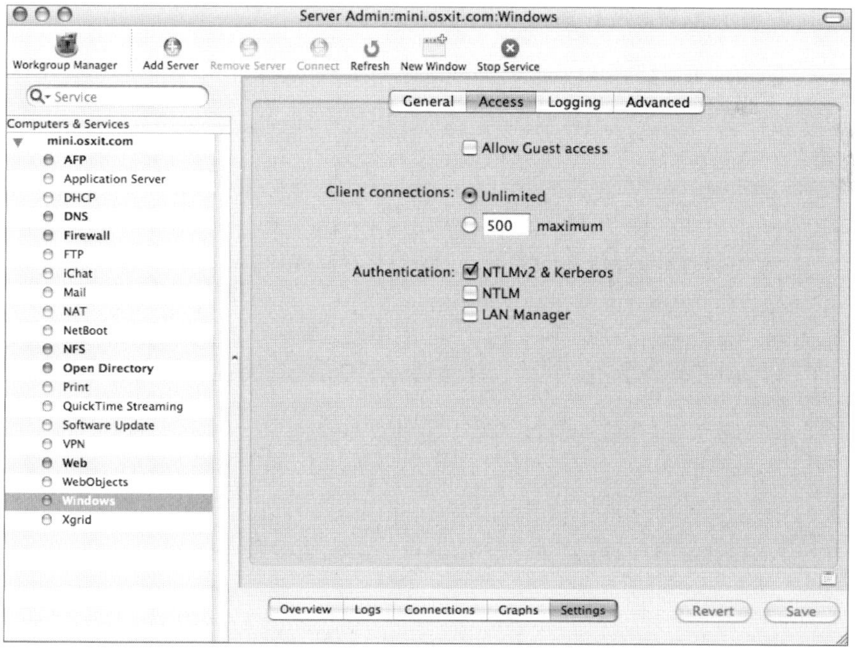

NOTE ▶ The authentication methods used when accessing share points over SMB should be similar to the global password policies established prior to creating Windows users. Keeping the authentication methods similar will reduce the chance of Windows users using insecure authentication methods.

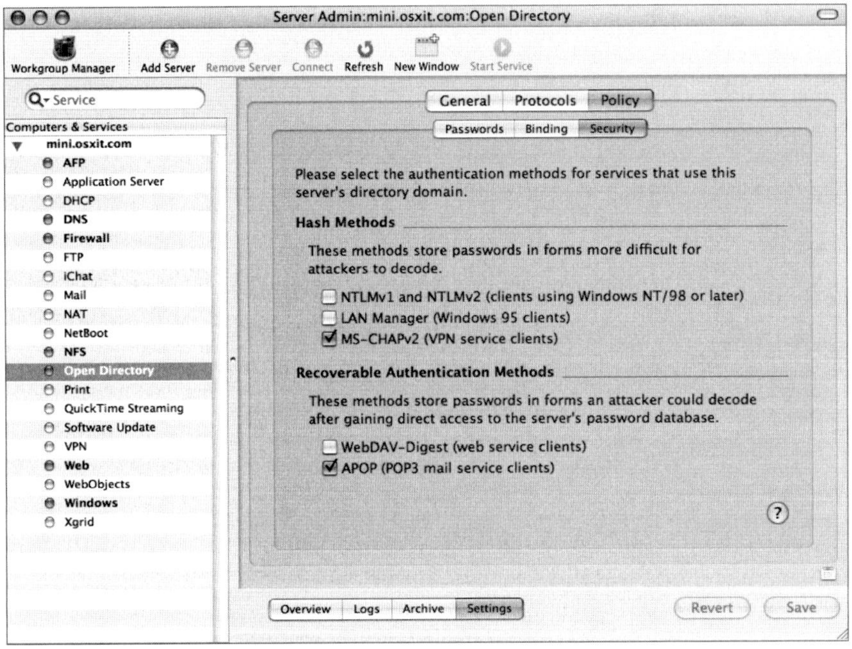

The Advanced pane of the Settings for Windows services should be viewed after the role for the server has been set. This is because certain roles will alter the possible settings in the Advanced pane. For example, choosing to make your server a PDC automatically will set it up as a Workgroup Master Browser and Domain Master Browser.

Other options include setting up the Mac OS X Server as a Windows Internet Naming Service (WINS) or connection to one. For more information on the various permutations possible, please refer to documentation from the Samba group at www.samba.org.

Enabling a Share Point Using SMB

Once the Windows service has been properly set up and started, you can choose which share points you want to enable with your Windows users. It is preferable to plan your share points in advance, to avoid having nested share points, which can lead to issues when users access those share points. It is also important to decide how your share points will be shared and which protocol will be used. Sharing a single share point over multiple protocols can lead to issues relating to access, especially when file-system access control is enabled.

Understanding SMB Permissions

When a share point is created, it is automatically enabled over three protocols: AFP, SMB, and FTP. The default SMB permissions for a share point are shown in the figure below.

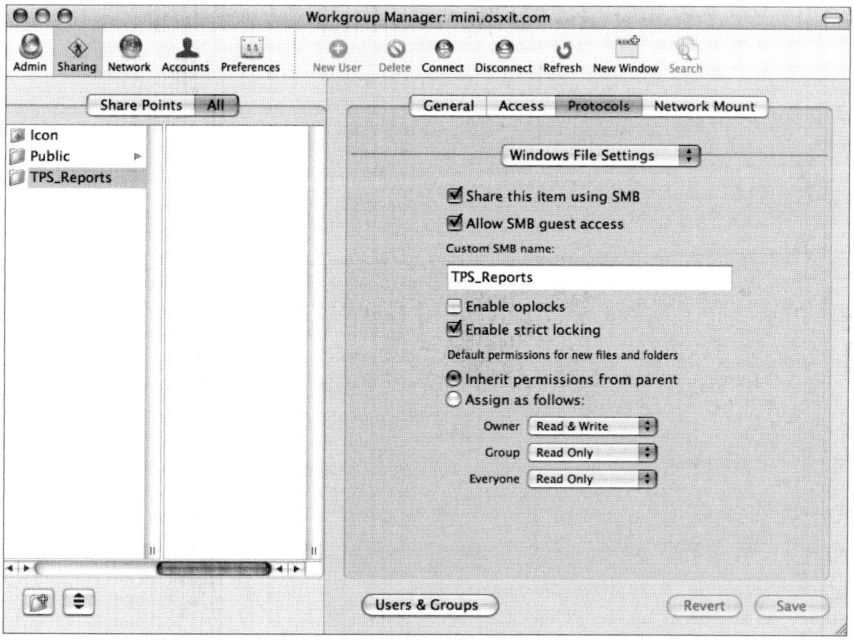

As you can see, guest access is on, and the share point is automatically shared. Even though guest access is on, if you have not allowed guest access via the entire Windows service, no one can connect as a guest. In other words, both check boxes must be checked to allow guest access.

You also have the option of changing the appearing name of the share point. The share point name could be TPS_Reports, as in the preceding figure, but could be renamed as Cover_Letter_Required, as in the figure below:

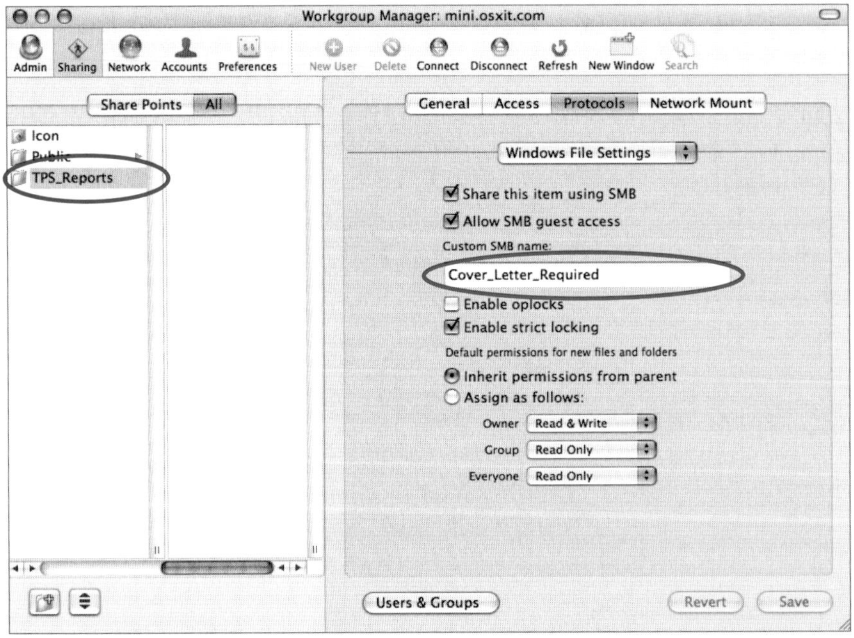

Make sure that you follow any changes you make by clicking the Save button to write the changes to the configuration file(s).

MORE INFO ▶ You can also use the sharing command-line tool to set up and manage share points on Mac OS X Server.

Using File Locking on SMB Share Points

Once a share point is enabled, the next step is to decide how to manage the permissions for that share point. SMB is not UNIX; therefore, the default permissions are slightly different. As seen in the preceding figure, the default SMB permissions for a share point are to inherit the permissions from the parent share point. You can change this to automatically assign permissions for the owner, the associated group, and everyone else.

You also have the option of setting file-system access controls, which further expand the options for the user. For more information on file-system access controls (ACLs), refer to *Apple Training Series: Mac OS X Server Essentials* and *Apple Training Series: Mac OS X System Administration Reference, Volume 1.*

Finally, you can enable locking on the share point. Locking prevents others from working with files opened by a specific user that are located inside the share point. The "Enable strict locking" box is selected by default and disallows simultaneous file access over varying protocols. The "Enable oplocks" option enables computers running Windows to ask Mac OS X Server if it can cache portions of the file on its local system. This feature is beneficial, as the Samba service running on Mac OS X Server is the one responsible for permitting access to the clients.

> **NOTE ▸** You should not enable oplocks if you are sharing over any protocol other than SMB.

Isolating and Resolving Windows Management Account Issues

Windows users who are having issues over their relationship with Mac OS X Server are likely to fall into a few main categories:

- The Windows service. Many issues can arise if a change has been made to the Windows (SMB) service. Make role changes sparingly, and if you are running a PDC and BDC scenario, treat the BDC as you would an Open Directory replica. That is, they are expendable and can be erased and set up again relatively quickly.

- Authentication. This can manifest as a result of a bad password or mistyped user name. Authentication issues can be tested if the user name(s) and password(s) are known to the administrator. Also, password policies may have the password about to expire, and the user may not be aware of an expired password.
- Poor user experience. It is possible that the user profile is corrupt or pointing to a different location, thereby negating any login scripts that may run. Rechecking the location of the profile and the path are excellent steps toward resolving this issue.
- Share points not showing up or are inaccessible. Provided the Windows service is operating normally and the user can authenticate, ownership and permissions discrepancies can thwart access to share points. Checking and rechecking the permissions and file-system access controls will help you to discover the anomaly. Should the share point still not be accessible, check service access controls in the Access pane of Server Admin to ensure that the appropriate group is allowed access over the Windows service, as seen below.

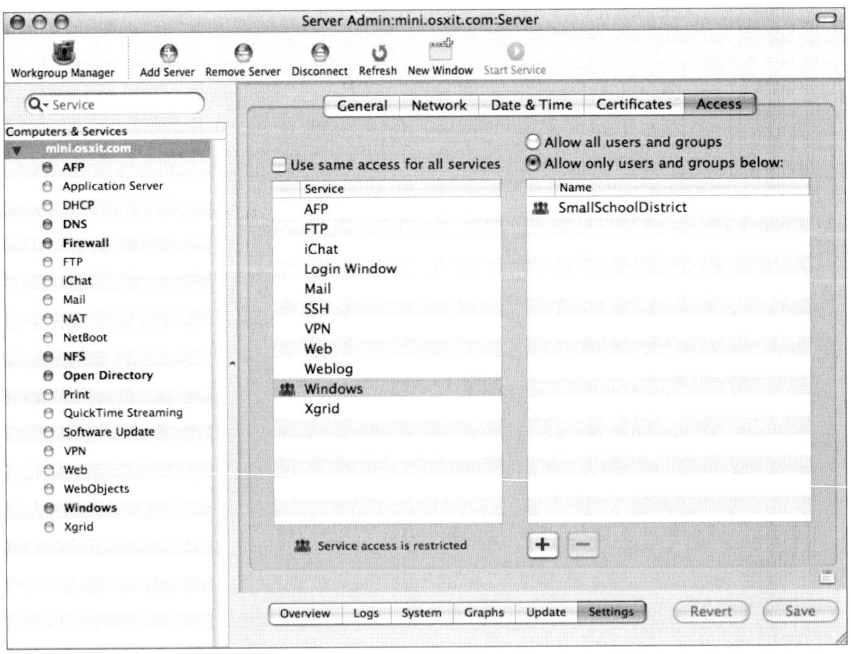

Exploring Network Home Folder Issues

Home folder issues can include any combination of the issues just listed and can be tested by attempting to create a new network connection to the Mac OS X Server using any other authorized computer running Windows, and viewing the Samba log files to examine the results.

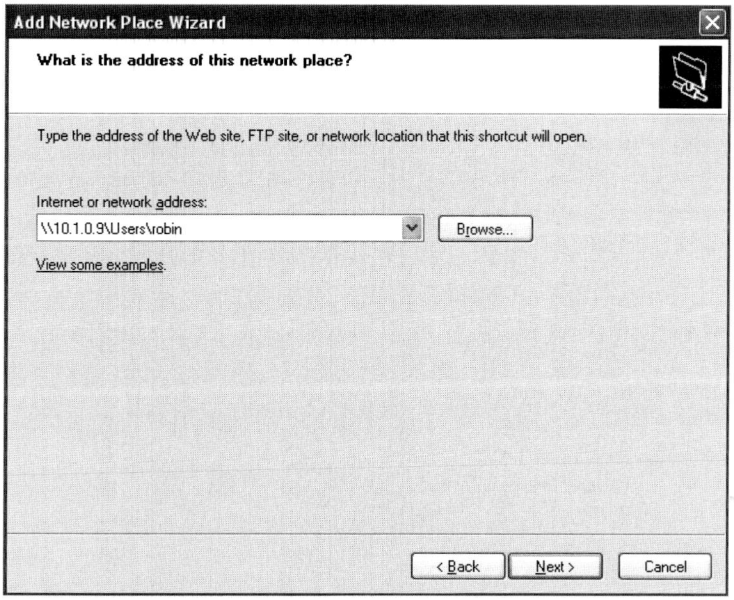

Finally, many additional options that can change the user experience when accessing share points on Mac OS X Server are offered via Samba. These can be examined in the Samba configuration file, which is called smb.conf and located in /etc/.

Managing Remote Windows User Environments

Another aspect of managing computers is running Windows remote access. Remote access can be enabled for Mac OS X computers using Apple Remote Desktop (ARD). As you will learn in Lesson 13, "Using Apple Remote Desktop," many capabilities include taking control of the keyboard and mouse of a remote computer, while allowing you to see the screen and control the computer as if you were sitting in front of that remote computer. It is also possible to use ARD to control a computer running Windows, thereby removing any instances of remote management of computers running Windows.

To control a computer running Windows with ARD, simply open the Remote Desktop administration application and add the Windows computer via the IP address. Prior to opening the Remote Desktop administration software, you should install OpenVNC (Virtual Network Client) software (or something similar that can access information over port 5900 (and port 5800 for Java applications that work with OpenVNC). It is also possible that the VNC software is incompatible with the Remote Desktop administration software. When choosing the computer running Windows from the list of available computers, you may receive a message saying that the software on the computer running Windows is not compatible with the keystroke encryption used with Remote Desktop. You have the options of tunneling the traffic over SSH if you wish.

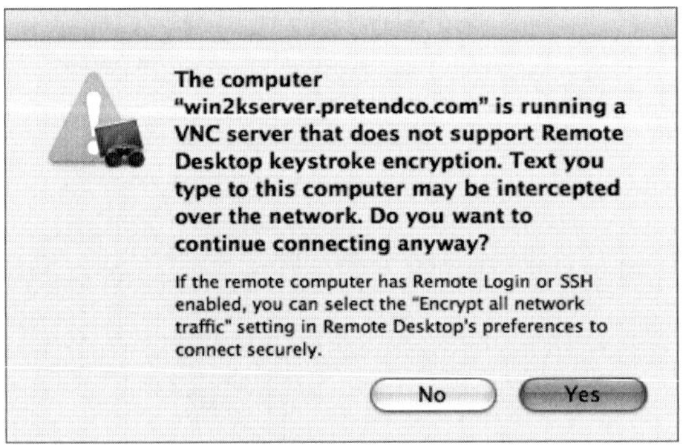

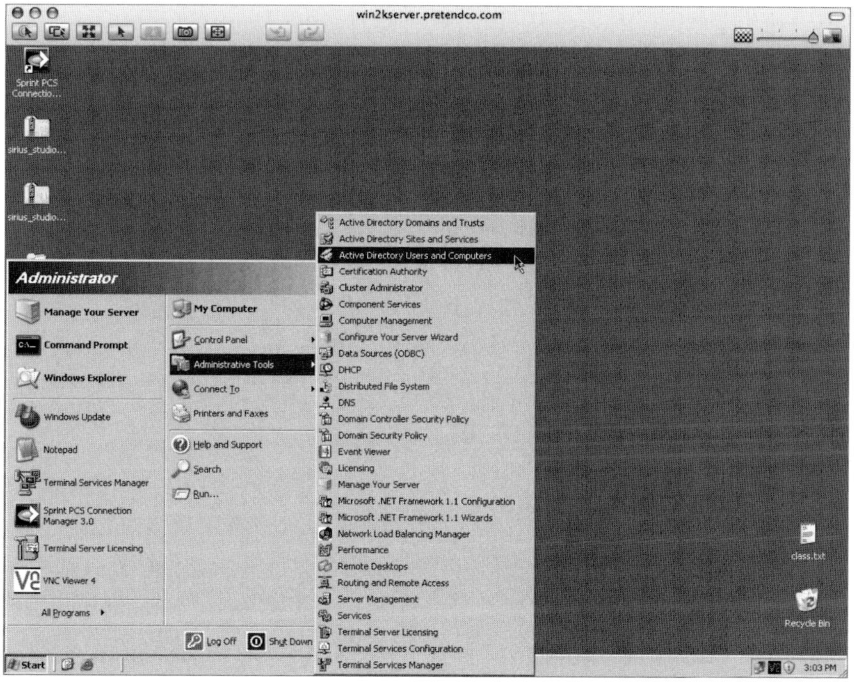

Controlling a computer running Windows via ARD

Lesson Review

1. What service must be active for Windows users to connect to Mac OS X Server share points?
2. Once a folder is shared, does SMB sharing need to be activated for that share point?
3. How do you set password policies for users logging in from computers running Windows?
4. What is an early step when attempting to troubleshoot why a home folder is not accessible for a Windows user?
5. What should be done prior to enabling your Mac OS X Server as a Primary Domain Controller?

Answers

1. The Windows service known as Samba, which is activated via the Server Admin tool.
2. No. Mac OS X Server automatically shares all share points over the following three protocols: AFP, SMB, and FTP.
3. Global policies are set in the Security pane of the Open Directory service with Server Admin. Per-user policies are set by selecting the user in Workgroup Manager and clicking the Options button in the Advanced pane.
4. Have the user attempt to mount the home folder manually via Windows.
5. To avoid any possible conflicts, check with your Windows administrator to ensure there is not another Primary Domain Controller on the network.

References

Administration Guides

"Mac OS X Server Windows Services Administration": http://images.apple.com/server/pdfs/Windows_Services_v10.4.pdf

"Mac OS X Server File Services Administration": http://images.apple.com/server/pdfs/File_Services_v10.4.pdf

Knowledge Base Articles

You can check for new and updated articles in the AppleCare Knowledge Base, at www.apple.com/support.

"Mac OS X Server 10.4: Windows users cannot modify ACL permissions on the server": http://docs.info.apple.com/article.html?artnum=301310

"Microsoft Windows users get an error when transferring certain files from a Mac OS X share point": http://docs.info.apple.com/article.html?artnum=301956

File Locking with SMB/CIFS Share Points: http://docs.info.apple.com/article.html?path=ServerAdmin/10.4/en/c3wn36.html

URLs

Visit the following sites for more information:

AFP548.com: www.afp548.com

MacEnterprise.org: www.macenterprise.org

Samba: www.samba.org

12

Time This lesson takes about 1 hour to complete.

Goals Learn how network views differ from the existing network browser

Understand the objects that can be in a network view

Create, manage, and assign network views

Lesson **12**

Managing Network Views

Managed *network views* allow you to take complete control over what the Mac OS X computers see on your network when browsing for file servers. Managed network views can supplement or completely replace the network view on each client machine. In addition, by controlling which machines are shown on a managed computer, you can also create a hierarchy of servers, in which you can group together similar servers into a network neighborhood, which just looks like a folder on the client machine.

Throughout this lesson, you'll learn about the different ways to configure a network view to create a custom list displayed to users browsing your network. By using network views, you can divide your flat view into a well-organized hierarchy.

Examining Flat and Managed Views

You can use the Mac OS X Finder to discover shared network file servers without knowing the names of the servers. This is referred to as network browsing, and it can be accessed with two methods:

- Open a new Finder window and click the Network icon.
- Choose Go > Connect to Server, and then click the Browse button.

This view presents all of the file servers for your workgroup in one flat list with no hierarchy. In a small organization, this may be desirable due to its simplicity; but as your organization grows, you'll quickly find that this view grows out of control. In most cases, you'll just have one workgroup, and all of your computers will be listed in that one workgroup.

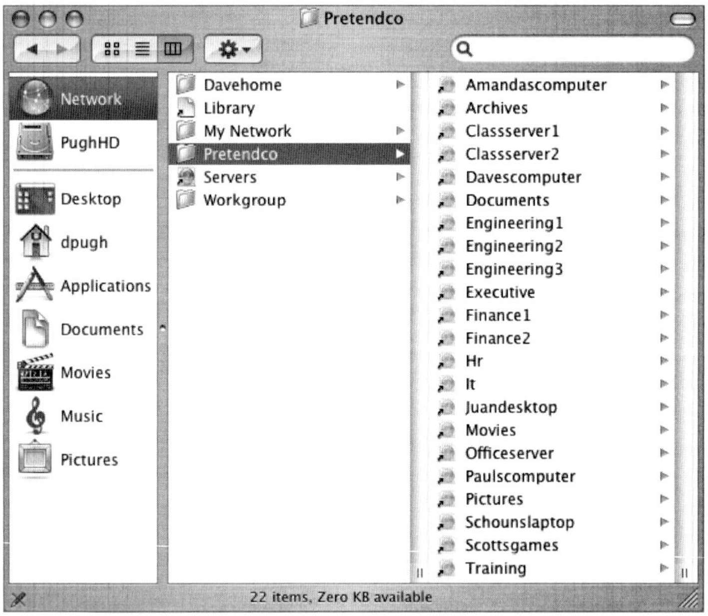

A flat view contains a list of all the AFP, SMB/CIFS/, and local NFS and FTP file servers that have elected to advertise their service. In an ideal world, you would see an accurate list reflecting all of the file servers that you need to access and none of the extra file servers that may be on your network. Unfortunately, flat network browsing isn't nearly that specific. In many cases, particularly if you have multiple subnets on your network, you may not see all of your file servers. In large organizations, you may see hundreds or thousands of servers, making it nearly impossible to find the one you're looking for in the list.

These are the problems that Apple has solved with managed network views.

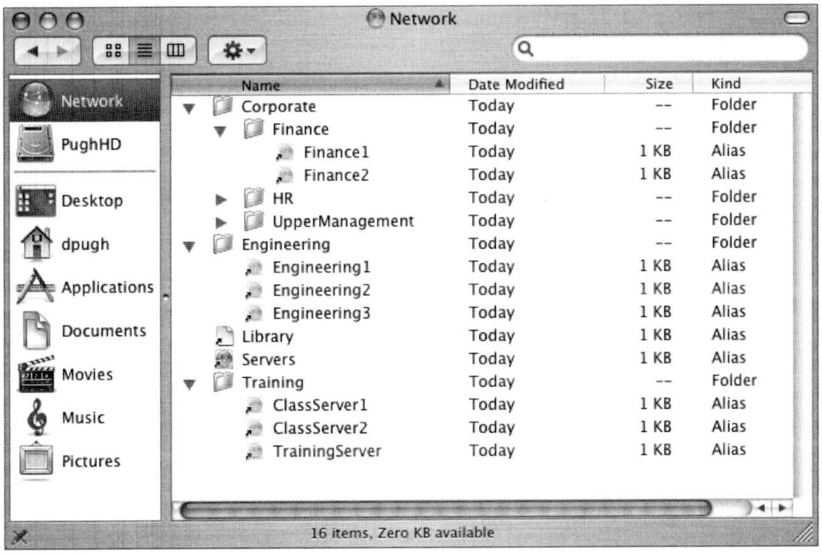

A more organized structure can be achieved through managed network views.

TIP As with many features of Workgroup Manager, you can also implement managed network views on your local computer without being connected to any directory service.

Planning Your Network View

The main advantage to using managed network views is that your clients can see a hierarchical view of your network resources rather than a flat view. Before implementing network views, you'll want to do some planning and organization. Here are some suggestions for tasks to do prior to creating your network views:

- Gather a list of all your network file servers and the URLs that clients use to access them, such as afp://fileserver.osxit.com/.

- Categorize all of your file servers into logical groupings. You may also wish to create groups of groupings.
- Categorize all of your client computers, and determine which groups of file servers should be shown to each group of client computers.
- Determine if you'd like your client machines to see only the network resources you list, or whether they should be able to browse to other network resources.

You may categorize some computers by the room they're in, by the skill level of their users, or by restrictions on what the users can do. Your organization might have hundreds of servers, but a given group of users might need to connect to only a few of those servers. You'll quickly discover that this is the case for most of your users.

Understanding Network Views

There are three types of network views:

- Named view
- Default view
- Public view

When a Mac OS X machine is turned on, it will search the directory servers for an appropriate network view in this order:

1. If there is a computer record present in the directory and it has a network view associated with it, the computer will use that network view.
2. Next, the computer will search every directory server in the search path (as defined in Directory Access) for a Named view that matches the computer.
3. If there is still no network view available, the computer will search every directory server in the search path for a view named Default.
4. Failing that, the computer will search through every directory server it knows about, including those not found in the Directory Access search path, for a view named Public. Each one it finds will be displayed in a folder named after the server.
5. If no Public views are found on the directory servers, the computer will search for views named Default on all of the directory servers, including those not found in the search path. Each one it finds will be displayed in a folder named after the server.

If all of these efforts fail, the computer will default to its original flat view.

Matching Named Views

When searching for a matching Named view, the client computer will search for each of the following, in this order, until a match is found:

1. A view whose name matches the *Ethernet MAC address* of this computer.
2. A view whose name matches the *IP address* of this computer.
3. A view whose name contains a *subnet* description that contains this computer.

   Subnet descriptions are in standard CIDR notation, such as 192.168.15.0/24.

Understanding a Network View

Each network view can contain many objects consisting of three types of entries:

- *Neighborhood*—A neighborhood acts like a folder. It is simply a collection of other computers, dynamic lists, or even other neighborhoods.
- *Computer*—A computer is any computer on the network that accepts remote file service connections.
- *Dynamic List*—A dynamic list is a list of network resources generated dynamically on the server, based on the computers seen from a specific group of computers. The contents of a dynamic list will depend on the service discovery configuration of the server for AppleTalk, Bonjour, SLP, and SMB/CIFS discovery protocols.

Creating Network Views

You'll start by using Workgroup Manager to control network views.

1. Launch Workgroup Manager.
2. Connect to your directory server and authenticate.
3. At the top of the Workgroup Manager window, click the Network button.
4. Choose Server > New Network View, or click the New Network View button at the top of the Workgroup Manager window.

5 Select the type of network view you wish to make and click Create.

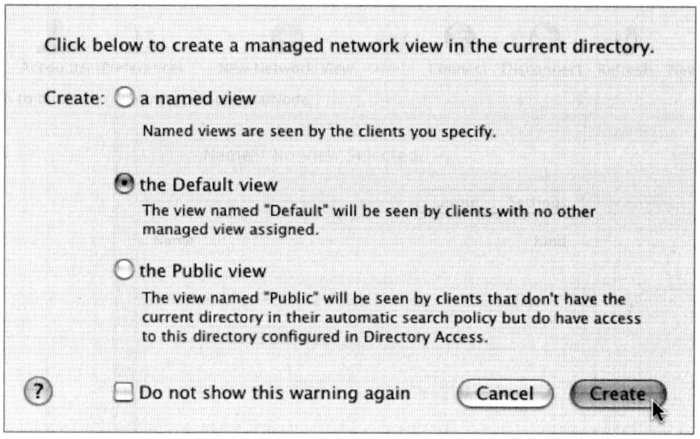

6 If you're creating a Named view (not a Default or Public view), type the name of the view. A Named view can have any name if you're assigning computers to it manually, or could have a special name in order to have computers matched to it automatically:

Matching Network Views

Type of Match	Example Network View Name
Ethernet MAC address	00:0d:93:09:21:02
IP address	192.168.15.165
Subnet	192.168.15.0/24

NOTE ▶ Do not set the name of a Named view to Default or Public, as it will behave as any Default or Public view would if you had chosen that type of view when creating it.

7 In the Layout pane, add objects that should be present in this view.

Adding a New Neighborhood

To add a new Neighborhood (folder) to your network view, choose New Neighborhood from the menu at the bottom of the window, and name it.

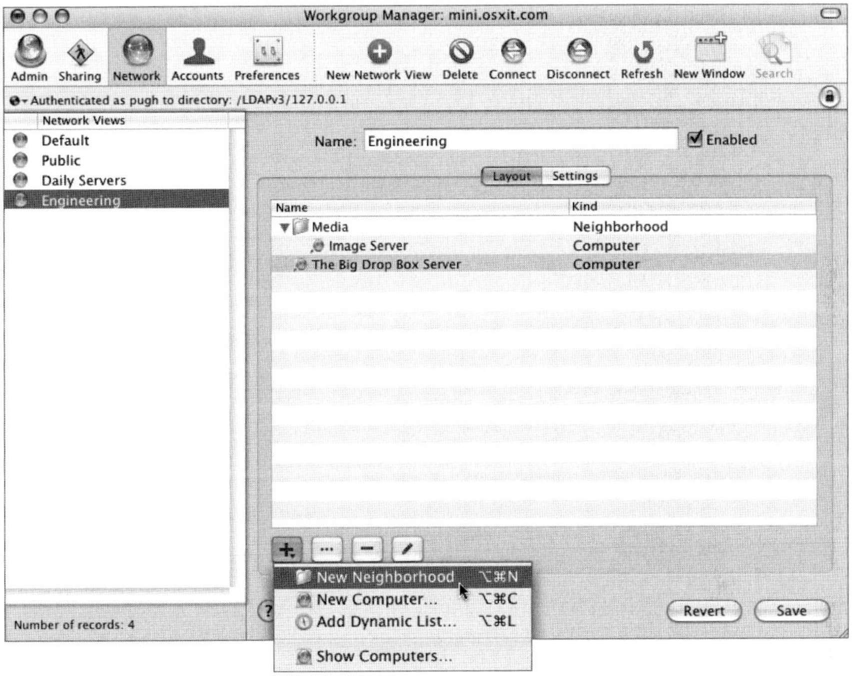

Adding a Computer

If the computer you wish to add to your network view has already been defined (such as in a computer list for managing preferences or for use in an existing network view), adding it to your view is simple.

1 From the Add (+) button menu, choose Show Computers to display the computer list drawer.

   It may take a few seconds to open the drawer if you have many computers defined in your directory.

2 Drag the computer into the layout.

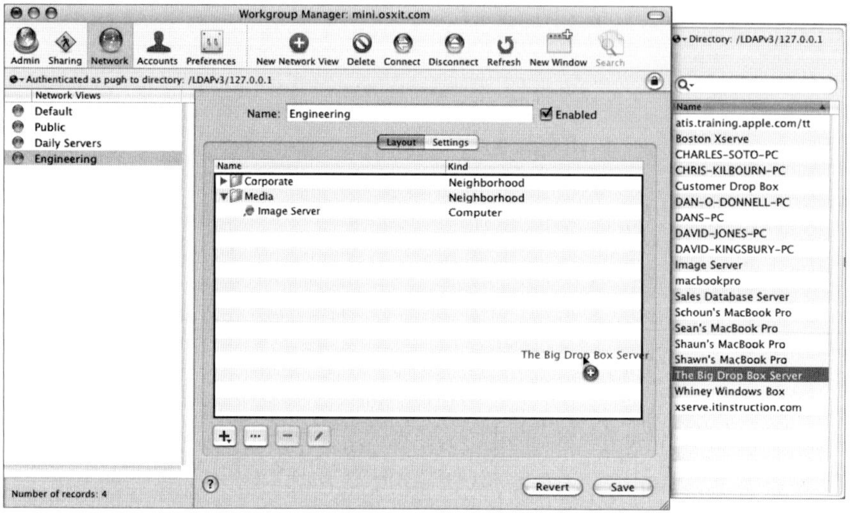

If the computer you wish to add isn't in the list, you can add a new computer.

1 From the Add (+) button menu, choose New Computer.

2 In the window that appears, type the name of the computer.

   This is a notable feature of using network views: You can type a more human-readable name for this network resource than the hostname that the user would normally see in a flat view.

3 Select the computer list (for managed preferences) to which this computer should be added.

4 Enter the Ethernet MAC address of this computer.

5 You can add this computer directly to a network view using the pop-up menu if desired, or add it later by dragging it from the computer list.

6 Enter all of the URLs you would like your users to use to access this computer.

7 If desired, you can click Show Options at the bottom of the window to reveal Comment and Keywords fields.

NOTE ▶ Be sure you aren't adding a computer that already exists in your directory. Workgroup Manager will allow this, but doing so will likely confuse many things after the computer has been added.

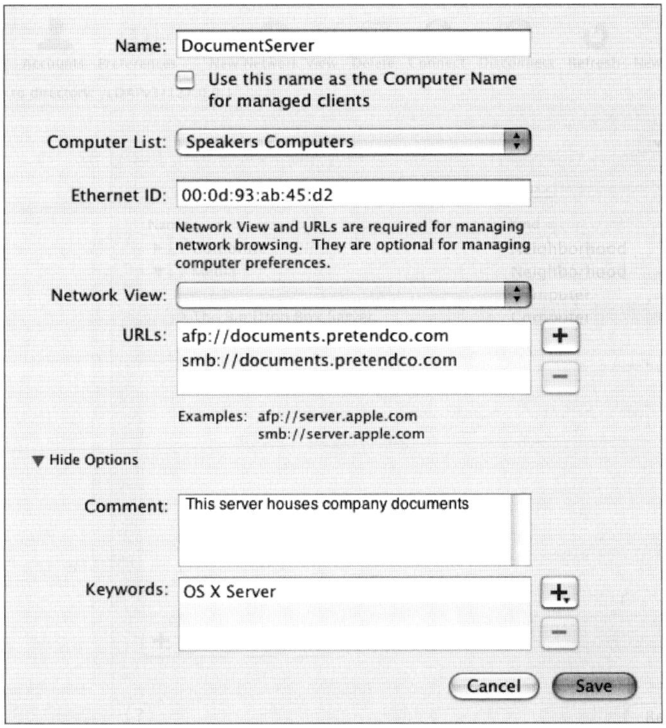

Adding a new computer to the computer list.

Last, if you have the ability to browse to the computer you wish to add to your view, you can click the Browse button (…) to browse for the computer. After you click Connect, the computer will be added to the computer list, if necessary, and to your view. As a shortcut, you also have your menu of recent and favorite servers at the top of the browsing window.

Adding a Dynamic List

If you wish to have your network view contain resources dynamically based on certain discovery protocols, you can add a dynamic list to your network view.

1 From the Add (+) button menu, choose Add Dynamic List.

2 Select all of the discovery protocols you wish to use. Press the Command or Shift key, and click to select multiple protocols. If a protocol is not in the list, you can configure it through Directory Access.

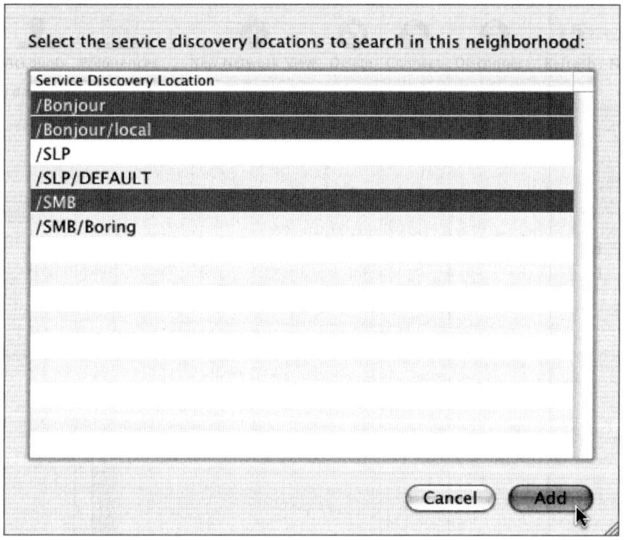

Configuring Clients to Use a Network View

After you've defined the layout of your network view, you need to tell the directory which clients should use it.

1 At the left of the Workgroup Manager window, select the network view.

2 Click the Settings tab.

3 In the Settings pane, click the Add (+) button and choose Show Computers to open the computer list drawer.

4 Drag each of the computers that should use this network view into the Clients list.

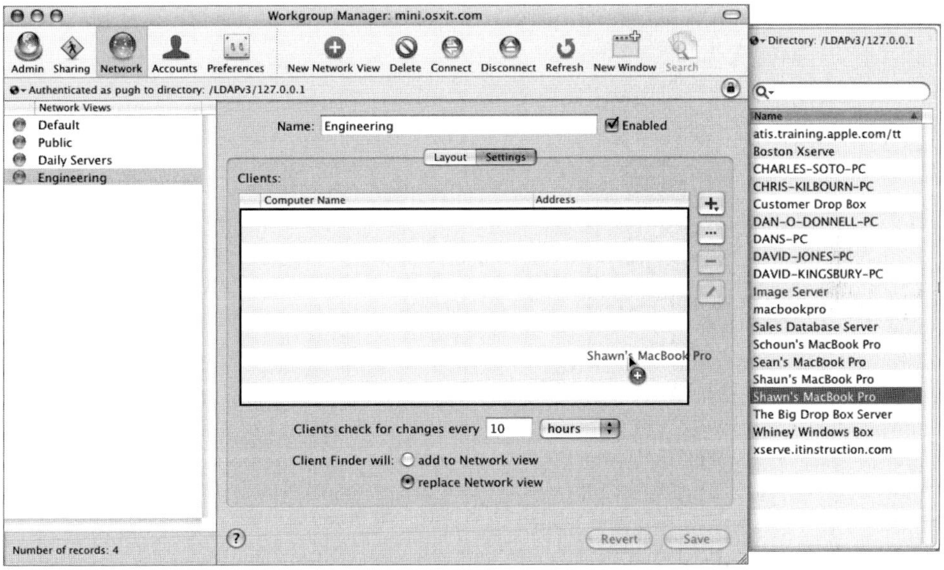

If a computer isn't available in the drawer, you can choose New Computer from the Add (+) button pop-up menu, or click the Browse (...) button to browse to the computer, in the same manner used to add new computers when defining the layout of the network view.

5 Select the interval at which a computer should check for updates to its managed view configuration. If your server configurations will remain relatively static, you can set this to a longer time period to reduce network traffic.

6 The last option to configure determines whether your network view is shown in addition to the client's normal network browser, or if it replaces it.

Renaming or Deleting a Network View

If you wish to rename a network view:

1. At the left of the Workgroup Manager window, select the network view that you wish to rename.
2. Change the name in the Name field.
3. Click the Save button.

Keep in mind that the names Default and Public have special meanings and should not be used as network view names unless you would like that network view to act as the Default or Public view for your domain.

If you'd like to delete a network view:

1. At the left of the Workgroup Manager window, select the network view that you wish to delete.
2. At the top of the window, click the Delete button.

   WARNING ▶ Deleting a network view cannot be undone, so use caution when deleting one. It may be wise to look through the Settings pane to see which clients are currently set to use that network view before deleting it.

Disabling a Network View

Instead of deleting a network view, you have the option to disable the view. This will cause clients to no longer use the view, but it will leave the network view and all of its settings on your server.

1. At the left of the Workgroup Manager window, select the network view that you wish to disable.
2. Next to the network view name in the Name field, uncheck the Enabled box.
3. Click Save.

If you wish to re-enable the view, simply check the same box again.

Modifying a Network View

You change any of your network views in the same ways that you configured the views.

1 At the left of the Workgroup Manager window, select the network view that you wish to disable.

2 Make any desired changes.

3 Click Save.

You can also edit any of the computer records by first selecting the computer in any of the lists and clicking the Pencil button. In this window, you can also change which network view this computer uses or which computer list this computer belongs to by selecting the desired items from the menus. This would be a quick technique when a computer is transferred to another employee in a different group.

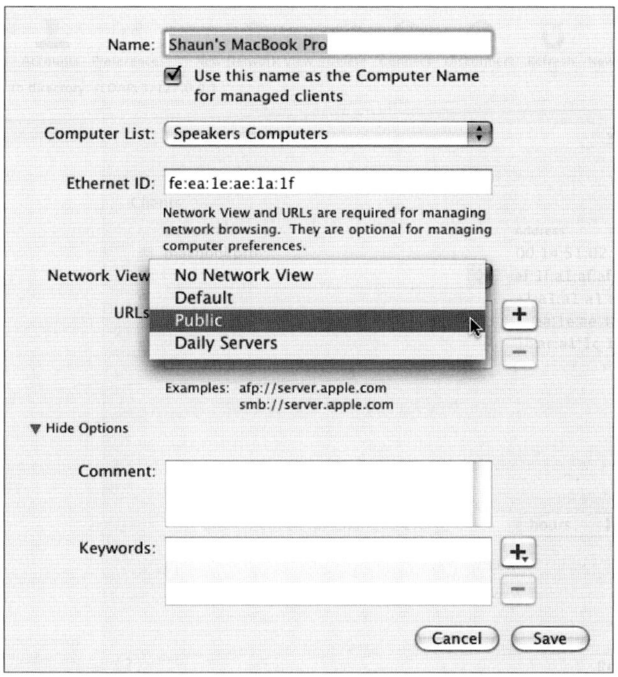

You can modify a network view to change parameters.

WARNING ► Use caution when making changes to a network view. If you select a computer, neighborhood, or dynamic list and press the Delete button at the top of the window, you'll actually be deleting the entire network view, which is irreversible.

Viewing the Results

Once your network views are configured, and after your client machines have rebooted, the Network icon in the Finder will use the network view configuration applicable to that computer. Below is a series of images that show what can be done with network views to organize what the user sees when browsing the network.

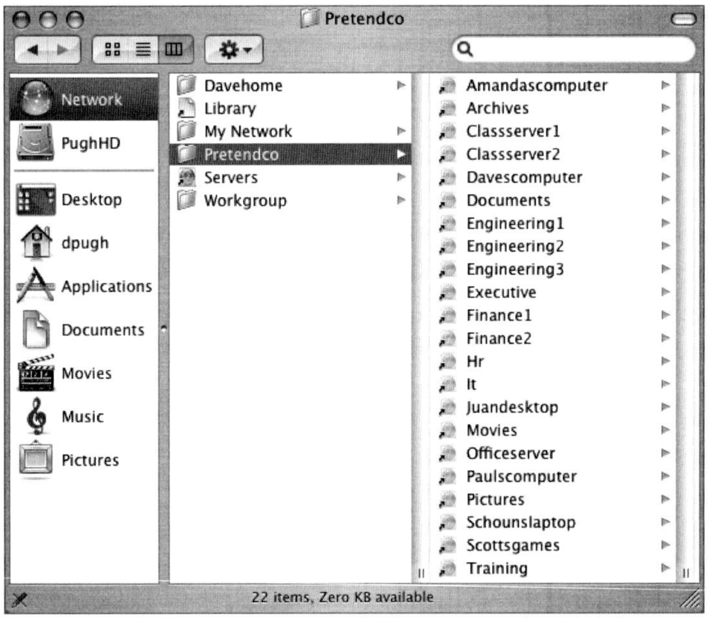

The original, flat network view.

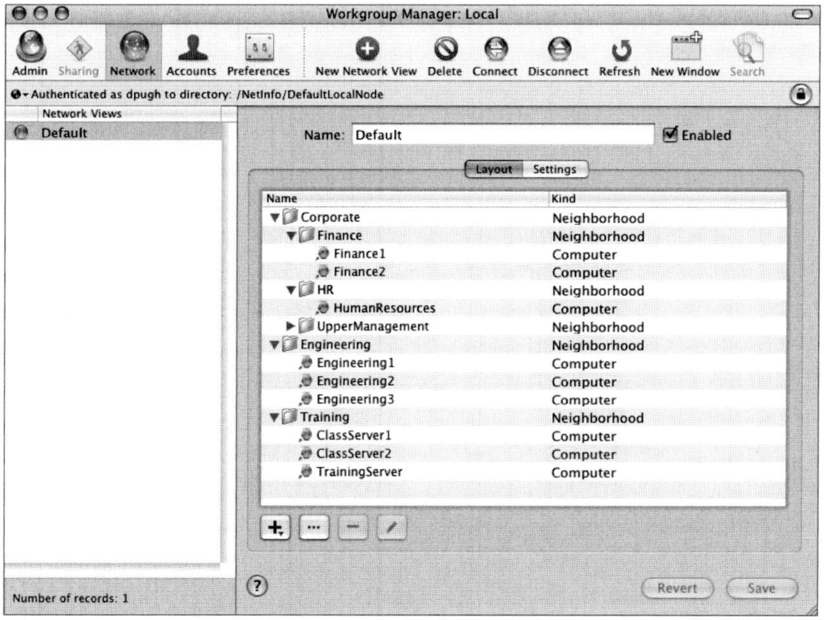

Using Workgroup Manager to create a new network view.

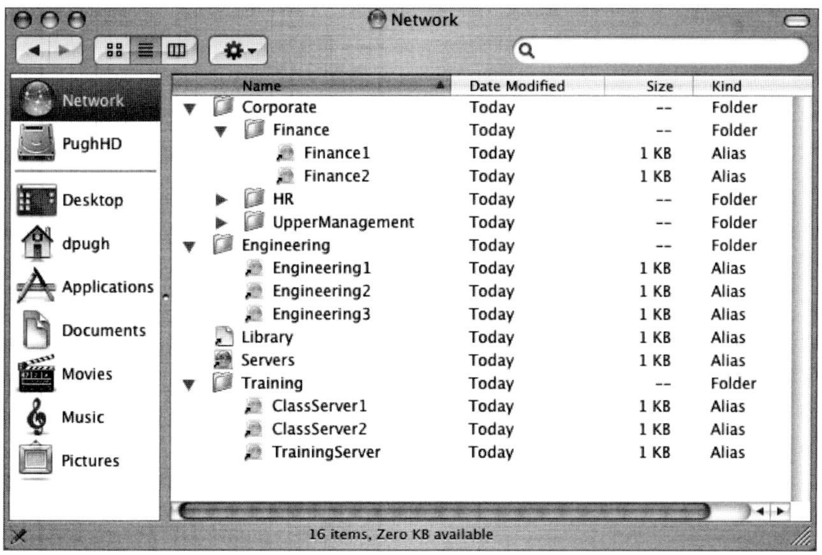

The resulting network view as seen on a client computer.

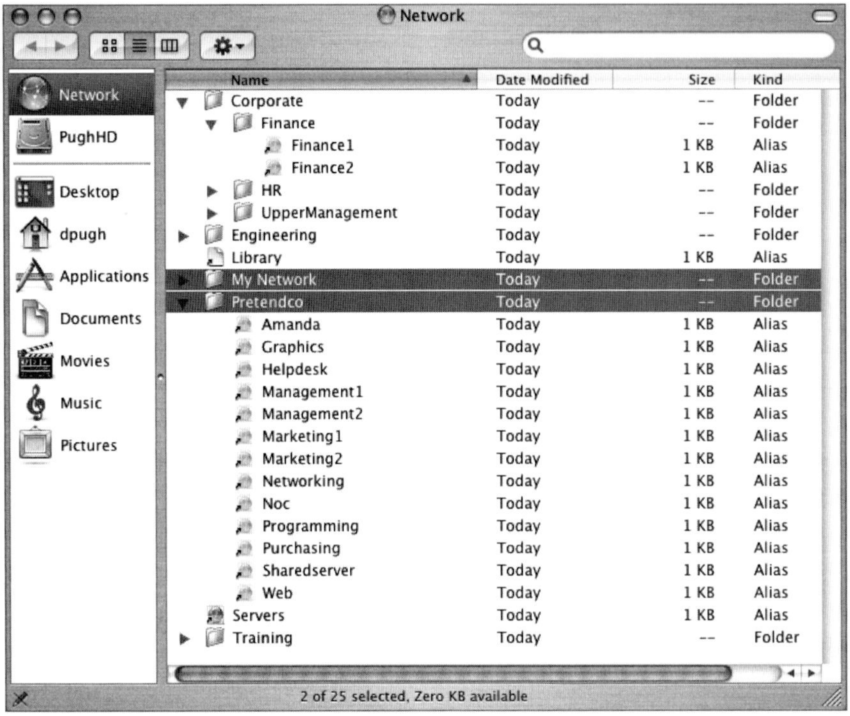

The same network view, but with "Add to Network view" having been selected instead of "Replace Network view." Notice the Pretendco workgroup that is present even though it wasn't defined in the network view.

Lesson Review

1. List the advantages of using managed network views over flat views.
2. What types of objects can appear in a network view?
3. List the special names for network views.

Answers

1. Managed network views are hierarchical and don't necessarily show every server that's available.
2. Neighborhoods, computers, dynamic lists.
3. Ethernet MAC address, IP address, Subnet, Public, Default.

References

Administration Guides

"Mac OS X Server User Management": http://images.apple.com/server/pdfs/User_Management_Admin_v10.4B.pdf

Apple Knowledge Base Documents

"About network browsing and connected servers in Mac OS X 10.3": http://docs.info.apple.com/article.html?artnum=107804

URLs

"Working with Managed Network Views": http://docs.info.apple.com/article.html?path=ServerAdmin/10.4/en/c8um.html

13

Time This lesson takes about 2 hours to complete.

Goals Install, configure, and enable Apple Remote Desktop (ARD)

Control and share screens using ARD

Manage computers using ARD

Use reports to manage your computer assets

Lesson **13**

Using Apple Remote Desktop

Apple Remote Desktop (ARD) is a versatile product that goes far beyond its well-known use of offering remote screen control. In addition to being able to control screens, you can observe screens, share screens, lock screens, gather reports, install software, run UNIX commands, and much more, all from your own workstation.

Although ARD is most commonly used in an enterprise environment for remote assistance, asset control, and computer maintenance, it is also a great tool for use in other environments. Educators use ARD in the classroom to lock everyone's screen, to monitor students' progress while working on a problem, and for displaying a solution on everyone's screen. Classrooms using Apple's NetBoot architecture benefit from ARD by simultaneously issuing startup disk selection and reboot commands to every classroom computer.

ARD has even found its way into the home. Parents can monitor a child's activity on another computer in the house, and individuals can assist a family member at a distant location in troubleshooting a computing problem.

ARD has a number of different uses no matter what type of user you are or how many computers you support. In this lesson, you'll learn how to effectively use ARD to assist both yourself and your users.

Installing ARD

ARD is composed of two pieces of software: the administrator utility and the client, or agent, software. The administrator utility is installed on one machine and controls all the clients. The client runs on every computer that will be controlled with ARD. The administrator utility, called Remote Desktop, must be purchased separately for each computer on which it will be installed. The client software is included with every Mac OS X installation since Mac OS X v10.3, but is disabled by default for security reasons. Additionally, you can install the ARD client software separately, as discussed later in this lesson.

As an option, you can also create a central task server. This computer must have a copy of the unlimited licensed administrator utility installed, and can act as a go-between for both installations and report gathering.

Installing the Administrator Utility

Installation of the administrator utility is a simple package installation. Find the RemoteDesktop.mpkg file and double-click it to install the program.

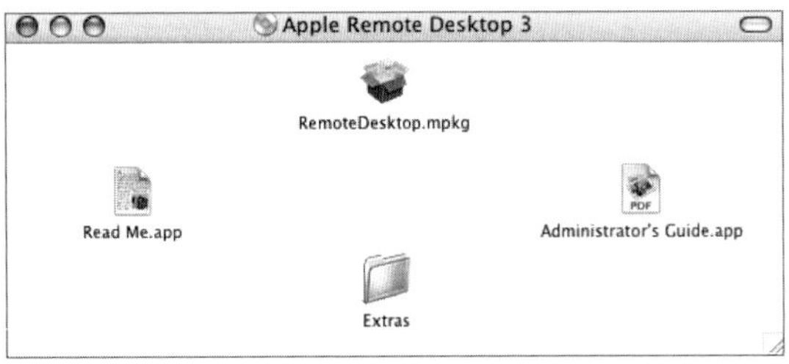

After it's installed, look in your Applications folder for the Remote Desktop application and double-click it to open the administrator utility.

Since the administrator utility is a licensed product, you will be asked to enter the serial number that came in the package. Each copy of the administrator utility will require a unique serial number. Certain features of ARD interact between installations on different systems and require that each system have a unique serial number to function. The main situation that requires this is using a central ARD task server, discussed later in this lesson.

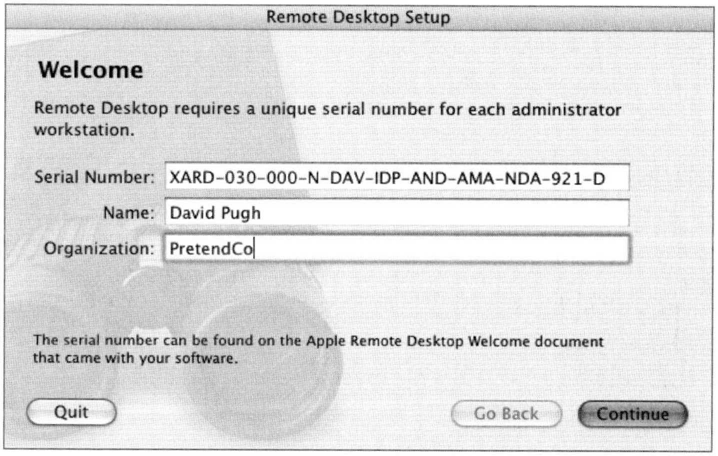

Next, you will be prompted for the password used to encrypt your client database. To perform actions on each of the clients, the administrator utility needs to know the username and password that will be used to access each of your clients.

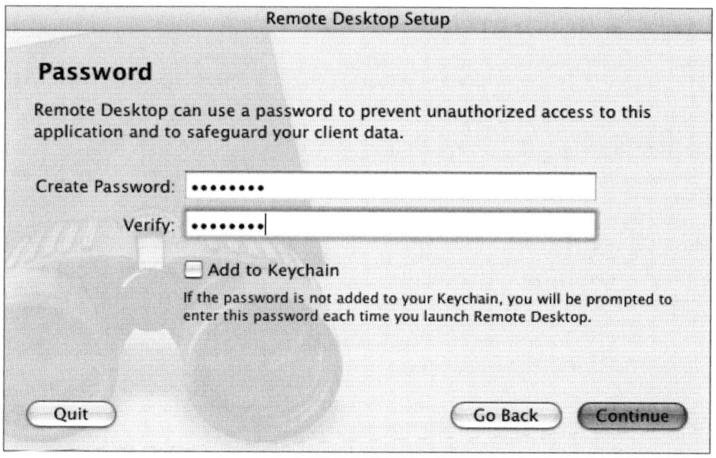

These usernames and passwords are stored locally on the Mac that is running the administrator utility. Since this list includes every one of your computers and its associated username and password, you'll want to keep it secured with a strong password. Although you can add this password to your keychain, you may not want to do so unless you're adding it to a secure keychain that locks itself quickly.

The next window asks if you wish to use a remote task server. If you already have a task server set up, enter its information now, otherwise just leave it blank and click Continue. If you set up a task server later, you can change this setting in the Remote Desktop preferences.

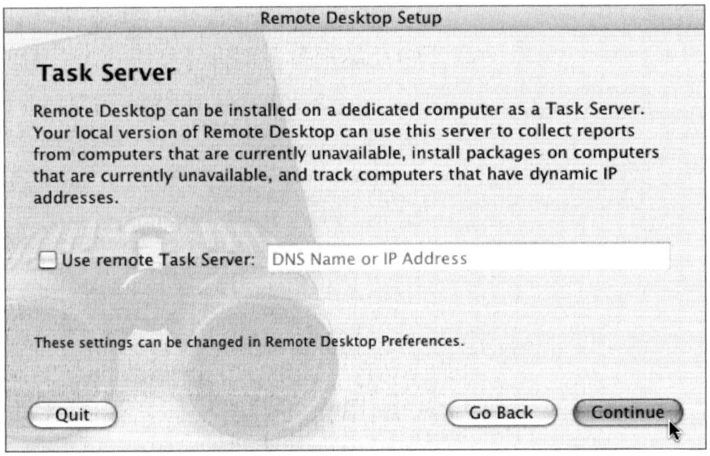

You can leave the Use remote Task Server field blank and enter the information later.

The final screen you'll see during initial setup of the administrator utility allows you to choose what information should be gathered on your clients.

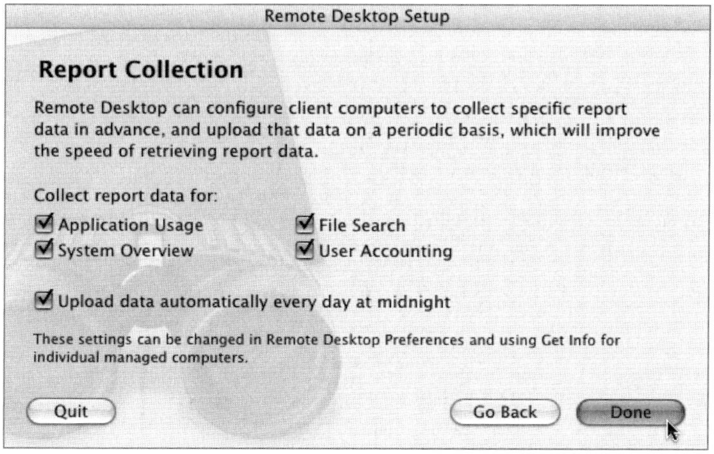

These settings will be sent to each ARD client when you configure it. This will speed up report generation by having the data already collected on the client and, if selected, will have already uploaded the data to your administrator client (or your task server) every night. This last option carries the added benefit of giving you access to reporting data whether the ARD client is turned on or off on your network. These settings are just the defaults assigned to new clients. You can change these settings for each individual computer later if you'd like.

Enabling the Client

The ARD client is pre-installed on every Mac OS X system since v10.3. In most cases, all you need to do is turn it on. This is can be done in the Sharing preferences, or by using the command line.

1 Open System Preferences.

2 Click the Sharing icon.

3 In the Services list, choose Apple Remote Desktop.

4 Click the Access Privileges button.

5 Select the checkbox next to the name of each user that you want to have access via ARD.

6 After enabling the user, select the types of access you want to assign to each user.

7 Click OK.

8 In the Sharing preferences, click the Start button to turn on Remote Desktop Control.

NOTE ▶ You can configure multiple ARD-specific user accounts, each with its own access privileges, so that different ARD administrators can have different levels of access.

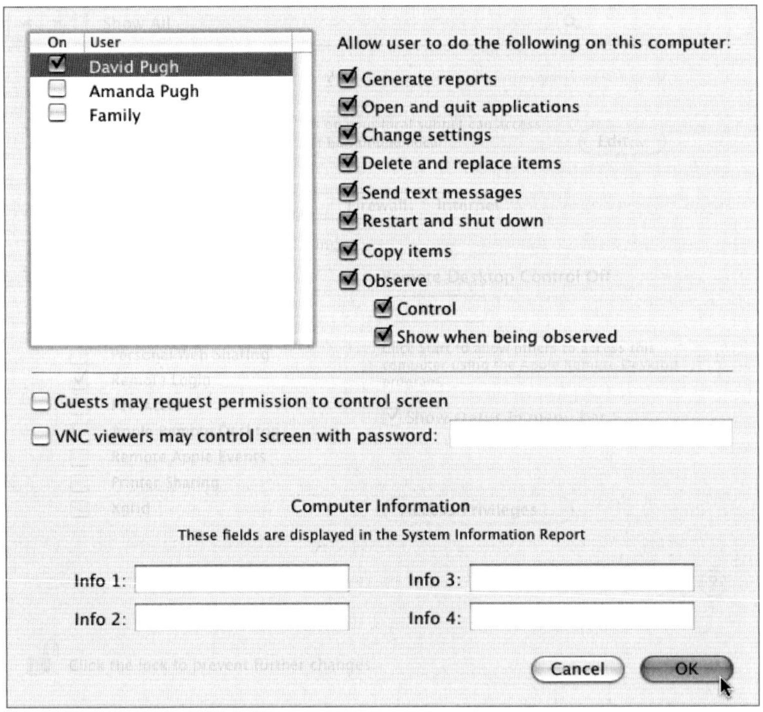

Enabling all the options for a user who will be remotely managing this Mac.

TIP If a user will have all ARD privileges enabled, you can save time by pressing the Option key while enabling that user. This will automatically check all privileges.

Virtual Network Computing (VNC) is a widely used remote screen control protocol. ARD includes support for this open standard. When configuring the ARD client through System Preferences, you have the option to indicate that VNC viewers may control your screen. You should only do this if you have non-ARD computers controlling this computer. VNC is less secure than native ARD because only one password controls access for everyone. If you have Windows or other UNIX machines, VNC might be a good option for your screen control needs.

There are also Mac OS X versions of VNC available if you wish to use VNC from another Macintosh. This is a free option for those Mac users who want screen control capabilities but don't need any of the other features of ARD.

If you aren't sitting in front of the client and you have remote login (SSH) access to that client, you can also enable ARD from the command-line using the `kickstart` command. A typical usage is:

```
sudo /System/Library/CoreServices/RemoteManagement/ARDAgent.app/Contents/Resources/kickstart -
activate -configure -access -on -users dave -privs -all -restart -agent -menu
```

This command configures the ARD client to allow the user, whose shortname is "dave", to connect via ARD with full privileges, and restarts the ARD agent and Menu Extra.

More information on the `kickstart` command can be found in Apple Knowledge Base article #108030, or by typing:

```
sudo /System/Library/CoreServices/RemoteManagement/ARDAgent.app/Contents/Resources/kickstart -h
```

An account is enabled for ARD access through the presence of the "naprivs" key in their account record. The numeric value associated with it determines what types of ARD access that user has.

One last method for configuring the ARD client is to use a Client Installer package. This is particularly useful as a quick alternative to guiding users through the configuration procedures over the phone. This option creates a normal Apple installation package that the user can double-click to install and configure the ARD client. Creating this package is a simple task accomplished by going through an Installer-like process.

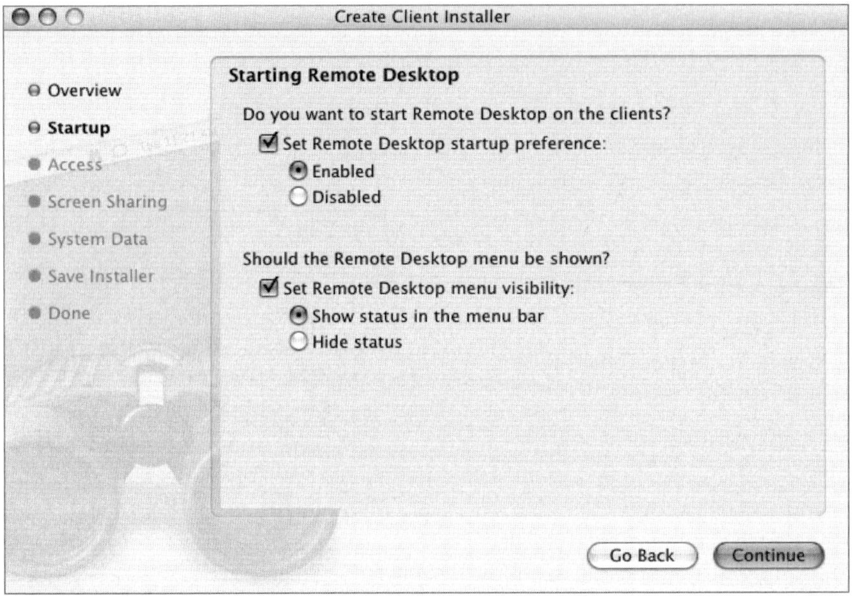

1 Run the Remote Desktop Admin utility.

2 Choose File > Create Client Installer.

3 When asked, "Would you like to Customize?", select Yes.

4 Select "Set Remote Desktop startup preference", and select Enabled.

5 Decide if you want to Set Remote Desktop menu visibility in the menu bar, then click Continue.

6 If you want the package to create a new user that will be given ARD access, select Yes to create users on the next screen. If you'll be using an existing user on the target system, just click Continue.

7 When asked "Do you want to set access privileges for local users?", select "Yes, specify access privileges."

   The option at the top of this window to "Enable directory-based administration" refers to using groups stored on a centralized Open Directory server. This will be described in "Giving Network Users ARD Access" later in this lesson.

8 On the resulting screen, add any users you desire and indicate the privileges they should have.

9 Select the options to Set request permission and Set VNC viewer access to Not allowed (unless you specifically want to enable those options).

10 You can leave the System Data fields blank unless your organization uses them for reports.

   The System Data fields are just blank text fields that you can fill in with whatever information you like. This could include the department this computer is used by, the physical location of the room, an asset tag number, or any other non-system data you'd like to see in your reports.

11 Click Continue to save the new package.

A new package called Custom Remote Desktop Installer.mpkg will be saved on your Desktop. You can send this to your users via email, by burning it on a CD, or by using any other package distribution method. If sending the metapackage over email or iChat, you will probably want to compress the package first by Control-clicking it and choosing Create Archive of "Custom Remote Desktop Installer.mpkg". This will compress the entire metapackage into a single zip file.

If SSH is enabled on your clients, you can copy the entire package to a remote machine with the command:

```
scp -r ~/Desktop/Custom\ Remote\ Desktop\ Installer.mpkg remote.hostname:/tmp
```

You can then SSH to the other machine and install it using the command:

```
sudo installer -pkg /tmp/Custom\ Remote\ Desktop\ Installer.mpkg -target /
```

> **NOTE ▶** ARD must match major version numbers between the administrator utility and the client. For example, ARD 3 can only be used to manage ARD 3 clients. If you have older clients on your network, you can choose Manage > Upgrade Client Software on all your older clients to upgrade them at once.

Giving Network Users ARD Access

If your computers are all bound to the same Open Directory system, you have another option for configuring access to your ARD clients. Simply add the users to these specially named groups in your directory:

- ard_admin: Membership permits full ARD access to the client.
- ard_interact: Membership only allows the user to control/observe the client's screen.
- ard_manage: Membership permits features like rebooting, software installation, sending UNIX commands, and other similar functions, but not screen control or observe.
- ard_reports: Membership permits only report generation, but no control of the ARD client.

These groups roughly correspond to the features given in the Interact, Manage, and Report menus available in the Remote Desktop Admin utility.

You'll then need to tell each of your ARD clients to use these groups for their access control. If you already have ARD access to these machines through an existing local account, you can choose Manage > Change Client Settings, which will guide you through the same process used to create custom client installers.

On the Incoming Access screen, select Set authorized groups. If you haven't yet installed or configured ARD on any of the machines, you can set the same option in your client installer package as discussed earlier in the lesson. Just choose File > Create Client Installer from the menus, but choose the option to Enable directory-based administration.

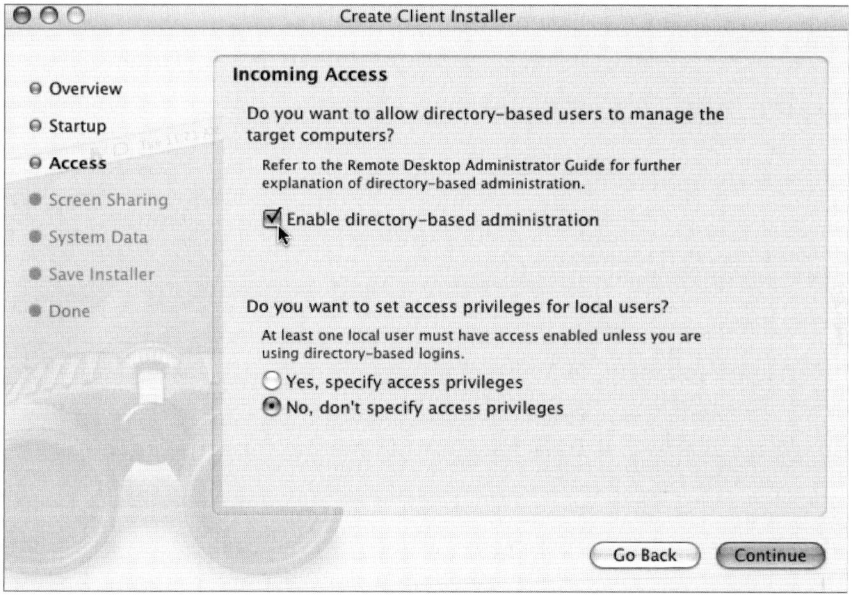

You can also use the `kickstart` command via SSH to enable ARD group access:

```
sudo /System/Library/CoreServices/RemoteManagement/ARDAgent.app/Contents/Resources/kickstart -
activate -clientopts -setdirlogins -dirlogins yes -setdirgroups -dirgroups "ard_admin, ard_interact,
ard_manage, ard_reports" -restart -agent -menu
```

ARD 3 introduces another option for using groups to control access to ARD. If you're using managed computers in Workgroup Manager, you can specify which groups of users have various levels of ARD access. Just as you can create computer lists and use them to manage preferences on a computer, you can use the same MCX settings to manage ARD, but you'll have to edit some XML code to do it. Currently there is no user interface to automate this task.

1 Launch Workgroup Manager.

2 In the Preferences, choose "Show All Records Tab and Inspector."

3 Find the computer list or computer you want to \ change.

4 Select the Inspector tab.

5 Select the MCXSettings attribute, and click the Edit button.

6 Merge the following MCXSettings into the existing text as appropriate. You may wish to copy any existing MCXSettings out and work with everything in PropertyList Editor outside of Workgroup Manager to ensure correct syntax.

```
<?xml version="1.0" encoding="UTF-8"?> <!DOCTYPE plist PUBLIC "-//Apple
Computer//DTD PLIST 1.0//EN" "http://www.apple.com/DTDs/PropertyList-
1.0.dtd"> <plist version="1.0"> <dict>
 <key>mcx_application_data</key>
 <dict>
 <key>com.apple.remotedesktop</key>
 <dict>
 <key>Forced</key>
 <array>
 <dict>
  <key>mcx_preference_settings</key>
  <dict>
  <key>ard_interact</key>
  <array>
  <string>some_group</string>
  <string>staff</string>
  </array>
  <key>ard_manage</key>
```

```
<array>
<string>staff</string>
</array>
<key>ard_admin</key>
<array>
<string>my_admin_group</string>
</array>
<key>ard_reports</key>
<array>
</array>
</dict>
</dict>
</array>
</dict>
        </dict>
        </dict> </plist>
```

Using ARD

Now that you've configured your ARD clients and your Remote Desktop Admin utility, you're almost ready to start managing your clients. Before you can perform actions on your clients, you need to tell the Remote Desktop Admin utility which computers it will be managing and what credentials will be used to access them.

Setting Up Computer Lists

To the left of the main window of Apple Remote Desktop's Admin utility are at least two computer lists. The Scanner list is a special list used to discover new computers. Most commonly, this is used to list all the devices on your local subnet, but you can also specify any single IP address or hostname, or a range of IP addresses if you wish to scan for machines not on your local subnet. The Scanner list will show every device that it finds, whether you have access to it or not, even if it's not a Mac OS X–based computer.

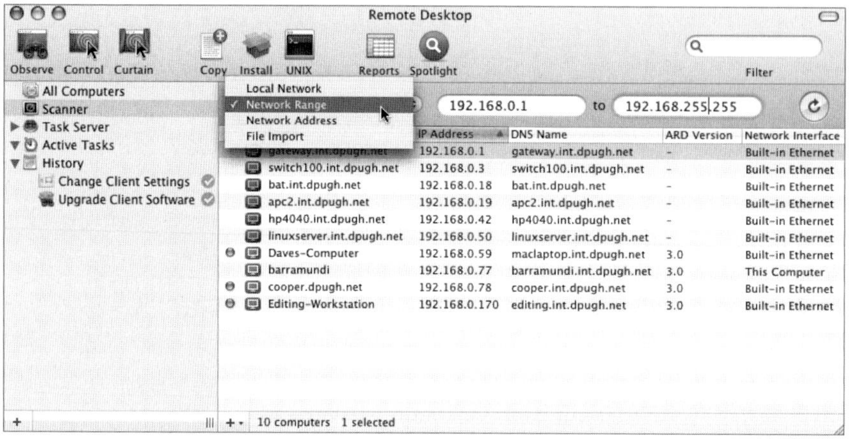

The All Computers list includes every computer that you have added to ARD. In most cases, this means every computer that you can access with ARD unless that computer is turned off or is otherwise unreachable. If you wish, you can create additional computer lists to contain subsets of the All Computers list. These lists can be used for different classes of machines (workstations, servers, kiosks, and so on), machines in different classrooms, or any grouping you wish to use.

You can add new items from the menus in the Add menus at the bottom of the main ARD window.

You can create new lists by choosing the Add menu in the bottom left corner of the window, or by selecting a number of computers from an existing list and clicking the other Add menu at the bottom of the window and choosing New List From Selection. Once you've created a list, you can add computers to that list by dragging them into the list from any other list, such as the All Computers list.

ARD also offers the option to export and import your computer lists, which is useful if you'd like to use the same computer list on your desktop and laptop, or if you'd like to give your computer lists to your peers. To export your computer lists, choose File > Export List. This will save a copy of your computer list, but will not include any of your authentication information. To import a list, choose File > Import List.

When you add a new computer to one of your lists, you'll be prompted for the username and password that you'll use to connect to that computer. These credentials will be saved in your computer list encrypted with your ARD password that you used when you first installed the administrator utility. If you're adding multiple computers simultaneously by selecting each one or using a file import, you have the option to use the same username and password for all of the computers. To take advantage of this, select the option to Use this name and password on remaining computers when the user name/password window is on your screen.

TIP You can customize which columns are displayed in your computer lists by Control-clicking the column headings. A menu will appear in which you can enable or disable individual columns. You can also drag columns to the left or right to reorder them in the window.

Controlling and Observing Screens

The most common use of ARD is to provide remote assistance to a user in another location. ARD is also commonly used to control the screens of servers in distant locations, or to control systems without video cards, such as Apple's Xserves. To control a screen, select the computer from one of your lists, and, from the menus at the top of the screen, choose Interact > Control, or click the Control button.

> **TIP** If you wish, you can modify the administrator utility preferences to make double-clicking a computer perform the Control screen or Observe screen function.

Once you initiate screen control, a resizable window will appear that contains a view of the remote computer's display as if you were sitting in front of the screen. Any mouse movements or keyboard actions you perform will be performed as if you were executing them on the remote keyboard and mouse. At the top of the window, buttons can be used while the remote screen is open. These buttons can be selected to do the following:

- Switch between control and observe mode
- Toggle on and off the function of the target computer's keyboard and mouse
- Fit the remote screen into the local window, or look at objects at full resolution
- Lock the remote screen, while you retain visibility through ARD. This is known as curtaining or cloaking.
- Take a snapshot of the remote screen and save the image on your computer
- Fit the remote screen to the full size of your display. This best simulates sitting in front of the remote computer's monitor, particularly if your screens are of the same resolution.
- Copy the remote user's clipboard contents into your local clipboard
- Copy your local clipboard contents into the remote user's clipboard

Controlling another computer from the Remote Desktop application.

In the top-right corner of the screen-control window is a quality control adjustment. If you have a high-speed connection between your computer and the computer you're controlling, such as a local Ethernet, you can keep the slider positioned to the right for a full-quality color display. However, if you're using ARD to control a screen over a slower Internet connection, such as a home broadband connection or a modem, adjust the slider to the left. This will lower the quality of the screen data, but will speed up the refresh rate and make ARD more usable on a slow connection.

To release control of the screen, simply close the window.

TIP Although you can't control multiple machines simultaneously by selecting them all at once in the computer list, you can control multiple machines by controlling them one at a time and leaving their control windows open.

Observing Screens

You can also observe screens without controlling them. This can be useful in a number of situations. You may just need to see what a user is seeing on her screen while she is controlling it, or you may be a teacher monitoring the progress of the students in your class. For observing, you can actually monitor multiple screens at once. This is particularly useful in a classroom situation. Select all the computers you wish to observe, and choose Interact > Observe, or click the Observe button.

This will create a tiled window displaying the screens of all the computers you selected.

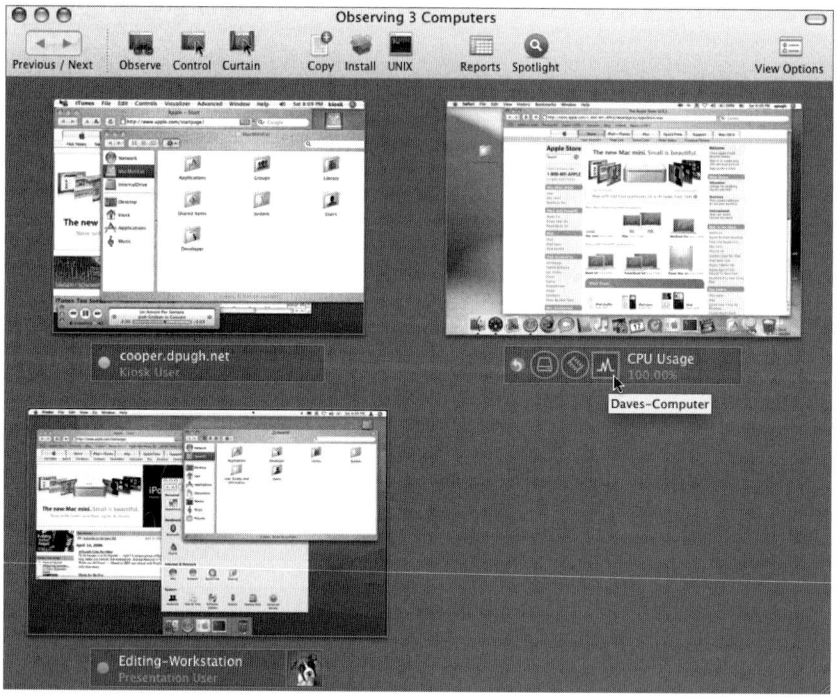

If you wish, you can perform any ARD action on one of the screens, such as initiating a control session, by selecting that screen and choosing any option from the menus as if it were a computer in the computer list.

Below each screen, you'll see an informational window that shows the name of the computer, the user that is currently logged in, and a colored dot indicating the health of the computer. By clicking the colored dot, you can flip the panel over to see the following at a quick glance:

- Disk usage
- Memory usage
- CPU usage

TIP If you would prefer to see users with their short names instead of long names in the computer lists and in the Observe windows, run this command from the terminal: `defaults write com.apple.RemoteDesktop showShortUserNames -bool true`. You may have to restart the Remote Desktop Admin utility for the change to take effect. If you'd like to return to the default of long names being shown, just repeat the same command but replace `true` with `false` at the end.

You can use the View Options button at the top of the window to change how many screens will be shown at once. If you are observing more screens than you can fit in the window at one time, you can also change the time interval at which the window will cycle through them. You are also given the option to customize what information is shown below each screen image.

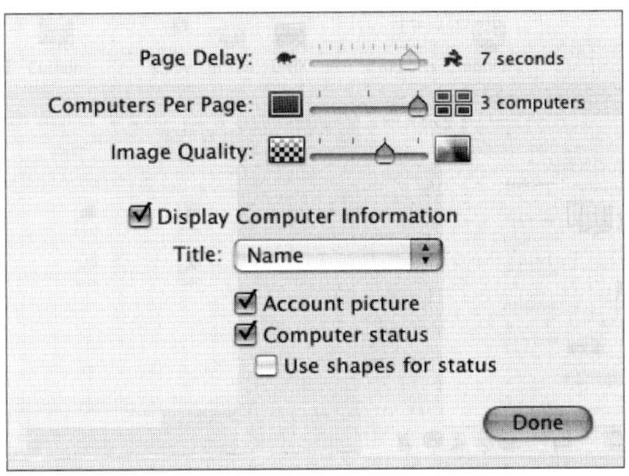

Using a Dashboard Widget to Observe

ARD 3 includes the installation of a Dashboard widget that you can use to observe screens. This can be particularly helpful for peeking at a screen that would visually indicate something requiring your attention. One example of this might be a monitoring server that has Apple's Server Monitor application running on it. An invocation of Dashboard will show you a miniature version of the screen in which you can quickly see if everything in Server Monitor is okay.

You can monitor multiple screens by dragging extra copies of the ARD Dashboard widget onto your Dashboard. Clicking an active ARD Dashboard widget will initiate a control session to that computer.

Locking Screens

Particularly useful in a classroom is the ability to lock a group of computers' screens. This implementation of screen lock differs from that provided by a screen saver. A screen saver lock allows a user to unlock the screen with his username and password, while the ARD screen lock can only be unlocked from ARD.

A teacher can use this when she wants the full concentration of her students, or if she wants to enforce a common start time for a test problem. To lock the screen, select the computer(s) in your computer list, and choose Interact > Lock Screen. If you find yourself using the Lock Screen feature often, you may wish to add it to your toolbar by Control-clicking the toolbar at the top of the Remote Desktop window and choosing Customize Toolbar.

A screen locked by a Remote Desktop administrator.

When the screen is locked, a picture of a lock is shown along with a custom text message and the name of the person who locked the screen.

> **NOTE ►** Don't forget to unlock the user's screen when you're done. The user has no way to do it on his own, and there is no obvious indication from your administrator utility that her screen is locked.

Closing the Curtain

In some cases, you may wish to control the remote computer but you may not want the person at the other end to be able to see what you're doing. This may be the case if you need to open a window of sensitive files on the other screen. By controlling the remote screen in curtain, or cloaking, mode, you see the screen as if you're performing a normal control action, but the other computer display is locked. To initiate curtain mode, select the computer from your computer list and click the Curtain button or choose Interact > Curtain from the menus. Curtain mode is actually just a combination of normal control mode and locking the user's screen. You can get the same functionality by locking the user's screen and then controlling it.

What you see...

What they see...

Sharing Screens

Another useful feature is the ability to share anyone's screen with others. There are two ways to use this feature. The first is to share your screen with others.

1 Select the machines in your computer list that will receive your screen image.

2 Choose Interact > Share Screen.

3 Select Share your screen (the default).

4 Click Share Screen.

Your screen will be shared with each of the target computers. Everything you do on your screen will be seen by others. This has a similar effect to using a projector in a room. However, instead of everyone looking at a big screen in the front of the room, they're seeing the image on their individual workstations.

Alternatively, if, for example, one student sitting at Computer14 has solved a class problem and you'd like to share his screen with the rest of the class, you can perform a similar procedure.

1 Select the machines in your computer list that will receive the screen image, but do not select Computer14.

2 Choose Interact > Share Screen.

3 Select Share other screen.

4 Drag Computer14 from the computer list into the box just below the Share other screen option.

5 Click Share Screen.

Now everyone in the class is seeing Computer14's display. To discontinue the screen sharing, click the Stop button in the Active Share Screen Tasks window that appeared on your screen.

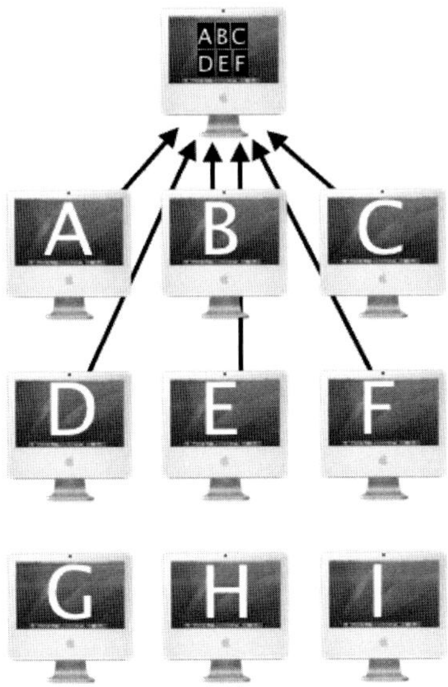

A teacher observing students A-F.

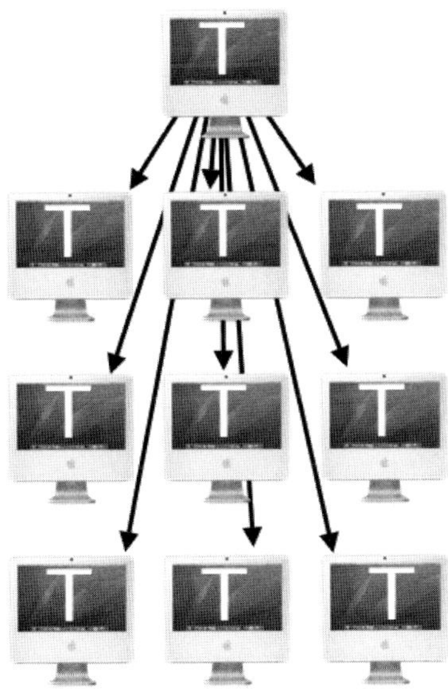

A teacher sharing her screen with all of the students.

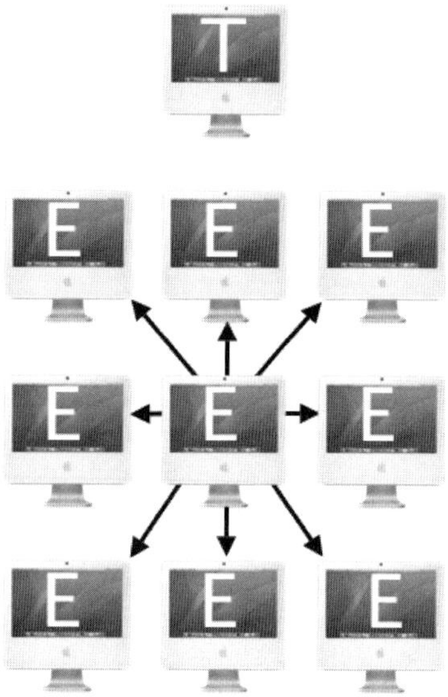

A teacher sharing student E's screen with the other students.

Managing Clients with ARD

As you learned at the beginning of this lesson, ARD can be used for much more than screen control. The Manage menu in ARD's administrator application contains a number of other options, including:

- Copy Items
- Install Packages
- Send UNIX Command
- Open Application
- Open Items
- Empty Trash

- Set Startup Disk
- Rename Computer
- Sleep
- Wake
- Restart
- Shut Down
- Log Out Current User
- Upgrade Client Software
- Change Client Settings

As you can see, ARD can control many functions of a target computer. Some of the basic ones can be very useful in computer lab situations. If your computer lab uses NetBoot, you can have a different NetBoot image for each of your classes. By using ARD, you can send a Set Startup Disk command between classes to switch the NetBoot image to that of the upcoming class. All of the machines are rebooted, and in a few minutes you have a lab ready for use by the next class. When the end of the day arrives, you can use ARD to send a Sleep command to all of your computers. It isn't a rare occurrence for students in a computer lab to leave themselves logged in after they leave. Using the Log Out Current User option in ARD can save you a trip over to that computer to fix the problem.

By using the options at the top of the Manage menu, you have some powerful management tools at your disposal. By combining these items, you can do almost anything on a target computer.

Installing Software

Installing software packages remotely is one of the more obvious features of ARD. If a user needs a new program on his computer, you can install it remotely as long as it comes in an Apple package file (*.pkg or *.mpkg). If the file is some other type of installer, you can use the Copy Items feature, followed by the Open Items option to open the installer you just copied.

Another way the Copy Items option can be used is to modify user interface settings. If you want all of your users to get a certain set of preferences for an application, configure them the way you want in your account, and use the Copy Items feature to copy all of the plists to the Preferences folder on the target machines. You could also use this functionality to deliver a shell script or other program to the remote client. The program could be used by the user or as an administrative tool for performing maintenance on or gathering statistics about a computer.

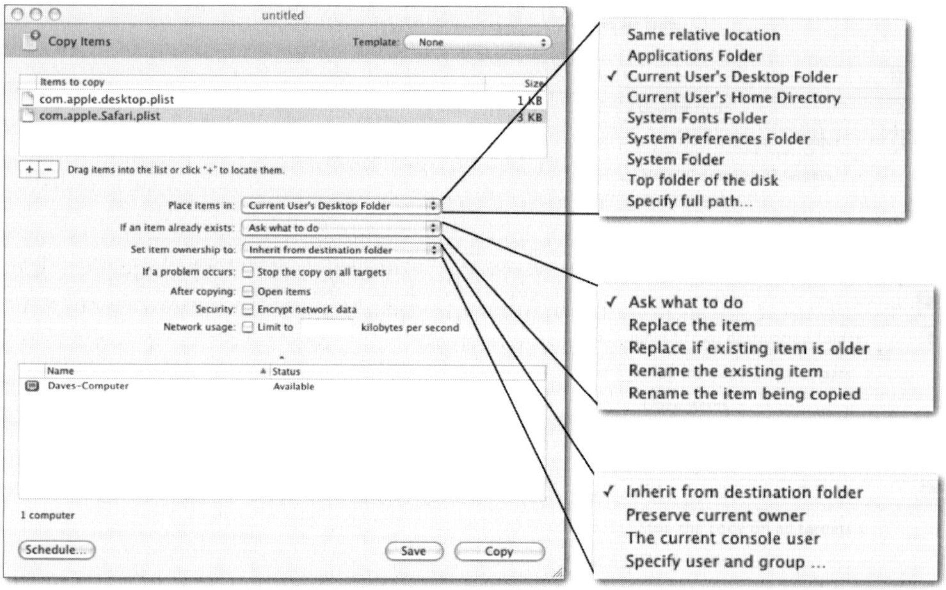

The options when copying items to a remote computer.

Running UNIX Commands Remotely

One of the most powerful items in the Manage menu is Send UNIX Command. As you know, Mac OS X is built on a UNIX foundation. Almost anything that you can do in the GUI also can be done with a UNIX command. With ARD, you can use the power of UNIX to simultaneously make changes to many computers.

For example, if a recent software installation changed some important permissions in your file system, you can use UNIX to issue Disk Utility's Repair Permissions command by sending it through a UNIX command.

```
diskutil repairPermissions /
```

This will run the permissions repair on each computer, and will also report the output from each invocation, providing you with even more report flexibility than is included in ARD.

One example of this might be to check the hard drive's SMART status. SMART is a predictive drive failure feature included on most modern hard drives. ARD's built-in Storage Report does not include SMART status, but with a simple UNIX command, you can get the SMART status of the boot drive of all of your computers.

```
diskutil info / | grep SMART
```

You can also use UNIX to send AppleScript commands. Perhaps someone left iTunes playing music through her speakers, and you can't figure out who it is. You can send the command to mute everyone's speakers using the UNIX interface to AppleScript, `osascript`.

```
osascript -e 'set volume 0'
```

You can combine many of these features to make powerful system administration tools. You could write a long shell script that you install on everyone's machines using the Copy Items feature, and execute as the root user with the Send UNIX Command feature.

Version 3 of ARD includes a number of UNIX command templates that provide common functionality. Although these templates will cover some of what you may want to do, it will benefit you greatly to expand your knowledge of UNIX to administer your computers. By using UNIX commands, you can do almost anything to each of your computers using ARD.

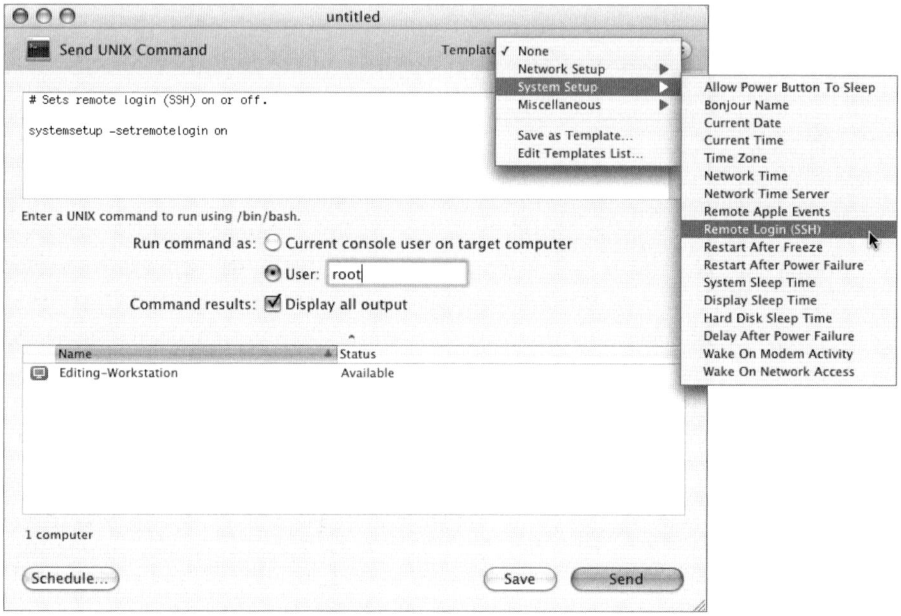

Some template scripts included with ARD 3.

Scheduling Tasks

You may find it desirable to schedule some of your tasks to execute at a later date, or on a recurring basis. ARD provides a simple and convenient interface to accomplish this.

At the bottom of almost every task that you execute on a remote computer is a Schedule button. Clicking this button opens a schedule dialog that allows you to indicate the exact date and time the command will run. You can also specify that this command should repeat at a specified frequency.

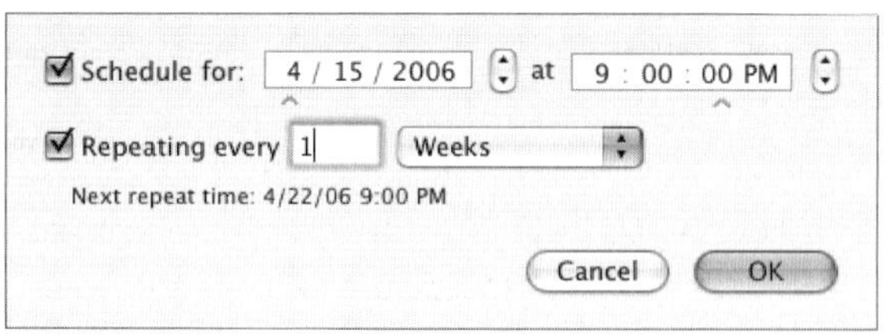

Saving Tasks

In addition to scheduling tasks, you can also save them. This comes in handy if you're issuing the same commands frequently, but not on a scheduled or recurring basis. An example of this might be to set the startup disk of a lab full of computers to a specified NetBoot image.

To save tasks, set up the task as you normally would to execute it, but instead of clicking the button to run the task, click Save. When you save the task, it will appear in the Sidebar of the main Remote Desktop window. To initiate the task later, select it and click the Play button on the right side of the window.

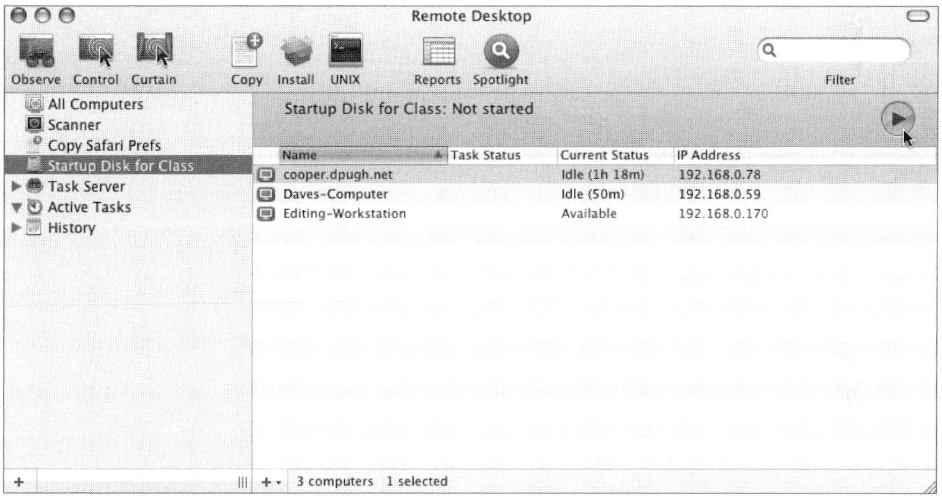

You can edit the task later if you wish by Control-clicking the saved task and choosing Edit Task. You can also rename the task or run the task by Control-clicking it.

Scripting Remote Desktop

AppleScript and Automator are two tools used to simplify repetitive tasks with Mac OS X applications. They both can be used to interact with ARD. AppleScript is a programming language in almost every respect, while Automator is a graphical tool used to create workflows by dragging individual actions into a chain of events. While you can use both

AppleScript and Automator with ARD, the basics of each tool are not within the scope of this book. In this lesson, you'll be concentrating specifically on the way each tool can be used to interact with ARD. Some additional sample scripts are available in the Administrator's Guide and from the ARD 3 Resources website.

Using AppleScript

AppleScript is generally harder for the novice to use and, in the case of Apple Remote Desktop, is more limited in capability. AppleScript may be the right choice, however, for a seasoned AppleScript programmer, or for someone who just needs to do some basic tasks. ARD's AppleScript dictionary contains many functions, such as:

- Add computers to a computer list
- Copy or install items
- Initiate or terminate a control, observe, share, or screen lock task
- Generate reports
- Open items
- Logout the current user
- Wake, sleep, restart, or shut down the computer, set startup disk

You can view the entire AppleScript dictionary for ARD from within Script Editor by choosing File > Open Dictionary, and selecting the Remote Desktop application.

Here is a simple AppleScript that could be used to put a list of computers to sleep for the night:

```
tell application "Remote Desktop"

        set tired_computers to computer list "Sleepers"

        execute (make new sleep task) on tired_computers

end tell
```

Just create a computer list called "Sleepers" that contains each computer that should be put to sleep, and then just run the AppleScript.

Using Automator

Automator is similar to AppleScript in a number of ways, but with an entirely different user interface. With Automator, you drag available actions into your workflow. Data passes from one action to the next until the workflow is complete. Many of the same things that are available in AppleScript are available in Automator, although you may find yourself writing AppleScript within Automator to do exactly what you need done.

Here is a sample Automator workflow that just connects to every machine in the "Kiosk Machines" computer list. First, it will close all open Finder windows, then it will run an AppleScript on each computer to instruct Safari to open the Apple Store's Web site.

Generating Reports

ARD contains a number of very useful reports:

- System Overview
- File Search
- Software Version
- Software Difference
- Storage
- USB Devices
- FireWire Devices
- Memory
- PCI Cards
- Network Interfaces
- Network Test
- Administration Settings
- Application Usage
- User History

Each of these reports can be useful for different users at different times. For example, software licensing managers will find the Software Version and Application Usage reports very convenient. They can use these reports to find out how many copies of each version of a package are installed throughout an entire organization, how often they are used, and by whom.

Each of these reports can also be exported into tab- or comma-separated files by clicking the Export button on the report output window. These files can be imported into many popular programs such as Microsoft Excel for further data refinement. The resulting data could be used to generate HTML documents in Pages or iWeb describing features of your network.

Gathering System Information

System Overview Reports can be used by most system administrators to gather information about the physical properties of all of the computers in your network, such as features and serial numbers.

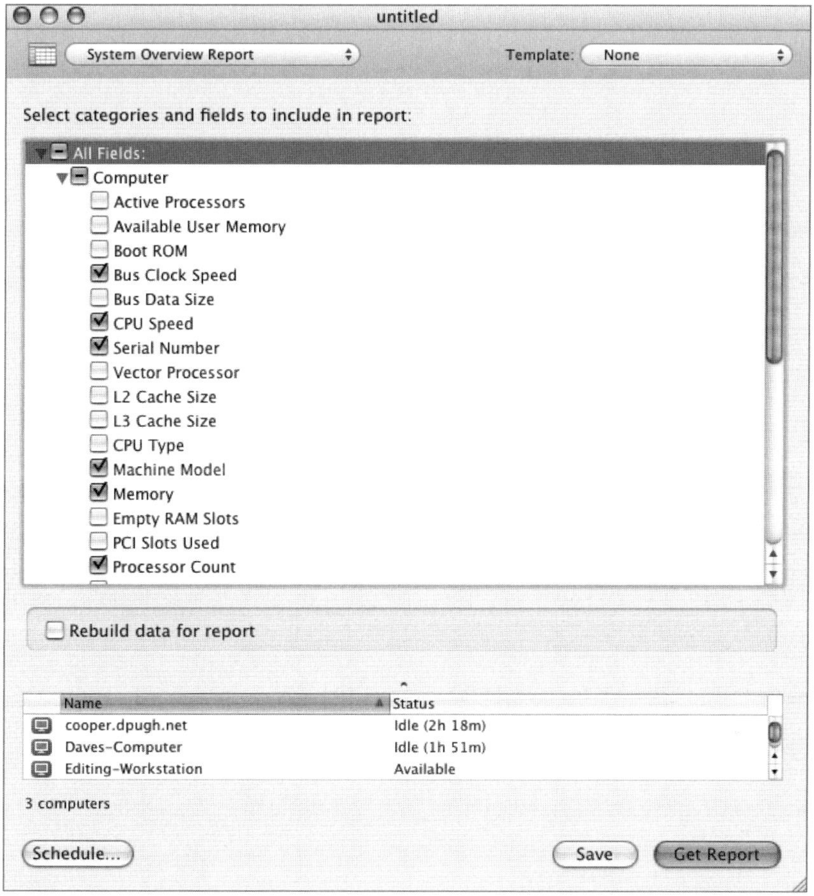

Not only is this useful for inventory control, but it can be used to determine if your computers meet the minimum hardware requirements for a piece of software.

Gathering Software Information

Many reports are available for gathering software information. The most basic of these is a simple Software Version Report. Running this report allows you to compare the versions of up to ten applications between your administrator computer and all of the selected target computers.

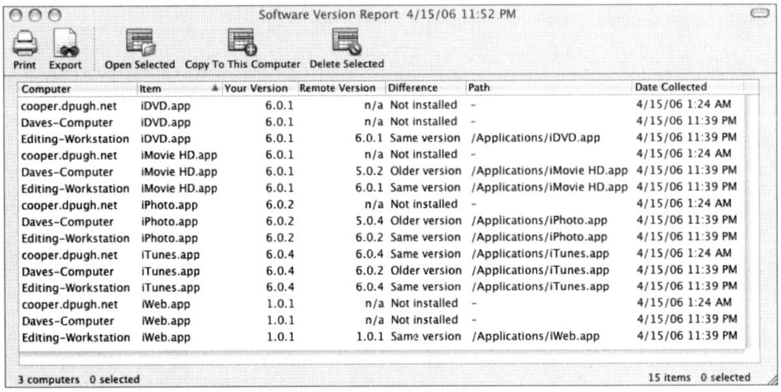

The Software Difference Report can provide a quick list of how your target computers differ from your administrator computer or, better yet, how they differ from an image that has been deployed to all client computers. Unlike the Software Version Report, which can only report on applications, the Software Difference Report can report on applications, fonts, packages, and more. Also, the Software Difference Report will list all of the applications that differ, not just the ten you select as in the Software Version Report.

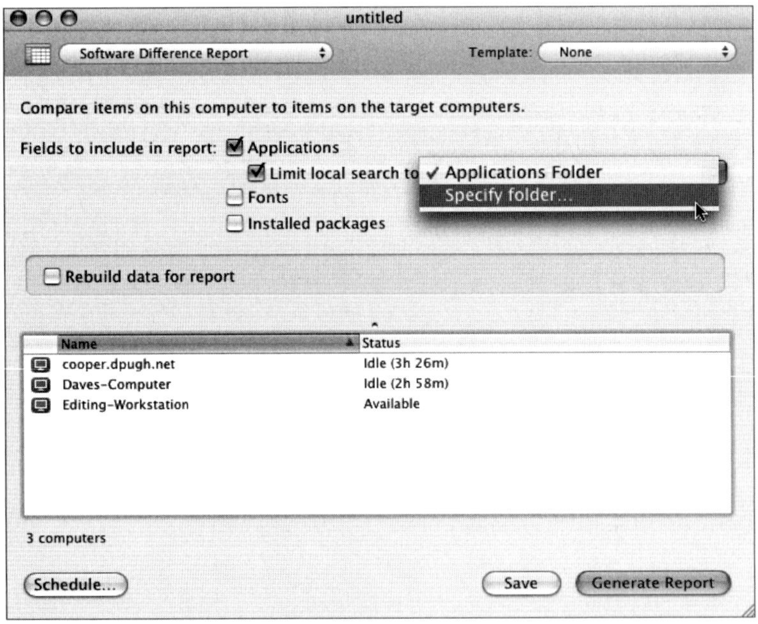

If you're just looking for the presence of one file, you can use the File Search report. This report possesses many of the same options as a local Find File operation.

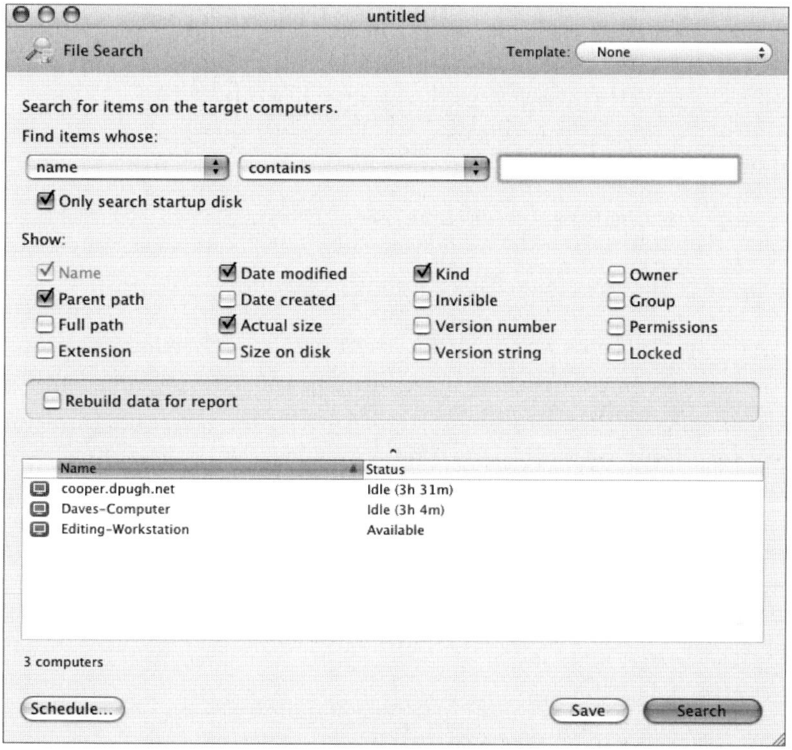

Lastly, you can use the Application Usage Report to find out how your software is being used. This report is very powerful in that it tells you the following about every use of the software on the target computers:

- Who ran the software?
- When was it started?
- How long was it running?
- How long was it in the foreground?

TIP Each computer builds a cache of all of its files and their versions once a day. Unless you need data that is current up to the minute, you should NOT select the option to "Rebuild data for reports" for file and software searches. Leaving this option deselected will result in reports that are nearly instant, while rebuilding the reports will take around 5 minutes on average, depending on the speed of your computers and the number of files on their drives.

Running Spotlight Searches

New in ARD 3 is the ability to carry out Spotlight Searches for files. As you may already know, Spotlight has the ability to search for much more than filenames. Spotlight can search the contents of files along with their metadata. Using Spotlight through ARD behaves the same as it does locally. You have the option to limit your search to the entire computer, the startup disk, the home folder, or a specified folder. While the search is being performed, you'll see a summary of how many hits were found on each of the target computers, and at the bottom you'll see the individual hits. By highlighting files, you also have the option of opening them, copying them to your administrator workstation, or deleting them from the target computers.

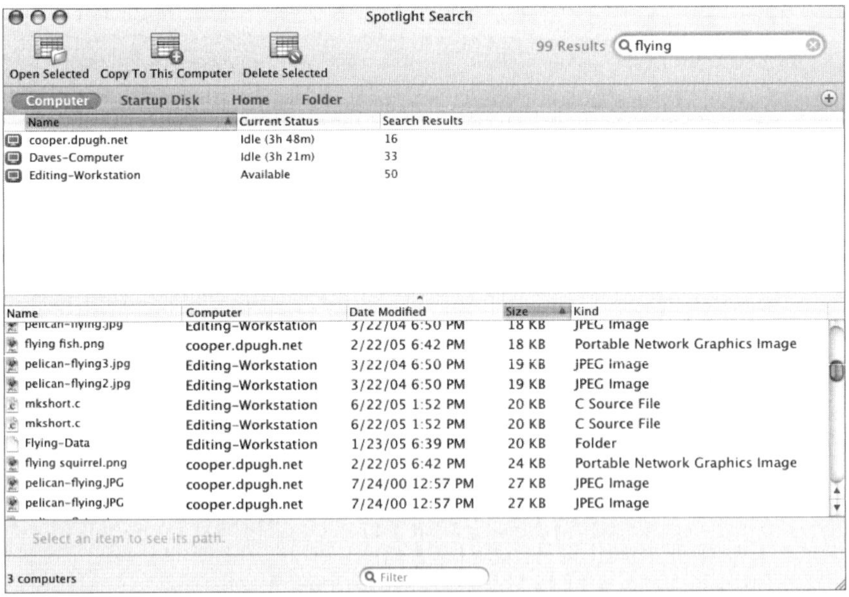

Using SQL to Access Report Data

ARD stores all of its report data in a PostgreSQL database on your administrator workstation (or on your central ARD task server, if used). With minor configuration changes, you can access all of your report data in custom ways from external applications or from your Web server. By default, only the ARD administrator utility has access to the PostgreSQL database. To allow others to connect, follow these steps.

1. Quit the Remote Desktop Admin utility.

2. In System Preferences > Sharing, deselect the Remote Desktop service if it is selected.

3. Enter the following command (you should know how to use the command line utility vi. If not, consult the vi man pages):

   ```
   sudo vi /var/db/RemoteManagement/RMDB/rmdb.data/pg_hba.conf
   ```

4. At the bottom of the file, enter the following line:

   ```
   host ard ard 127.0.0.1 255.255.255.255 password
   ```

5. Save the file.

6. Enter the command:

   ```
   sudo vi /var/db/RemoteManagement/RMDB/rmdb.data/postgresql.conf
   ```

7. Find the line that contains "#tcpip_socket = false". Remove the "#" at the beginning of the line, and change "false" to "true" so the line looks like this:

   ```
   tcpip_socket = true
   ```

8. Save the file.

9. In System Preferences > Sharing, select the Remote Desktop service, if desired.

10 Launch the Remote Desktop Admin utility.

11 Run some reports to populate the database.

12 Find your local PostgreSQL database password by typing:

```
sudo cat /private/var/db/RemoteManagement/RMDB/passwd.txt
```

Make a note of the output of this command. This is the password you'll need to connect to your PostgreSQL database.

You can now run SQL commands against the PostgreSQL database on your machine. This could come from Web applications on a local Web server, or from the command line with commands such as this:

```
/System/Library/CoreServices/RemoteManagement/rmdb.bundle/bin/psql -p 5433 -h localhost -U ard -c
"SELECT * FROM systeminformation" ard
```

When prompted, type the password you found in the passwd.txt file.

You can modify the above command to output the data in other formats. To output the data in an HTML table, add `-H` to the arguments for `psql`, or to output the data in a tab-separated list, add `-A -F $'\t'`.

For more information on the `psql` command, consult its man page with the command

```
man -M /System/Library/CoreServices/RemoteManagement/rmdb.bundle/man psql
```

TIP The configuration steps and usage outlined above provide the most generic interface to your PostgreSQL data. If your usage of the PostgreSQL database is limited to only human interaction by those who are administrators on your system, you can simplify the above steps significantly. Don't modify either of the conf files. Preface the `psql` command with `sudo`, and omit the `-p 5433 -h localhost` arguments. This will create a local domain socket connection to your database rather than a TCP/IP connection. This is more secure and requires fewer changes, but is more difficult to access by other systems such as your Web server.

By harnessing the full power of SQL, you can create any custom report you desire based on the data stored in the PostgreSQL database. A sample query showing how you can join many fields together into one report is shown below:

```
barramundi — bash — 80x23
barramundi:~ dpugh$ cat /tmp/query
SELECT SI1.value AS Name,  SI2.value AS OS,
       SI3.value AS Model, SI4.value AS SerialNum
FROM systeminformation SI1,
     systeminformation SI2,
     systeminformation SI3,
     systeminformation SI4
WHERE
   SI1.computerid=SI2.computerid AND
   SI1.computerid=SI3.computerid AND
   SI1.computerid=SI4.computerid AND
   SI1.propertyName='ComputerName' AND
   SI2.propertyName='SystemVersionString' AND
   SI3.propertyName='MachineModel' AND
   SI4.propertyName='MachineSerialNumber'
barramundi:~ dpugh$ /System/Library/CoreServices/RemoteManagement/rmdb.bundle/bi
n/psql -U ard < /tmp/query
Password:
       name       |               os               |     model     |  serialnum
------------------+--------------------------------+---------------+-------------
 Daves-Computer   | Mac OS X 10.4.4 (8G32)         | PowerBook3,5  | G2YK01VAPQV
 Web-Server       | Mac OS X Server 10.4.4 (8G32)  | PowerMac10,1  | GTW84HZ0PVX
(2 rows)
```

Using a Task Server

With ARD 3, you can designate one administrator workstation as a central task server. A task server is nothing more than a normal ARD administrator workstation that has been told it's a task server. Configuring a computer to be a task server requires selecting only one checkbox but using a task server has a number of advantages.

The first benefit is centralization. By using a task server, all of your reports are funneled through one host. This allows all of the ARD administrators in your organization to use the same set of cached data. Not only does this save disk space, it also saves network traffic and CPU utilization on the target computers. With a central report repository, you can collate data for your entire organization when gathering statistics, rather than for only those computers you are administering.

The second main benefit of using a task server is to deal with offline clients. Offline clients can be machines that are powered off, or sleeping, or laptops that are off-site and not on the network. By using a task server, you retain access to all of the reporting data for these offline clients. Also, many tasks can be set to run through the task server. By doing this, any offline clients automatically will run their queued tasks the next time they check-in to the task server. This is particularly important for package installation. If you have an updated version of a package or an important security update, you can tell ARD to install it on all clients using the task server. Every client will eventually get it, so long as they are eventually reachable by the task server.

A third benefit is to allow scheduled tasks to be performed at later times when the remote administrator is running, such as with late night events.

Configuring the Task Server

To designate a computer as a task server, follow these steps:

1. Install the Remote Desktop Admin utility.
2. Configure it normally; being sure you've given it a unique serial number for an unlimited client version of ARD.
3. Choose Remote Desktop > Preferences.
4. Select the Task Server tab.
5. Select the "Use Task Server on this computer" checkbox.
6. Select the "Allow remote connections to this server" checkbox.

You may now quit the Remote Desktop Admin utility on your task server if desired. For the task server to function, you need not have the administrator utility running. In fact, you don't even need anyone logged in. Once configured, the task server will just continue running as long as the ARD service is enabled in the Sharing System Preferences.

Using the Task Server

Assuming that the task server is not running on your local administrator workstation, you next need to configure your computer to use the new task server.

1. Launch the Remote Desktop Admin utility.
2. Choose Remote Desktop > Preferences.
3. Select the Task Server tab.
4. Select "Use remote Task Server."

5 Type the hostname or IP address of your task server.

6 Click Select.

7 If you have not already added this host to your computer list, you will be prompted for a username and password that has ARD access to your task server.

To use a task server, you must have an account on that task server and be given "Generate reports" access to the task server.

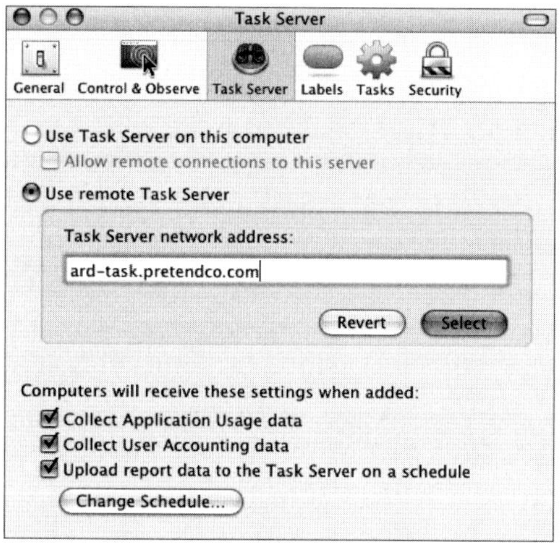

Configuring Clients to Use the Task Server

When you add new computers to your computer lists, they will be configured to use the task server and default reporting policy saved on your administrator workstation at the time the computer was added. You can change these defaults using the same procedure outlined in the previous section, "Using the Task Server."

To configure existing computers to use your task server, follow these steps:

1 Launch the Remote Desktop Admin utility on your computer. Be sure it's configured to use your task server.

2 Select the computers that should use your task server in your computer list. This is likely all of your computers.

3 Press Command-I, or select File > Get Info.

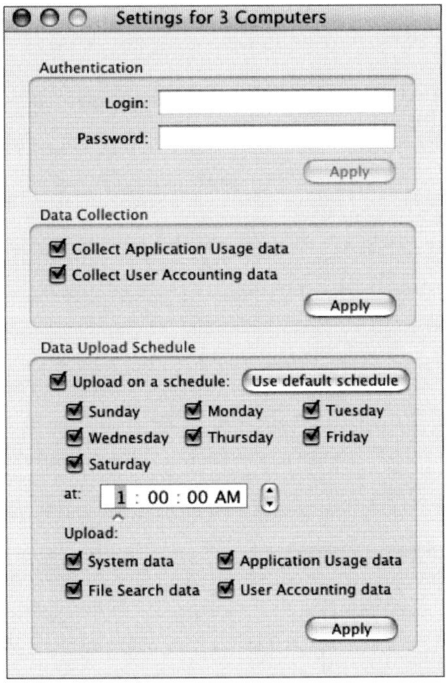

4 Make your changes to the Data Collection or Data Upload Schedule.

5 Click Apply.

When you apply the settings to your clients, they will also be configured to use the same task server as your administrator workstation. You may wish to run a report on all of your computers to pre-populate the task server, or you can just wait until the next reporting interval.

Lesson Review

1. What methods can be used to configure and enable the ARD client?
2. Describe the difference between the All Computers and Scanner computer lists.
3. Describe the three types of screen sharing.
4. How would you initiate Disk Utility's Repair Permissions function using ARD?
5. Name five types of data that can be collected when generating reports.

Answers

1. Sharing preferences pane, custom client installer package, `kickstart` utility.
2. The All Computers list contains hosts that you've added to your list and have access to control via ARD. The Scanner lists all of the hosts found during a network scan. This could include hosts that you don't have access to and machines that are not even Macs.
3. A teacher can observe multiple computers, a teacher can share his screen with the entire class, or a teacher can share a student's screen with the rest of the class.
4. Select the target computers, and send it the UNIX command: `diskutil repairPermissions /`.
5. System Overview, File searches, Storage information, Memory information, Software Differences, Software Versions, Application Usage, User History.

References

Administration Guides

Apple Remote Desktop 3 Administrator's Guide: http://images.apple.com/remotedesktop/pdf/ARD 3_AdminGuide.pdf

Apple Knowledge Base Documents

Document 106807, "How to Create a Custom Locked Screen Picture": http://docs.info.apple.com/article.html?artnum=106807

Document 108030, "Configuring remotely via command line (kickstart)": http://docs.info.apple.com/article.html?artnum=108030

Document 108021, "How to uninstall or disable ARD 2": http://docs.info.apple.com/article.html?artnum=108021

Document 302262, "Unable to add remote computer for Data Collection": http://docs.info.apple.com/article.html?artnum=302262

URLs

Apple—Apple Remote Desktop: http://www.apple.com/remotedesktop/

Remote Desktop Resources: http://www.apple.com/remotedesktop/resources.html

Providing Application Access to SQL Data in Apple Rremote Desktop 2: http://developer.apple.com/appleapplications/ardsql.html

OpenWBEM: http://openwbem.sourceforge.net/

ARD 3 script collection: http://homepage.mac.com/jcwelch/ardscriptcollections.zip

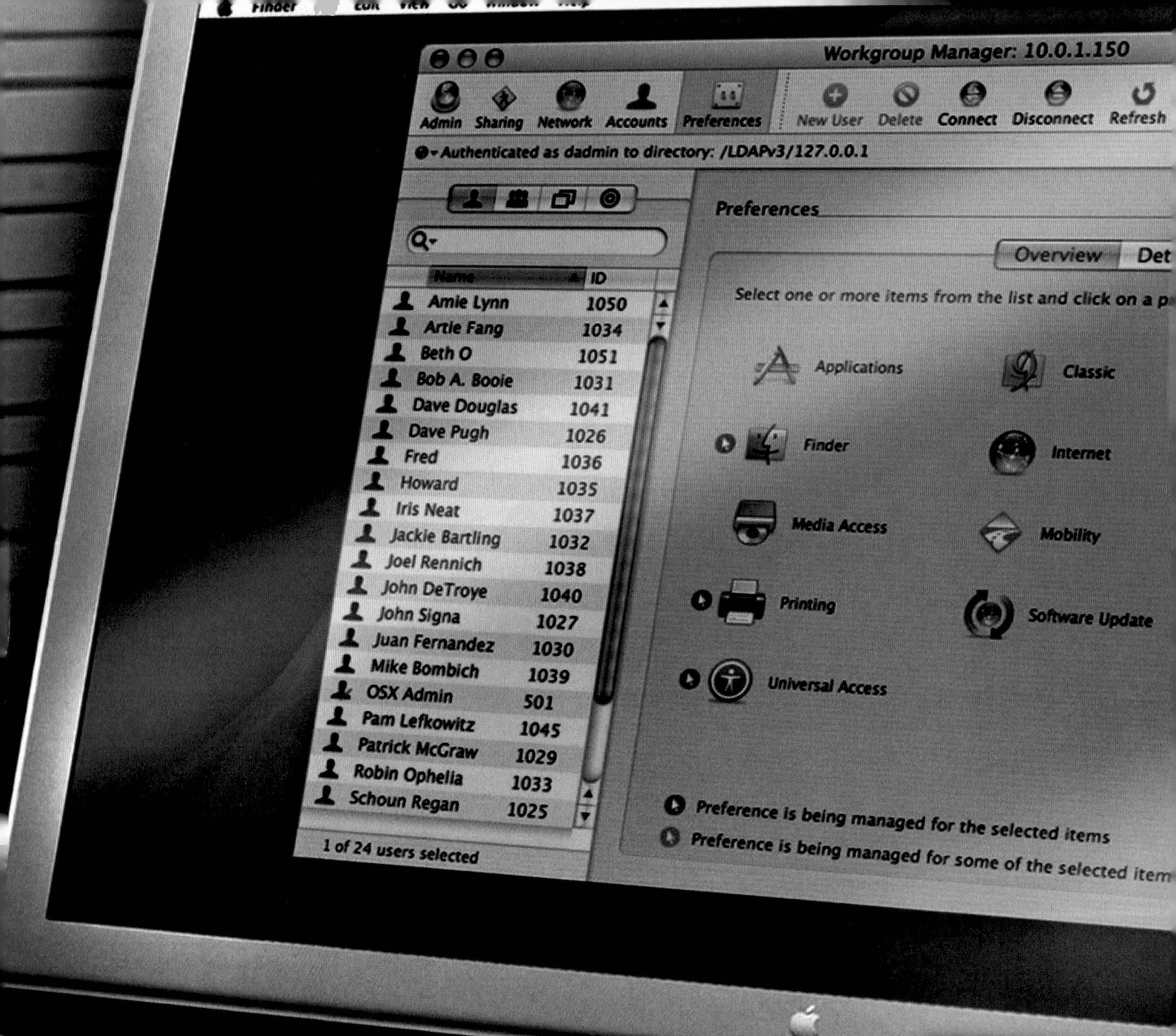
Workgroup Manager: 10.0.1.150
Admin
Sharing
Network
Accounts
Preferences
New User
Delete
Connect
Disconnect
Refresh
Authenticated as dadmin to directory: /LDAPv3/127.0.0.1
Name
ID
Amie Lynn 1050
Artie Fang 1034
Beth O 1051
Bob A. Booie 1031
Dave Douglas 1041
Dave Pugh 1026
Fred 1036
Howard 1035
Iris Neat 1037
Jackie Bartling 1032
Joel Rennich 1038
John DeTroye 1040
John Signa 1027
Juan Fernandez 1030
Mike Bombich 1039
OSX Admin 501
Pam Lefkowitz 1045
Patrick McGraw 1029
Robin Ophelia 1033
Schoun Regan 1025
1 of 24 users selected
Preferences
Overview
Applications
Classic
Finder
Internet
Media Access
Mobility
Printing
Software Update
Universal Access
Preference is being managed for the selected items

System Administrat
Name:
Password:
NAT
NetBoot
NFS
Open Directory
Print
QuickTime Streaming
Software Update
VPN
VPN

Appendix

Using Radmind

Radmind is a client/server system for maintaining UNIX systems, including Mac OS X. It is from the Research Systems UNIX Group of the University of Michigan. The Macintosh version can be run entirely within a graphical user interface, within a command-line interface, or using a combination of both.

Radmind runs on the client using a tripwire-like mechanism that detects changes to file system objects (such as files, directories, links), and creates a *transcript* of any objects that did not pass the integrity check. Any files that have changed can be retrieved from a Radmind server and replaced on the client, restoring the system to its previous state.

If the transcript contains new files that you'd like to keep on the client, the new files can be uploaded to your Radmind server, and the transcript becomes an *overload*. A Radmind server easily scales to support hundreds of clients and can be based on any UNIX server. It need not be a Mac OS X Server, or even Mac OS X.

The *Radmind Assistant* GUI offers additional functionality such as installing the Radmind tools, configuring Radmind to run automatically, setting up your template user, and enabling lab user management shell scripts. You can also use the Radmind Assistant just to set up lab user management, even if you don't run Radmind.

Radmind, which is available at no cost under a BSD-style license, provides a good balance of benefits for maintaining multiple Mac OS X clients:

- No license fee
- File-level maintenance
- Intrusion detection
- Low network usage
- IP address or certificate-based access control
- TLS encryption
- Multiple machine configurations with different combinations of overloads

Understanding Radmind

Radmind uses transcripts to list all file system objects to be managed. *Positive transcripts* list objects that must match filename, date, privileges, size, and an optional checksum of the file contents. *Negative transcripts* list objects that must match only certain attributes depending on the object type. For example, the /Users directory is listed in the negative transcript. Radmind ensures its ownership and privileges are correct, but does not check its contents. This allows you to preserve the contents of users' home directories.

Initially, a client starts with a positive base load transcript, and a negative transcript. This combination tells Radmind what files to manage, and provides a basic system on the client, or *loadset*. Overload transcripts then can be added in any combination. For example, all of the clients may get security update overloads, but only the video-editing clients get video editing software overloads. All of the administrative clients could get office productivity overloads, while the kiosk clients get a locked-down browser overload.

The list of overloads each client gets is called a *command file*, with a *.K* extension, and is simply a list of precedence-ordered transcripts. When a client is first updated, it retrieves its command file. This tells the client what transcripts it needs, and the client retrieves them. Next, Radmind on the client cross checks every hard drive file 'against the transcripts and creates a list of each file that needs to be reset or replaced. Finally, the client loads those files from the Radmind server and replaces them. As in all of Mac OS X, Radmind consists of a number of shell scripts, so a filesystem check can be initiated on the client in any number of ways:

- Automated scripts that are run periodically during off-hours
- After each logout
- On startup
- When a user named "radmind" logs in
- Manually by an administrator

The server runs the Radmind service that listens for client requests. The server data includes a configuration list of all the clients it manages, the command file for each of those clients, a copy of all the transcripts, and a copy of each of the files that should be managed on the clients.

Setting Up Radmind

Creating a basic setup to maintain multiple Mac OS X computers with Radmind is a fairly straightforward process. In this exercise, you will set up a base load and an overload for a desktop Mac OS X client. You will:

- Install the Radmind software on your Radmind server and client
- Make a base load on a client Mac OS X computer and upload it to the server
- Make an overload on the client and upload it to the Radmind server
- Add additional clients to the system

TIP Radmind Assistant lets you see which UNIX commands are being issued by the GUI, as well as other command-line information. While the Radmind Assistant is running, type Command-L to open a drawer showing the UNIX command that corresponds to the current action.

Installing and Configuring the Radmind Server

You can use Mac OS X or Mac OS X Server (or any UNIX system) for your Radmind server; it doesn't matter.

1 On the Macintosh that will be your Radmind server, open a Web browser and go to www.radmind.org. Find and download the latest version of Radmind Assistant.

2 Drag the Radmind Assistant application to /Applications/Utilities, and double-click it to start the Radmind Assistant.

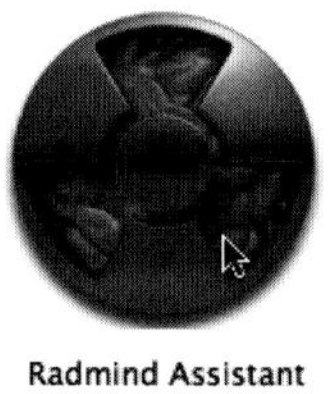

3 A dialog appears notifying you that you must install the Radmind Tools. Click OK to install the Radmind Tools

4 In the "Radmind Assistant: First Run" window, make sure the radio button for "I'm new, and I want to set up a radmind server" is selected, then click Continue.

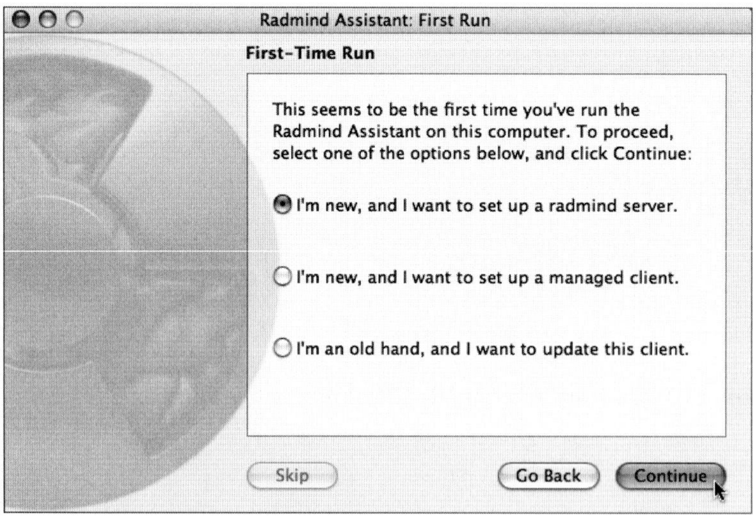

5 Make sure the radio button "Start the radmind server with Rendezvous on" is selected and click Continue. You will be asked to provide an administrator password.

The assistant displays a window showing how it is configured. Notice that the Radmind server service runs on port 6662—make sure this port is not blocked by your firewall.

6 Click Finish. You are asked to provide an administrator password to start the Radmind Server Manager application.

Installing and Configuring a Radmind Client

You will now need to set up a Mac OS X client computer with a base load—that is, install the operating system along with the files that will be common to all of your Radmind-managed client computers.

1 On the Macintosh that will be your Radmind client, perform a clean install of Mac OS X, erasing the contents of the hard drive.

2 Configure the computer with the startup assistant.

3 Open a web browser and go to www.radmind.org. Find and download the latest version of Radmind Assistant.

4 Drag the Radmind Assistant application to /Applications/Utilities, and double-click it to start the application.

5 A dialog will appear to notify you that you must install the Radmind Tools. Click OK to install the Radmind Tools

6 In the Radmind Assistant: First Run window, select "I'm new, and I want to set up a managed client", and click Continue.

7 The Radmind Assistant: First Run—Set Up a New Radmind Client window appears. In the Radmind Server field, enter the fully qualified domain name or the IP address

of your Radmind server. Leave the Comparison Path set to /, leave the SSL Security Level set to *0 - None*, and select "Disable checksums globally" button. Click Continue and enter your administrative password when prompted.

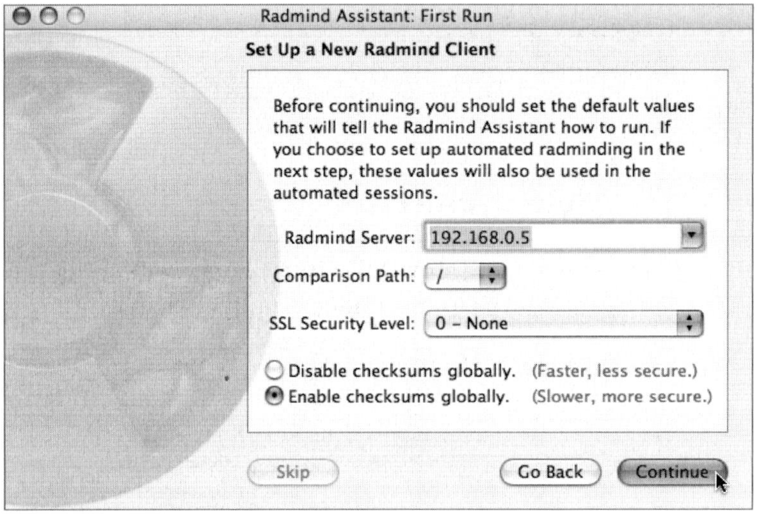

8 At this point, you are given the option of Configuring Radmind Automation. If you want to add this functionality, you can always add it later as an overload. For now, click Continue

9 Select 10.4-desktop-negative from the transcripts listed, click Edit Negative and provide your administrative password when prompted. This opens the negative transcript in the Radmind Transcript Editor

10 Because you will be using / for your base path (as specified in step 7), click Edit > Select all to select every item in the negative transcript. In the Transcript Editor toolbar, click Convert and choose /.

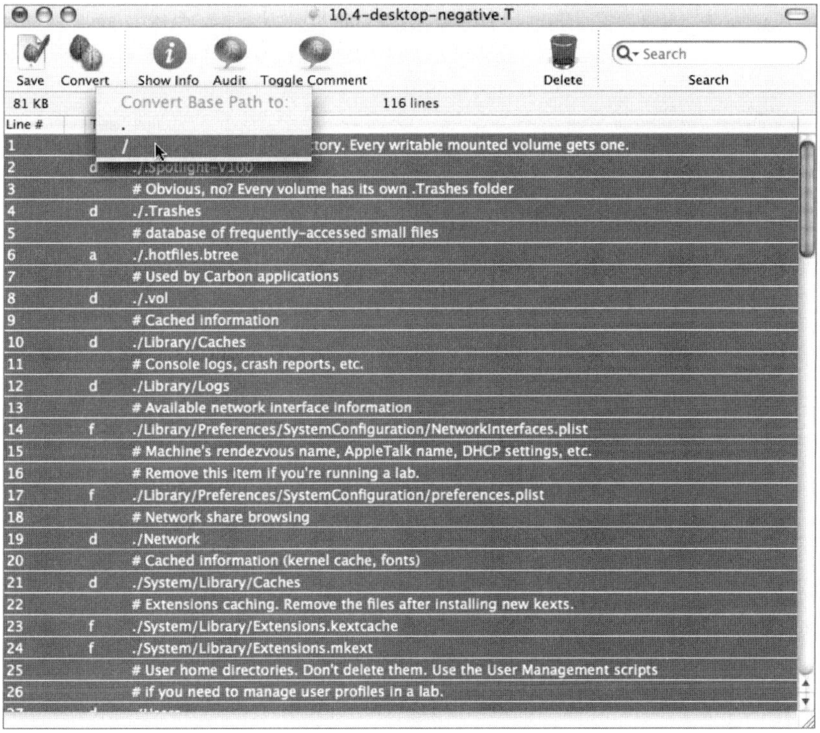

11 In the toolbar, click the Save button and quit the Transcript Editor.

12 In Radmind Assistant, click Continue.

13 Because you configured the Radmind server to use Rendezvous/Bonjour, a dialog may appear, Radmind Server Detected. If the information provided matches your Radmind server, you should select Set Default. Then click Continue.

14 If you had any other applications open, you will see a dialog asking if you want to quit those open applications. Select Quit Other. Authenticate if requested to do so.

The Radmind Assistant should report that the negative transcript was successfully uploaded to the server.

Checking in the Negative Transcript on the Radmind Server

Now that you've uploaded your negative transcript to the server, you need to check it in to approve its use.

1. If Radmind Server Manager is not currently running on your Radmind Server, open /Applications/Utilities/Radmind Assistant. From the Session menu, choose Open Server Manager.

2. The Radmind Loadsets window displays a dialog after detecting your newly-uploaded negative transcript. If a dialog doesn't appear, click the Refresh button in the toolbar. Click OK and authenticate.

3. Another dialog appears asking if you would like to add the negative transcript to your client's command file. Click OK.

   Your Radmind Loadsets window should now show your negative transcript, and your Radmind Command File Editor window should show a base.K Command File with the 10.4-desktop-negative.T transcript file in it.

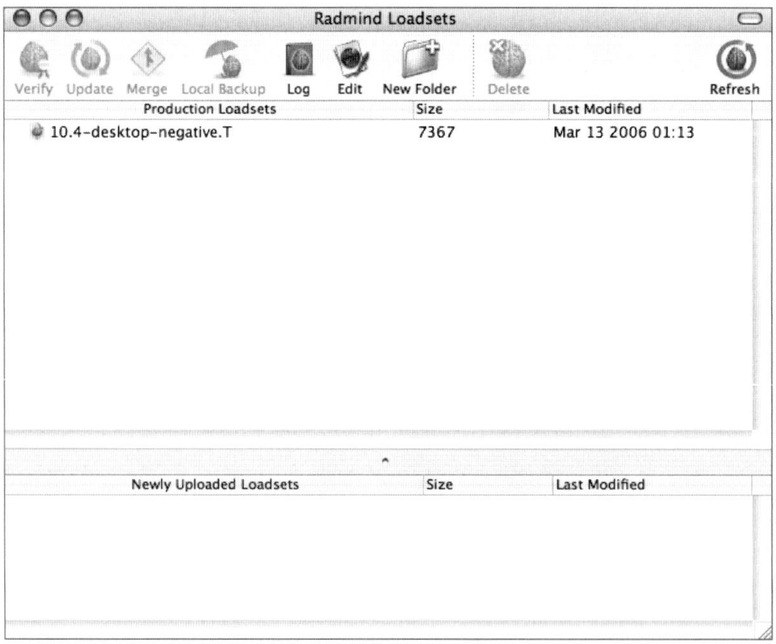

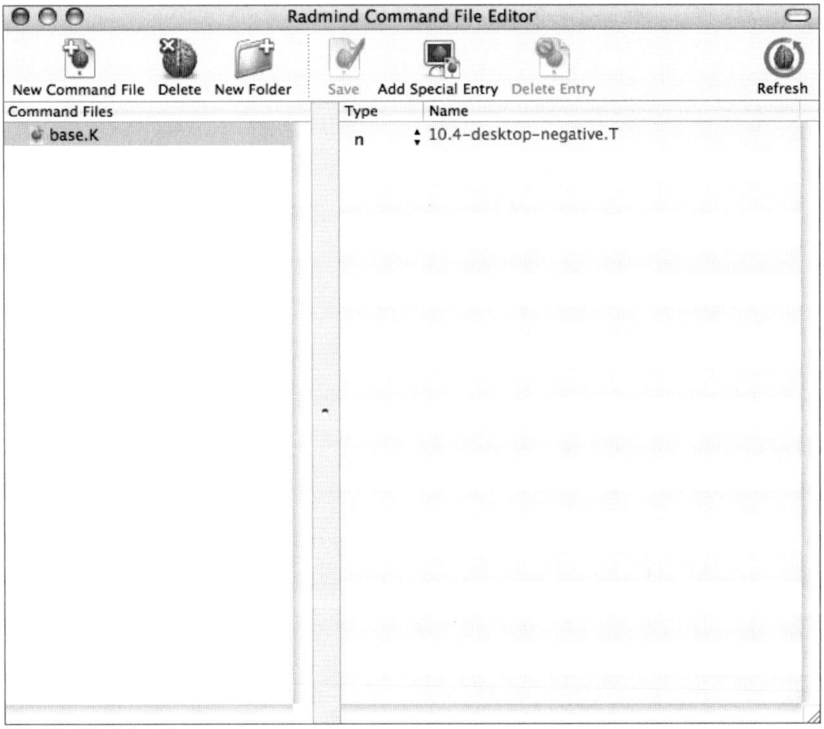

Creating the Positive Transcript on the Client

So far, you've created a negative transcript that lists which files and directories will be ignored. Next, you'll create the positive transcript that lists the files that should be present, along with all of their attributes.

1 The Radmind Assistant should still be reporting that the negative transcript was successfully uploaded to the server. Click Continue.

2 The Radmind Assistant offers to check the Radmind server for updates. Make sure the Radmind host is either the IP address or the fully qualified domain name of your Radmind server, click Continue and authenticate, if necessary.

3 The Radmind Assistant offers to create a new transcript and loadset. Select "Enable checksums" and click Continue.

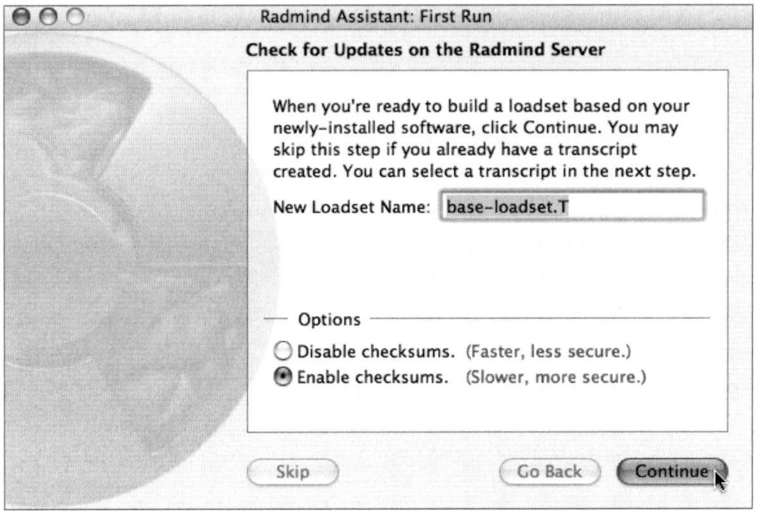

The Radmind Assistant now begins to scan the entire file system and creates a positive transcript of every file system object

TIP You should use checksums whenever possible to ensure the integrity of your files. This is especially important when building your transcripts and loading the files up to the Radmind server. You may want to run client updates without checksums at times when users are waiting, but during idle times, such as overnight, run a full Radmind update with checksums—this will ensure the integrity of their files.

4 When the Radmind Assistant has finished scanning the file system, click Review Loadset and authenticate. The Transcript Editor opens, allowing you to inspect and, if necessary, edit your transcript before uploading it and its files to the Radmind Server.

5 When you have finished inspecting and editing the transcript, click the Save button in the toolbar, and quit the Transcript editor. In the Radmind Assistant window, make sure Enable checksums is selected and click Continue, Authenticate, if necessary.

The Radmind Assistant begins uploading your positive transcript and all associated files to the Radmind server.

6 When the Radmind Assistant has successfully completed the upload, click Finish.

Checking in the Positive Transcript on the Radmind Server

After the positive transcript is uploaded to the server, you need to check it in to approve its use.

1 If Radmind Server Manager is not currently running on your Radmind Server, open /Applications/Utilities/Radmind Assistant. From the Session menu, select Open Server Manager.

2 The Radmind Loadsets window displays a dialog after detecting your newly-uploaded positive transcript. If a dialog doesn't appear, click the Refresh button in the toolbar. Click OK and authenticate.

3 A dialog appears noting the newly-uploaded loadset. Click the Verify and Check In button and authenticate.

4 When the verification process has completed, you asked to authenticate again. You are then asked if you want this loadset added to your client's command file; click OK.

Updating the Client

Now that you have your negative and positive transcripts on the server, your client needs to use them to verify that nothing has changed since they were created. It does this by updating itself with what's on the server. In theory, there should be nothing to update, but this process must be followed so the client knows that. This process is also necessary if you used multiple machines to create transcripts. The process of updating the client will find any additional transcripts that this machine doesn't already know about.

1 Open /Applications/Utilities/Radmind Assistant. The Radmind Assistant offers to guide you through the update process. Click Continue and authenticate.

2 In the window that appears, confirm the correct Radmind Host, click Continue and authenticate.

3 The Radmind Assistant checks the Radmind server for any updates in the command or transcript files and download them, if there are any. Select "Enable checksums" and click Continue.

4 After scanning the filesystem, if any changes need to be made, the Radmind Assistant offers to perform the update. Select "Enable checksums" and click Continue.

5 When the changes have been applied, click Finish, then click Reboot.

Creating an Overload

With your client's file system perfectly matching the files stored on the server, you are ready to create an overload. Overloads are used to reflect any optional files that may not be present on every computer, such as for applications, or even for updates to the original base load, such as with system software updates. For this exercise, you are going to set up Radmind's automation features, and install iHook, a GUI for running shell scripts. You will then make an overload of these changes.

1 Open /Applications/Utilities/Radmind Assistant. From the Radmind Assistant menu, choose Preferences, and in the toolbar click the Automation button.

2 Select all of the checkboxes in the Automation Preferences window. Then click the Download iHook button.

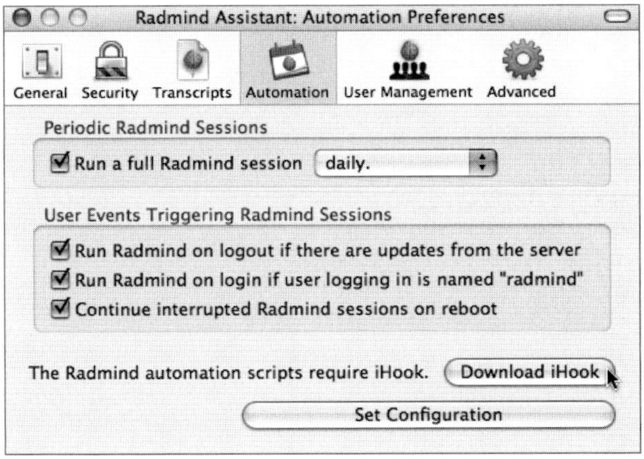

3 A browser opens. Download iHook and install it by dragging it to the /Applications/Utilities folder.

4 Return to the Radmind Assistant: Automation Preferences window. Click Set Configuration and authenticate.

5 Click the Advanced button in the toolbar. Then click "Make Preferences Global."

6 Close the Radmind Assistant preferences, and return to the Radmind Assistant. From the Session menu, select Create New Radmind Loadset, then click Continue.

7 Because you just updated the client, you don't need to do so now. In fact, doing so would erase the changes you've just made. Click Continue.

8 Name the new transcript *rad-automation.T*, and select "Enable checksums". Click Continue and authenticate as needed.

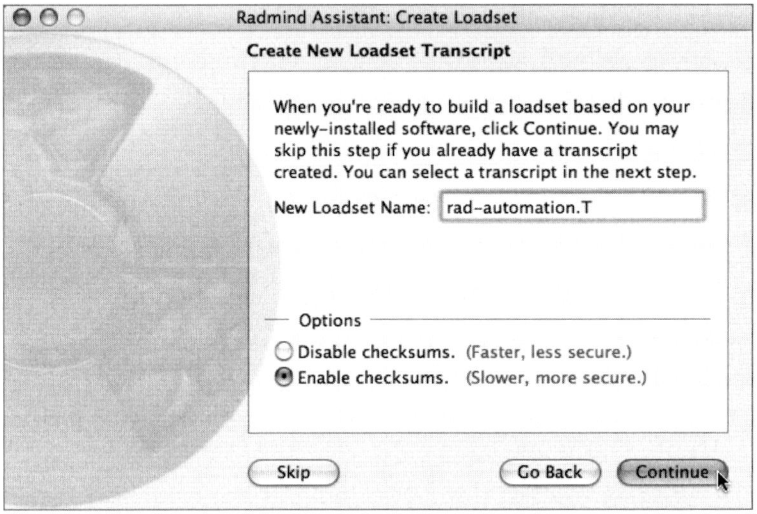

9 When the Radmind Assistant has finished scanning the file system, click Review Loadset and authenticate. This opens the Transcript Editor, allowing you to inspect and, if necessary, edit your transcript before uploading it and its associated files to the Radmind server.

10 When you have finished inspecting and editing your transcript, click the Save button in the toolbar, and quit the Transcript Editor. In the Radmind Assistant window, make sure "Enable checksums" is selected. Click Continue and authenticate if necessary. If a dialog appears suggesting that you quit other open applications, click Quit Other.

The Radmind Assistant uploads your positive transcript and all associated files to the Radmind server.

11 When the Radmind Assistant has successfully completed the upload, click Finish.

Checking in the Positive Transcript on the Radmind Server

Your overload transcript is another positive transcript that must be checked in on the server to approve its use, just like the original positive transcript used as your base load.

1. If Radmind Server Manager is not running on your Radmind Server, open /Applications/Utilities/Radmind Assistant. From the Session menu, choose Open Server Manager.

2. The Radmind Loadsets window displays a dialog after detecting your newly-uploaded positive transcript. If a dialog doesn't appear, click the Refresh button in the toolbar. Click OK and authenticate.

3. A dialog appears noting the newly-uploaded loadset. Click the Verify and Check-in button. Authenticate, if necessary.

4. With both the Radmind Loadsets window and the Radmind Command File Editor open, drag the new loadset from the Radmind Loadsets window to the Radmind Command File Editor window. Drop the file between the base-loadset.T and the 10.4-desktop-negative.T transcripts. In the toolbar, click the Save button and authenticate.

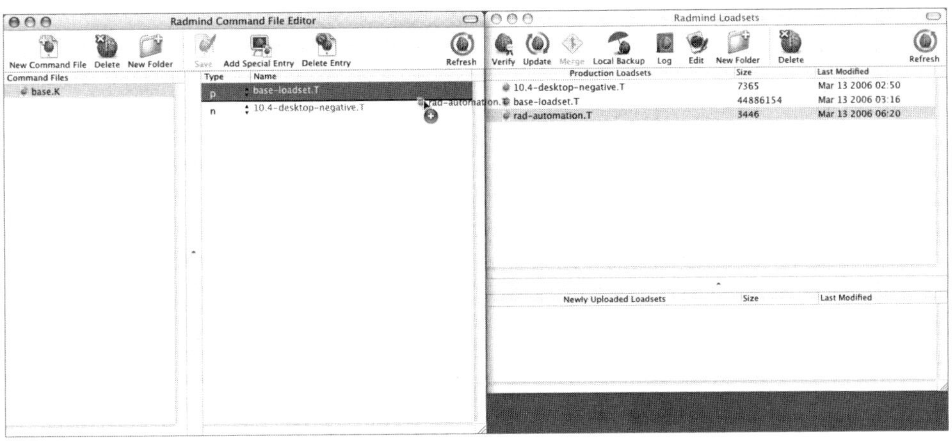

Loading Additional Clients

Loading any number of additional clients is now a simple task.

1 On each additional client you want to manage, open a web browser and go to http://radmind.org. Find and download the latest version of Radmind Assistant.

2 Drag the Radmind Assistant application to /Applications/Utilities, and double-click it to start the Radmind Assistant.

3 A dialog notifies you that you must install the Radmind Tools. Click OK and install the Radmind Tools.

4 The Radmind Assistant: First-Time Run window is displayed. Select the "I'm an old hand, and I want to update this client" button and click Continue.

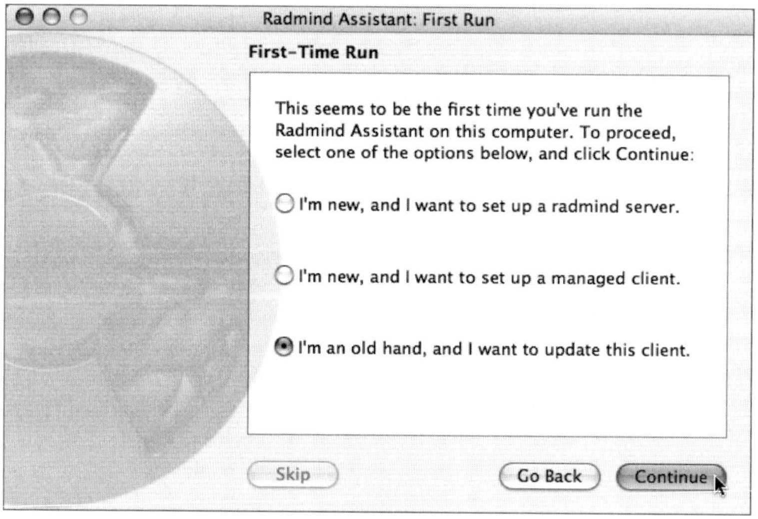

5 Click Continue to dismiss the welcome window.

6 Enter the fully qualified domain name or IP address of your Radmind server, and click Continue. Authenticate, if necessary.

7 In the Check Filesystem for Changes to Make window, select Enable checksums, and click Continue.

8 In the Apply Necessary Changes to This Machine window, select "Enable checksums", and click Continue to apply the changes.

9 When your client has been successfully updated, click Finish and then reboot.

The steps you've performed in this appendix serve to outline some of the key features of Radmind. As you become a seasoned Radmind administrator, you'll learn that there's much more that can be done with Radmind. When you perform these steps in the GUI, you should also open the drawer that shows the associated UNIX commands for each action. Becoming familiar with these UNIX commands will allow you to perform these actions remotely using SSH or ARD.

Workgroup Manager: 10.0.1.150
Admin
Sharing
Network
Accounts
Preferences
New User
Delete
Connect
Disconnect
Refresh
Authenticated as dadmin to directory: /LDAPv3/127.0.0.1
Name
ID
Amie Lynn 1050
Artie Fang 1034
Beth O 1051
Bob A. Booie 1031
Dave Douglas 1041
Dave Pugh 1026
Fred 1036
Howard 1035
Iris Neat 1037
Jackie Bartling 1032
Joel Rennich 1038
John DeTroye 1040
John Signa 1027
Juan Fernandez 1030
Mike Bombich 1039
OSX Admin 501
Pam Lefkowitz 1045
Patrick McGraw 1029
Robin Ophelia 1033
Schoun Regan 1025
1 of 24 users selected
Preferences
Overview
Select one or more items from the list and click on a pre
Applications
Classic
Finder
Internet
Media Access
Mobility
Printing
Software Update
Universal Access
Preference is being managed for the selected items
Preference is being managed for some of the selected items
Name: cdadmin
Password:
NAT
NetBoot
NFS
Open Directory
Print
QuickTime Streaming
Software Update
VPN
VPN
Web

Index

> console option, 215–216
100Base-T Ethernet connections, 84
100Base-T switched network, 84

A

Access Control Lists (ACLs), 139–141, 269
Access pane, 265–266
accessibility options, 220–223
account creation, 155–181
  in Accounts preference pane, 156–157, 159
  computer list accounts, 176–179
  groups, 174–176
  guest accounts, 179
  with NetInfo Manager, 157–158
  with Passenger, 146
  policy for, 135–137
  presets for, 145, 168, 233
  procedure for, 170–174
  relocating user accounts, 161–174
  tools for, 156–160
  with Workgroup Manager, 158–160
account data, 151, 152. *See also* data
account management, 131–153
  described, 131
  directory/folder structure, 138–139
  documenting policy, 147
  home folders, 8–9, 31, 141–142
  levels of, 132–137
  managing users, 142–146
  optimizing user management, 142–146
  organization management, 138–139
  permissions, 139–141
  planning for, 150–152
  user documentation, 148–150
  with Xserve, 150–152
accounts. *See also* users
  administrator. *See* administrator accounts
  computer list, 176–179
  creating. *See* account creation
  deleting, 28, 32, 239
  growth management, 137–142
  guest, 177, 179, 197
  Guest Computers, 179
  LDAP, 163–168
  levels of, 132–137
  local, 132–133
  Mac OS X, 255, 256, 260
  managing. *See* account management
  mobile. *See* mobile accounts
  NetInfo, 161–163
  network, 43, 133, 238
  presets, 145
  root, 27
  searching for, 144
  setting policy components, 135–137
  synchronizing, 242–252
  types of, 132–134
  user. *See* user accounts
  Windows. *See* Windows accounts
Accounts preference pane, 156–157, 159
ACLs (Access Control Lists), 139–141, 269
ACSA (Apple Certified System Administrator) certification, xxi
actions, 297, 310, 323, 325
Active Directory, 113–114, 213, 242, 263
Active Directory server, 242

administration
    directory-based, 303, 305
    levels of, 27
    remote. *See* ARD (Apple Remote Desktop)
    Universal applications for, 84
    Windows accounts, 255–275
administrative groups, 134
administrative users, 7, 134
Administrator Account pane, xix
administrator accounts
    creating, xix, 27–31, 135
    deleting, 28
    hidden, 27–31
    modifying, 28–29
    passwords, xix, 29, 30, 70
    user name, xix, 70
    vs. root account, 27
administrator utility. *See* ARD (Apple Remote Desktop)
administrators
    described, 132
    First Administrator, xxi
    folder/directory management, 138
    policies for, 135
    restricting to given workgroup, 136
Advanced pane, 171, 266
AFP (Apple Filing Protocol), 85, 115
AFP server, 98, 140
AirPort wireless technology, 84
All Computers list, 308
anacron utility, 124
Apple Authorized Training Centers, xxii
Apple Certified System Administrator (ACSA) certification, xxi
Apple Filing Protocol. *See* AFP
Apple Partition Map, 79
Apple Remote Desktop. *See* ARD
Apple Software Restore. *See* ASR
Apple technical certification, xxi–xxii
Apple Training Series books, xii
AppleScript, 321, 323–325
AppleScript dictionary, 324
.AppleSetupDone file, 32
Application Usage Reports, 329
applications. *See also* software
    auto-start, 6
    baseline for, 107
    Classic, 218–219
    distributing, 12
    on Dock, 202, 207
    installing, 6, 123
    Java, 272
    licensing of, 112
    limiting user access to, 217–218
    parental controls, 188–191
    Preference Manifests, 193–194
    preferences, 107, 217–218, 242
    problems with, 103, 106–108, 111–115
    required, 6
    starting at login, 211
    testing, 107
    Universal, 84
    updates and, 9–10, 13
    usage reports, 329
    versions, 327–328
archive file, 55
archiving account data, 151
ARD (Apple Remote Desktop), 295–339
    administrator utility, 296–299
    advantages of, 16–17
    client management, 318–323
    client software, 296, 299–304
    common tasks, 307–318
    components of, 296
    computer list setup, 307–309
    controlling screens, 301, 310–318
    controlling Windows computers, 272–273
    corporate environment, 16
    described, 16, 295, 296
    desktop publishing environment, 17
    education environment, 16–17
    enabling client, 299–304
    enabling screen sharing, 316–318
    enterprise environment, 16

generating reports, 326–333
initiating Curtain mode, 315
installing, 296–299, 296–307
installing software with, 97, 123, 319–320
locking screens, 314–315
managing with MCX settings, 305–307
network access to, 304–307
observing screens, 310, 312–314
opening, 296–297
password, 297–298
performing remote administration, 96–98
running UNIX commands, 320–322
saving tasks, 323
scheduling tasks, 322
serial number, 297
setting boot volume, 17, 88
software updates, 122–123, 229
Spotlight Searches, 330–331
system maintenance with, 122–123, 127
username, 297–298
uses for, 16–17, 295–296
using scripts with, 323–325
using task servers, 333–337

ARD Admin, 96–98

ARD clients. *See also* clients
- ARD 3 version, 304
- corporate environment, 16
- described, 296
- desktop publishing environment, 17
- education environment, 16–17
- enabling, 299–304
- enterprise environment, 16
- information about, 298–299
- managing, 318–323
- uses for, 16–17

ARD Dashboard Widget, 314

ASR (Apple Software Restore)
- delivering images with, 79–80
- system maintenance and, 127
- using over networks, 93–96
- working with, 36–39

ASR images, 79–80, 93, 106, 114

ASR multicast, 93–96

asr tool, 36, 38

assistive devices, 223

authentication. *See also* permissions
- Active Directory, 113
- LDAP, 150, 163
- Mac OS X Server, 256–260
- mobile accounts, 240
- network, 108
- Open Directory, 108
- options for, 70
- passwords, 256–260
- policies for, 256–260
- synchronization and, 243, 251
- users, 150, 161, 166
- Windows accounts, 265–266, 270

Automater, 325

automating client maintenance, 120–125

B

Backup Domain Controller (BDC), 264, 269

bandwidth
- Internet, 97, 228
- network, 38, 142
- synchronization and, 251

base images, 6

Basic pane, 170

batch editing, 145

Battery Menu pane, 231

battery status, 231

BDC (Backup Domain Controller), 264, 269

bill of material. *See* BOM

binding to Active Directory, 113–114

bless command, 88

BOM (bill of material), 107

BOM files, 54–55, 110–111

boot disks, 79, 84. *See also* startup disks

boot drives, 321

boot ROM file (booter), 85

bootable DVDs/CDs, 22, 41, 82, 93

bootpd configuration, 89

bootpd manual page, 91

bootpd process, 89
Bourne shell, 232
BSD files, 27, 29–31
BSD Open Directory plug-in, 29–31
ByHost files, 87

C

C Shell, 232
caches, 91, 330
CD drives, 33, 206
CD/DVD burners, 23
CDs
  bootable, 22, 41, 82, 93
  ejecting at logout, 206
  emergency, 38, 41, 239
  image delivery on, 82
  running Disk Utility from, 25
certification programs, xxi–xxii
checksum information, 38
Chooser, 219
chown command, 28
Classic applications, 218–219
Classic environment
  disk images, 34–36
  including, 33–36
  permissions, 112
  preferences, 34–36, 218–219
  printing from, 219
  security and, 33
Classic System Folder, 34–35, 112
click matrix, 109
Client Data Rate, 94
clients. *See also* ARD clients
  automating maintenance for, 120–125
  booting, 84, 85
  client computer setup, xiv–xv
  configuring for task server, 336–337
  information about, 298–299
  installing software remotely, 97, 319–320
  managing, 318–323
  MCX settings, 188–200
  names, 44
  network view, 286–287, 288
  number of, 84, 85
  offline, 334
  older, 304
  passwords, 297
  running UNIX commands, 320–322
  saving tasks, 323
  scheduling tasks, 322
  usernames, 297
client/server applications, 108
com.apple.loginwindow.plist file, 29
commands
  restricting, 203–204
  running remotely, 320–322
  scheduling, 322
  SQL, 332
  UNIX, 98, 124, 320–322
comments, 144–145, 178
Composer tool, 72
compressed images, 38
computer labs, 7–8, 206, 319
computer list accounts, 176–179
computer lists
  adding computers to, 308, 309
  All Computers, 308
  changing, 289
  creating, 308
  customizing columns in, 309
  described, 176
  importing/exporting, 309
  passwords, 309
  Scanner, 307–308
  setting up in Workgroup manager, 176–177
  setting up with ARD, 307–309
  settings, 176–177
  usernames, 309
  Windows, 261–262
computers
  adding to network view, 283–285
  client computer setup, xiv–xv
  comparing, 328
  Curtain mode, 315

descriptions, 177
desktop, 132, 237, 238
disk images for, 10–11
disk imaging environment, 23–25
energy saver settings, 230–231
guest, 177, 179, 197
identifiers for, 91
information about, 177–178, 313, 326–327
initial setup, 4–6
Intel-based. *See* Intel-based Macs
in lab setting, 7–8
laptop. *See* laptop computers
locking screens, 314–315
managed settings, 196–201
models, 91
modifying records, 289
names, 44, 90, 113–114, 177, 178, 313
network views, 281
numbers, 90
observing screens, 310, 312–314
platforms, 132
PowerPC. *See* PowerPC-based Macs
presets, 196
restricting workgroup access, 179
screen control, 301, 310–318
screen sharing, 316–318
sharing preferences, 44, 299–300
sleep options, 230–231, 324
types of, 132

Concurrent Versioning System (CVS), 150
configuration
bootpd, 89
client computer, xiv–xv
initial setup, xix–xxi, 4–6
network views, 286–287
packages, 68–71
presets, 54
task servers, 334–337
Windows accounts, 260–261
Workgroup Manager, xviii

configuration files, 25, 56, 94, 268, 332
Configuration pane, 69–71
Contents folder, 54–55
Copy Items feature, 319–320
corporate environment, 6, 8, 16
cross-platform issues, 256–263
Custom Remote Desktop Installer.mpkg, 303–304
CVS (Concurrent Versioning System), 150

D

Dashboard widget, 314
data
account, 151, 152
archiving, 151
client, 86
importing, 168–170
PostgreSQL, 331–333
report, 331–333
restoring, 152
theft of, 8

Data Collection settings, 337
data rate, 94
Data Upload Collection settings, 337
Date & Time pane, xvi, xxi
Deep Freeze, 17
Default views, 280, 282, 288
defaults command, 29
deleting
accounts, 28, 32, 239
administrator accounts, 28
files, 330
firmware password, 113
network views, 288, 290

delivery. *See* image delivery
deployment
computer labs, 7–8
disk images. *See* disk images
key points, 18
scenarios for, 4–12
strategies for, 3–19

deployment server solution, 6
desktop computers, 132, 237, 238
Desktop image, 26–27

Desktop pane, 230
desktop publishing environment, 6, 8, 10, 17
Developer Tools (Xcode), xiv, xvii, 12, 52, 55, 63, 184
devices
  assistive, 223
  boot, 88, 112
  bootable, 33
  creating images from, 37
  FireWire, 326
  listing on subnet, 326
  media, 93
  USB, 326
DHCP servers, 84–85
dictionary, AppleScript, 324
directories
  creation of, 138
  home. *See* home directories
  overview, 8–9
  permissions, 71
  RTF, 56
Directory Access utility, 29–30
directory domains, 179
directory services
  described, 44
  importing users and, 161
  local accounts associated with, 132–133
  mobile accounts and, 242
  using Active Directory for, 213
Directory Usage pane, xx
directory-based administration, 303, 305
discovery protocols, 286
disk image (.dmg) files, 22–23, 41, 115
disk images, 21–49. *See also* images
  active image, 26–27
  ASR, 36–39, 93, 106, 114
  base image, 6
  Classic environment, 34–36
  click matrix, 109
  compressed, 38
  creating from device, 37
  creating from folder, 37
  creating imaging environment, 23–27
  creating with Disk Utility, 37–38
  creating with NetRestore Helper, 38–39
  delivery of. *See* image delivery
  described, 10–11, 21
  documenting, 25–26
  format options, 22, 38
  hiding, 22–23
  imaging environment for, 23–25
  managing with hdiutil, 22–23
  NetBoot, 40–48, 319
  Network Install, 40–47, 61, 86–87
  number of, 6
  planning, 6
  rollback, 7
  solutions for, 10–18
  System Image Utility, 43–45
  testing, 104–111
  types of, 22–23
  uses for, 21
  versions, 26–27
Disk Utility
  creating disk images with, 37–38
  image types supported, 22–23
  repairing permissions, 321
  running from CD/DVD, 25
  starting Classic from disk image, 34–35
  using for image delivery, 80–81
disks. *See also* drives; volumes
  erasing, xiii, xiv, xix, 80, 81, 87
  external, 206
  hard, 39–43, 92, 93, 204, 230, 321
  internal, 206
  startup. *See* startup disks
  virtual, 22
.dist files, 56
distribution projects, 64–65
distribution scripts, 56–58
.dmg (disk image) files, 22–23, 41, 115
DNS Service Discovery, 94
Dock
  group shares, 208–210
  items in, 207

managed settings, 197
preferences, 202, 207–208
documentation
account management policy, 147–148
delivering, 149–150
imaging environment, 25–26
key items, 148
troubleshooting and, 25–26
updating, 149–150
user, 148–150
drivers, 10, 17, 33, 96, 106
drives. *See also* disks; volumes
boot, 321
CD, 33, 206
erasing, xiii, xiv, xix, 80, 81, 87
FireWire, 33, 39, 78–79
hard, 39–43, 92, 93, 204, 230, 321
USB, 78–79
drutil tool, 23
.DS_Store files, 68
DVD burners, 23
DVDs
bootable, 22, 41, 82, 93
ejecting at logout, 206
image delivery on, 82
running Disk Utility from, 25
dynamic lists, 281, 286

E

education environment
ARD client, 16–17
considerations, 3, 6, 134, 137
deployment issues, 6
screen sharing, 316–318
upgrade issues, 10
Eggplant, 17
email, 173, 225, 251, 303
Email pane, 225
email preferences, 225–226
Energy Saver preferences, 230–231
enterprise environment, 10, 16, 295
environment-test scripts, 58–60
erasing drives, xiii, xiv, xix, 80, 81, 87
error messages, 62, 110, 251
/etc/master.passwd file, 29
Ethernet address, 177, 178
exporting
computer lists, 309
LDAP accounts, 163–168
NetInfo accounts, 161–163
reports, 326
users, 161–168

F

Fast User Switching option, xvi
file filters, 68
File Search Reports, 329
file servers, 43, 93, 278–280
files
BOM, 54–55, 110–111
BSD, 27, 29–31
ByHost, 87
configuration, 25, 56, 94, 268, 332
deleting, 330
.dist, 56
.dmg, 22–23, 115
.DS_Store, 68
hiding, 116
.img, 22
log, 152, 271
managing preferences with, 184–187
.mpkg, 56, 319
ownership, 55, 68, 70, 162
permissions. *See* permissions
.pkg, 56, 99, 319
.plist, 29, 55, 94, 184–185, 320
Preference Manifest, 186–187
property list, 184–187
receipt, 61–62, 110–111
ROM, 85
searching for, 114, 330–331
securing issues, 8
shadow, 35–36, 42–43, 90
size, 8
.smi, 22

storing, 8
support, 54
temporary, 91
Update ByHost, 44
.zip, 115
FileWave, 17
find command, 114
Finder preferences, 202–205
finding items
files, 114, 330–331
with keywords, 143–145
Named views, 281
Search dialog, 144
Spotlight Searches, 330–331
firewalls, 13, 120, 228
FireWire drives, 33, 78–79
firmware, 84
firmware passwords, 112–113
flags, 57, 70–71, 120
flat views, 278–279
folders
aliases to, 67
creating images from, 37
default location, 70
group, 175–176
hiding, 116
hierarchy, 68
home. *See* home folders
Installer, 66–67
local, 8
names, 67
out of sync, 251
ownership, 70, 139
paths, 67–68
permissions. *See* permissions
scripts in, 68
structure of, 138–139
symbolic links, 67, 71
synchronized, 245–247
System Folder, 34–35, 112, 218
font management, 10

G

GBT (GUID Partition Table), 79
generateduid attribute, 161–162
Gigabit Ethernet, 84
Go to Folder setting, 204
Group Folder pane, 175–176
group folders, 175–176
group IDs, 28, 157–160, 168, 171–172
group shares, 208–210
groups, 133–134. *See also* workgroups
administrative, 134
creation of, 138–139, 174–176
described, 174
folder structure, 138–139
share points, 175, 176, 208–210
viewing group associations, 171–172
Groups pane, 171–172
guest computers, 177, 179, 197
Guest Computers account, 179
GUID Partition Table (GBT), 79

H

hard drives, 39–43, 92, 93, 204, 230, 321
hardware
disk imaging environment, 23–24
OS versions and, 24
planning growth management, 137
software updates and, 24
system requirements, xiv–xxi
testing images with, 104–106
upgrading. *See* upgrades
hdiutil utility, 22–23, 38
Hearing pane, 220
Help feature, 69
home directories
creation of, 162
mobile accounts, 238–240
network, 107, 184
preferences, 196
synchronization and, 251–253
Windows accounts, 260, 263–264

home folders
described, 8
location of, 141–142, 172–173
management of, 8–9, 31, 141–142
modifying info for, 28–29
network, 8, 107, 108, 142, 211, 251
synchronization and, 242–245
user customization of, 31
Windows accounts, 271
Home pane, 172–173
HTML tables, 332
HTTP protocol, 85, 88, 95, 115
HTTPS protocol, 43, 85, 95

I

Iceberg tool, 12, 72
icon properties, 204–205
id command, 28
image delivery, 77–101
with ASR, 79–80
with bootable DVDs, 82
with Disk Utility, 80–81
on FireWire drive, 78–79
installer tool, 98–99
local, 78–79
over network, 83–96
with radmind, 100
with Remote Desktop, 96–98
Image from Folder command, 36
images. *See also* disk images
ASR, 79–80, 93, 106, 114
base, 6
compressed, 38
delivery of. *See* image delivery
imagescan command, 38
.img files, 22
importing
LDAP accounts, 168–170
NetInfo accounts, 168
with Passenger, 146
passwords and, 169–170
user data, 168–170
users, 161–170
Info pane, 173
installation packages, 11–12, 51, 52. *See also* packages
installation scripts, 58–60
InstallationCheck script, 58
Installer application
distribution scripts, 56–58
folder structure for, 66–67
initial setups, 4–6
packages, 11–12, 301–304
testing packages with, 110–111
installer tool, 98–99
installers, 114–115
installing
administrator utility, 296–299
applications, 6, 123
ARD, 296–307
initial installation, 4–6
Mac OS X, 4–6
packages, 11–12, 51, 52
post-install actions, 70
software packages with ARD, 97, 319–320
Intel-based Macs
boot disks, 79, 84
Classic not supported on, 33
disk images, 24, 36, 86, 87, 106
NetBoot images, 40, 42
updates for, 87
Internet. *See also* Web
bandwidth, 97, 228
preferences, 225–226
IP addresses, 84–85, 88

J

Java applications, 272
JavaScript, 56, 57, 64
Java-style packages, 69

K

Kerberos, 265
Keyboard pane, 221–222
keyboard shortcuts, 223
keyboard-based options, 221–222
keywords, 142–145
kickstart command, 301, 305

L

LAN Manager, 265
languages, 71
laptop computers
    Energy Saver settings, 106
    levels of management, 132
    mobile accounts, 133, 237–242
    preferences, 196, 230
    testing disk images, 106
LDAP (Lightweight Directory Access Protocol), 163
LDAP accounts
    authentication, 150, 163
    exporting, 163–168
    importing, 168–170
LDAP database, 150, 160, 163
LDAP directory, 163, 168–170
LDIF (Lightweight Directory Interchange Format), 167
lessons
    prerequisites, xiii
    structure, xii–xiii
    system requirements, xiv–xxi
lifecycle, 119
Lightweight Directory Access Protocol. *See* LDAP
Lightweight Directory Interchange Format (LDIF), 167
loadsets, 14–15, 125–126
local accounts, 132–133
local folders, 8
local volumes, 11, 42–43, 61, 93, 175
locator definitions, 68
Lock Screen feature, 314–315
locking
    files, 269
    screens, 314–315
    share points, 269
log files, 152, 271
logGen utility, 71, 107, 114, 115
Login Items pane, 211–216
Login window, 29, 214–216
login/logout operations, xvi, 211–216
login/logout scripts, 212–214, 260, 261
.lproj extension, 56
lsbom command, 55, 61, 111

M

MAC (Media Access Control) addresses, 44, 112, 114, 177
Mac OS 9. *See* Classic environment
Mac OS X
    certification programs, xxi–xxii
    configuring. *See* configuration
    cross-platform issues, 256–262
    deployment of. *See* deployment
    disk images, 10–11
    initial setup, 4–6
    installing, 4–6
    password policies, 256–260
    users account requirements, 263
    versions, 24, 26–27, 104
Mac OS X accounts, 255, 256, 260
Mac OS X Certification Alliance, xxii
Mac OS X Deployment Exam, xxi
Mac OS X Installer
    distribution scripts, 56–58
    folder structure for, 66–67
    initial setups, 4–6
    packages, 11–12, 301–304
    testing packages with, 110–111
Mac OS X Open Directory server, 242
Mac OS X Server
    enabling SMB services on, 263–264
    growth management, 137

initial setup, xix–xxi, 4–6
user authentication policies, 256–260
Mac OS X Server Assistant, 4–6
Mac OS X Server Combo Update package, xiv, xxi
Macintosh computers. *See* computers
mail information, 173
Mail pane, 173
maintenance, 119–128
with ARD, 122–123, 127
automating, 120–125
with packages, 127
with Radmind, 125–126
with shell scripts, 123–125
Managed Client for Mac OS X (MCX) settings, 188–200
managed network views, 278–279
MCX settings
editing, 212, 214
Energy Saver preferences, 230
managing ARD with, 305–307
managing preferences with, 188–200, 210
mobile accounts, 240, 242
parental controls, 188–191
printer access, 227
synchronizing accounts, 242
Universal Access, 220
MCXScriptTrust setting, 212–213
Media Access Control (MAC) addresses, 44, 112, 114, 177
media preferences, 205–206
memory, 84, 91, 113, 313
metapackages, 12, 52–54, 87
mobile accounts, 237–253
authentication, 240
home directories, 238–240
implementing, 240–242
overview, 133, 238–242
passwords, 241–242
preferences, 240–245
synchronizing, 133, 242–252
uses for, 238–240
Mouse pane, 222–223
mouse settings, 222–223
.mpkg files, 56, 319
Multicast TTL, 94

N

Named views, 280, 281, 282
NBImageInfo.plist file, 90
NDIF (New Disk Image Format), 22
neighborhoods, 281, 283
NetBoot
ARD and, 127
disk images, 40–48
image delivery via, 83–86
settings, 88–91
NetBoot Across Subnets application, 88
NetBoot environment, 26
NetBoot images, 40–48, 319
NetBoot servers, 26
NetInfo accounts, 161–163
NetInfo database (NIDB), 32, 89, 158, 161–163
NetInfo Manager, 28–29, 157–158
NetInfo users, 161–163, 168
Netinstall settings, 88–91
NetRestore, 38–39, 92–93
NetRestore Helper, 36, 38–40, 46–48
network accounts, 43, 133, 238
network home folders, 8, 107, 108, 142, 211, 251
Network Image Utility. *See* System Image Utility
Network Install, 41
Network Install images, 40–47, 61, 86–87
Network Interfaces list, xx
Network Names pane, xix
Network preferences, 224
Network Restore, 41
Network Time pane, xx
network users, 31, 107, 133, 304–307
network views, 277–293
adding dynamic lists to, 286
configuring clients for, 286–287
creating, 281–285
deleting, 288, 290

- disabling, 288
- matching, 282
- modifying, 289–290
- overview, 277, 280–281
- planning, 279–280
- renaming, 288
- types of, 280, 282
- viewing results, 290–292

networks
- AirPort, 84
- ARD access, 304–307
- authentication, 108
- browsing, 278–279
- image delivery over, 83–96
- preferences, 224
- static value, 114
- using ASR over, 93–96
- wireless, 84

New Disk Image Format (NDIF), 22
NFS protocol, 43, 85, 88
NFS servers, 88, 278
nicl command, 32, 157–158
NIDB (NetInfo database), 32, 89, 158, 161–163
nidump utility, 162
-nobrowse flag, 22–23
NTLMv1, 255, 265
NTLMv2, 255, 265
nvram command, 88

O

OD/AD (Open Directory/Active Directory), 242
OD/AD triangle, 242
offline clients, 334
Online Documentation menu option, 69
Open Directory
- ARD access, 304–307
- attribute names, 261
- authentication, 108
- user customization, 31

Open Directory masters, 108, 163
Open Directory replica servers, 152
Open Directory/Active Directory (OD/AD), 242
Open Firmware password, 33, 92
Open Firmware Password utility, 33, 113
OpenLDAP attribute names, 261
OpenVNC, 272
operating systems. *See also specific operating systems*
- cross-platform issues, 256–263
- integrity of, 100
- maintaining. *See* maintenance
- updates to. *See* software updates
- upgrading. *See* upgrades
- versions of, 10, 12, 58, 149

oplocks, 269
Options pane, 216, 223
osascript, 321
ownership. *See also* permissions
- files, 55, 68, 70, 162
- folders, 70, 139
- share points, 270
- UNIX-style, 139
- vs. permissions, 139

P

Pacifist tool, 72–73
package file structure, 66–67
package projects, 63, 66–67
package scripts, 58–60
Package Setup Assistant, 64
PackageMaker
- components of, 67–69
- creating package manually in, 67–69
- custom installation packages, 114–115
- described, 12, 63
- flags/functions, 57
- obtaining, 52
- opening packages in, 64
- version, 52, 63

packages, 51–75
- adding description information to, 67
- configuration options, 69–71
- configuring package contents, 68
- contents of, 54–56

creating, 63–73
deployment of, 6
Installer, 301–304
installing, 11–12
installing remotely, 319–320
Java-style, 69
maintaining with, 127
metapackages, 12, 52–54, 87
modifying, 67
Network Install image, 87
overview, 11, 52–54
payload-free, 60–61
receipts, 61–62, 107
reverting to earlier version of, 71
testing, 110–111
third-party utilities for, 71
unique identifiers for, 69
versions, 69
parental controls, 188–191
Passenger application, 146
passwd command, 29, 30
passwd utility, 29, 30
passwd.txt file, 29, 30, 332
passwords
administrator, xix, 29, 30, 70
authentication policies, 256–260
changing, 30, 113
clients, 297
cross-platform issues, 256–260
exporting users and, 161–168
firmware, 112–113
guidelines for, 259–260
hidden administrator account, 29, 30
hints for, 215
importing users and, 169–170
mobile accounts, 241–242
Open Firmware, 33, 92
Remote Desktop utility, 297–298
removing, 113
user, 161–163
PasswordServer, 164
paths, 60
payload, 55, 58
payload-free packages, 60–61
PDC (Primary Domain Controller), 261–262, 264, 269
permissions. *See also* authentication; ownership
Classic applications, 112
directory, 71
establishing, 139–141
file, 67–68
folder, 71, 111–112, 176
repairing, 321
requiring, 111–112
SMB, 267–269
UNIX-style, 139
vs. ownership, 139
.pkg extension, 52
.pkg files, 56, 99, 319
.plist files, 29, 55, 94, 184–187, 320
plug-ins, 54
Portable pane, 230
ports, 94
postflight script, 59
PostgreSQL database, 331–333
postinstall script, 59
postupgrade script, 59
PowerPC-based Macs
boot disks, 79, 84
disk images, 24, 36, 86, 87, 106
NetBoot images, 40, 42
updates for, 87
PRAM, resetting, 113
Preference Manifests, 186–187, 193–194, 200
preferences, 184–200
Accounts pane, 156–157, 159
application, 107, 217–218, 242
Classic, 34–36, 218–219
Dock, 202, 207–208
Energy Saver, 230–231
Finder, 202–205
Guest Computer, 179
Internet, 225–226
location for, 184

login, 211–216
managed, 196–201
managing with files, 184–187
managing with MCX settings, 188–200
media access, 205–206
mobile accounts, 240–245
network, 224
printing, 227
setting up, xvi–xvii
sharing, 44, 299–300
Software Update, 228–229
System Preferences access, 210–211
Universal Access, 220–223
Web, 226
preflight script, 58
preinstall script, 58
prerequisites, xiii
presets
account, 145, 233
computers, 196
configuration, 54
keys, 186
user account creation, 145, 168, 233
preupgrade script, 59
Primary Domain Controller (PDC), 261–262, 264, 269
printers
drivers, 10, 17
quotas, 173–174
restricting access to, 227
printing
from Classic, 219
preferences, 227
problems. *See* troubleshooting
processor, 106
processor types, 91
Property List Editor, 55, 94, 184
property list (.plist) files, 29, 55, 94, 184–187, 320
Proxies pane, 224
psql command, 332
Public views, 280, 282, 288
pwpolicy command, 256–259

R

Radmind, 100, 125–126
Radmind Assistant, 14–15
Radmind server, 126
RAM, 84, 91, 113, 137, 313
"Rebuild data for reports" option, 330
receipt files, 61–62, 110–111
receipts, 61–62, 107
remote access. *See* ARD (Apple Remote Desktop)
remote administration, 96–98
Remote Desktop utility. *See* ARD (Apple Remote Desktop)
Repair Permissions command, 321
replicas, 150, 152
replication, 150
reports, 326–333
rescue images, 91
rescue/diagnostic applications, 91
resource forks, 68, 115
Resources folder, 55–56
Restart button, 215
Restart Print Quota button, 173–174
restoring archived data, 152
rollback, 7
ROM files, 85
root account, 27
root folder (/), 66–67
root-only installers, 115
RTF format, 56

S

Safari browser, 187
Samba service, 266, 269, 271
Scanner list, 307–308
Schedule button, 322
Schedule pane, 231
Script Editor, 324
scripts
AppleScript, 321, 324–325
Automater, 325
distribution, 56–58

environment-test, 58–60
example, 60
FireWire drive startup, 78
folders for, 68
installation, 58–60
login/logout, 212–214, 260, 261
maintenance with, 123–125
package, 58–60
payload-free packages, 60–61
shell, 56–58, 98, 123–125
sleep, 324
UNIX, 98
using with ARD, 323–325
Scripts pane, 212–214
Search dialog, 144
searches
for files, 114, 330–331
with keywords, 143–145
Named views, 281
Spotlight Searches, 330–331
security. *See also* authentication
Classic environment, 33, 219
data theft, 8
file storage, 8
firewalls, 13, 120, 228
Mac OS 9, 33, 219
Mac OS X, 256–260
passwords. *See* passwords
permissions and, 112
policies for, 256–260, 265
System Preference access, 210–211
Windows, 256–260, 265
Seeing pane, 220
Send UNIX Command, 124, 320–321
serial numbers, 41, 112, 297
Server Admin Tools package, xiv, xvii, 158
Server Admin utility, 89, 120, 151, 152
Server Assistant, xx, 4, 5
Server Manager, 126
Server Message Block. *See* SMB
server replication, 150
serveradmin command, 89
servers. *See also* Mac OS X Server
Active Directory, 242
AFP, 98, 140
DHCP, 84–85
file, 43, 93, 278–280
NetBoot, 26
NFS, 88, 278
Open Directory, 152
PasswordServer, 164
Radmind, 126
replica, 152
Software Update, 228–229
task, 296, 298, 333–337
Web, 95–96
Services pane, xx
Set Startup Disk command, 319
SetFile tool, 116
Setup Assistant, 4, 32
shadow files, 35–36, 42–43, 90
ShadowClassic, 35–36, 112
share points. *See also* sharing
enabling with SMB, 267–269
group, 175, 176, 208–210
home folders, 31, 172
locking, 269
ownership, 270
Windows, 255, 263, 267–270
sharing. *See also* share points
load sharing, 150
preferences, 44, 299–300
report data, 331
screens, 316–318
with SMB, 255, 267–269
unique names for, 44
Sharing pane, 29
shell scripts, 56–58, 98, 123–125
shells
configuring, 232
default, 29, 232
preferred, 232
types of, 171, 232
Shut Down button, 215

Skills Assessment Guide, xxi
slapconfig log file, 152
sleep options, 230–231, 319
sleep script, 324
SMART status, 321
SMB (Server Message Block)
  Open Directory attribute names, 261
  permissions, 267–269
  sharing with, 255, 267–269
SMB services, 263–264
.smi files, 22
software. *See also* applications
  information about, 327–330
  installing with ARD, 319–320
  planning growth management, 137
  restoring, 94–96
  site license of, 112
  testing images with, 106–108
  updates. *See* software updates
  upgrading. *See* upgrades
  usage reports, 329
Software Difference Reports, 328
Software Update server, 228–229
Software Update utility, 13–14, 120–121
software updates
  automating with shell scripts, 123–125
  checking for, 121
  considerations, 10
  controlling, 120–121
  installing with ARD, 122–123, 229
  installing with Software Update, 13–14
  new hardware and, 24
  packages. *See* packages
  preferences for, 228–229
  regular schedule for, 13–14
Software Version Reports, 327–328
softwareupdate command-line utility, 13, 120–121, 123–125
sound options, hearing-impaired users, 220
Spotlight Searches, 330–331
SQL, accessing report data with, 331–333
SSH connections, 38, 124, 301, 304, 305
ssh keys, 38, 114
Startup Disk preference pane, 90–91
startup disks
  changing, 32, 42–43, 93, 113
  Classic mode and, 33
  diskless NetBoot, 42–43
  Intel-based Macs, 79, 84
  network, 122–123
  PowerPC-based Macs, 79, 84
  preferences, 43, 90–91
  remote volumes, 10–11
  setting, 97, 319, 323, 324
  shadow files and, 42–43
startup (bootable) DVDs/CDs, 22, 41, 82, 93
static network values, 114
Storage Report, 321
.strings extension, 56
.strings file, 56
subnets, 88
support files, 54
sw_vers command, 96
symbolic links, 71
synchronization
  directories, 8
  folders, 8–9, 245–247
  mobile accounts, 133, 242–252
synchronization services, 8–9
System Data fields, 303
System Folder, 34–35, 112, 218
System Image Utility, 40, 43–45, 82, 114
System Overview Reports, 326–327
System Preferences, 210–211. *See also* preferences
system requirements, xiv–xxi

T

Target Disk Mode, 25
task servers, 296, 298, 333–337
tasks, 109, 110, 123, 322–324, 334
TCP/IP connections, xx, 331, 332
templates
  home folder, 173

UNIX, 321–322
user account, 133, 167, 238
temporary files, 91
Terminal window, 116, 185
testing, 10, 13–18, 103–111
TFTP (Trivial File Transfer Protocol), 85
time zones, xv, xx, xxi
training centers, xxii
tripwire, 14–15
Trivial File Transfer Protocol (TFTP), 85
troubleshooting
applications, 103, 106–108, 111–115
common problems, 111–116
documenting, 25–26
error messages, 62, 110, 251
synchronization issues, 250–252
Windows accounts, 269–273

U

UDIF (Universal Disk Image Format), 22
uid (user ID), 28, 157, 159–160, 168
undo actions, 221
Universal Access, 220–223
Universal Disk Image Format (UDIF), 22
UNIX commands, 98, 124, 320–322
UNIX shell scripts, 98
UNIX utilities, 217, 234
UNIX-style ownership/permissions, 139
Update ByHost preference files, 44
updates, software. *See* software updates
upgrades
client software, 304, 319
hardware, 105, 127, 161
importing/exporting users, 161–170
installation scripts, 58–60
license for, 41
overview, 9–10
packages. *See* packages
planning for, 10–18
regular schedule for, 13–14
software, 105, 127, 161, 304, 319
USB drives, 78–79
user accounts. *See also* accounts; users
creating. *See* account creation
Mac, 263
relocating, 161–174
requirements for, 134
security policies, 256–260
user name, 29
Windows. *See* Windows accounts
user authentication policies, 256–260
user documents, 148–150
user ID (uid), 28, 157, 159–160, 168
user management policies, 134–137
users. *See also* accounts; user accounts
accessibility options, 220–223
adding basic information for, 170
adding to BSD flat user file, 29–31
advanced options for, 171
creating with Passenger, 146
default, 44
described, 132
exporting, 161–168
Fast User Switching option, xvi
folder structure, 138–139
groups of. *See* groups
importing, 161–170
importing data, 168–170
importing with Passenger, 146
limiting application access, 217–218
managed settings, 196–201
managing, 142–146
NetInfo, 161–163
passwords, 161–163
personal info about, 173
searching for, 144
training, 147

V

View Directories command, 158
viewing options, visually impaired users, 220
views
default, 280, 282, 288
flat, 278–279

managed, 278–279
named, 280, 281
network. *See* network views
public, 280, 282, 288
Virtual Network Computing (VNC), 272, 301, 303
VISE, 114
VNC (Virtual Network Computing), 272, 301, 303
VoiceOver Utility, 187
volume license key, 41
VolumeCheck script, 58
volumes. *See also* disks; drives
erasing, xiii, xiv, xix, 80, 81, 87
local, 11, 42–43, 61, 93, 175
names, 43, 60
startup. *See* startup disks

W

Web browsers, 95–96
Web pane, 226
Web preferences, 226
Web servers, 95–96
Windows accounts, 255–275
authentication, 265, 270
configuring, 260–261
cross-platform issues, 256–262
home directories, 260, 263–264
home folders, 271
login scripts, 260, 261
password policies, 259
problems with, 269–273
remote access, 272–273
security policies, 265
share points, 255, 263, 267–270
SMB services, 263–264
user account requirements, 263
Windows computer list, 261–262
Windows Internet Naming Service (WINS), 277
Windows services, 264–270
Windows tab, 260–261
WINS (Windows Internet Naming Service), 277
wireless networks, 84
Workgroup Manager
Application preferences, 217–218
assigning administrative privileges, 136
computer list setup, 176–179
creating accounts with, 158–160
creating group shares, 208–210
defining scripts, 213
exporting LDAP accounts, 163–168
initial setup, xviii
managed settings, 196–200
managing Classic preferences, 218
managing preferences, 191–196
network views, 281–282
setting up group folders, 175–176
Universal Access settings, 220–223
workgroups. *See also* groups
managed settings, 196–201
restricting computer access to, 179
searching for, 144
types of, 132

X

Xcode Developer Tools, xiv, xvii, 12, 52, 55, 63, 184
XML code, 305–307
Xserve, 150–152
Xserve Remote Diagnostics, 91

Z

.zip files, 115
Zoom features, 220, 221

Apple Certified

The Apple Pro Training Series

Apple Pro Training Series: Final Cut Pro 5
0-321-33481-7

In this best-selling guide, Diana Weynand starts with basic video editing techniques and takes you all the way through Final Cut Pro's powerful advanced features. Using world-class documentary footage, you'll learn to mark and edit clips, color correct sequences, create transitions, apply filters and effects, add titles, work with audio, and more.

Apple Pro Training Series: Advanced Editing Techniques in Final Cut Pro 5
0-321-33549-X

Director and editor Michael Wohl shares must-know professional techniques for cutting dialogue scenes, action scenes, fight and chase scenes, documentaries, comedy, music videos, multi-camera projects, and more. Also covers Soundtrack Pro, audio finishing, managing clips and media, and working with film.

Apple Pro Training Series: Advanced Color Correction and Effects in Final Cut Pro 5
0-321-33548-1

This Apple-authorized guide delivers hard-to-find training in real-world color correction and effects techniques, including motion effects, keying and compositing, titling, scene-to-scene color matching, and correcting for broadcast specifications.

Apple Pro Training Series: Optimizing Your Final Cut Pro System
0-321-26871-7

Written and field-tested by industry pros Sean Cullen, Matthew Geller, Charles Roberts, and Adam Wilt, this is the ultimate guide for installing, configuring, optimizing, and trouble-shooting Final Cut Pro in real-world post-production environments.

Apple Pro Training Series: Final Cut Pro for Avid Editors
0-321-24577-6

Master trainer Diana Weynand takes you through a comprehensive "translation course" designed for professional video and film editors who already know their way around Avid nonlinear systems.

Apple Pro Training Series: Getting Started with Final Cut Studio
0-321-36991-2

This Apple-authorized guide provides newcomers with an excellent overview of all products in Final Cut Studio: Final Cut Pro 5, Motion 2, Soundtrack Pro and DVD Studio Pro 4.

Apple Pro Training Series: Final Cut Express HD
0-321-33533-3

The only Apple-authorized guide to Final Cut Express HD, this book delivers the techniques you need to make movie magic from the comfort of your Mac.

Apple Pro Training Series: Xsan 2/E
0-321-43232-0

Apple's exciting new enterprise-class file system offers high-speed access to centralized shared data. This handy booklet provides invaluable setup, configuration, and troubleshooting tips.

To order books or find out about the Apple Pro Training Series, visit: **www.peachpit.com/appleprotraining**

Apple Pro Training Series: DVD Studio Pro 4
0-321-33482-5

Learn to author professional interactive DVDs with this best-selling guide.

Apple Pro Training Series: Shake 4
0-321-25609-3

Apple-certified guide uses stunning real world sequences to reveal the wizardry of Shake 4.

Apple Pro Training Series: Shake 4 Quick Reference Guide
0-321-38246-3

Compact reference guide to Apple's leading compositing software.

Apple Pro Training Series: Getting Started with Motion
0-321-30533-7

Apple-certified guide makes sophisticated motion graphics accessible to newcomers.

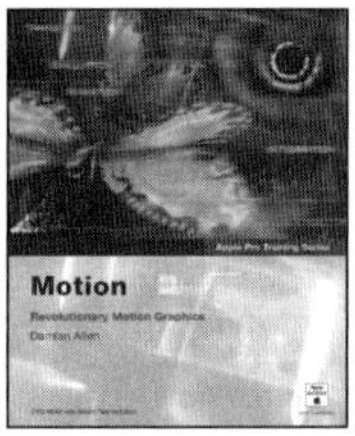

Apple Pro Training Series: Motion
0-321-27826-7

Comprehensive guide to Apple's revolutionary motion graphics software.

Encyclopedia of Visual Effects
0-321-30334-2

Ultimate recipe book for visual effects artists working in Shake, Motion and Adobe After Effects.

Apple Pro Training Series: Soundtrack Pro
0-321-35757-4

Create original soundtrack's with Apple's exciting new sound design software.

Apple Pro Training Series: Logic Pro 7 and Logic Express 7
0-321-25614-X

Create, mix, and polish your musical creations using Apple's pro audio software.

Apple Pro Training Series: Advanced Logic Pro 7
0-321-25607-7

Comprehensive guide takes you through Logic's powerful advanced features.

Apple Pro Training Series: Color Management with Mac OS X
0-321-24576-8

Project-based guide shows how to set up real-world color management workflows.

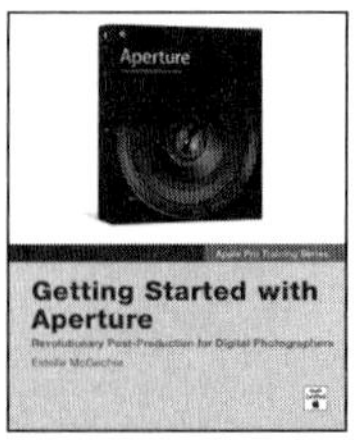

Apple Pro Training Series: Getting Started with Aperture
0-321-42275-9

Introduction to Apple's revolutionary workflow tool for professional photographers.

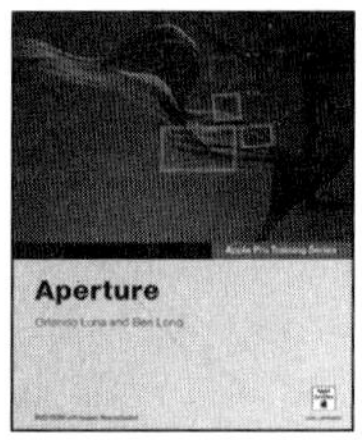

Apple Pro Training Series: Aperture
0-321-42276-7

Comprehensive book-DVD combo takes you step by step all the way through Aperture.

The Apple Training Series

Designed for system administrators, IT professionals, AppleCare technicians, and Mac enthusiasts, the Apple Training Series is both a self-paced learning tool and the official curriculum of the Apple Training and Certification program. For more information, go to **http://train.apple.com.**

Apple Training Series: Mac OS X Support Essentials
0-321-33547-3

Apple Training Series: Mac OS X Server Essentials
0-321-35758-2

Apple Training Series: Desktop and Portable Systems, Second Edition
0-321-33546-5

Apple Training Series: iWork '06
0-321-44225-3

Apple Training Series: Mac OS X System Administration Guide, Volume 1
0-321-36984-X

Apple Training Series: Mac OS X System Administration Guide, Volume 2
0-321-42315-1

Apple Training Series: iLife '06
0-321-42164-7

Apple Training Series: GarageBand 3
0-321-42165-5